Encyclopedia of

SACRED
PLACES

Encyclopedia of

SACRED PLACES

Norbert C. Brockman

ABC-CLIO

Santa Barbara, California
Denver, Colorado
Oxford, England

Library of Congress Cataloging-in-Publication Data
Brockman, Norbert C., 1934–
        Encyclopedia of sacred places / Norbert C. Brockman.
            p.   cm.
        Includes bibliographical references and index.
        ISBN 0-87436-830-8 (alk. paper)
        1. Sacred space—Encyclopedias. I. Title.
    BL580.B76   1997
    291.3'5'03—dc21   96-53652

ISBN 0-87436-830-8

02 01 00 99 98 97 10 9 8 7 6 5 4 3 2 1

ABC-CLIO, Inc.
130 Cremona Drive, P.O. Box 1911
Santa Barbara, California 93116-1911

This book is printed on acid free paper ∞ .
Manufactured in the United States of America

CONTENTS

PREFACE

Places dedicated to sacred memories are a part of all the world's religious and spiritual traditions. In these sacred places the seeker encounters the holy and, through rituals, meditation, and revelation, experiences a call to move beyond the self.

The reverence for sacred places has existed as long as people have formed communities. In recent decades, however, it has enjoyed a powerful reawakening. Not only does this rebirth take the form of religious conversion, it also takes the form of a quest for new means of experiencing ancient ways of knowing. Pilgrimage routes that, over the past 200 years, attracted only a trickle of pilgrims now draw tens of thousands. Spain, for example, has reopened the medieval pilgrim hostels on the route to Santiago de Compostela, one of Europe's most important pilgrimage places, and many make the months-long trek there. Jerusalem and Rome continue to attract streams of believers and seekers. And the quest for insight from outside Western traditions has sparked a new fascination with the ancient traditions of Native American Indians and the way of the Buddha.

What are these sacred places? They are the shrines where apparitions of angels, saints, or a god have been reported. They are the sites of miraculous cures. They are locales of particular significance in the natural world, such as sacred mountains or rivers. Sacred sites also include places associated with the life of a prophet or religious founder.

The sacred sites described in this book fall into nine general categories.

1. Places sanctified by events in the life of a prophet, saint, or deity
2. Sites of miracles and healing
3. Places of apparitions or visions
4. Locales dedicated to special religious rituals
5. Tombs of saints
6. Shrines of a miraculous statue, icon, or relic
7. The ancestral or mythical abodes of the gods
8. Places that manifest the energies or mystical powers of nature
9. Places marked by evil that have been a turning point for a religious community

There are so many acknowledged holy places in the world that it is impossible to mention them all here. In Japan, for example, over 2,000 Shinto shrines exist, and the listing of Marian shrines in Spain alone fills three volumes. However, I have included all internationally known sacred places, such as Lourdes and the Golden Temple at Amritsar. In addition to these well-known sites, each religious and spiritual tradition is represented by its own notable sacred places. I also gave consideration to achieving worldwide geographic coverage and attempted to include leading examples of types of sacred places. Readers will find examples of sacred mountains, wells, and relic shrines in addition to sites of apparitions, miracles, and other forms of divine intervention. Most of the sites described are active, although some represent historical cultures or religions that no longer exist, such as Delos, Machu Picchu, and Rapa Nui.

Finally, I have included a number of sites like Auschwitz and the Peace Memorial at Hiroshima that are not "sacred" in the conventional sense. Yet these places, where horrible events of great magnitude took place, exert a powerful hold on our spiritual sensibilities. They are memorials that mark the triumph of enduring faith over evil. To visit Gorée Island, for instance, is to stand in the presence of the spirits of the enslaved taken to the Americas. To make such a visit in the company of African Americans is to be touched deeply by the call of these ancestor spirits across time. Without belonging to a specific religious tradition, the slave depots are shrines of the spirit world.

Secular ideologies, too, have their sacred places: the Communists once had Lenin's Tomb, Americans have the Lincoln and Vietnam memorials, and the Afrikaners their Vortrekker Monument. At these monuments to national identity, the spirit of a people can be experienced. However, I decided to leave out national civic shrines such as these. Only one example of a secular shrine, the Père Lachaise Cemetery in Paris, has been included, and that because of its international appeal. But since the meaning of the spiritual is complex, places of importance to some will seem marginal to others.

No single author can share the faith of the wide-ranging collection of traditions represented here. But I approached each site with respect for the devotion of those whose faith is enshrined there. Some accounts come from fable or legend and challenge the rational and scientific mind. However, I attempted to understand and to accept the explanations offered by believers, and to present them here without judgment.

Entries are followed by suggested background readings on the site or the tradition that it reflects. In some cases, videos are mentioned; as of 1997, all those referred to in the book were available from distributors. In deference to the fact that a wide range of traditions are included here, the Christian dating system BC/AD has been replaced by the system more commonly used in comparative religion: BCE/CE, "before the common era" and "common era."

Compiling a book such as this requires the help of many people. First I must thank Henry Rasof, my editor, who proposed this project to me and followed through at every step, and the wonderful people at ABC-CLIO, who are a delight to work with. Many people from tourist offices answered my questions and sent material and photos for use.

I visited most of the sites in the book in person, and along the way caretakers, taxi drivers, innkeepers, and pilgrims offered information and guidance. Above all, believers offered stories, for the oral traditions surrounding these holy places remain alive and vibrant. People shared accounts of their own spiritual journeys and confided the small or dramatic miracles they had received and the inner peace they had found. Many told of lives set on new paths.

A number of friends and associates offered special assistance of various kinds:

PREFACE

Kazuki Yasumura in Tokyo; Judith Yamada, SSND, in Kyoto; Dennis Schmitz, SM, in Seoul; and Ronald Macfarlane in Penang. The Marianists in Fulda (Germany), Tokyo, and Rome were generous in hospitality and suggestions. I would also like to acknowledge Bro. William Fackovec, SM (Marian Library of the University of Dayton); George Nuñez, my translator in Spain and Portugal; Dr. Nancy Sahli of the National Historical Publications and Records Commission for early suggestions; and innumerable librarians, curators, and shrine personnel.

MAPS

AFRICA

1   Axum
2   Lalibela
3   Debra Libanos
4   Gorée
5   Touba
6   Slave Depots
7   Djenné
8   Dogon Cliffs
9   Mount Kenya
10 Morija
11 Uganda Martyrs' Shrines
12 Kibeho
13 Kairouan

NORTH & CENTRAL AMERICA

SOUTH AMERICA

1 Padre Cicero
2 Cuzco
3 Machu Picchu

ASIA & THE SOUTH PACIFIC

1 Uluru and Kata Tjuta
2 Borobudur
3 Gunung Agung
4 Kek Lok Si
5 Cao Dai Temple
6 Shwe Dagon Pagoda
7 Pagan
8 Angkor Wat
9 Bangkok: Wat Po, Lakmuang Shrine,
  Erawan Shrine, Emerald Buddha

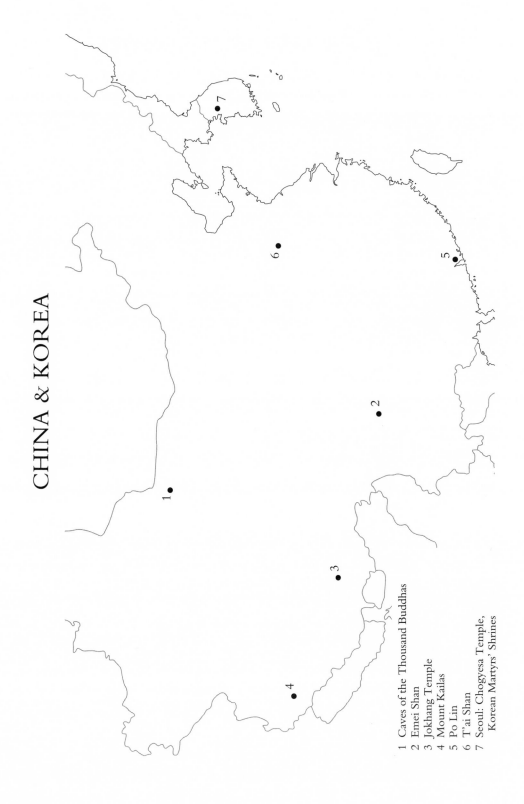

CHINA & KOREA

1 Caves of the Thousand Buddhas
2 Emei Shan
3 Jokhang Temple
4 Mount Kailas
5 Po Lin
6 T'ai Shan
7 Seoul: Chogyesa Temple,
    Korean Martyrs' Shrines

NORTHERN EUROPE

SOUTHERN EUROPE

WESTERN EUROPE

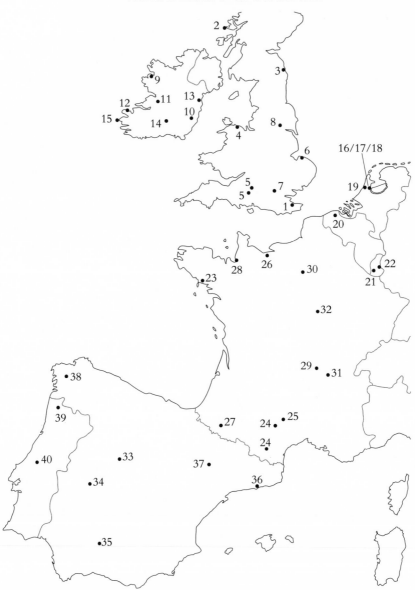

INDIA, SRI LANKA, & NEPAL

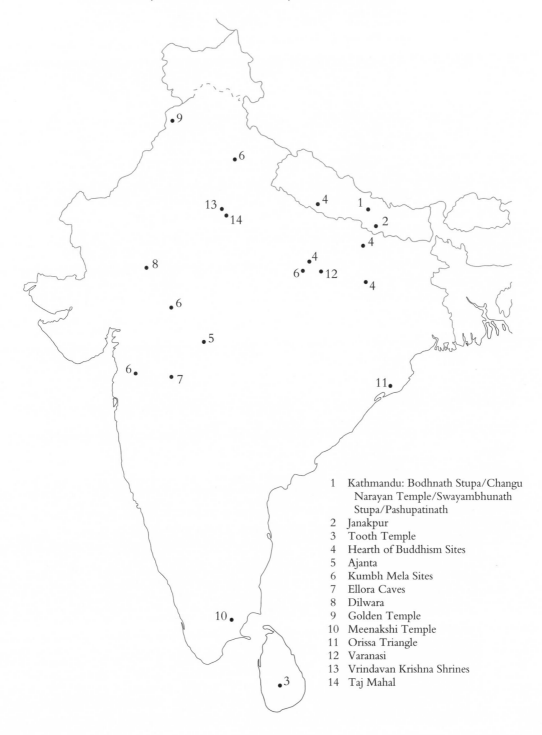

1 Kathmandu: Bodhnath Stupa/Changu
   Narayan Temple/Swayambhunath
   Stupa/Pashupatinath
2 Janakpur
3 Tooth Temple
4 Hearth of Buddhism Sites
5 Ajanta
6 Kumbh Mela Sites
7 Ellora Caves
8 Dilwara
9 Golden Temple
10 Meenakshi Temple
11 Orissa Triangle
12 Varanasi
13 Vrindavan Krishna Shrines
14 Taj Mahal

JAPAN

1 Eighty-Eight Temples
2 Hiroshima Peace Memorial
3 Hasadera Temple
4 Kyoto
5 Mount Fuji
6 Tokyo
7 Nagasaki
8 Nikko
9 Nara
10 Ise
11 Izumo Taisha Shrine

MIDDLE EAST

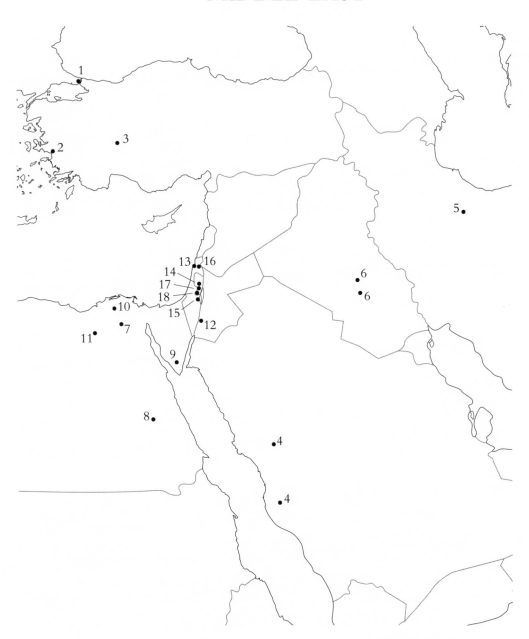

PACIFIC

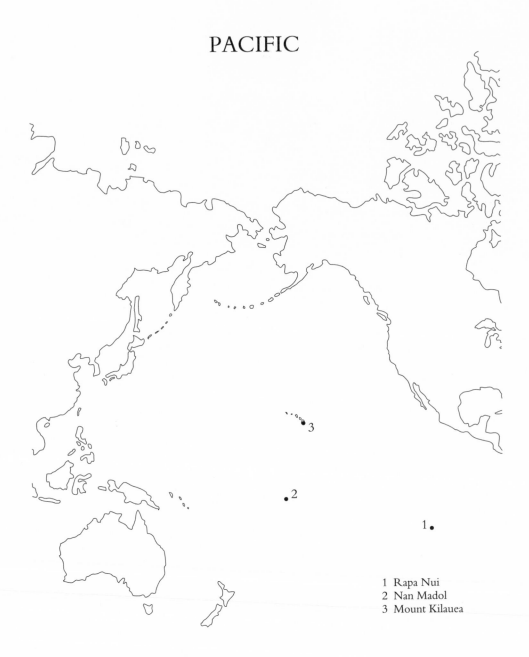

1 Rapa Nui
2 Nan Madol
3 Mount Kilauea

Encyclopedia of

SACRED
PLACES

AACHEN CATHEDRAL, Germany

Since the dawn of recorded history, the town of Aachen, located where modern Germany, Belgium, and the Netherlands meet, has been a worship site. The Celtic healing god Granus was worshipped at the Aachen hot springs. The less spiritual Roman conquerors turned the spring into public baths, but also built a sacred well and sanctuary. King Pippin, the father of Charlemagne, built his capital at Aachen and constructed the cathedral over the ancient Roman well and sanctuary. Charlemagne, intent on creating a great empire, built a palace with a vast royal hall and his own royal chapel next to the cathedral. It is now incorporated into the cathedral.

Charlemagne took the throne in 768 and began a series of campaigns that made him master of northern Europe. With his many concubines and the encouragement he gave to the sexual escapades of his daughters, he would hardly pass the scrutiny of modern tests of holiness. Yet his genuine religious fervor and missionary zeal caused him to be recognized as a saint in 1165, and his relics are kept in a shrine in the chapel. Because of his notorious lifestyle, his cult is merely tolerated by the Church and is kept to a minimum. Ceremonies in his honor are limited to one Mass celebrated annually in the chapel on his feast day.

The Palatine Chapel, Charlemagne's im-perial church, is the heart of the cathedral. (His tomb is believed to be under the center of the main floor.) Charlemagne built the church in 794 with marble from the palace of Ravenna in northern Italy, seat of the last Roman emperors. He modeled it on Ravenna's San Vitale, which was in turn based on another imperial church, Justinian's Hagia Sophia in Constantinople. The eight-sided Palatine Chapel has three tiers crowned by a mosaic dome 50 feet in diameter and twice that in height. It is surrounded by an ambulatory—a covered arcade where pilgrims can circle the main shrine, in this case the central altar. In Charlemagne's day, the men sat in this gallery during services. The emperor with his family and courtiers sat in the upper mezzanine, which also circles the church. A lower mezzanine was reserved for women and small children. At one time there was a tower near the throne from which Charlemagne spoke to assemblies in the courtyard below. Because of its cultural importance, the Palatine Chapel is on the UNESCO World Heritage List (*see* appendix C).

The chapel continued as a coronation church until 1531, a year after the Diet of Augsburg, which resulted in a majority of the German princes choosing the then-new Protestant faith. Through the centuries there were additions and changes in the chapel. In 1168, Frederick Barbarossa added a 48-lamp chandelier, a symbol of the Heavenly Jerusalem. A Gothic choir was built in the fourteenth century.

The church treasury is the finest in Germany and includes some of the most fantastic relics in Christendom. The collection was begun by Charlemagne, and it drew countless swarms of pilgrims from the Germanies, England, Scandinavia, Austria, and Hungary. Four "great relics" have been ex-

3

Throne of Charlemagne, Aachen Cathedral, Aachen, Germany.

posed to the public every seven years from 1349 to 1992: the cloak of the Virgin Mary, the swaddling-clothes of the Infant Jesus, the loin cloth worn by Jesus on the Cross, and the cloth on which the head of John the Baptist lay after his beheading. These are often cited by critics as the most pretentious frauds created by greedy fakers in the Middle Ages, and in modern times they attract more of the curious than the pious.

4

But their antiquity alone places them in the front rank of Christian artifacts.

The octagonal shape of the chapel has attracted the interest of New Age groups, who regard the cathedral as the preservation of ancient occult knowledge in stone. They argue that the Palatine Chapel was built on the model of Stonehenge rather than San Vitale and that it incorporates Stonehenge's supernatural knowledge. Much of this argument is based on astrology; but there is no question that at the spring and autumn equinoxes, the emperor's throne is illuminated, and at noon on the summer solstice the gold ball of the chandelier is struck by a sunbeam.

References Flavio Conti, *The Closed Faith.* Boston, HBJ Press, 1979, 105–120. Paul Devereux, *Secrets of Ancient and Sacred Places.* London, Blandford, 1992. Richard Sullivan, *Aix-la-Chapelle in the Age of Charlemagne.* Norman, University of Oklahoma, 1963.

ACROPOLIS, Greece

The Acropolis, a complex that overlooks the city of Athens, contained both the civic and religious buildings of the Athenian state, including the temple of Athena, patroness of Athens. Its remains, impressive even as ruins, are the city's most enduring symbol.

Before 1000 BCE, there was a temple and there were numerous shrines on the hill. In 480 BCE, Athens was overrun by the Persians, who razed the temple and burned all the shrines on the hill. Pericles built a fleet of 200 vessels and defeated the Persians. With peace secured, the city was rebuilt and the fleet was used to expand Athenian colonies around the Mediterranean Sea. When Athens became the dominant Greek state, Pericles taxed the other Greek states the equivalent of 14 tons of gold to pay for a new Acropolis.

The Parthenon, which dominates the Acropolis, was the chief temple dedicated to Athena Parthenos (Athena the Virgin). Majestic Athena—who was merely a local goddess until her worship became the official cult of Athens—represented the triumph of the mind over the chaotic forces of nature and the taming of the ancient fertility cults by the pantheon of Greek gods and goddesses. Her feast day in July was observed with special ceremonies. Every fourth year the festivities expanded into the Panathenaea, a procession conducted with special splendor to bring a new woven robe to dress the statue. The walls of the Parthenon are covered with a continuous carved scene showing this procession.

From 447 to 442 BCE, Phidias, the greatest sculptor of ancient Greece, supervised the Parthenon's construction. The temple measures 228 feet by 101 feet and stands 65 feet high. Along each side, seventeen columns support its length, eight columns support each end. Originally, its marble exterior was decorated with red, blue, and ocher paint and covered by a roof of blue with gold stars. Phidias also created a 40-foot gold and ivory statue of Athena for the new Parthenon. The warrior virgin was shown standing with her shield and sacred snake at her left side, her right hand extended and holding a small carving of Winged Victory. The statue represented intelligence—the combination of divine knowledge and human wisdom.

Since the Acropolis sits on a plateau with steep cliffs, there is only one possible entrance, a processional path up from the surrounding streets through a majestic gateway with attached wings. From this gate the visitor sees the whole of the Acropolis and the harmony of the structures and the landscape. The Sacred Way gives visitors a feeling of ritual propriety, wending its course

Young men carry water jugs in a Parthenon frieze carved by Phidias, 442–438 BCE. The carving is one of the numerous friezes covering the walls of the Parthenon, which depict the Panathenaea, an elaborate procession conducted to dress the 40-foot gold and ivory statue of the goddess Athena.

up to the Parthenon. On one side it passes the Erechtheum, a small temple with lovely, slender, fluted columns and several porches. The Porch of the Maidens faces the Parthenon; it has five columns (one was removed) of sculpted female figures intended as ex-votos, or offerings to Athena. They represent the maidens who carried offerings to the Parthenon during the processions.

All of daily life during the Athenian period clustered under the shadow of the Acropolis and the protection of Athena. Two ancient theaters sit just below the Acropolis, each with a horseshoe ring of marble seats for the priests of the Dionysian cult. The Agora, or civic and commercial center of Athens, was located adjacent to the Areopagus, where the Council of Nobles and Court sat.

Athens was conquered in turn by the Macedonians, Romans, Byzantines, Franks, Florentines, and Ottoman Turks. Athena was evicted from her temple during the Byzantine period and taken to Constantinople, where the statue was destroyed in 1203 by the Crusaders. Later, the Parthenon was used as an ammunition dump. A naval bombardment by the Venetian fleet in 1687 hit the gunpowder storage and blew off the roof, smashing half the columns, collapsing the interior walls, and leaving the ruin that now remains. The last degradation was the flying of the swastika flag by Nazi occupiers in 1941. The Parthenon's survival remains a symbol of Greece itself.

References Flavio Conti, *The Focus on Democracy*. Boston, HBJ Press, 1978, 9–40. Spencer Harrington, "Rebuilding the Monuments of Pericles," *Archaeology* 48:1, 4–56 (January-February 1995). Robert Hopper, *The Acropolis*. New York, Macmillan, 1971.

AJANTA, India

Ajanta is a series of 29 caves carved in the basalt cliffs that overlook a bend in the Waghore River of central India. Seven waterfalls cascade down at the head of the gorge. The approach and setting are breathtaking, and the remoteness of the place adds an air of mystery. The caves themselves are famous for their beautiful and varied wall paintings.

Both Buddhists and Hindus built many rock-cut caves in central India. The oldest are Buddhist and are of two kinds: cave temples (*chaityas*) and monastery residences (*viharas*). The temples have a stupa at the end of a rather narrow passage, while the monks' residences are usually lined with cells and have simple but adequate living spaces.

The first caves at Ajanta were carved about 200 BCE, and building continued until 650 CE. Ajanta was built before the Ellora Caves, and some believe that the same peoples who built Ajanta went on to Ellora. However, there are important differences between the two sites: Ajanta is noted for its paintings, Ellora for its sculpture; Ajanta is a Buddhist site, while Ellora is Buddhist, Jain, and Hindu.

The Ajanta complex was built under the sponsorship of wealthy patrons, and some caves represent bodhisattvas (Buddhist teacher-saints) dear to some member of the court. Five of the Ajanta caves are temples and 24 are monasteries. The temples, though not vast, are roomy, with intricately carved pillars and arched ceilings. Some of the caves have sculptured fronts, pillars forming aisles, and altars. Because the cliff face is very steep, a few of the viharas even have small galleries at the entrance.

The Ajanta wall paintings rival the best religious frescoes of Assisi or Florence. Accidentally rediscovered in 1819 by a British hunting party, they immediately began to attract visitors. In their prime—until a hundred years ago, that is—the paintings remained bright and colorful. But a combination of petty vandalism, poor restoration techniques, and the use of harsh electric lights resulted in inevitable deterioration. However, in 1922, Italian conservators used scientific methods to preserve the paintings, and their decline has been stopped.

The themes of the paintings vary. The walls of the first cave are decorated with four representations of the banquet of the god of wealth, as well as other scenes. Many paintings portray bodhisattvas, or saints who have turned away from buddhahood in order to help others on the spiritual path. A repeated scene is The Dying Princess, showing Buddha's sister-in-law dying from sorrow when she learns that her husband has chosen to leave her to become a monk. In one cave, the paintings depict scenes of the Buddha's previous lives; another cave has a fine collection of secular paintings: a woman putting on cosmetics, a royal procession, and a couple making love. Outstanding among the numerous wall paintings is *The Bodhisattva with the Blue Lotus*. Here, wearing jasmine and lotus blossoms, sits the Bodhisattva Padmapani, an archetype of serenity. Close by is his spirit in female form. The figures are life size, and the effect is of holiness and other-worldliness.

Large numbers of Indians come to Ajanta on weekends and holidays, some as tourists but many as devotees to honor Buddha by leaving offerings of flowers and incense. There is no operating monastery today, however, and no services are conducted.

See also Ellora Caves.

References James Burgers and James Fergusson, *The Cave Temples of India*. Philadelphia, Coronet, 2d edition, 1969. Satcheverell Sitwell, *Great Temples of the East*. New York, Ivan Obolensky, 1963. Walter Spink, "The Caves at Ajanta," *Archaeology* 45:6, 52–60 (November-December 1992).

ANGKOR WAT, Cambodia

The approach to Angkor Wat, the magnificent shrine tribute to a god-king in northeast Cambodia, prepares one for an experience of awe. The visitor advances along 200 yards of causeway across a moat with a high balustrade of *nagas* (stone seven-headed cobra-protectors) on either side. The causeway ends at a five-story gate with colonnades along four sides of an outer court. A second raised causeway leads on for 400 yards to the entrance of the inner shrine. Looming ahead is a five-towered temple, fantastically shaped and intricately carved, giving the impression of a living, moving body. It rises above a double wall that completely surrounds it. A maze of galleries and stairs leads up the central tower (180 feet). The sandstone walls and staircases were originally painted and had gold highlights,

but they are extensively worn today. The large central tower is flanked by four smaller towers. Each anchors four courtyards with shaded galleries running around them. The highest point contains the main sanctuary, a small empty room.

The scale of the complex is enormous. The shrine building is the size of a medieval European cathedral and was built at the same time as the first Gothic cathedrals. A rectangular stone platform with sides 1,000 yards long serves as a base for the sanctuary. But the most striking aspect of Angkor Wat is the detail work covering every exposed surface, generating the sense of movement in the stone.

The shrine was built as a tomb for the ashes of Suryavarman II (1113–1150), one of the greatest of the Khmer rulers. Known as the Sun King, Suryavarman was regarded as a god by his people. Angkor's five towers represent the five peaks of fabled Mount Meru, a mountain that in Hindu myth was the legendary home of the gods. Angkor was thus a mountain home for the deified spirit of Suryavarman, so that his soul might communicate as an equal with the gods of Meru. During Suryavarman's life, Angkor Wat also enshrined the *lingam*, a carved stone pillar representing his penis, a symbol of his potency and dominance over the nation. Since it was believed that the security of the country and the continuation of the dynasty depended upon protecting the lingam, the courtyard sanctuary was a way to guard this sacred emblem. The lingam has long since been lost or destroyed.

Angkor Wat is an unusual shrine in that there is nothing to enter. It is pure architecture. Doubtless throngs of Khmer people came here to pay homage both during the king's life and after, but there are no places where sacrifice was offered. The galleries are covered with 700 yards of carved reliefs of

The central tower of Angkor Wat stands 180 feet and contains the main sanctuary, which is a small empty room. Angkor Wat was built as a shrine for the Khmer ruler Suryavarman II (1113–1150), who was regarded as a god by his people.

scenes from Hindu religious epics involving some 18,000 characters. The thousands of carvings of female dancers suggest the kinds of ceremonies that must have been conducted, all of them centered about the praise and adulation of the king and father of the nation.

Angkor evidently provided for a large population. Its water reservoir is sufficient for a fair-sized city, and doubtless large herds of ceremonial elephants were kept. But Angkor began to decline within a century of its completion. When the canals were no longer used for irrigation, malaria spread, crops failed, and people left for other areas. In 1432 the site was abandoned and jungle vines closed around it.

In the 1850s French archaeologists rediscovered Angkor Wat and restoration began. The latest work was completed with United Nations support, and Angkor Wat is on the UNESCO World Heritage List. During the Cambodian terror in the 1970s, Angkor Wat was used as a communications center by the Khmer Rouge. It was not damaged by war, however, and since the establishment of a new government it has been reopened in an attempt to earn tourist foreign exchange. Even though Angkor itself is well secured, the area surrounding it is dangerous, subject to raids from bandits and former guerrillas. There are a number of other temples and ruins in the rainforest surrounding Angkor Wat, though none rivals it in importance or magnificence.

References Russel Ciochon and Jamie James, "The Glory That Was Angkor," *Archaeology* 47:2, 38–49 (March–April 1994). Flavio Conti, *Tribute to Religion*. Boston, HBJ Press, 1979, 153–168. Michael Freeman and Roger Warner, *Ankor*. Boston, Houghton Mifflin, 1990. Dawn Rooney, *Ankor*. Lincolnwood, IL, Passport Books, 1994. Sacheverell Sitwell, *Great Temples of the East*. New York, Ivan Obolensky, 1963.

ANNE FRANK HOUSE, Netherlands

During the German occupation of the Netherlands, Anne Frank, a young Jewish girl, and her family hid in a secret apartment in Amsterdam. The Franks had fled Nazi Germany in 1933, after Adolf Hitler came to power, but the occupation of the Netherlands left them no further refuge. The apartment was their last hope. Anne Frank was 13 when the family went into hiding in 1942; she was 15 when she died.

On August 4, 1944, acting on a tip from a collaborator, the Nazi police broke into a secret annex built above Mr. Frank's spice business in Amsterdam and captured the two Jewish families that had been in hiding there. After terrorizing the employees and vandalizing the hidden apartment, they left. Shortly after the raid, Miep Gies, one of those who had smuggled food to the families, sneaked into the apartment and gathered up the scattered pages of a diary the young daughter, Anne Frank, had been keeping. Fearful that the Gestapo would find it and hunt down those mentioned in it, she kept it in her home in an open drawer, which she guessed would cause the least suspicion.

The Franks and their companions, a family named Van Damme, were sent to concentration camps on the last transport to leave Holland with Jews bound for their deaths. Only Anne's father, Otto Frank, lived to be liberated from Auschwitz. All the others perished within a few days of one another. Anne and her sister, Margot, died of typhus at Bergen-Belsen.

Anne Frank's story is only one among thousands of similar stories during World War II. What set it apart and made Anne Frank a symbol of suffering Jews during the

Holocaust was her diary. Returned to Otto Frank, it was published in an edited edition and became an immediate international bestseller. It has appeared in 50 languages and was made into both a play and a film. In 1995, the complete edition appeared. Personal and touching, the diary records the family's life and her own maturing. It also relates the horrors of the Nazi occupation reflected in the lives of a small group of people who take on personality as the diary unfolds.

The diary is surprisingly well written for a young person, detailing Anne's emergence from childhood to early womanhood. She explores her developing romantic feelings and her adolescent tensions with her mother. She speaks of her fear and the atmosphere of oppression that lay upon them in the annex. Prophetically, she writes, "The perfect round spot on which we're standing is still safe, but the clouds are moving in on us, and the ring between us and the approaching danger is being pulled tighter and tighter."

The Anne Frank House was established in 1960, after a public outcry prevented the building's demolition. Every year it draws over 600,000 visitors. Many of them are merely curious when they enter but fall silent as they move through the annex. The apartment has been left as it was at the end of the war, stripped of furniture but with many little reminders of the family. Anne's movie star posters are still pasted on the wall, along with a few mementos. The feeling of the place, above all, is claustrophobic. But somehow, what rings through is Anne Frank's triumphant testimony: "In spite of everything I still believe that people are really good at heart." The Anne Frank Foundation, which owns the building, also engages in antiracist education programs and organizes traveling exhibits.

See also Auschwitz-Birkenau; Holocaust Sites.

References Anne Frank, *The Diary of a Young Girl.* New York, Doubleday, 1995. Miep Gies, *Anne Frank Remembered.* New York, Simon and Schuster, 1987. Israel Gutman (ed.), *Encyclopedia of the Holocaust.* New York, Macmillan, 4 vols., 1990. Ruud van der Rol, *Anne Frank: Beyond the Diary.* New York, Viking, 1993 (young adult).

ASSISI, Italy

Assisi is the hometown of St. Francis of Assisi, one of the most popular Christian saints. Assisi is perhaps the only place commonly revered by Christians of all expressions and by Buddhists, Muslims, and animists as well. Buddhist and yoga retreats have even been established in the surrounding hills.

The focus of this reverence is St. Francis of Assisi, a humble man who chose to live poor as a wandering poet and prophet while building up a community of simple but devout friars. Francis is today celebrated throughout the world. The center of his devotion is the town of Assisi in the Tuscan hills.

Francis (1182–1226) and his close friend and disciple Clare (1193?–1253) are the soul of Assisi. A soldier and something of a wastrel, Francis had a profound conversion experience when an inner voice led him to rebuild ruined chapels. His father sued him for using the family's money for chapels, and in a dramatic scene, Francis cast off his rich clothing and returned it, revealing himself clad in a penitent's hair shirt. Francis spent a period as a hermit, and toward the end of his life received the stigmata, the bleeding wounds of Christ, on his hands and body. Yet his poetry, especially the ecstatic *Canticle of the Sun* and the *Canticle of the Creatures,* which are among the finest poems in Italian, reveals no melancholy but only joy.

Francis gathered together a group of followers whose numbers swelled until there were thousands across Europe. They lived lives of simplicity and poverty, often sleeping on the ground or in caves, yet after Francis's death his followers built a magnificent church in Assisi in his honor.

The church is built in Romanesque style, which blends well with the Umbrian hill country surrounding it. In the crypt beneath it lie the remains of Francis. When they were brought there four years after his death, the friars bolted the doors against the crowds that pressed to see and touch the relics. A few trusted friars buried the body secretly in the lower church, and it was not rediscovered until the nineteenth century. The lower church is the site of some of the most valuable frescoes, although many are now damaged by damp and age. In 1996, the Chapel of St. Mary Magdalen was reopened after restoration, revealing splendid frescoes by Giotto, previously hidden under layers of smoke and wax from votive candles.

The upper church is a grand, vaulted, 60-foot space, more Gothic in style. It, too, is frescoed, including 28 panels by Giotto of the life and legend of St. Francis. These include the famous scene of Francis preaching to the birds along with a scene of his taming a wolf and another of Francis before the Turkish sultan (he had gone to Turkey, hoping for martyrdom). The choir stalls, of intricately carved woodwork, are masterpieces. Each is inlaid with wood mosaics, portraits of early disciples of Francis. They also reflect the irony of the splendid church in honor of *il poverello,* the man of poverty, for Franciscan friars are not monks and do not use choir stalls.

The Church of San Francesco, with its attached monastery, is a beacon for pilgrims of many faiths from all over the world, and they are received in a constant stream. Many of them make the same round of stops: the Basilicas of St. Francis and of St. Clare, the hermitage, and the Portiuncula.

St. Clare was the beautiful daughter of a nobleman, Francis's closest friend, and the foundress of the Franciscan nuns. Homes in Assisi had two doors, one for regular use and the Door of the Dead, only used for funerals. When Clare left home, she went through it as a sign that she had died to this world and chosen a new one. Francis and some friars met her at the Portiuncula, a tiny chapel they had restored, where they cut off her long hair. After 42 years as head of the Order of St. Clare, she was buried in the church named for her.

Another shrine is Francis's hermitage, a cave in the forested hills above the church. Francis's cell is preserved along with the stone altar from which he preached to the birds. Its simplicity and austerity are a better reflection of Francis than the grander churches of Assisi.

The Portiuncula is rather tiny, and to preserve it, a church, the Basilica of St. Mary of the Angels, was built around it. The annual Feast of Forgiveness is held here. It was begun by Francis, who was vexed that warriors were forgiven their sins by the Church if they joined the Crusades. Francis established his feast with a pilgrimage as a more peaceful way to seek forgiveness and expiation. It is thronged with pilgrims, especially youth groups and charismatic Catholics, singing, dancing, and celebrating in a very Franciscan way. The Portiuncula is kept as a Franciscan shrine because as he was dying, Francis asked to be taken there. Then, singing the last verse of his *Canticle of the Sun,* Francis passed to eternity.

References Line Gorgon, *The Story of Assisi*. New York, Gorgon, 1977. Marian Habig, OFM (ed.), *St. Francis of Assisi: Writings and Early Biographies.* Chicago, Franciscan Herald, 1972. Nest de Rabic, *Life of St. Francis of Assisi*. Assisi, Case Editrice, 1975.

AUSCHWITZ-BIRKENAU, Poland

Auschwitz (Oświęcim in Polish), the largest and most vicious of the Nazi extermination camps during the Holocaust, lies in a desolate area 35 miles outside Kraków in southern Poland. Although the Nazis destroyed part of the camp when they fled before the advance of the Soviet armies, much of Auschwitz remains as it was when the Germans left.

Today, Auschwitz is well cared for and receives numbers of visitors daily, while its twin camp at Birkenau (two miles away) has been deliberately left in ruins. A rail line separates the two camps. Here the unfortunate deportees and their meager goods were unloaded and sorted out. The healthy were set aside for work while the elderly, the weak, and the children were immediately sent off to the gas chambers. Under the pretext of delousing, the women prisoners had their hair cut off. The prisoners were then herded into large rooms disguised to look like public showers. (The Germans cynically called them "the saunas.") When the doors were sealed, gas pellets dropped into the room, and soon all were dead. The bodies were stripped of any rings and gold teeth and then taken to the crematoria to be burned.

One of the barracks at Auschwitz has been refitted as a museum to display eerie piles of shoes, eyeglasses, luggage, and dentures confiscated from the prisoners. Seven tons of human hair represent the many tons that were shipped away for use in making felt for the German war effort.

Those who were held back for labor were tattooed with identification numbers. They worked long hours under brutal conditions and ate little more than bread and watery soup. The barracks, which are still standing, were unheated in the freezing Polish winter, and the only clothing was thin. In the summer the climate was humid and malarial. There were no facilities for laundry, and underwear was changed at intervals of weeks or even months. Typhus, tuberculosis, scabies, and typhoid fever flourished under these conditions. The average prisoner survived only a few months, and many of the prisoners were simply worked to death. At the end, some survivors weighed only 60 pounds. But even under extreme conditions, there was resistance in the camp. In 1944, for example, an uprising by the camp leaders blew up one crematorium at Birkenau.

Auschwitz was established in 1940 as a Polish prison camp, following the Nazi policy of destroying Polish culture by eliminating its intellectual leadership and reducing the nation to slavery. Many priests were executed at Auschwitz. Candles and a marker indicate the small cell where St. Maximilian Kolbe, a priest-martyr who is popular in Poland, was starved to death after he offered himself in exchange for a condemned prisoner with a wife and family.

Within a year, Auschwitz became the main depot for Jews from throughout Eastern Europe, and then from the entire continent. Birkenau was built in 1942. Forty branch camps, mostly slave labor centers, were also built. It was the most efficient killing machine ever developed, using the latest German technology to eradicate almost two million people, 80 percent of them Jews. Dr. Josef Mengele, nicknamed "the Angel of Death," selected children, especially twins, for cruel medical experi-

German civilians view a line of bodies at Auschwitz following the Russian liberation of the camp in 1945.

ments. Then, as the Soviet forces closed in, the Nazis drove 58,000 prisoners on forced marches toward Germany. Almost none survived. Those who were left behind, about 7,000, were freed by the Russians. The coldness and remorseless evil involved makes Auschwitz-Birkenau a monument to depravity.

The Polish government restored the camp as a monument after World War II, although, under Communism, government policy was often anti-Semitic. Although Auschwitz guides refer to the Jews who died there, displays still concentrate on Polish Christians. Along one hallway several hundred photos of the dead stare down from the walls, but not one is Jewish. Polish nationalism, in its desire to proclaim the suffering of the Poles during the Nazi occupation, has chosen to relegate the Jewish

slaughter to a minor position and to continue to distort history.

Auschwitz has the atmosphere of a museum, with throngs of visitors, a documentary film, and signboards in five languages. Birkenau, which has never been restored, is a stark contrast. One negotiates its broken ground to the one restored barracks, an austere and cheerless place. Once there were 300 people packed into one of these hovels, built directly on swampy ground and infested with rats. Shelves held eight people sleeping squeezed together on rotten straw. One wooden stable originally built for 52 horses was used to hold 1,000 prisoners. There were four massive gas chambers, each with its crematorium. A small pond contains the ashes of 100,000 people consumed in the crematoria, and a little scratching at the earth soon brings up splinters of human bone. The crematoria still impress by their size, but it is the memorials that attract most visitors. There is a hush as people lay flowers and light candles.

Historians, Jewish survivors, and the Polish government are debating the future of Auschwitz. Many favor making it into a museum to educate the public, while others seek a religious memorial. The first group wants to rebuild one gas chamber complex to allow visitors the harrowing experience of entering the "shower rooms" and then seeing the crematorium. Many find this offensive, turning visitors into voyeurs and cheapening what they regard as holy ground. Controversy flared for a decade when Carmelite nuns built a convent next to the camp, angering many Jews who felt it was a further attempt to make Auschwitz a Christian Polish shrine. Incidents led to the appointment of a Church commission, led by a French cardinal of Jewish extraction, and the sisters were finally ordered to relocate in 1993.

See also Holocaust Sites.

References Lucie Adelsberger, *Auschwitz: A Doctor's Story*. Boston, Northeastern University, 1996. Danuta Czech, *Auschwitz Chronicle, 1939-1945*. New York, Henry Holt, 1990. Israel Gutman, *Anatomy of the Auschwitz Death Camp*. Bloomington, Indiana University, 1994. Israel Gutman (ed.), *Encyclopedia of the Holocaust*. New York, Macmillan, 4 vols., 1990.

AVILA, Spain

One of the finest medieval cities in Spain, the walled town of Ávila breathes the spirit of its patron, St. Teresa (1515–1582). She dominates not only the religious soul of the city but also its history and cultural life.

A native of Ávila who spent her entire life in the town, St. Teresa became one of the principal forces in the Spanish religious and national revival of the sixteenth century. Signs of her influence are everywhere. She was associated with several of the churches and powerful convents of the city and became reformer and mistress of most of the Carmelite convents in the country. With her friend, St. John of the Cross, she reformed the men's order as well, and her essays and spiritual diary are considered some of the most exalted mystical writings in the Spanish language. A woman of intense religious feeling and rigor, she also had a charming sense of humor and everyday common sense. When she founded her first convent, based on poverty and hardship, she chose only women of intelligence and common sense. "God preserve us from stupid nuns," she commented tartly.

It is evident that Teresa is both revered and beloved in Ávila. Even the local candy, usually made in the enclosed convents, is named for her. The first woman recognized as a Doctor of the Church for her outstanding theology, she was likewise a major figure in the Catholic Reformation, which brought new direction and new life to the decadent Catholic church of the sixteenth century.

Ávila is a popular stop for religious tours of Spain. It is not a shrine town, so visitors seek out the places of Teresa's life along a kind of pilgrimage route. Teresa spent 27 years as a nun and 3 as a superior in the *Convento de la Encarnación*. Her austere cell, furnished with her things, may be visited. The first of the 16 convents she founded, *Convento de las Madres*, preserves the coffin in which she slept as an act of penance. The *Convento de Santa Teresa*, built over her birthplace, has paintings of miraculous events during her life, such as being raised off the ground and encountering Christ.

All of these convents have museums devoted to her.

Teresa's attraction is the way she combined her down-to-earth practicality (*Encarnación* has a display of her pithy sayings) with a mystical life. Her books constitute the classic description of the mystical experience. Together with the exalted poetry of her intimate friend John, they constitute a major contribution to Spanish literature. Teresa's *Interior Castle*, far from being obscure, is a highly accessible pathway to contact with God, requiring neither great learning nor occult practices. Pope John Paul II once referred to Teresa and John as "the spiritual teachers of my interior life."

References Jodi Bilinkoff, *The Avila of St. Teresa*. Ithaca, Cornell University, 1992. Francis Gross, *The Making of a Mystic*. Albany, State University of New York, 1993. Victoria Lincoln, *Teresa, a Woman*. Albany, State University of New York, 1984.

AXUM, Ethiopia

The holiest city of the Ethiopian Orthodox faith, Axum was founded over 2,000 years ago. It was here in the fourth century that Christianity first came to the highlands, the heartland of Ethiopia. Prince Ezana, instructed in Christianity by two Syrian brothers shipwrecked on the Red Sea coast, promoted the faith when he became king. He is regarded as a saint in both the Ethiopian Orthodox and Catholic churches.

Axum was the first Christian kingdom in the world and the largest outside the Roman Empire. It sat astride the caravan routes to Arabia, Nubia, and Egypt, trading as far away as Greece, Rome, and Constantinople. In the sixth century, King St. Kaleb built Axum into a military power and took on the role of protector of Christians in the region, including Arabia. Kaleb conquered several small Jewish kingdoms in Arabia. As a result, Jewish customs crossed the Red Sea and were incorporated into Ethiopian Christianity.

The most sacred shrine in Ethiopia is the church of *St. Mary of Zion*, first dedicated to the Virgin Mary in the 300s CE and reconstructed in the seventeenth century on the ruins of the church destroyed by the Muslims. The destruction and rebuilding of the church is an important part of its meaning for Ethiopians. Surrounded by Muslim countries, overrun several times, and brought to the brink of extinction, Orthodox Christianity in Ethiopia sees itself as a militant bastion against Islam. St. Mary of Zion's rise from the ashes serves as a symbol of the nation. The emperors of Ethiopia were all crowned there. Until the 1930s, criminals could receive sanctuary in the church precincts by ringing the bell on the porch.

The present church was rebuilt with Portuguese aid and shows a Syrian influence. It is a squat, square structure with a colonnade around it, used for dancing by the priests during services. Inside is a vestibule, and beyond this is the Holy of Holies, closed to everyone but the priests. Male pilgrims do not go beyond the vestibule and women are confined to the courtyard. The small church is soon overwhelmed by the crowds, whose sonorous chanting flows like a tide, rising and falling in a wave of sound. When the priests emerge from the Holy of Holies to carry the Gospel book in procession or bring the Eucharist to the people, they are garbed in bright robes and shielded by ornate ceremonial umbrellas.

Next to the church is a relic chapel (built in 1965 by Emperor Haile Selassie) that contains the royal crowns and church treasures. It is also believed to contain the biblical Ark of the Covenant with the tablets of the Ten Commandments given to Moses on Mount Sinai. Copies of the ark and the tablets are taken out on feast days and paraded around the towns, though the originals are seen by no one except a single guardian priest. He takes up this task for life, standing alone before the Holy of Holies. On his deathbed he is expected to name his successor.

Accounts dating to the fourteenth century say that Menelik, legendary son of King Solomon of ancient Israel and the Queen of Sheba, brought the Ark of the Covenant to Ethiopia. A recent study traced this tradition and argues that although Lalibela was built to house the Ark, it came to Axum instead. Ethiopians firmly believe this argument and flock to St. Mary of Zion in pilgrimage, especially for feasts of the Virgin. The Ark is said to be a box covered with fine cloth, with winged figures on each corner.

Also at Axum is a series of 11 granite columns or stelae, one of which—now fallen—is the tallest in the world at 90 feet. These had some religious purpose in pre-Christian times, and some have altars at the base with grooves cut into them to carry away blood from sacrifices. The Ethiopian Orthodox Church has retained many Jew-

ish and ancient customs, and in rural areas, animal sacrifice is not unknown, though there is no evidence of it being practiced here. Monoliths continued to be erected after the arrival of Christianity, and several with Christian inscriptions can be found. Some say that one of the fallen stelae covers the site of the Queen of Sheba's grave. A large reservoir is called her "bath," and pilgrims collect water from it to take home.

A short distance away from the stelae is a fortress containing the tomb of St. Kaleb. The cover stone is a granite piece weighing 100 tons. Nearby is a stone slab with inscriptions in Greek, Saebean, and Ge'ez, the ancient liturgical language of Ethiopia. It describes St. Ezana's conversion of Ethiopia.

Axum was in the battle zone during much of the liberation war against the central government in the 1980s. Marxist forces were accused of plundering 83 churches in the area and killing a number of priests, but the ancient shrines of Axum were not seriously damaged.

See also Lalibela.

References James Bent, *The Sacred City of the Ethiopians*. New York, Longmans, 1896. Graham Hancock, *Historic Ethiopia*. Nairobi, Camerapix, 1994. ———, *The Sign and the Seal: Quest for the Lost Ark of the Covenant*. New York, Crown, 1992.

BABI YAR, Ukraine

The site of one of the worst Nazi atrocities, Babi Yar, a wooded ravine outside Kiev, has become the symbol of the Holocaust in the Ukraine and Russia.

As the World War II Nazi armies swept across Europe in their first flush of victory, they gathered Jews together, registered them, and persecuted them. Then, when the Nazis decided on the "final solution"—the genocide of the Jews—massive numbers were either executed or deported to work at death camps. The Nazi campaign against the Jews was especially vicious in the Ukraine, where the Nazis killed most of the Jewish population during their occupation.

Between 1941 and 1943, over 100,000 people, almost all Jews, were executed at Babi Yar. In the most horrific incident, on September 29, 1941, 33,000 Jews were marched to the ravine, stripped, and executed by machine gun fire. Their bodies were buried, both the dead and those still living. Then the Nazis decided to execute all the Jews left in Kiev, and they summoned them to a gathering point for "deportation and resettlement," then marched them to their deaths.

As Soviet forces advanced on Kiev in 1943, a Nazi team was formed to cover over all traces of Babi Yar. Prisoners from a nearby concentration camp were forced to exhume and burn the bodies, then crush the bones with headstones taken from neighboring Jewish cemeteries. Finally the Nazis were expelled and the Soviet government reestablished, but a cloak of silence was wrapped around Babi Yar. Though many Jews who had fled the advance of the Nazis returned, all attempts at memorializing the dead met bureaucratic opposition, and Jews who prayed at the site were often arrested. Among the causes of this bureaucratic resistance was the embarrassing fact, long suppressed and denied by the Communists, that a number of Ukrainians had defected to the Nazis, hoping to escape communism. The Ukrainian tradition of anti-Semitism was well-established, and many of the Ukrainian police had taken part in the atrocities as allies of the Nazis. In the months following the September massacre, more executions took place at Babi Yar, and Nazi officials testified that reports from the Ukrainians betraying Jews came in "by the bushelful." This fact, though officially ignored, was never quite forgotten. In 1961 it finally received international attention with the publication of a lengthy poem, "Babi Yar," by the distinguished writer Yevgeny Yevtushenko. In one passage, its haunting lines read:

> No gravestone stands on Babi Yar;
> Only coarse earth heaped roughly on the
> gash:
> Such dread comes over me.

Immediately, both Russian and international attention focused on Babi Yar. Dmitri Shostakovich incorporated the poem into his Thirteenth Symphony. Still, a memorial was not erected until 1974, and it made no mention of the Jewish dead. Instead it centered on a wartime resistance hero and vaguely referred to the "victims of fascism." It was built away from the ravine, and pilgrimages and demonstrations were discouraged. Finally, on the fiftieth anniversary of the September slaughter, during the disintegration of the Soviet system and in a newly independent Ukraine, a new memorial was put up. It was accompanied by a campaign of education in Kiev about the Holocaust and Babi Yar's part in it. The memorial itself is set in a large park at the end of a brick road leading up to a menorah, the traditional seven-branched candlestick used in Jewish ceremonies.

See also Holocaust Sites.

References A. Anatoli, *Babi Yar.* Cambridge, MA, Bently, 1979 (fiction). Israel Gutman (ed.), *Encyclopedia of the Holocaust.* New York, Macmillan, 4 vols., 1990. Yevgeny Yevtushenko, *Collected Poems, 1952–1990.* New York, Henry Holt, 1991.

BAHA'I WORLD CENTRE, Israel

Members of the Baha'i faith throughout the world make pilgrimages to Haifa, Israel, to the shrines of their founders.

In the 1840s a young Shiite Muslim mystic who was a *siyyid*, a descendant of the Prophet Mohammed, began preaching and took the title Bab, the "Gateway of Divine Perfection." Soon he proclaimed himself the *mahdi*, the divinely sent leader who was to deliver his people from oppression. When he also implied that he was a prophet, the Shiite leadership denounced him as a heretic and executed him in 1850. His remains were taken to Palestine by his followers and entombed near present-day Haifa.

The Bab taught that God would raise up a World Teacher who would usher in a new age of peace and bring religious unity. This teacher was later revealed to be a disciple

named Baha'u'llah, who expanded the Bab's teaching into what has become known as Baha'i and made it into a world religion. Baha'u'llah announced that he was the Promised One whom all the prophets had predicted. But when his teachings were warmly embraced by the common people in Persia, the Muslim leaders drove him into exile. He wandered through the Middle East and ended up in Acre in Palestine, where he was imprisoned by the Turks and died in 1892. His son, Abdul Baha, succeeded him and took the faith to Europe and America, where it received its final transformation, becoming more socially conscious. Baha'i teaches that since God is one, all religions contain manifestations of the truth. Nine is a sacred number, a symbol of unity that stands for the nine manifestations of God: Moses, Buddha, Zoroaster, Confucius, Jesus, Mohammed, Hare Krishna, the Bab, and Baha'u'llah.

Every Baha'i is encouraged to fulfill the wish of Baha'u'llah to visit the shrines of the faith in Israel. The first pilgrimage came from America in 1898, six years after Baha'u'llah's death. Today, nine-day pilgrimages are organized in groups that are put together from Baha'i communities around the world as a sign of universality. Baha'i followers believe that in the pilgrimage they come as close to the divine as possible in this life, and the pilgrimage experience is intense.

The main sites for the pilgrimage are the tombs of the Bab and of Baha'u'llah. The tomb of the Bab is on the slopes of Mount Carmel near Haifa, in a breathtaking setting that overlooks the Mediterranean Sea. The shrine is a soaring, nine-sided dome of white marble and colored tiles, with nine pillars and nine sections, a masterpiece of Near Eastern architecture. A few miles away is the tomb of Baha'u'llah, a squat building surrounded by formal gardens intended to reflect the peace and harmony of the Garden of Eden. The gardens are divided by rows of trees and shrubs radiating out from the shoreline, symbolizing the coming together of all peoples into world unity.

In a nearby building, Baha'u'llah spent his last years under house arrest during the Ottoman Turkish colonial period. Here, pilgrims are permitted to see pictures of the Bab and Baha'u'llah, the only time their portraits are ever revealed. A museum focuses on the martyrs of the faith, especially the many who have died in the genocide against them in Iran in recent years. Pilgrims visit all these sites, but an important part of the pilgrimage is the interaction among the pilgrims themselves, affirming their unity across lines of nation, race, and gender.

References *The Baha'i Faith.* Cos Cob, CT, Hartley, 1989 (video). Francis Beckwith, *Baha'i.* Minneapolis MN, Bethany, 1985. Eunice Braun and Hugh Chance, *A Crown of Beauty: The Baha'i Faith and the Holy Land.* London, G. Ronald, 1982.

BEGIJNHOF, Netherlands

Located in bustling central Amsterdam, Begijnhof was built as a residence for Beguines, a community of women that arose in the Lowlands during the thirteenth century to devote themselves to good works. Of 20 convents and monasteries in Amsterdam at the time of the Reformation, only Begijnhof continued to operate after the suppression of Catholicism. It is built as a large cloister, a circle of small townhouses around a lovely quadrant of gardens and park. The last Beguine died there in 1974. For some years it has been a residence for elderly widows.

The ability of the Beguines to operate during times of persecution was a result of their religious position. They did not take religious vows and were not nuns. The sisters worked as seamstresses, taught children, and cared for widows and for the homeless, as well as travelers. By the sixteenth century there were many of these religious settlements, and several with thousands of members. The Amsterdam Begijnhof, built in the fourteenth century, was more modest.

In 1578, with the banning of Catholic worship in Holland after the victory of the Protestants, the garden chapel of the Begijnhof, dating from 1346, was taken from the Beguines and assigned to English Calvinist refugees who had fled both Catholic and Anglican persecution. The Engelsekerk (English Church) remains Presbyterian and is today a center for Amsterdam's English-speaking Protestant community. A stained-glass window in the church shows John Robinson's followers leaving for Plymouth in 1620 to join the Pilgrims who sought religious freedom in America.

The Beguines, who continued to minister to Catholics through clandestine chapels, resisted the suppression of Catholicism. As Sister Cornalitgen Arents neared death, for instance, she rejected burial in the Protestant chapel and asked to be placed beneath the gutter. Her gravestone can still be seen on the curbstone. In 1665, the Catholics built a clandestine chapel by converting two houses in the Begijnhof. Dedicated to Ss. John and Ursula, its stained-glass windows commemorate a Eucharistic miracle that supposedly took place around the time of the foundation of the Begijnhof. In 1345 a sick man, given the sacred host as he was dying, vomited it up. When the nurse cast the refuse into a fire, the host emerged intact and pure. From that time, many pilgrims have visited the site of the miracle, and the processional passes by the Begijnhof. Today the Catholic chapel is the

Dating from the fourteenth century, the Begijnhof was the only one out of 20 convents and monasteries in Amsterdam that continued to operate after the suppression of Catholicism in 1578.

gathering place of the English-speaking Catholic community, celebrating Mass a few yards from the Presbyterian church. Clearly, the Catholic chapel was clandestine in name only. The two religious communities, Protestant and Catholic, have worshipped side by side for over three centuries.

See also Our Lord in the Attic.

References Ernest McDonnell, *Beguines and Beghards in Medieval Culture*. New York, Octagon, 1969. Ephraim Mizruchi, *Regulating Society: Beguines, Bohemians, and Other Marginals*. Chicago, University of Chicago, 1987. Marguerite Porete, *The Mirror of Simple Souls*. Mahwah NJ, Paulist, 1993.

BENARES

See Varanasi.

BETHLEHEM, Palestinian Authority

The biblical birthplace of Jesus of Nazareth is Bethlehem of Judah, five miles south of Jerusalem. Its importance comes from the infancy narratives, those sections of Luke's and Matthew's Gospels that recount the birth of Jesus. These legends, among the best known in western civilization, are the basis of the Christmas celebration. According to Luke 2:1–39, Mary and Joseph traveled from their home in Nazareth to Bethlehem to be registered for the imperial census. Mary delivered the child in a manger because inns were full, and shepherds and angels came to worship him. He was circumcised and then presented at the Temple. Matthew 1:18–2:23 adds the account of a star seen in the East by three magi, or wise men, who followed it to find Jesus and honored him with gifts of gold, frankincense, and myrrh.

After the Roman destruction of Jerusalem, the imperial government tried to erase the memory of those places important in the life of Jesus by building pagan shrines over them. In Bethlehem they planted a grove consecrated to Adonis, the god of love, around the cave where Jesus was born. But this shrine only served to mark the place with certainty, and in 326 CE the first Christian emperor, Constantine, built a basilica there. In a nearby cave, St. Jerome lived for many years while he prepared his Latin translation of the Bible. During a revolt in 529 CE the basilica was destroyed, but it was soon rebuilt.

The Persians invaded Palestine in 614, and their armies advanced as far as Bethlehem. There they stopped before the basilica and refused to damage it because above the entrance was a large mosaic portrait of the three magi in Persian attire. The Persian soldiers recognized their own sages. Nor did the Muslims who came in the following century disturb the Basilica of the Nativity. When the Christians won back the Holy Land during the Crusades, the church was used for the coronations of the Christian kings for two centuries. In 1852, Emperor Louis Napoleon claimed the Church of the Nativity for France, and this conflict with the ruling Turks became a pretext for the Crimean War.

Greek Orthodox, Catholics, and Armenians may each worship at the basilica, but the Greek Orthodox church handles the administration. The main entrance, the Door of Humility, requires one to bend over to enter. It was built to keep the Muslims from entering on horseback, but Jews refuse to use it rather than bow their heads to a Christian shrine. Trap doors in the ground floor reveal the remnants of the mosaic floor of the original Byzantine church. The impressive icons before the altar were a gift of the Russian imperial family in 1764. Alongside the altar are stairs leading down to the Grotto of the Nativity, where Jesus' birthplace is marked by a star, which many pilgrims kiss.

The major celebration in Bethlehem occurs at Christmas, when the Latin patriarch comes from Jerusalem for midnight Mass at the Church of St. Catherine. (St. Catherine's is the Catholic church, built by the Franciscans in 1881, next to the Church of the Nativity. Below it is the cave of St. Jerome and his tomb, along with those of his companions.) In former times, the Patriarch rode on a donkey or in a carriage, with hundreds of people walking alongside, but today, political tensions make such a procession impossible. Instead, an Israeli military escort takes the Patriarch, who is Palestinian, to a checkpoint, where Palestinian police receive him.

On the northern outskirts of the town is the Tomb of Rachel, beloved wife of Jacob and matriarch of the tribe of Benjamin. Her love story is told in Genesis 30. She died giving birth to Benjamin, and her tomb is mentioned in Genesis 35:20. However, the Bible mentions two locations for Rachel's tomb, and scholars agree that Bethlehem is not the correct one. Even so, popular tradition insists on the Bethlehem site. Rachel's tomb is one of the holiest shrines of Judaism and is visited by many pilgrims, including some Muslims and Christians. Because Rachel was the mother of her people and died in childbirth, a visit to her tomb is especially favored by women praying for the blessing of a large family or for safe delivery.

See also Nazareth.

References Raymond Brown, SS, *The Birth of the Messiah*. New York, Doubleday, rev. ed., 1993. Joe Cauthen, *Come to Bethlehem*. New York, Viking, 1975 (juvenile). *Christmas Experience in Bethlehem.*

Clarksburg NJ, Alden Films, 1987 (video).

BIGHORN MEDICINE WHEEL, Wyoming, USA

The most important of the many medicine wheels found in high mountain areas throughout the American West, the Bighorn Medicine Wheel is located in the Bighorn National Forest of north-central Wyoming. Located at an elevation of almost 10,000 feet on Medicine Mountain, the Bighorn Medicine Wheel is inaccessible much of the year due to snow pack and winter weather. Its rim is about 80 feet in diameter, its circumference 245 feet. The central cairn (stone pile), about 10 feet across and 2 feet high, is made simply of gathered rocks. Twenty-eight spokes radiate out, and six smaller cairns are spaced along the rim. Four of the cairns line up with the rising and setting sun of the summer solstice, and the others with the three bright stars of summer mornings that fade as the sun rises: Aldebaran, Rigel, and Sirius. The 28 spokes are assumed to relate to the lunar month.

For the Native Americans of the Great Plains, medicine wheels were apparently both religious ritual places and a means of determining the seasons and religious ritual places. Each medicine wheel includes a cairn at the center of a circle, with lines of stones radiating out along the solstice lines. The Bighorn Medicine Wheel has long been used by Crow youth as a place to fast and seek their vision. Native Americans go to Bighorn Medicine Wheel to offer thanks for all of creation, especially the plant and animal life that has sustained them, placing a buffalo skull on the center cairn as part of a prayer offering. The Wheel is protected by a wire fence, to which prayer bundles are often found attached. Prayers are offered for healing, and atonement is made for harm done to others, or reparation for the harm done to Mother Earth by others. Great chiefs, including Chief Joseph of the Nez Percé, have come to Bighorn for guidance and prayed for the wisdom to lead their people in the transition from freedom to reservation life.

The Bighorn Medicine Wheel is several hundred years old—possibly 700. Its original ceremonial use is not connected with any American Indian tribe in the region. In fact, it predates them. Crow mythology ascribes the creation of the medicine wheel to a boy named Burnt Face, who was scarred when he fell into a fire as a baby. When he reached his teen years, Burnt Face went on his vision quest into the mountains, where he fasted and built the first medicine wheel. The story says that he was carried off by an eagle, after he helped it drive away an animal who attacked the baby eaglets before they could fly. In return, his face was made smooth.

The vision quest and other practices have also attracted a number of practitioners of New Age religions, who consider medicine wheels centers of earth energy connected with the spiritual powers of the sun. However, the presence of New Age pilgrims is resented by many Native Americans. Today, some young warriors are reluctant to go to the wheel because of the presence of white visitors.

See also Black Hills; Medicine Wheels.
References John Eddy, "Probing the Mystery of the Medicine Wheels," *National Geographic* 151:1, 140–146 (January 1977). Sam Gill, *Native American Religion.* Belmont CA, Wadsworth, 1982. Courtney Milne, *Sacred Places in North America.* New York, Stewart, Tabori & Chang, 1994.

BLACK HILLS, South Dakota/ Wyoming, USA

The Black Hills (*Paha Sapa* in Lakota) have been sacred lands for the Plains Indians for hundreds of years. Stretching across 6,000 square miles of the borderlands between Wyoming and South Dakota, they include mountains, caves, and timberland. Native American Indians have begun a campaign to keep the Black Hills free of development and prevent access by tourists. The federal government has offered $108 million to buy out Sioux rights, but the Sioux have refused. To them sacred land is a trust that cannot be alienated.

After the Civil War, the West was opened to white settlement and buffalo were slaughtered commercially. For the Plains Indians, this meant the destruction of their economy and their way of life. As reservations were imposed upon them, the Black Hills became one of the few places where traditional life was possible. The U.S. government guaranteed the inviolability of the Black Hills in an 1868 treaty. Just six years later, however, Col. George Custer precipitated a gold rush in violation of the treaty. Indian resistance was led by a Sioux holy man, prophet, and warrior named Sitting Bull. Following a vision, he and Crazy Horse led the victorious Sioux and Cheyenne in the Battle of the Little Big Horn, in which Custer died. Black Elk, the Oglala Sioux holy man, dreamed a prophecy foretelling that a foreign race would weave a spider's web around the Black Hills, rendering the lands barren.

Bear Butte in South Dakota—*Mato Paha* (Sleeping Bear Mountain) to the Sioux—is an ancient sacred mountain. The bear has symbolic meaning to the Plains Indians, its hibernation a sign that it is the "keeper of dreams." In the Sioux creation myth, a girl escaping the primordial flood was rescued by an eagle who carried her to Bear Butte and married her. The twins she bore were the ancestors of the Sioux Nation. For the Cheyenne, Bear Butte is the most sacred spot in the Black Hills, a place of such spiritual intensity that they will not camp there, because it is the abode of the Creator God, Maheo. In Cheyenne tradition, a cave on Bear Butte was where the great shaman, Sweet Medicine, spent four years (1693–1696) in a vision quest before Maheo gave him four taboos—murder, theft, adultery, and incest—in the form of sacred arrows. Two of the arrows endowed the people with authority over the buffalo and the other two with power over men. Thus the Cheyenne believe that they became a chosen people.

Another sacred mountain is Harney Peak, where Black Elk was carried in a vision and shown good and evil from the center of a great circle of the four directions. Devil's Tower, a huge monolith in Wyoming that rises 865 feet above its base and 1,280 above the valley of the River Fourche below, is also considered sacred. The Kiowa tell the tale of a boy who turned into a fierce bear and chased his seven sisters until they climbed a tree. The tree lifted them up to safety and turned into the Devil's Tower, with the bear's claw marks still scoring the sides. Devil's Tower has become a popular destination for rock climbers, to the horror of the Sioux, who believe it is the place of creation.

The Lakota Sioux, Cheyenne, and Arapaho still build sweat lodges in the mountains of the *Paha Sapa*. When a young man begins his vision quest, he prays to the forces of nature, begging them for support. As he enters the sweat lodge, he must begin a ritual of attentiveness and reverence to everything about him. As he pours water on hot stones, he asks their voices to speak to him in the steam. Once the sweat lodge has purified his body of poisons and cleared his mind, he begins "crying for a vision." His hair combed out, he sets forth wearing only a breechcloth and carrying a blanket. His nakedness and unbraided hair announce his humble acceptance of whatever vision is given him. High places are necessary for the vision quest, and the mountain is chosen with care. It will test him, and his perseverance and indifference to suffering are signs of his worthiness to become a warrior. He will be fasting, and hunger and thirst, extremes of climate, insects and snakes may test his resolve. He is alone. The vision may come in a dream or while he is awake, and it brings with it a power he will have the rest of his life. He will reflect and meditate on its meaning, ask wise men for interpretations, and from the vision determine much of his future life and his responsibilities in the tribe. At ceremonies, including the sacred Ghost Dance, men wear special shirts with emblems and decorations recalling their vision from the mountains.

The Black Hills have also attracted many New Age devotees, although the Sioux have asked that their access to the butte be limited during ceremonial periods. At the New Age ceremonial of the summer solstice in 1994, the Sioux confronted them with this demand. Native Americans have also been offended by the appropriation of their rituals by New Agers, whom they scornfully call "plastic medicine men." The bitterest of the conflicts, however, has been with Kevin Costner. Costner made the film *Dances with Wolves*, which earned him a place of honor among the Sioux for its fair portrayal of their history. So when Costner began building a $100 million casino at the edge of the Black Hills in 1995, the sense of betrayal among the Sioux was deep. Costner's actions confirmed their worst suspicions of

white society's lack of respect for American Indian sacred places.

See also Bighorn Medicine Wheel; Sweat Lodge.

References Don Doll, SJ, *Vision Quest*. New York, Crown, 1994. Martha Geores, *Common Ground*. Lanham MD, Rowman & Littlefield, 1996. Edward Lazarus, *Black Hills/White Justice: The Sioux Nations versus the United States*. New York, HarperCollins, 1991.

BODHNATH STUPA, Nepal

Called the Great Stupa, this is the largest in Nepal and is dedicated to the god of wisdom. An immense structure that covers several acres in Kathmandu, its circular base is 100 yards in diameter. Set on shelves along the outer wall of the base are two-foot prayer wheels, each containing the sacred mantra, "Hail Jewel of the Lotus." Devotees circle the stupa, giving each wheel a spin as they pass it, thus causing the mantra to be repeated as many times as the wheel turns. There are thirteen steps up the side of the base, symbolizing the thirteen levels of wisdom needed to attain nirvana. The structure of the stupa itself, alternating levels of squares and circles as it rises, has religious symbolism. On the four sides of the topmost level are painted pairs of eyes, which can be seen from a great distance. They are bow-shaped and all-seeing.

Inside the stupa are several shrines to holy men, and a relic of the Buddha is also buried there. Pilgrims circle the stupa clockwise before entering the precincts and visiting the shrines. They come to seek a blessing before a journey or to earn merit. Ceremonies involve processions around the stupa, accompanied by trumpet-blowing monks in saffron and red robes. Handfuls of wheat flour are thrown in the air in celebration. On the Buddha's birthday, his image is carried around the stupa on the back of an elephant.

Legend has it that a wealthy prostitute asked for a small piece of land, whatever could be covered by a buffalo robe. When the king granted the wish, she cut the robe into narrow strips and outlined a huge plot. Forced to grant her wish by this trick, the king permitted her to build the stupa. It is served by Tibetan monks from six monasteries and caters largely to Tibetan refugees, although Buddhist pilgrims come from across the region—Nepal, Ladakh, Bhutan, and Tibet. The Great Stupa is a center for Tibetan Buddhism, with some 100,000 Tibetan refugees settled in the area. Pictures of the Dalai Lama are seen throughout. Twice a day the monks perform *puja,* the basic Tibetan worship consisting of chanting, offerings, and caring for the idols in the temple.

References Trilok Majupuria and Indra Majupuria, *Holy Places of Buddhism in Nepal and India.* Bangkok, Tecpress, 2d ed., 1993. Ormond McGill, *Religious Mysteries of the Orient.* South Brunswick NJ, Barnes, 1976. *Nepal: Land of the Gods.* New York, Mystic Fire, 1976 (video).

BOM JESUS, Portugal

Bom Jesus (Good Jesus) is the most important of three churches that form a triangle east of the city of Braga, the religious heart of Portugal. It stands on a high hill overlooking the city. Built in 1811 in the architectural style called Minho Baroque, the church is set in a large park within a lush northern rainforest. In the park itself are several chapels and a number of statues. The chapels in one section are dedicated to the biblical themes of the Ascension, the Meeting at Emmaus, and the appearance of Jesus to Mary Magdalene. Separating them are fountains in honor of the four Evangelists: Matthew, Mark, Luke, and John.

The most notable feature of Bom Jesus, however, is the Stairway to Paradise, completed in 1723, much earlier than the church. Through terraced gardens the Stairway to Paradise winds, via a series of switchbacks, up a 31 percent grade. From the bottom, it creates the impression of a huge fan. At the first two landings are small chapels featuring life-size scenes of the Passion of Christ: the Garden of Gethsemane and the Last Supper, the Flagellation and Crowning with Thorns, Simon of Cyrene carrying the Cross, the Crucifixion, and the like. Above these are five landings with pre-Christian themes: fountains representing the five senses, the first understanding of which is ascribed to the pagan Greeks. To these are added statues of figures from the Hebrew scriptures: Moses, David, Joseph, Solomon, Isaac, and Isaiah. The next three flights constitute the Stairway of the Virtues, where Faith, Hope, and Charity are represented allegorically. At the top, the stairway opens to a magnificent fountain, capping one of the finest examples of garden architecture in Europe. Pilgrims climb the stairs, stopping at each shrine or chapel to pray, often lighting votive candles. The most devout, or those seeking special favors, ascend on their knees. The less devout may take the easier route—riding to the top in a cable-car, then walking down the stairs.

In front of Bom Jesus are two formal gardens with scenes of the Crucifixion and Descent from the Cross. The church is the last station, showing Jesus on the Cross. All the tableaux are made of life-size polychrome figures, with the focus in all the Passion scenes on the person of Jesus. The church has a relic altar with over 50 busts of saints containing their relics. The mummified body of St. Clement is laid in the altar, which is covered with a plain white cloth on which pilgrims write petitions and prayers.

Bom Jesus is a family place, and many family groups—parents, children, and grandparents—climb the stairs praying together. At the top, superb views and a large picnic area reward the children for their diligence. The spirit of the place includes prayer on the Passion of Christ as well as family unity and celebration.

References Helder Carita and Homem Cardoso, *Portuguese Gardens*. Woodbridge, UK, Antique Collectors' Club, 1989. Marion Kaplan, *The Portuguese: The Land and Its People*. New York, Viking Penguin, 1991. René Laurentin, *Pilgrimages, Sanctuaries, Icons, and Apparitions*. Milford, OH, Faith, 1994.

BOROBUDUR, Indonesia

The great temple of Borobudur is the first and greatest of many monuments built by ancient Javanese kings to demonstrate their status as intermediaries between this world and the world of the gods. Borobudur lies in the center of the island of Java, 40 miles northwest of Yogyakarta.

Borobudur was begun in 775 CE as a Hindu temple and finally completed about a century later. After the first ten years of construction, the king was overthrown by a Buddhist ruler who built further levels of the temple on top of the two Hindu ones. Despite its mixed heritage, Borobudur is regarded as one of the greatest Buddhist masterpieces in the world. By 1100 it was abandoned, as power shifted to East Java and away from the central plains. Eventually it was overgrown by the surrounding jungle. In a ten-year restoration that was sponsored by UNESCO, the terraces were strengthened and all 1,300 reliefs were removed and cleaned. Borobudur was finally opened to the public in 1984.

Borobudur is actually a small hill representing a sacred mountain—the home of the gods, according to the Buddhist tradition. The hill is covered by a skin of huge stones; some 60,000 cubic yards of stone were quarried and cut to build Borobudur. The three spheres of Buddhist creation figure in the design and decoration: the first or lowest is the world of the flesh and everyday life; the second, the world of the spirit; and the third, total detachment from the world. The original base, 200 yards square, was decorated with carvings of the first sphere, with its lusty delights and passions. But this base was soon covered, perhaps as a means of keeping the pilgrim's vision on higher things. Now, however, the south side of the base has become exposed, and some of these carvings can be seen.

Borobudur's walls and balustrades are covered with three miles of detailed, well-preserved relief carvings that are followed clockwise along the pilgrim route from the east entrance. The carvings are especially fine on the next five levels, which display the life of Prince Siddhartha, who became the Buddha. The carvings show what must have been typical scenes of early Java: entertainers, dancers, family scenes, magicians, and worshippers all jumbled together with the story of the Buddha. Here we see the Buddhist ideal of surrendering one's desires and urgent longings, all told in Buddha's life from the sutras. In niches along the balustrades are many statues of Buddha—432 in all.

Above the five square terraces lie three circular ones, without carvings but surmounted by 72 miniature *stupas*, or relic shrines. There are no relics here, but each stupa, which is latticed, holds a small statue of the Buddha. To touch the statue through one of the holes in the lattice is considered good luck. However, as one progresses, the openings become smaller and fewer, to indicate that the Buddha becomes less

Perforated stupas, or relic shrines, at Borobudur, Indonesia, hold small statues of the Buddha, which can be touched by reaching through the holes in the lattice.

accessible as one progresses toward spiritual wholeness. The first of the three circular terraces is a bit off center; the second is closer, and the third achieves perfect roundness. The topmost level, which represents ultimate truth, is a large bell-shaped stupa with two small rooms. The rooms have always been empty—a sign of total absorption into the supreme being and the ultimate emptiness of all sensual appearances.

Borobudur is not only a temple, but a grand mandala, a cosmic image symbolizing Buddhist thought. The structure even takes the basic shape of the mandala: the square first levels are symbols of earth, with the circular superstructure symbolizing the sky.

Together they total nine levels, the sacred number of Buddhism. So too, the number of statues on the square and concentric terraces are a play on the numbers three and nine (3 x 3) in a grand scheme of symbolism.

Borobudur has not been a place of pilgrimage since its abandonment, but it has become the major tourist site in Indonesia. Among the visitors are many Asian Buddhists, who come in a spirit of reverence to see the fabled scene. Each year on Waicak Day, the celebration of the birth and death of the Buddha, a formal pilgrimage is held by full moon, with priests making offerings of flowers and incense. Two temples on an eastern alignment with Borobudur—Mendut and Pawon—are thought to have been early purification temples for pilgrims going to the sanctuary. The Waicak Day procession goes to these temples before proceeding to Borobudur. In the centuries since the construction of Borobudur, Indonesia has become 90 percent Muslim, making it the largest Muslim country in the world. Buddhists represent a tiny minority, mostly of Asian foreigners, although some ancient Buddhist customs still linger in Indonesian culture.

References Flavio Conti, *Centers of Belief*. Boston, HBJ Press, 1978, 121–136. Bedérich Forman, *Borobudur: The Buddhist Legend in Stone*. London, Octopus, 1980. W. Brown Morton III, "Indonesia Rescues Ancient Borobudur," *National Geographic* 163:1, 127–142 (January 1983). *Wonders, Sacred and Mysterious*. Pleasantville, NY, Reader's Digest, 1993 (video).

BUCHENWALD, Germany

Buchenwald, located outside Weimar, south of Berlin, was the largest Nazi concentration camp on German soil.

As at the site of every former Nazi concentration camp, debate rages over the meaning of the site and how it should be presented. One position considers all Holocaust sites holy ground to be left untouched as a memorial to those who died there. Others see the moral and educational value of showing the details of the Holocaust to future generations; they want the camps preserved and restored to the state they were in as part of the Nazi attempt to destroy the Jewish people. Both sides agree that as the remaining survivors age and die, the camps are the most important tangible reminder of the Holocaust.

At Buchenwald this conflict is especially acute. For 40 years Buchenwald was part of Communist East Germany. The Communists denied any responsibility for the Holocaust, blaming it on the Nazis, whom they identified with the West Germans. With the unification of Germany, Buchenwald generated furious argument until Communist administrators were removed from their jobs. It is gradually being restored.

Buchenwald was established in 1937, and from then until 1945 it held 239,000 Jews, Gypsies, homosexuals, and political prisoners. By 1938 the majority were Jews, although at first German policy was to pressure Jews into leaving Germany by 15-hour days of forced labor in the quarries. About 10,000 were freed when their families arranged emigration. After 1942, when the Nazis had decided on the "final solution"—the total destruction of the Jews—all Jewish prisoners were either shipped to their deaths at Auschwitz or placed in permanent slave labor, often worked to death. A thousand children were also kept at Buchenwald in special barracks, and most of them survived the war.

Buchenwald was not an extermination camp like Auschwitz. It was a labor camp, where the slave laborers were exploited as thoroughly as possible. Most worked in a stone quarry or an armaments factory operated by the camp; some were shipped out from Buchenwald to 130 factories to aid the German war effort. But labor camps were only marginally better than extermination camps. Prisoners were often beaten to death, and many died from malnutrition and exhaustion. Some were subjected to gruesome medical experiments. The evil of Buchenwald has often been symbolized by the camp commandant's wife, who made lampshades from the skins of Jewish victims, particularly those with interesting tatoos. In April 1945, as the Soviet army advanced toward Weimar, the Nazis began evacuating Jewish prisoners. In the forced march to the west that followed, 25,000 died. At liberation Buchenwald still held 25,000 prisoners, of whom 4,000 were Jews. A total of 44,000 people perished at Buchenwald.

The present-day camp reflects the ambiguities of modern German attitudes toward the Holocaust. The administration uses the former SS officers' rooms, and a back-packers' youth hostel has been placed in the camp guards' barracks. A museum recounts in pictures and artifacts the stark realities of camp life and shows a documentary film. The film, a relic of the Communist past, tells more about Communist political prisoners than about Jews. In a recent about-face that still manages to avoid the full hor-

ror of Buchenwald's place in the Holocaust, the present German authorities have focused on Buchenwald's history after the liberation. From 1945 to 1950, occupying Soviet forces ran an internment camp there for 32,000 Germans; at first it was for suspected war criminals, but it soon turned into a prison for anti-Communists. Ten thousand died of neglect and disease; they are remembered with a simple memorial. There is also a memorial at the site of the children's barracks.

See also Holocaust Sites.

References Israel Gutman (ed.), *Encyclopedia of the Holocaust*. New York, Macmillan, 4 vols., 1990. David Hackett (ed.), *The Buchenwald Report*. Boulder, CO, Westview, 1995. Poller, *Medical Block Buchenwald*. New York, Carol, 1987.

CAHOKIA MOUNDS, Illinois, USA

Cahokia Mounds, located in southern Illinois, is the remains of a large city built by the people of the Mississippian culture. It includes a complex of huge, flat-topped pyramids, some of which were used for burial, others as the foundations of temples and grand residences. The Mississippians apparently took over an earlier Hopewell settlement around 900 CE and immediately began building their characteristic earthworks. By 1500 Cahokia was abandoned; evidence suggests long droughts and malnutrition, probably due to environmental degradation from the deforested hillsides.

Cahokia lay at a major trade crossroads. At its height, it covered six square miles and had a population of over 20,000, making it the largest city north of Mexico. Agriculture provided its economic base, producing the corn surpluses that were its primary trade goods. Cahokia residents lived in thatched huts made of poles and sealed with mud. The atmosphere of the city was pleasant, with open parks and plazas scattered about and family gardens and farms on the edge of the settlement.

At Cahokia there are 68 mounds in the central area alone, mostly platform mounds used for the homes of the elite. But the main structure is a pyramid known as Monks' Mound, after the Trappist monks who lived there from 1809 to 1813. It is the largest earthwork in the Western Hemisphere—over 100 feet high on a base of 14 acres, larger than the Great Pyramid of Egypt. On its top was the traditional home of the chief, who was raised up to be close to his god-brother, the sun. The chief was housed in a wooden building 100 by 48 feet, and 50 feet high. By 1200 CE, Cahokia had become a society built on sharp class divisions: farmers and workers, artisans, nobility, and priests. A wall was built around the central sacred precincts, probably to separate the elite class of priests and rulers.

The similarity between artifacts found at Cahokia and designs from Mayan culture suggests trade or cultural relations between the two peoples. Since Mississippian settlements stretched from present-day Illinois to the Gulf Coast, contact between the Mayans and Cahokians is not improbable. The Mayans may have been the source of the Cahokian practice of human sacrifice and cannibalism, both of which were unknown among the Native American Indians of the United States. These practices may have spread along the trade routes during the Mayan Revival (1150 to 1400), to be taken up by the Buzzard Cult, a Mississippian elite who controlled the lives of the people and practiced torture as well as human sacrifice.

The heart of Mississippian religion was the Southern Cult, and many Cahokia artifacts bear its symbols: weeping eyes, sun circles, crosses, skulls, and sun rays. Elaborately carved soapstone pipes were used in rituals. The main focus of this Cahokia religion was death. Funeral rites for a god-king were elaborate and lengthy. Mound 72, one of the most interesting burial mounds, contains the remains of over 350 women around the grave of a god-king, who lay on a bed of 50,000 seashell beads. Whether the women were persons honored in the society or blood offerings in some funeral sacrifice is unknown. At the death of a king, his wife (always a commoner) was strangled, along with many of his household, so that they might accompany him into the next life.

The ruler was a god-like representative of the sun on earth. If the Cahokians followed other Mississippian traditions, which is likely, he communed with the sun each morning in the temple, and messages from the sun were passed on to the people through the priests. The Mississippians worshipped the sun, and the locations for the mounds relate to the points of the compass. Monks' Mound is on a north-south axis leading to Mound 72, and several other important mounds were constructed along the same line. Not far from Monks' Mound are four (perhaps five) circular sun calendars, originally made of log posts. Called Woodhenge because of their similarity to Stonehenge, they were used for ceremonies and for determining planting and harvesting seasons. New Age groups continue to hold ceremonies there for sunrises at both the solstices and the equinoxes.

New Age practitioners identified Cahokia Mounds as one of the major centers of earth energy for the Harmonic Convergence in 1987. At this event, thousands gathered to observe the conjunction of astronomy and the ancient Mayan calendar. It was argued that if 144,000 persons (a sacred number) gathered at a series of sacred power sites worldwide, their combined spiritual energy could cause a shift in the earth's alignment to place it in harmony with the rest of the universe. This would bring an age of peace and harmony and stave off the advent of an age of destruction. The day chosen was determined to be the last of a series of nine "infernos" that began in 1519, when the Spaniards conquered the Aztecs. Through Harmonic Convergence, the Aztec god of death could be persuaded to lift his mask and reveal his opposite and usher in the new age. During the Harmonic Convergence, 4,000 people gathered on the top of Monks' Mound, an indication of its size.

Today there are an interpretive museum and a wide variety of activities at Cahokia, including classes, programs, and sample digs.

See also Mound Builders.

References Melvin Fowler, *Cahokia: Ancient Capital of the Midwest.* Reading, MA, Addison-Wesley, 1974. William Iseminger, "Mighty Cahokia," *Archaeology* 49:3, 30–37 (May-June, 1996). Claudia Mink, *Cahokia: City of the Sun.* Cahokia, IL, Cahokia Museum Society, 1992.

CANTERBURY CATHEDRAL, England

Canterbury Cathedral, in southern England, contains the shrine of St. Thomas à Becket, which has been the destination of pilgrims since the twelfth century. This pilgrimage is the setting for Geoffrey Chaucer's *Canterbury Tales,* one of the oldest and best-known works in English literature, and Canterbury remains a center of Christian worship and pilgrimage to this day.

England had already accepted Celtic Christianity when Pope St. Gregory the Great sent St. Austin (Augustine) to reorganize church life in 597. He baptized the king of Kent and built the first cathedral and a monastery at Canterbury. The archbishop of Canterbury became the head of the English Church with authority over the other bishops. After the Reformation, the archbishop continued as head of the Church of England, which has developed into the worldwide Anglican Communion. The cathedral

Built in the twelfth century, Canterbury Cathedral became a popular place of pilgrimage after the archbishop Thomas à Becket was murdered by four of the king's knights in 1170.

has been used without interruption since the first church was built in the early seventh century. Destroyed by fire in 1064, the present cathedral replaced it. Today it is the official cathedral of the archbishop of Canterbury, head of the worldwide Anglican Communion, to which the American Episcopal Church belongs. Canterbury also serves as an important national shrine. It contains many monuments and memorials to British war heroes, as well as battle standards.

In 1170, the event took place that transformed Canterbury into a popular place of pilgrimage. King Henry II had chosen a close friend, Thomas à Becket, to be archbishop. The appointment assured the king's control of the Church, or so it seemed. Once in office, however, Becket began to challenge the king and uphold the rights of religion. Exasperated, the king cried out one day, "Who will rid me of this troublemaking priest?" Four knights took his suggestion literally and murdered Becket on the high altar of the cathedral, cutting the top from his skull and scattering his brains on the stone floor. That night people began assembling to revere the body and touch bits of cloth to the bloodstains. Immediately Canterbury became a place of pilgrimage. People demanded that Becket be named a martyr and a saint, which he was in 1173. The place of Becket's martyrdom is marked by an inscribed stone slab in the floor of the cathedral. In the crypt is the chapel where Becket was first buried and where Henry completed the penance imposed on him for causing his death. After walking barefoot into the town and following a long fast on bread and water, Henry spent the night in prayer in the crypt chapel, at dawn receiving three lashes on his bare back from each of the monks.

Immediately after Becket's death, and for the 350 years that followed, springtime in England brought groups of pilgrims to Canterbury. The cathedral is 55 miles from London, three to four days' ride—for those rich enough to have a horse. Penitents walked. All, however, traveled in groups for security from robbers. They crossed London Bridge and, along the way, stopped at various, stations. One station was at the shrine of St. William the Baker, a pilgrim stabbed to death by outlaws on the road in 1201. Those coming from France disembarked at Southampton and rested at a hospice in Winchester. Each was given a horn of beer and a slice of bread, a custom continued today for anyone who requests it while on the way to Canterbury. The medieval horn mugs are still used for this ancient rite of hospitality.

In 1220, Becket's body was placed in a sumptuous shrine in the Trinity Chapel, just behind the high altar. The shrine was an oak chest covered with gold and precious stones, resting on a marble table. Pilgrims viewed it through an ironwork grill. Accounts of miracles had begun within days of the saint's assassination, and the lame, blind, and insane were brought to the shrine. Many were left overnight in prayer, the demented chained to the grill. Penitents could request strokes with a rod to atone for their sins. The sick brought with them a candle matching their height, as an ex-voto. Water from a well was mixed with a drop of the saint's blood; pilgrims carried it away in vials. One of these vials on a chain around the neck was the sign of the Canterbury pilgrim. Stained-glass windows from 1220 still recount the miracles of St. Thomas, but the shrine was dismantled in 1538 by King Henry VIII, who confiscated its treasury, which filled 26 wagons. The hundreds of relics, including the beard of St. Dunstan and the arm with which St. George slew the dragon, were destroyed.

See also Westminster Abbey; York Minster.

References John Adair, *The Pilgrims' Way*. London, Thames & Hudson, 1978. Shirley du Boulay, *A Road to Canterbury*. Ridgefield, CT, Morehouse, 1995. Geoffrey Chaucer, *Canterbury Tales*. New York, Random House, 1994. Jonathan Keates and Angelo Hornak, *Canterbury Cathedral*. London, Summerfield Press, 1980.

CAO DAI TEMPLE, Vietnam

This temple is the main worship center, shrine, and headquarters of the Cao Dai sect, popularly known as the "Holy See." In a series of visions during the years following World War I, a Vietnamese bureaucrat in the French colonial service received revelations from Cao Dai, whom he identified as the Reigning God. At one seance a corrupt businessman, Le van Trung, was converted and changed his life. He soon became head of the new movement that flourished under his leadership and spread throughout the country.

Cao Dai is symbolized by the Eye of God, which figures prominently in all of the sect's temples. The religion has taken much of its style of worship from Catholicism, but its doctrines come from its revelations and various borrowings from eastern faiths. The "five faiths"—animism, Buddhism, Catholicism, Confucianism, and Taoism—combine in Cao Dai to form the "greater path to perfection." Its organizational structure, too, is modeled on Roman Catholicism, with cardinals, bishops, and priests, though any of these offices may be held by women as well as men. Women have a special role in Cao Dai, since all the revelations are interpreted by female spirit mediums who have been recognized by the sect's hierarchy.

Because of Cao Dai's belief in uniting truth regardless of its source, the temple enshrines Lao Tsu, Buddha, Joan of Arc, Mohammed, the French novelist Victor Hugo, and Jesus Christ. Spirit mediums transmit messages from such luminaries as Sun Yat-Sen (the founder of modern China), Lenin, and Shakespeare. Received while the mediums are in a trance, the messages are "caught" in a basket, then written down for the faithful.

The temple building is like a telescope, larger at the entrance and progressively smaller toward its far end. At the same time, it is stepped. Thus it both rises and narrows to a focus on the altar at the rear. This configuration symbolizes the journey of the soul toward enlightenment. The temple is ornate and colorful. Twisted pink columns entwined by dragons reach up to a blue tin ceiling covered with mirrored glass reflectors. Clergy wear bright robes of yellow, red, and turquoise, while the laity are gowned in white. Above everything is the all-seeing Eye of God, the symbol of Cao Dai. It is painted on a huge green globe decorated with 3,000 stars, all resting on an elaborately carved golden altar. The Eye—"mover of the heart, sovereign master of visual perception"—is the presence of God. The faithful fill the temple four times daily, with men and women kneeling in separate groups. Services are highly stylized, including chants and offerings of incense, fruit, and wine. The priests may also offer sacrifice during ceremonies. Festivals are marked by very elaborate rituals, but the seances by the spirit mediums are held privately.

All Cao Daists are vegetarians. One prophecy says that between 1996 and 1998 a new age will begin where wars will cease and all humanity will be divided into flesh-eaters and vegetarians. The vegetarians, "with pure souls in their bodies," will be saved, while the carnivores, "fattened by foulness of the flesh," will perish at the coming of the Consoler, a messiah figure who will usher in the new age.

Cao Dai has always been a nationalist movement. It has long dominated the province of Tay Ninh, where it introduced progressive social and agricultural reforms. At its greatest, Cao Dai membership was about 2 million. At one time it had a private army of 35,000, which was allied with the Japanese during World War II and opposed the government of South Vietnam in later years. In 1956 the Cao Dai army was suppressed. Under Communist rule, the sect's properties were confiscated, the seances forbidden, and the leader of the church beheaded. In 1985, the Holy See and several hundred chapels were returned to the sect, which is now slowly reviving.

References Ormond McGill, *Religious Mysteries of the Orient.* South Brunswick, NJ, Barnes, 1976. Edward Rice, *Ten Religions of the East.* New York, Four Winds Press, 1978. Jayne Werner, *Peasant Politics and Religious Sectarianism.* New Haven, Yale University, 1981.

CARNAC, France

The world's largest collection of menhirs, mounds, and dolmens is found on the southern shores of Brittany at Carnac. Menhirs are standing stones that can be found either alone, in rows, or in circles. Dolmens are table stones made by setting a capstone across two menhirs; they mark the tombs of chieftains from pre-Celtic times. Though menhirs, mounds, and dolmens are found throughout Brittany, the finest examples are around Carnac.

The Ménec Lines, named for a nearby hamlet, consist of 1,099 menhirs in 11 parallel avenues. They stretch across the landscape for hundreds of yards, ending at the town, which is bordered by a *cromlech,* or circle, of 70 menhirs. The Kermario alignment consists of 10 rows of 1,029 stones; the Kerlescan, 13 rows of 555 stones with an intact cromlech; but the last, the Petit Ménec, has been largely vandalized, its stones used for constructing a lighthouse in the nineteenth century. These four alignments extend for five miles, an amazing building feat,

since the stones are up to 20 feet high and weigh up to 350 tons. The cromlechs are focal points in the lines, and all are found on small rises, where they served as some sort of sacred center. Their diameters range from 70 to 100 yards. They may once have been incorporated into timber structures or altars that have long since disappeared.

In total, there are some 5,000 menhirs at Carnac, the largest stone alignment in Europe. But archaeologists believe that there were once over 10,000. They have been dated between 4000 and 2500 BCE. Though the lines and dolmens begin around 4000 BCE, some of the burial mounds scattered through the area had been established by 5000 BCE. The French government purchased the land in the 1880s, and the local road surveyor began re-erecting the fallen stones, though some were mistakenly placed upside-down.

The stone formations at Carnac are cultic, but their use is a mystery. One guess is that they were part of a cattle cult that continued into Christian times; remains of buried bulls and a ceremonial bull statue have been found, and the patron saint of cattle, St. Cornély, has been honored in Carnac's parish church from the earliest Christian times. These speculations connect the cattle cult with an ancient pagan cult of the Celtic horned god, Cernunnos. When the local saint, Cornély, was first honored, it was natural to make him the patron of horned animals in order to attract the pagans to Christianity.

It is more likely, though, that the stones were used in some sort of megalithic observatory. The lines of the largest stones produce astronomical information, specifically the rising and setting of the moon. Another theory suggests that the entire complex of four alignments was some sort of huge outdoor worship center, though no altar stones have ever been found. A Breton legend says that the menhirs are ancient statues of God, but since no one knew what form to give them, the ancients left the great granite rocks uncarved as a sign of the mystery of God.

Followers of New Age movements have been attracted to Carnac because of its astronomical aspects, though it has not become the center for seasonal observances that Stonehenge or Externsteine have.

References Aubrey Burl, *Megalithic Brittany.* London, Thames & Hudson, 1985. ———, *From Carnac to Callanish.* New Haven, CT, Yale University, 1996. M. Scott Peck, *In Search of Stones: A Pilgrimage of Faith, Reason, and Discovery.* New York, Hyperion, 1995.

CATACOMBS, Rome, Italy

Outside the walls of imperial Rome lie underground burial grounds, extensive complexes that include tombs, chapels, and small meeting rooms. These are the catacombs. Their place in Christian history is so important that most pilgrims to the Holy City visit at least one of them. Popes and peasants, nobles and slaves are buried there.

Since burial within the city walls was forbidden by imperial law, tombs were built along the prominent roads leading into the city. There are 60 miles of underground passages with 500,000 tombs, all of which are now, centuries later, incorporated into the modern city of Rome. Contrary to popular modern belief, the catacombs were not secret places. Christians did not hold services in them habitually, and they were rarely used as hiding places during persecution. In fact, the catacombs were usually well marked; often churches were built above their entrances.

Although catacombs were used before the Christian period, they are closely associated with the early Christians. Their strong belief in the afterlife led Christians to consider burial an important rite. During periods of persecution, Christians exposed themselves to considerable risk to retrieve the bodies of their martyrs and give them a proper burial. Tombs, in pagan tradition, were used for family memorial services, gatherings that included storytelling about the deceased and a family meal. For Christians, it was a short step to the sacred meal that was the memorial of the Last Supper. By 150 CE celebrations of the Eucharist at the tombs of the martyrs were recorded. Later, altars were built with openings to hold the bones of the martyr, and thus the altar became the burial place. From this tradition comes the present-day custom observed by Catholics and Orthodox of incorporating the relics of the martyrs into the altars of churches or sewing them into cloths laid on the table where the Eucharist is celebrated.

Despite the severe persecutions of Christians during the first three centuries after Christ, there were long periods of relative calm when relations among different religious groups were peaceful. Pagan, Jewish, and Christian tombs are usually found together in the same catacomb, and the tombs of one group were never disturbed by another. With the arrival of the Goths in 537 CE, however, this peaceful coexistence came to an end. The Goths vandalized the tombs or pillaged them in search of treasure. The popes gradually began transferring the relics of the martyrs to the churches, and the barbarian invasions effectively ended the creation of further catacombs.

In the Middle Ages the tombs of the martyrs were the focus of pilgrimages, and medieval pilgrim guides were written to help lead the pious on their journeys. They describe a circular route around the city.

Tombs, many of which are now empty, and elaborate tomb inscriptions line the walls of one of the over 50 catacombs in Rome, Italy. These underground cemeteries stretch 60 miles and contain the burials of 500,000 clergy, nobles, peasants, and slaves.

This round-about approach was incorporated into the architecture of shrine churches throughout Europe, where one may still see ambulatories, circular passageways around a shrine that the pilgrim walks before visiting the relics of a saint. By 1100 most relics had been moved out of the catacombs, and pilgrims' attention shifted to the churches themselves. A drop in population caused the Roman suburbs to be abandoned, and the entrances to the catacombs gradually crumbled and disappeared. Only in the nineteenth century did systematic exploration begin. With the rise of modern religious tourism, the catacombs have again become an important point of interest. When the Vatican signed the 1929 treaty with Italy giving it international standing as a state, Article 33 entrusted the catacombs to the papacy.

More than 50 catacombs have been identified, and others have come to light regularly. Seven catacombs are open to the public: Santa Domitilla, San Callisto, St. Sebastian, St. Laurence, St. Agnes, St. Pancras, and Priscilla. The first three are on the Appian Way and are the most visited by pilgrims.

The stairway to the subterranean walkways can be claustrophobic. The passages are seven to ten feet tall and a yard wide. Lesser passages run off at right angles to the main corridors, all filled with burial niches. The widened spaces used for early gatherings are not large, although tombs of important people can be very elaborate, faced with marble and decorated with wall paintings. Ordinary graves simply had a space for a body to be laid out; the front was sealed and marked with a coin or bit of ceramic so it could be identified later. The catacombs contain many small graves for children, sometimes marked by a child's toy.

Santa Domitilla contains several important paintings and a large number of tomb inscriptions. The catacomb was originally four smaller units that were later joined together. It has a room for funeral meals and a well. Most striking, though, is the Basilica of Ss. Nereus and Achilleus—a full church entirely underground. No other catacomb has such a structure.

San Callisto is the largest catacomb, with over 13 miles of underground passages. Many wall paintings of Christian symbols, such as the anchor, fish, dove, lamb, ship, or a praying figure, decorate its five levels of passages. Nine early popes are buried there, but it is the inscriptions on the graves of the ordinary folk that are the most touching in their affectionate simplicity. The tomb of the popular virgin martyr, St. Cecilia, patroness of musicians, draws a number of pilgrims. She converted her fiancé, and both were martyred. Her body was later removed to a church, and in 1599, when the tomb was opened, the body was found incorrupt. At the original spot is a lovely marble statue of the body as it was found—lying on its side, head turned away and arms outstretched. The cut of the executioner's sword is plainly visible.

St. Sebastian was reputed to be the temporary resting place of saints Peter and Paul before they were reburied at St. Peter's and St. Paul's, respectively. There are many memorials of the two apostles in St. Sebastian, even an early banquet room with third-century graffiti in honor of the saints. Numerous mosaics and carvings including the initials for *Jesus Christ, Son of God, Saviour*. The letters form the Greek word for "fish" and the fish symbol are found on tombs in all the catacombs.

St. Laurence is the burial place of the Deacon Laurence, who was martyred by being strapped to a grill and roasted over a fire. *St. Agnes*, in the northwest quadrant of the city, is a shrine church built over the saint's tomb. The shrine of Agnes, another popular virgin martyr, is well visited, although many pilgrims are unaware of the catacombs beneath the church. *St. Pancras* is the patron of the newly baptized, but little is known of him. *The Catacomb of Priscilla* is the oldest. Seven popes were buried there as well as many prominent martyrs. In its upper level is some of the oldest Christian art in existence, including the earliest paintings of the Virgin Mary, dating from the third century.

See also Petra; Relics; Rome; Saint Peter's.

References Rodney Griffin, *The Catacombs of Rome.* Lima, PA, CSS Publishing, 1982. James Stevenson, *The Catacombs: Rediscovered Monuments of Early Christianity.* London, Thames & Hudson, 1978. Pasquale Testini, *The Christian Catacombs in Rome.* Rome, Turismo di Roma, 1970.

CATHAR SITES, France

High on a peak in southern France is Montségur, the last outpost of a medieval sect, the Cathars. Although it is a fortified stronghold, many Cathar settlements were in towns and villages.

The Cathars (the name means "puritans") are sometimes called Albigensians after the town of Albi where they were particularly strong. Their religion originated in eastern Europe, but they flourished in France and Italy in the twelfth and thirteenth centuries until they were destroyed in a crusade against them in 1208. The ruins of their religious centers are found in several places in southern France.

The Cathars taught that there were two gods, a good god who created the spiritual world, and an evil one, the creator of the material world. To live in the physical world

was hell, because the god of evil had captured the soul and imprisoned it in a physical body. Christ, whose human body was only an illusion, was sent by the good god to free humanity from this miserable condition. The Cathars denied the death of Christ, the sacraments, and the Resurrection, which made the medieval Church their bitter enemy. The Cathars were led by a sect called the Perfect, who renounced sex and lived a common life. They ate no meat because it was the product of sexual generation. Their only prayer was the Lord's Prayer, which they recited up to 40 times a day. Most ordinary Cathars could not live according to these strict rules, but as they neared death, they could be enrolled among the Perfects. They would then begin the *endura,* refusing food and drink until they starved to death. The Cathar faith was passed on within families under the influence of grandmothers, who were the guides of people's consciences.

When the crusade armies marched against the Cathars, they were terribly harsh. In one town alone, 20,000 Cathars were slaughtered—after they had surrendered. In 1232 the surviving Cathars moved their headquarters to Montségur, a castle built by Esclarmonde, one of the holiest of the women Perfects. Set on a limestone outcrop in the Pyrenees Mountains, the castle is extremely inaccessible and thus was able to survive siege for several years until forced to surrender in 1244. Given two weeks to consider abandoning their faith, the Perfects spent the time praying and preparing for death. After their capture, 207 defenders were burned alive on a huge pyre for their heresies. Although a number of Cathar sites survive, Montségur became the symbol of Cathar resistance.

The Cathars have always inspired spiritualist interpretations. In the nineteenth century, a mishmash of mysticism and occultism surrounded the history of the cult. One historian even proclaimed that Montségur was the location of the Holy Grail, the cup that Jesus used at the Last Supper. The assertion was taken up by Heinrich Himmler, the Nazi leader, who commissioned a book about the Cathars. He portrayed them as anti-Semitic, when in fact the Cathars had protected Jews as fellow outsiders in medieval society. In the 1960s a more scientific analysis was made, but it suggested that Montségur was the work of a clever astronomer who built a temple to the sun.

Despite the fact that sun worship would have deeply offended Cathar beliefs, Montségur has become the focus of New Age cults, vegetarians, and feminists. It also attracts various anti-Catholics and neo-fascists from Spain, Italy, and France who are interested in the revival of paganism. At the summer solstice (June 21), groups gather for the first rays of the sun, and on one recent occasion, the Nazi flag was raised.

About 100,000 visitors come to Montségur each year. Historians argue that the original castle was probably demolished, since church law required that heretics' buildings be destroyed, and the present structures may be of a later date. There is no medieval account of this destruction, however, and it may be that the sheer difficulty of demolishing the remote mountain-top castle saved it. The Cathar village that surrounded the castle ruins is now being excavated.

References Zoë Oldenbourg, *The Massacre at Montsegur*. New York, Marboro, 1990. Steven Runciman, *The Medieval Manichee*. New York, Cambridge University, 1947. Joseph Strayer, *The Albigensian Crusades*. Ann Arbor, University of Michigan, 1992.

CAVES OF THE THOUSAND BUDDHAS, China

In 366 CE, a monk traveling in northwest China near the Mongolian border had a vision of a thousand golden Buddhas, which inspired him to carve a cave out of the nearby sandstone cliffs as a sanctuary. Over the next 1,000 years, hundreds of caves were cut in these cliffs in a honeycomb pattern, connected by ladders and walkways. They became the Caves of the Thousand Buddhas.

The caves were used for meditation and for rest along the Silk Road, the world's oldest continuous trade route. It crossed harsh, waterless terrain, connecting China with the Mediterranean. A southern branch originated in India and became the route over which Buddhism was brought to China. The caves are sacred because they mark the place where Buddhism entered China and from which it spread. The Silk Road was a major path for the expansion of Buddhism, and many travelers stopped at the caves to renew their faith as they pushed on to unknown lands. Wealthy traders often commissioned the decoration of a cave as a thank-offering for a safe and prosperous trip. Stencils were invented at the caves, and devout traders took images of the Buddha with them, either as mementos or as aids to help them teach their religion on their journey. The decline of the caves began when Vasco da Gama's discovery of a sea route to the East made the Silk Road less important.

Once richly decorated with paintings and embroidered silk wall hangings, the caves and their attached monasteries were gradually abandoned and lay forgotten by the outside world from the eighth century CE until around 1900. At that time, western explorers and adventurers began to bribe the few remaining monks to allow them to carry off priceless artworks. Over the following 50 years, the caves were plundered for their invaluable artifacts, scrolls, paintings, and embroideries, which were taken to museums or sold piecemeal on the art market. The most valuable item remaining is the *Diamond Sutra*, the first printed book in the world (868 CE). The Communist government ended this practice of plundering in 1949 and began restoration of the caves.

The caves, which vary in size, are all marked, numbered, and dated. Most have vivid wall paintings of the life of the Buddha and the *bodhisattvas*, Buddhist saints who have sacrificed the highest stages of religious growth in order to bring blessings and help to ordinary people. Done on a thin layer of porcelain china laid over plaster, the wall paintings cover 484,000 square feet and reveal a great deal about Buddhist popular religion. One large mural shows thousands of treasures raining down like heavenly flowers on 72,000 devotees as one of the bodhisattvas preaches. Some temples are painted with guardian figures—barechested, muscular and aggressive—to keep the evil spirits at bay.

All the caves originally contained brightly painted statues, and 2,300 of these remain in the 492 caves that have endured erosion and pillage. The caves are artistically important because they show the distinctive styles of each of the eight dynasties during which they were carved. The most striking sculpture is a 108-foot statue of the Buddha in a cave that is fronted by a pagoda-like entrance seven stories high. The seated Buddha there is 85 feet high, and a Sleeping Buddha, 55 feet long, though most of the statues and paintings are much smaller.

A previously unexplored set of caves is now being opened by scholars, who have discovered worship caves, burial chambers, and storage areas for the monks.

References Jan Myrdal, *The Silk Road*. New York, Pantheon, 1979. Reza, "Pilgrimage to China's Buddhist Caves," *National Geographic* 189:4, 53-63 (April 1996). Roderick Whitfield, *Caves of the Thousand Buddhas*. New York, Braziller, 1990.

CHACO, New Mexico, USA

Chaco Canyon in northern New Mexico contains a complex of Anasazi villages surrounding a great ceremonial center. A network of roads connected outlying settlements up to 100 miles away. Between 20 and 30 feet wide, laid out in straight lines, regardless of the terrain, these thoroughfares were constructed without the benefit of either the horse or the wheel.

The Chaco people, a nomadic clan of the Anasazi, settled the area in the tenth century CE, hundreds of years before the Navajo arrived, and became farmers. They worshipped the plumed serpent, as did the Mayans and Aztecs, and its sacred image is found at various spots in the canyon. Many Chaco wall paintings portray humans as well as animal figures that may have been totems. Women are shown giving birth, and youths are depicted playing the flute. Some paintings include handprints, which are believed to indicate especially sacred spots. The meaning of other scenes is unclear.

Fajada Butte, a flat-topped plateau 450 feet high, seems to have been a sun-watching station for the Chaco. Rooms have been found that were used by shamans to observe movements of the sun and the play of light and shadow on certain stone outcrops. Carvings mark some of these sun points. At the crest of the butte, slabs of rock rest before a carved spiral, permitting only a small finger of light. The light beam points to the center of the spiral at the summer solstice, touches both sides of it at

The ruins of Chaco Canyon testify to the amazing abilities of the Chaco people, who constructed a complex village that included a four-storied pueblo, without the use of horses or the wheel. The Chaco people settled in New Mexico in the tenth century CE.

the winter solstice, and also defines the equinoxes and shows the phases of the moon.

Pueblo Bonito contains 800 rooms and 37 kivas (worship rooms), three of them major. A four-story pueblo built around 920 CE, Pueblo Bonito is one of 13 separate "great houses" still preserved, probably the largest medieval dwelling in the Southwest. It is built as a series of concentric semicircles that covers three acres and housed 1,500 people. Its kivas are round, with a bench along the wall, and were intended for family use. Most have a *sipapu* or spirit tunnel, an opening in the floor used as a passage between this world and the spirit netherworld. The spirits of the ancestors were believed to live in the sipapu. The Great Kiva, 53 feet in diameter, is perfectly circular, a symbol of the womb of mother earth from which the community was born. The Chaco mastered irrigation, and the evidence of trade goods indicates that they were prosperous. Bonito was abandoned in the thirteenth century due to drought.

Casa Riconada, built as a worship center, lies across the canyon from Pueblo Bonito. Its kiva is 66 feet across, perfectly circular, and 12 to 14 feet deep. At the solstices, light plays across its east window. Although its purpose is uncertain, it may have been a priestly gathering place, a sun watch, or a place for special ceremonies not conducted on a regular basis.

The Navajo who live in the area today are not related to the Chaco people, but they regard Chaco Canyon as sacred ground, a special opening from the heart of

Mother Earth, from which the spirit of the place is reborn periodically.

Chaco Canyon is located over two tectonic fault lines, causing followers of New Age spiritualities to consider it a place of focused energy and the scene of paranormal mystical phenomena, such as a luminescent blue light that hovers over the sipapus. New Agers regard the straight Chaco roads as ley lines (lines between geographical features, believed to have spiritual force). They made Chaco one of the centers of the 1987 Harmonic Convergence, in which various New Age groups gathered at "power sites" around the world to channel and direct cosmic energy in order to avert ecological calamity.

References Kendrick Frazier, *People of Chaco*. New York, W.W. Norton, 1986. Stephen Lekson et al., *Chaco Canyon*. Santa Fe, Museum of New Mexico, 1994. David Roberts, *In Search of the Old Ones: Exploring the Anasazi World of the Southwest*. New York, Simon & Schuster, 1996. ———, "The Old Ones of the Southwest," *National Geographic* 189:4, 86–109 (April 1996).

CHANGU NARAYAN TEMPLE,
Nepal

Both a pilgrimage site and a feast of Nepali art and temple architecture, Changu Narayan contains some of the most intricate bronze castings found in the Hindu world. Originally built in 325 CE to honor the Hindu god Vishnu, it was destroyed by fire in 1702 and then immediately rebuilt, with every detail precisely re-created.

Changu Narayan lies in a valley about eight miles east of Kathmandu. It is built as a pagoda with an open temple compound. Within this compound are a number of small shrines to various Hindu gods, especially Vishnu, who is presented in all ten of his incarnations. One of these incarnations,

in the Hindu system, is the Buddha, who is portrayed in various poses.

Narayan is the name given Vishnu in his manifestation as a cosmic, archetypical man. At Changu Narayan, this powerful myth is re-created in a stunning eighth-century tableau showing Vishnu revealing himself in his Universal Form. The ten-headed god stands on Garuda (the man-bird that serves as Vishnu's vehicle), with legions of adoring lesser gods surrounding them. Below this scene, Vishnu is seen again, asleep within the coils of the sacred serpent, Ananta. The temple shrine itself is a riot of painted carvings in bright primary colors. While non-Hindus may enter the compound and visit the minor shrines, the temple is open only to Hindus, and it is there that the sacred Narayan image is kept.

Statues, ornate carvings, gilded metalwork, and wall sculptures all compete for the eye of the visitor. Several are lingams, the phallic statues representing Shiva's potency. The artwork is of the highest quality, with masterpieces of religious art found at every turn. Among these are several statues of Garuda. One of these statues is reputed to have been created by Garuda himself, and on the feast of Nag Panchami it is said to sweat in memory of his wrestling with a great serpent. (Nag Panchami honors the great snake in whose coils Vishnu rested between universes.) The miraculous sweat is gathered and used for anointing against leprosy.

References Douglas Chadwick, "At the Crossroads of Kathmandu," *National Geographic* 172:1, 32–65 (July 1987). Klaus Klostermaier, *A Survey of Hinduism*. Albany, State University of New York, 1994. *Nepal: Land of the Gods*. New York, Mystic Fire, 1976 (video). Mary Slusser, *Nepal Mandala*. Princeton, NJ, Princeton University, 2 vols., 1982.

CHICHEN ITZA, Mexico

Wedged between the tourist destinations of Mérida and Cancún on Mexico's Gulf Coast are the temple ruins of Chichen Itza, first used as a Mayan worship center from 500 to 900 CE.

After an abandonment that lasted 200 years, Chichen Itza was taken over by the Toltecs, who introduced the cult of Quetzalcóatl, the feathered serpent. Quetzalcóatl, according to an ancient legend, had been driven out of the home, and his return would usher in a new age of peace. He was to arrive on white ships from far away. It was this part of the legend that would later make it possible for Cortés to conquer Mexico, since many Indians thought that the white sails of the Spaniards were a sign of the returning god.

Thus Chichen Itza has been the shrine of two gods: Chac, the Mayan rain god, and later Quetzalcóatl. Sculptures of both are found throughout the ruins. The compound contains a large number of shrines and temples, but it is dominated by the 75-foot pyramid that the Spaniards called "The Castle." Inside the pyramid is a second pyramid containing a red jaguar throne set with jade.

The pyramid had a role in the establishment of the Mayan calendar, which was more accurate than any other of its time and as good as any today. It has 52 panels for the 52 years of the Mayan "century," and 365 steps for the days of the year. During the equinoxes on March 21 and September 21, when day and night are equal, a serpent seems to uncoil and undulate along one side of the pyramid as the shadows fall on a stairway leading to the top.

The Toltecs practiced human sacrifice on a grand scale, and scenes of these grisly ceremonies are found in numerous rock carvings. The main task of special companies of soldiers was to capture prisoners from other tribes for sacrifice. The Temple of Skulls, a grim place where the heads of victims were displayed, is decorated with stone skulls and carvings of eagles tearing the hearts of men from their chests. On a nearby platform similar carvings portray eagles and jaguars with hearts in their claws. A second platform is dedicated to a goddess shown as a feathered serpent with a human head in its jaws. From there, a long path—once a causeway—leads to a sacred well (*cenote*) 60 yards across and 35 yards deep. The skeletons of sacrificial victims have been found in the deeps, along with gold and jade jewelry offerings to the gods.

There are eight ball courts in Chichen Itza, with stone hoops above them, but these arenas were not merely for games of pleasure. It is thought that the Toltecs sacrificed the losing teams, and the wall carvings show the beheading of players. At either end of the main court are temples, both with elaborate carvings and one with murals.

The many buildings at Chichen Itza include two sweat houses used for purification rites and a celestial observatory used for reading the stars in order to determine the most propitious times for planting, harvest, and rituals. Several residences for priests and nobles are preserved, though those of the common people, not being stone, have long ago disappeared. A fertility shrine features a series of stone phalluses. Evidence also suggests that a network of sacred ways may have connected Chichen Itza with other ceremonial centers.

Even though the Toltecs also abandoned the place after 200 years, its religious power was such that Mayan pilgrimages continued for centuries. The daily presence of so many tourists has kept most devotees away, but folk healers and other descendants of the Mayans still come to pray for rain or other needs. Food offerings are made to the gods

The Toltecs of Chichen Itza practiced human sacrifice on a grand scale. Numerous rock carvings, such as the wall of skulls pictured here, testify to the gruesome ceremonies.

on makeshift altars lit with candles. One of the petitioners may act the part of the rain god Chac. After the ceremony, when the gods have feasted on the spirits of the sacrifice, the participants share the food in a ritual meal.

References Clemency Coggins, *Cenote of Sacrifice*. Austin, University of Texas, 1984. Andrew Slayman, "Seeing with Maya Eyes," *Archaeology* 49:3, 30–37 (May-June 1996). Edward Thompson, *People of the Serpent*. New York, Capricorn, 1965.

CHIMAYO, New Mexico, USA

El Sanctuario de Chimayó, formally known as Nuestra Señor de Esquípulas, is a sanctuary in the foothills of the Sangre de Cristo Mountains in northern New Mexico that brings together the practices of the area's traditional religion and Roman Catholicism. It was built over land that the Native American Indians regarded as sacred because of a healing well. Although the well has dried up, its soil is still regarded as miraculous.

According to the Christian legend of Chimayó, an Indian farmer was plowing the area in 1810 when he had a vision of an angel, who told him that the land was consecrated by the blood of two missionaries martyred there. The farmer dug up a cross he found in the mud pit where the well had been and took it to the local parish. Overnight it disappeared and turned up back at the pit. When this happened three times, it was taken as a sign, and a small chapel was built for the cross at the site of the well.

The shrine is named for an older shrine in Esquípulas, Guatemala, dedicated to El Cristo Negro, the Black Christ. The crucified Christ—a large, 1810 crucifix—presides over the main altar of Chimayó. The altars, statues, and other decorations at Chimayó are all in traditional Mexican folk style. The altar features a large gold backdrop, or *reredos,* decorated with paintings of various religious symbols. It was painted by Molleno, "The Chili Painter," so called because the backgrounds of his work resemble chili pods. The four other reredos in the church feature paintings of saints. Several small shrines are dedicated to Santo Niño de Atocha, a statue of the Child Jesus. Local people believe that Santo Niño leaves the chapel and wanders in the area at night, often wearing out his shoes, so pilgrims bring baby shoes (or even pairs of tiny sneakers!) as ex-voto offerings.

The *santos*—statues of favorite saints—receive numerous ex-votos in the form of flowers, letters, prayer cards, and candles. These represent the spiritual favors received at the sanctuary, such as consolation in grief, conversion of loved ones, and an end to marital problems. The focus of most pilgrims, however, is the sacred earth from the pit (*posito*) where the crucifix was found. The soil is used for healing, and tradition has it that no matter how much soil is removed from it by the devout, the posito always remains filled. Those who have been cured leave behind the signs of the cures; piles of crutches, hospital ID bracelets, and eye patches line the left wall. The walls are also decorated with *milagros*, small metal stampings in the shape of arms, hands, legs, or ears to indicate the part of the body that was healed at the miraculous shrine. Because of the healings, Chimayó is known as the "Lourdes of America."

About 300,000 pilgrims come to Chimayó each year. On Good Friday a major pilgrimage brings 30,000 from across the region, many walking for days to reach the shrine. Most make a three-hour walk from the town of Española. Traditionally the archbishop of Santa Fe makes this pilgrimage, not as its leader but as a participant.

References Stephen De Borhegy, *El Sanctuario de Chimayó.* Santa Fe, Ancient City Press, 1987. Lebaron Prince, *Spanish Mission Churches of New Mexico.* Glorieta, NM, Rio Grande Press, 1977. *The Shrine.* Berkeley, University of California, 1990 (video).

CHOGYESA TEMPLE, Korea

The only major temple within the city walls of Seoul, Korea's capital, Chogyesa is the spiritual and administrative center of Chogye Buddhism. The Chogye Order, with over 15 million adherents and over 1,600 temples with 12,000 monks, makes up 70 percent of Korea's Buddhists.

The temple was built in 1395 but took on its present status only in 1910, with the rebirth of Buddhism during the Japanese occupation. In 1954, during a national drive to remove all signs of the Japanese colonialist period (1910–1945), Chogyesa took its present name, after a mountain sacred to its revered master, Hui-neng (638–713). Chogye is a Zen sect that follows a Buddhism stripped of most formal elements, emphasizing the spiritual life. It is also missionary, sending monks overseas to establish temples in the United States, Japan, and Europe.

Hemmed in by the narrow streets of Seoul, the temple is a refreshing refuge from the traffic and bustle of the city. It is entered by a narrow alley that opens onto a leafy square with many rare trees, including a 550-year-old white pine listed as a national monument. On the square are a number of shrines and buildings, along with souvenir shops and vendors of religious offerings. The focus of activity is the main hall. By day, a steady stream of the faithful offers incense and prayers, and almost every evening a lecture, ceremony, or class in chanting or bowing rituals is scheduled. In front of the main hall is a seven-story pagoda containing a relic of the Buddha, brought to Korea in 1914 by a Sri Lankan monk. Nearby is a bell pavilion, used to call all living beings to hear the wisdom of the Buddha. It holds a drum for calling all animals, a bell to call the sinful and corrupt, a cloud-shaped gong for calling the birds; and a log shaped like a fish to call water creatures.

A large monastery is attached to the Chogyesa Temple, and the monks of the Chogye Order provide the temple's leadership and publish a newspaper. The monks are celibate, forbidden the use of alcohol or tobacco, and practice strict vegetarianism. However, far from otherworldly, the monastery has always been a bastion of political activism, supporting student strikes against the government and upholding the rights of workers. Visitors usually see riot police posted on the surrounding streets as a precaution. Occasionally, democratic dissidents take refuge in the temple, and it has been raided a number of times. A major rift within the Chogye sect caused a 1994 raid in which 476 reform monks were arrested. In a final settlement, the reform group won and cut back the authority of the chief administrator. In 1997, Chogyesa was one of the centers of workers' resistance during a series of violent strikes.

Faithful to the Zen tradition, the temple built a meditation center on the grounds in 1991, where free instruction in meditation is given daily to all, Buddhist and non-Buddhist. There is also a two-year Buddhist college in the temple compound. A cultural center completes the temple's educational facilities, offering seminars, theater, concerts, and exhibitions. Weddings are also performed there.

The eighth day of the fourth lunar month (around May) is the feast of lanterns, or Buddha's Birthday. Crowds of people assemble at the Temple at sundown with paper lanterns, until the grounds are lit by thousands of flickering paper lanterns. Then the procession winds through the city streets.

References *Korea: The Circle of Life.* Buffalo Grove, IL, Coronet, 1980 (video). *Korea Buddhism.* Seoul, Chogye Order, 1986. Earl Phillips and Eui-Young Yu, *Religions in Korea.* Los Angeles, California State University, 1982.

EL COBRE, Cuba

Named after the Cuban mining town where her shrine is located, El Cobre is a statue of the Virgin of Charity, patroness of Cuba.

The town of El Cobre began as a copper mine in 1550, worked by slaves and Indians. According to the legend, as two Indians and a slave boy (each named John) were gathering salt on the coast one day in 1608, they sighted something floating in the water. It turned out to be a small statue of the Virgin, carrying the Christ child and a gold cross. The statue rode on a board with the inscription, "Yo soy la Virgen de la Caridad" (I am the Virgin of Charity).

At that time, a statue of Santiago Matamoras presided over the church in the village. Santiago—St. James the Great—was an apostle of Jesus and the powerful patron of the Spanish conquest. So the Virgin statue was not placed in the church, but was put in a thatched hut nearby. On three succeeding nights, the statue disappeared and was found on top of the hill above El Cobre. In 1630, the mine was closed and the slaves freed, and the statue of Mary took Santiago's place above the high altar in the church, a symbol of the triumph of the people over the Spanish conquerers.

The statue is of a mestiza woman, and the affectionate title of El Cobre ("the copper one") is both a reference to the mining economy of the town and a wordplay on her dusky complexion. When an attempt was made in 1731 to reintroduce slavery, she became a rallying image and symbol of emancipation for one of Cuba's largest slave insurrections. Church authorities mediated the uprising, and the slaves were declared free. Devotion to Our Lady of Charity spread, and in 1916, at the request of veterans of the War of Independence (1868–1878), the pope declared her the patroness of Cuba.

The shrine is Cuba's only basilica, a cream-colored square church on the hill overlooking the town. The statue is in a small chapel above the high altar, where pilgrims have left ex-votos and testimonials of miracles and prayers answered. During Mass, the statue, is turned to face out into the church. The statue is revered not only by Catholics, but also by followers of Santería, a blending of Christianity and African traditional religion. In Santería, El Cobre is identified with Ochún, the powerful Yoruba goddess of rivers and womanly love.

References Raul Gomez-Treto, *The Church and Socialism in Cuba*. Maryknoll, NY, Orbis, 1988. René Laurentin, *Pilgrimages, Sanctuaries, Icons, and Apparitions*. Milford, OH, Faith, 1994. Levi Marrero, *Los esclavos y la Virgen del Cobre*. Miami, Editiones Universal, 1982.

CONQUES, France

High in the southern hills of France lies Conques, the town that contains St. Foy, the only medieval shrine on the pilgrimage routes to Spain that survived both the Wars of Religion and the French Revolution.

Throughout the Middle Ages, pilgrims followed several well-defined routes through France to the great Spanish shrine of St. James, Santiago de Compostela. One of these routes began in Le Puy in eastern France. From there, pilgrims proceeded west through steep, mountainous terrain before arriving, exhausted and footsore, at the town of Conques. The tiny village, which sits precariously on the side of a narrow gorge overlooking the torrents of the Dourdou River, is built around the massive shrine church of St. Foy.

A monastery was built at Conques in 819, providing isolation for prayer and meditation. But the lure of success and fame proved too great for the monks, who conspired to obtain some miracle-working relics to attract pilgrims. In 866, a brother was dispatched secretly to join a monastery in Agen, where he acted as a faithful monk for ten years until he was able to steal the relics of St. Foy, a virgin martyred in 303 CE by the Romans. As a result, the pilgrim road soon shifted from Agen to Conques.

In the eleventh century a shrine church was built for the hundreds of pilgrims who flowed through the town each day. The monastery prospered, and the best goldsmiths vied to create ornamental items and beautiful containers for the relics. Pilgrims left jewels to be added to the statues and sacred vessels. The relics were exposed for veneration in a shrine surrounded by an ambulatory, or circular aisle. Medieval pilgrims circled the shrine three times before stopping in front of the golden reliquary of St. Foy to entrust her with the success of their long trek to Spain, a journey that would take them up to a year of hard and dangerous travel. The floor of the church slopes toward the door to make it easier to hose down the mud tracked in by pilgrim feet.

Today the church is rather bare, although each of its 212 columns is topped with a different carved capital—palm leaves, birds, monsters, scenes of the life of St. Foy, and symbols. Around the former shrine is the wrought-iron screen that protected the relics from thieves. It was forged from the fetters left by pilgrims who had been freed from Muslim slavery in occupied Spain through the intercession of St. Foy. The one modern addition is a stained-glass window in honor of the only saint to live at the monastery, St. George of Conques, a simple monk revered locally for his holy life.

Over the entrance to the church is its most notable feature, a large carved panel of the Last Judgment. Christ in majesty presides over the scene, while the Archangel Michael and a demon weigh the souls of the dead on scales at his feet. The damned

are swallowed by the biblical monster Leviathan, who excretes them into Hell. The tortures of the condemned are shown in gruesome detail. A bishop who governed the area (and did not get along with the monks) is shown caught in a net, while some poachers on abbey property are being roasted by the very rabbit they had caught. The saved, on Jesus' right hand, are portrayed less vividly, perhaps because goodness is less colorful than sin.

The centerpiece of Conques is the treasury, kept safe since 1955 in a small museum. Dominating the room is the stubby seated statue of the saint, the Majesty of St. Foy, which holds her relics. It is the only surviving example of what was common in the Middle Ages. The statue is thought to be based on a pagan Roman model. The figure is covered in gold and decorated with jewels and cameos, some from the Greek and Roman periods. The effect is not gaudy but

Last Judgment, *tympanum of the west facade of the church of St. Foy, 1130–1135, located in Conques, France.*

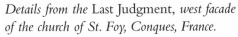

Details from the Last Judgment, *west facade of the church of St. Foy, Conques, France.*

awe-inspiring. The statue's face is almost expressionless, and its head (dating from the fifth century) contains part of the saint's skull, which has been authenticated. A glimpse of this statue was the goal of the pilgrims in visiting Conques.

The treasury also contains over 20 other gold masterpieces, including a ninth-century chest donated by King Pepin and Charlemagne's "A." Legend has it that Charlemagne had 24 golden letters made for 24 major monasteries in his kingdom, and that Conques, as his favorite, received the "A." Among the reliquaries is one containing the arm of St. George the Dragon-Slayer, supposedly the very arm that slew the dragon.

See also Santiago de Compostela.
References Patrick Geary, *Furta Sacra: Thefts of Relics in the Middle Ages.* Princeton, NJ, Princeton University, 1978. Rob Neillands, *The Road to Compostela.* Ashbourne, UK, Moorland, 1985. Pamela Sheingorn (ed.), *The Book of Sainte-Foy.* Philadelphia, University of Pennsylvania, 1995.

CONSOLATRICE, Luxembourg

The Consolatrice is a statue of Mary, Comforter of the Afflicted, the patroness of the capital of Luxembourg. In 1624 several students from the Jesuit College, now the cathedral, discovered the statue in an oak tree. A shrine was built by the oak tree, and after prayer to Mary during an outbreak of the plague the following year, the Virgin was credited with delivering the city from pestilence. In 1666 the statue was presented with the keys to the city. The Consolatrice is regarded as a miracle-worker, but not of physical cures; instead, she is said to produce conversion of the hard-hearted.

During the French Revolution the chapel was burned and the statue relocated to the cathedral. When Napoleon occupied Luxembourg, a little girl was chosen to present him with the keys of the city as a sign of surrender. But Napoleon ordered the keys returned to the statue, where they have remained. Five weeks after Easter each year, a festival is held throughout the city, lasting from one to two weeks. The main procession is led by the children making their first communion that year, followed by the statue (robed in dark blue velvet embroidered in gold and jewels), the royal family, officials, and a large gold reliquary (monstrance) containing the sacramental bread.

The devotion to the Consolatrice has spread in the region. In 1642, a shopkeeper in the Lower Rhine heard a voice asking that a shrine be built in Mary's honor. Some months later, his wife had a vision of Mary, whom she recognized from pictures of the Consolatrice that two runaway soldiers had tried to sell her. She located the soldiers and obtained a picture, and a shrine was built around it. The shrine is an exact copy of that in Luxembourg Cathedral, as is the statue which has replaced the picture.

References René Laurentin, *Pilgrimages, Sanctuaries, Icons, and Apparitions.* Milford, OH, Faith, 1994. Dorothy Spicer, *Festivals of Western Europe.* New York, H.W. Wilson, 1958.

COPTIC CAIRO, Egypt

Coptic Cairo is the religious and cultural hub of the Coptic faith, a distinctly Egyptian form of Christianity founded by St. Mark, a close disciple of St. Peter the Apostle.

Originally built by the Romans, Coptic Cairo is three miles south of the center of the city, away from where the Islamic invaders established their capital in 642 CE. The Romans built a fortress at the site, and Coptic Cairo first flourished as a trading center on the Nile. In the first century CE, Christianity was introduced by St. Mark, the author of one of the Gospels of the New Testament. It soon developed an identity of its own and customs quite distinct from either Western (Roman Catholic) or Byzantine (Greek) Christianity. Egypt became predominantly Coptic Christian, but Islamic Arab persecution and intermarriage gradually eroded the faith until today its followers number about ten million, 10 to 15 percent of the population. However, census figures are fudged, and the number of Copts is controversial in Egypt because Islamic harassment continues, including job and school quotas for Copts, as well as terrorism against Coptic centers by Muslim extremists.

Coptic Cairo has been considered a holy place from early in the Christian era. Today Copts from the Christian towns in Upper Egypt come regularly to make the rounds of the holy places. It is also a major tourist destination, which has helped to keep it protected and safe. For those unfamiliar with Coptic Christianity, the Coptic Museum provides an excellent introduction to the culture. It is the churches, however, that attract the faithful.

Sitt Mariam, also known as the Church of al-Moallaka or the "Hanging Church," is the oldest house of worship in Egypt; in the eleventh century it was the seat of the Patriarch, the head of the Coptic Church. It is suspended over a gatehouse of the old fortress walls, and its lovely decorated courtyard is adorned with icons. Inside the church is a striking pulpit (used only for Palm Sunday) set on 13 pillars representing Jesus and his apostles. One is made from black marble to symbolize Judas the betrayer. Small shrines are set into the walls, and the faithful leave petitions and notes to the saints whose icons are enshrined there. The icon is regarded as an abiding presence of the saint. Notable, therefore, is the iconostasis, an ebony partition that separates the people's area from that of the priests and is covered with icons. Sitt Mariam's iconostasis, inlaid with ivory, is a magnificent tribute to the saints who are "written" on its icons, most of them very ancient and sacred. Students who speak European languages spend their Sundays at the church to explain the faith to visitors.

The second station on the pilgrim route is the *Convent of St. George,* dedicated to one of the most popular Eastern saints. Through the centuries the level of the streets has been raised; thus, the oldest buildings are below street level. Pilgrims descend to the convent, passing through an underground corridor. Out of respect, they remove their shoes before entering the church. Inside is the "chain-wrapping" room, symbolic of St. George's imprisonment. In the sacred presence of a 1,000-year-old icon, the pilgrim is wrapped in chains while the attending nun chants prayers for his or her deliverance from sin.

Abu Serga is one of the many sites believed by Copts to have been a resting place of the Holy Family during the flight into Egypt, as told in Matthew, chapter two. The church, small but very attractive, was built in the 900s and was, until recent years, the

major shrine on the Coptic pilgrimage. The courtyard has 24 marble columns, but the striking interior is the main focus. The iconostasis is elaborate. Above it are 12 icons, over 700 years old, of the 12 Apostles of Jesus. In a crypt chapel where the Holy Family is supposed to have rested, a special Mass is celebrated every year on June 1 to mark the anniversary.

Sitt Barbara is a relic church containing the remains of Ss. Barbara and Catherine, the patroness of Alexandria and one of the most popular early Coptic martyrs. The church was built in 684 CE and receives pilgrims regularly. Pilgrims traditionally touch the reliquary with a cloth or handkerchief, which they taken home as an extended presence of the saints. The iconostasis in the church dates from the thirteenth century. Seven steps lead up to a niche, perhaps used for the presiding priest's chair during Mass.

References Pierre Du Bourguet, *The Art of the Copts.* New York, Crown, 1971. Jill Kamil, "The Coptic Museum in Old Cairo," *Archaeology* 40:3, 39–45 (May-June 1987). S.H. Leeder, *Modern Sons of the Pharaohs.* North Stratford, NH, Ayer, 1973.

CORRIE TEN BOOM HOUSE,
Netherlands

The Corrie Ten Boom House is the preserved apartment of Corrie Ten Boom who, along with the members of her family and a network of helpers, helped many Jews escape from Nazi-occupied Holland.

A simple watch-and-clock shop in Haarlem, with the proprietor's apartment above it, was the scene of quiet but firm resistance to Nazi oppression during the 1940s. Casper Ten Boom, then 84 years old and a solid evangelical Christian, was disgusted by Nazi racist doctrine and began to welcome Jews and members of the resistance movement into his home. He constructed a small hiding place behind a wall in his daughter Corrie's bedroom, hardly space enough for two or three people, but useful for emergencies in case of a Gestapo raid. Motivated by deep faith in the providence of God, the family (which included two sons and two daughters) began to take in and protect Jews. At one point, Corrie, who was the leader, had 80 people working within her network, placing Jews with farm families who disguised them as refugee relatives. Since the house had so little space, it was used as a transit point. Crammed into the little home, the fugitives amused themselves with cultural lectures, songfests led by the ebullient Casper, and earnest discussions. The Jews taught the devout evangelicals to sing Hanukkah songs, and Casper loved to talk of God's love and mercy with a young synagogue cantor he was hosting.

In 1944 the family was betrayed and sent to concentration camps. About 30 of their friends were also rounded up, but six Jews, who crammed into the hiding place by standing, survived by outlasting the Gestapo, which stayed in the house for several days looking for them. Casper, a daughter, and a son perished in the camp; the other son died shortly after liberation. Corrie was sent to Ravensbrück women's camp, where she saw her sister die. This terrible event was a call to further conversion, to forgive the guards who caused her death.

Corrie spent the rest of her life (she died in 1983) preaching and witnessing to her faith around the world, especially to children. In 1973, the popular preacher Rev. Billy Graham sponsored a film of her autobiography, *The Hiding Place,* which spread her message worldwide. The site of the Ten Boom store and apartment in Haarlem was purchased by a foundation in 1987 and is maintained as a shrine to Corrie Ten Boom and the family. Despite the fact that it is listed in no tourist guide, it receives a constant stream of visitors.

References Carole Carlson, *Corrie Ten Boom*. Old Tappan, NJ, Revell, 1983. Hans Poley, *Return to the Hiding Place*. Elgin, IL, David Cook, 1994. Corrie Ten Boom, *The Hiding Place*. New York, Random House, 1988.

CROAGH PATRICK, Ireland

A graceful cone of quartzite rising 2,510 feet over Clew Bay near the Atlantic Ocean, Croagh Patrick is the holy mountain of Ireland. It draws hundreds of thousands of pilgrims each year to its topside chapel to commemorate the legend of St. Patrick driving the serpents from the island, which he is supposed to have done while spending Lent of 441 CE on the mountain.

According to the tale, Patrick climbed Croagh Patrick and rang a bell, which caused the snakes to leap from the crest of the mountain to their deaths. The Devil then transformed the snakes into crows, and Patrick routed them by hurling the bell at them. Another version replaces the crows with the Devil's mother, Caora, who tried to cast a spell on Patrick by throwing garlic water on him. The bell is returned to Croagh Patrick each year, where the pilgrims pass it three times with the sun at their backs (the shadow side was the Devil's) and then kiss a cross engraved on it. The cross has been worn away by these exercises, and the bell is now kept in the National Museum in Dublin. But the myth has placed Patrick among those with the power to expel demons and evil spirits, demonstrating the triumph of Christianity in replacing the pre-Christian gods. The pilgrimage is held on the anniversary of the ancient Celtic observance in honor of Lughnasa, a pagan fertility god.

The last Sunday in July (Garlic Sunday) is the time of the great pilgrimage, which draws up to 80,000 people. They follow a series of stations up the mountain, several of which are stone "beds," so called because of legends that saints once slept on them. This is a pilgrimage of penitence in which pilgrims seek to atone for their sins by physical sacrifice. The pilgrim circles each station seven times, each time reciting the Our Father, Hail Mary, and Creed. Many go barefoot, despite the sharp rocks that cover the hillside, and by midday the path is marked with blood. Croagh Patrick and Lough Derg are the only harsh penitential journeys that continue today the rigor that was common to pilgrimages in the Middle Ages. At the top of Croagh Patrick, Mass is celebrated continually during the pilgrimage. But before taking part, the pilgrims circle a small chapel there 15 times. Most pilgrims also confess their sins, and pilgrims can be seen all along the arduous climb on their knees before some priest who is also making the pilgrimage. The last station is a cairn of stones resembling a burial mound; it is circled seven times.

References Paul Gallico, *The Steadfast Man: A Life of St. Patrick*. London, New English Library, 1967. Daphne Mould, *Irish Pilgrimage*. New York, Devin-Adair, 1957. Oliver St.-John Gogarty, *I Follow St. Patrick*. New York, Reynal & Hitchcock, 1938.

CUZCO, Peru

Twelve thousand feet up in the Andes lies Cuzco, the ancient holy city of the Inca peoples and the oldest continuously inhabited city in the Western Hemisphere. Each year on June 24 an Inca festival is held there.

The Incas, who were among the great empires to fall to Spanish conquest in the sixteenth century, had established themselves in what is now Peru around 1200 CE. In 1438 they began a process of conquest that resulted in an empire that stretched 2,500 miles down the cordillera of the Andes. The Sapa Inca was a god-king, the Son of the Sun, who presided over a strict social hierarchy. The Inca policy of cultural genocide obliterated the traces of the conquered peoples, who were absorbed into Inca society. Cuzco remained under Inca rule until 1533, when the Spaniards under Francisco Pizarro conquered it.

Cuzco was laid out on a grid plan in the shape of a puma, a sacred animal. The Inca fortress of Sacsahuamán, on a plateau on the northern edge of the city, forms the head of the sacred puma. Two sacred rivers were channeled through the city, which was laid out in quadrants that radiated out through the kingdom. The angles of the quadrants are uneven and seem to have been based on astrological lines in the Milky Way. Any visitor to the city was required to stay in the quadrant assigned to his home village. The center of the scheme was the Temple of the Sun, Corycancha, founded in legend when the first Inca was sent to earth by the Sun. He struck the ground with a gold rod until the rod was drawn into the earth at the proper spot for the building of the temple. The temple was oriented to the summer solstice, and the niche where the first solstice rays fell each year still remains. The Inca would sit in the niche at the solstice to receive the rays of the sun as it rose. Then a priest would light a sacred fire from the first solstice rays by reflecting them from a gold mirror. Corycancha was the "pivot of heaven," where the lines of sky and earth came together near the crossing of the sacred rivers. Cuzco means "navel of the world" in Quechua, the Inca language, which is still spoken there.

The Spaniards had little respect for the

Inca monuments and stripped them of their gold, which was extensive. The Temple of the Sun, for example, had 700 panels, each weighing five pounds—all of pure gold. The temple walls remain, although some have been incorporated into colonial Christian churches. The base of the Church of Santo Domingo consists of a section of the curved Inca wall that rises 20 feet high. Three chambers dedicated to the moon, the rainbow, and thunder can be visited in the church, and other elements of the temple are still visible though no longer complete. During the Inca period, the temple was surrounded by an ornamental garden of corn, potatoes, and other local foods, each plant made of gold and jewels.

Cuzco has become a city of dual religious legacies. The colonial churches themselves are beautiful and reflect the blending of Spanish and Inca heritages. The cathedral, one of the largest in the world, has many paintings with marked Indian influences, including a Last Supper scene showing Jesus and his disciples feasting on guinea pig and corn beer!

References John Reinhard, "Sacred Peaks of the Andes," *National Geographic* 181:3, 85–111 (March 1992). Michael Sallnow, *Pilgrims of the Andes: Regional Cults in Cuzco.* Washington, DC, Smithsonian Institution, 1987. Victor von Hagen, *Highway of the Sun.* New York, Duell, Sloan & Pearce, 1955.

ence in leadership made it possible to control the criminal element that preyed upon the weak in many other camps.

Among the 206,206 prisoners registered at Dachau during its existence, 31,591 deaths were recorded, though the number is certainly higher. This figure does not include the mass executions of Soviet and French prisoners-of-war; nor does it include the invalids shipped away and executed elsewhere. Most of the Dachau prisoners were used as slave labor, with upwards of 37,000 working in armament factories in 36 subsidiary camps. Both work and living conditions were harsh, with insufficient food, regular beatings, and unsanitary crowding. Each barracks housed some 1,500 people in unheated wooden buildings built for 200.

Many also suffered in the medical experiments performed on living prisoners. Some were kept in freezing water to see how long they could survive and still be revived. Over a thousand were infected with malaria, including numbers of Polish priests, and some with tuberculosis. Experiments with pressurization left their victims permanently deaf and disfigured.

The camp, with over 30,000 prisoners (almost 10,000 had been marched off three days earlier), was liberated by the U.S. 7th Army. The shocked and infuriated American commanding officer ordered the citizens of Dachau to march through the camp to see its devastation so that they could never deny the evil that had existed among them. Forty camp staff were tried for war crimes, and 36 sentenced to death.

Dachau is probably the most visited of the Nazi concentration camps. One barracks has been reconstructed to show the living conditions, and an introductory film and display convey the horror of the place.

DACHAU, Germany

In Dachau, a pleasant suburb outside Munich, the first Nazi concentration camp was built in 1933, two months after Adolf Hitler took power. Dachau was used as a training camp for SS camp personnel, instilling in them the attitude that prisoners were *Untermenschen*, or subhumans, and creating a climate of fear through intimidation and violence. At Dachau, the discipline and organization of the camps that would be built all over Europe was developed and honed to a fine edge.

During its 12 years of existence, Dachau was a camp for political prisoners, and its population was largely made up of dissidents and members of groups considered inferior. The former included Socialists, Christian leaders, and Jehovah's Witnesses, while the latter was largely made up of Gypsies, homosexuals, criminals, and Polish intellectuals. Dachau was not an extermination camp, so German Jewish prisoners were quickly shipped to the death camps in Poland. However, Hungarian and other Jews were brought to Dachau in 1944 to work as slave labor in munitions factories. At the liberation, about 30 percent of the camp population was Jewish. The "politicals" were made up of prominent leaders from every country invaded by the Nazis. In all camps, the prisoners formed an internal government, but at Dachau the prisoners' experi-

The gas chamber (never used), the gallows, and the crematorium have been maintained. Where the ashes of the dead were thrown is a park marked with a Star of David and a Cross. Three memorials—a Protestant chapel, the Catholic Christ in Agony church, and a Jewish memorial— honor the dead. Behind the camp is a Carmelite convent to offer prayers for reparation. In the field used for roll call each day is a sculptured memorial to the dead.

See also Holocaust Sites.

References *Dachau: Time To Forget.* UPI, 1970 (video). Barbara Distel, *Dachau Concentration Camp.* Brussels, International Committee of Dachau, 1972. Israel Gutman (ed.), *Encyclopedia of the Holocaust.* New York, Macmillan, 4 vols., 1990. Bedrich Hoffman, *And Who Will Kill You.* Poznan, Pallottinum, 1994.

DEBRA LIBANOS, Ethiopia

North of Addis Ababa lies Ethiopia's main monastery, Debra Libanos, founded in 1275 by the national saint, Tekla Haymanot. Until after World War II, all Ethiopian bishops were Egyptians appointed by the Coptic Patriarch of Alexandria, and few of them spoke Amharic very well. Consequently, the abbot of Debra Libanos became the most powerful religious figure in the country because he was the highest-ranking native.

Originally a missionary outpost of Christianity, Debra Libanos was based in a small cave from which St. Tekla expelled a pagan magician. In it he installed a model of the Ark of the Covenant, which the Ethiopians believe rests in a shrine in Axum. A model of this sacred relic is what makes an Ethiopian church holy, and every local church and monastery had one. St. Tekla's shrine and monastery became an important place of pilgrimage long before

the capital was built in Addis Ababa in the early 1900s.

Debra Libanos is set in a steep gorge, and the pilgrim's first sight on descending from the plateau above is the massive silver dome of the shrine built by the Emperor Haile Selassie to house Tekla's model of the Ark and his blessing cross. These are kept in an inner room, guarded and protected as national treasures. In legend, St. Tekla is credited with restoring the imperial family, which traced itself from Solomon, King of Israel, and the Queen of Sheba. Because of St. Tekla's importance to Ethiopian national consciousness, almost every emperor in the Solomonic line (Haile Selassie was the last, ruling until 1974) built a shrine over the place of his relics. This involved tearing down the preceding churches, so the present shrine is a twentieth-century building. The earlier churches figure prominently in Ethiopian history.

In 1531, a Muslim invader destroyed a church that had recently been completed. It was burned down with several hundred monks in it, and in an orgy of murder and looting, the ancient manuscripts of the monastery were lost. Another massacre took place barely 50 years later at the hands of a wandering tribe. When the Ethiopian capital was established at Gondar, the monks accompanied the emperor there, only to suffer another mass execution at the hands of the emperor. The valley was deserted for many years, and when the monks began returning shortly before 1800, the location of the saint's relics had been long forgotten. A boy revealed that the secret had been passed down in his family, and he led officials to a wooded area. Digging, laborers found a metal object, and the ground miraculously heaved up in a great earthquake. Following this sign from heaven that they had found the tomb, the sixth church of St. Tekla was completed on the site in 1884. Emperor Menilek II (1844–1913) tore down this church and built another in 1906, and during the construction, the burned medieval church was discovered under the foundations, along with the bones of many martyrs. With this discovery, Debra Libanos entered a period of revival.

This golden age was brought to a vicious end with the massacre of the monks by Italian Fascist troops in 1937. Deliberately choosing May 20, the day of one of the three annual pilgrimages, the Italians machine-gunned all the monks and deacons, several hundred men in total. A small mausoleum to hold their remains was built in 1966. The church was looted by the Italians and some of its treasures were placed in the Vatican museums. Menilek's church survived the pillaging only to be demolished to make room for the present one, built by Emperor Haile Selassie in 1963. Surprisingly, this latest church survived Communist rule (1974–1991) and has become again a place of pilgrimage. Its long and bloody history has made the monastery and shrine symbols of the triumph of Ethiopian Christianity over every adversity and trial.

The legend of St. Tekla says that Christ once promised that a pilgrimage to the saint's tomb would be as meritorious as one to Jesus' tomb. The three annual pilgrimages mix together poor peasants, nobles, the educated, and urban sophisticates. Some walk for days to Debra Libanos, often to fulfill a vow or give thanks. Most bring gifts, either for the monastery (candles, incense, or umbrellas, which are used in ceremonies) or to distribute to beggars. They bring back water from a sacred spring or mud from its banks. A few climb the sides of the gorge to honor the dead, whose bones are interred on ledges in the cliff face. Many pious Ethiopians believe that those buried near St. Tekla's tomb will ascend to heaven to be with him, and so pilgrims bring the bones of their dead to rest in the valley. The shrine has long been associated with healing, too, especially for lepers. During the Communist period, however, the ritual healing baths were taken down.

See also Axum; Lalibela.

References Elizabeth Laird, *The Miracle Child*. New York, Holt, Rinehart & Winston, 1985 (young adult). Alula Pankhurst, "Däbrä Libanos Pilgrimages Past and Present," *Sociology Ethnology Bulletin*. 1:3 (February 1994). Tadesse Tamrat, *Church and State in Ethiopia, 1270–1527*. Oxford, Oxford University Press, 1972.

DELOS, Greece

A small, waterless, and uninhabited island dedicated to the twin Greek gods, Artemis and Apollo, Delos was the cultural and religious hub of the Aegean Sea for over a thousand years. The Ionian States, including Athens, worshipped here. Today Delos is a great archaeological site visited each year by tens of thousands, although no one other than a few caretakers is permitted to remain overnight.

Pilgrims to Delos landed at the Sacred Port and followed the splendid Sacred Way to the Sanctuary of Apollo, which was surrounded by smaller temples, votive monuments, and treasuries. Many Greek city-states built treasuries along the Sacred Way (as they did at Delphi), and a massive statue of Apollo can still be seen, originally part of the treasury of the Island of Naxos. Four temples were dedicated to Apollo (now all in ruins), and a Sanctuary of Artemis was erected, along with several gymnasiums. The gymnasiums, too, were sacred places, since a healthy body was considered a form of perfection and a sign of virtue. What made them especially fitting at Delos was the honor they gave to Apollo, who was god of physical beauty.

Worship of Leto, mother of the twin deities, was well established on Delos by 1000 BCE. Her temple is finely crafted of small stones fitted closely together. The temple of Artemis, called the Artemision, is the best-known site on the island. The remaining ruins are of a 175 BCE shrine built over earlier ones on a granite foundation. During the annual festival of Theoria, dancers would present the story of Artemis' and Apollo's birth, accompanied by a sacred hymn that recounted the legend.

According to legend, Apollo left Delphi each winter and took up residence in Delos. Thus, each year on the birthday of the twin deities, the Delian Games were held. Besides temple ceremonies, musical competitions were held, along with wrestling matches, horse races, and plays. The stadium and open-air theater can still to be seen. During the Delian Games executions were forbidden anywhere in Greece, and after his sentencing, Socrates' death was postponed for this reason.

A few minor shrines were also built on Delos, including one where marvelous mosaic floors have been found, one showing dolphins (associated with Apollo) and another picturing Dionysus, god of wine and sexual revelry, riding a tiger. The House of Dionysus includes two large marble male sex organs. A lake (now drained because of malaria) is the legendary place where Leto gave birth to the twin gods. Along one side is a flanking row of mountain lions, erected by Naxos. Away from the main shrines is the Terrace of the Foreign Gods, a series of smaller temples of Egyptian and Syrian gods.

When the Athenians took control of the island, they decreed that no one could die or give birth there, and in 426 BCE they expelled the residents and dug up all the graves, making the island only a sanctuary. Protected by Rome after 166 BCE, people returned and made the island a bustling and wealthy port, largely through the slave trade. In 88 BCE a slave revolt led to the capture of Delos by a rebel general and the massacre of the entire population. Delos never recovered. By the early Christian era it was prey to pirates and was looted, much of the fine statuary carried off. Some of the best existing pieces are in the National Museum in Athens.

See also Delphi; Ephesus.

References Walter Burkert, *Greek Religion*. Cambridge, MA, Harvard University, 1985. Robin Osborne and Susan Alcock, *Placing the Gods: Sanctuaries and Sacred Space in Ancient Greece*. New York, Oxford University Press, 1994. Arianna Stassinopoulos and Roloff Beny, *The Gods of Greece*. Toronto, McClelland & Stewart, 1983.

DELPHI, Greece

The ancient Greek shrine of Apollo rests on the side of Mount Parnassus. Mount Parnassus rises in a long arc from the Gulf of Corinth above a valley whose sides held the groves, caves, and ravines sacred to the gods of ancient Greece. Parnassus itself was sacred to Apollo, god of the fine arts, and to the muses, the nine daughters of Zeus. The muses were considered demi-gods and were the guardian spirits of writers and artists. The most important of the mountain's places of worship was the Delphic shrine where the most famous oracle of ancient times presided and prophesied.

Greek legend recounts how Apollo chose Delphi as one of his chief places of worship, along with Delos. Greek mythology tells of a time when the gods of the sky

Three columns are all that remain of the Athena Pronaia, a sanctuary constructed in Delphi in 370–360 BCE. According to Greek legend, Apollo selected Delphi, along with Delos, as his central place of worship.

overcame those of the earth. Then the infant Apollo took control of Parnassus by killing Python, the dragon snake that had possessed it. Apollo took the form of a dolphin and swam out to sea to capture a group of sailors, whom he appointed the first priests of his cult.

Apollo spoke through his oracle, who had to be an older woman of blameless life chosen from among the peasants of the area. The sibyl or prophetess took the name Pythia and sat on a tripod seat over an opening in the earth. When Apollo slew Python, its body fell into this fissure, according to legend, and fumes arose from its decomposing body. Intoxicated by the vapors, the sibyl would fall into a trance, allowing Apollo to possess her spirit. In this state she prophesied. She spoke in riddles, which were interpreted by the priests of the temple, and people consulted her on everything from important matters of public policy to personal affairs.

Upon arriving at Delphi, the suppliants registered and paid a fee; when their appointments neared, they purified themselves at the Castalian Spring, where the bathing trough is still visible. They then proceeded along the Sacred Way, a zigzag flagstone walk up the hill. The Sacred Way was lined with statues and offerings, most of which have long disappeared, although a few surviving examples can be seen in the Delphi Museum. Also along the way were a series of treasuries, small shrines sponsored by various Greek cities as thank-offerings for important victories. The best preserved of these is the Athenian treasury, built in 490 BCE to celebrate the Athenian victory at the Battle of Marathon. Because of its balance, harmony, and purity of line, it is regarded as the finest example of ancient Doric style.

The Sacred Way ended outside the temple. There the pilgrims would sacrifice a sheep or goat, whose entrails were examined by the priests for omens. Then the pilgrims entered one by one to ask the sibyl their question. A carved domed rock, the *omphalos*, or navel of the earth, was kept at the place of prophecy. In an ancient flood story about the creation of the human race, the omphalos was the first thing to emerge from the waters as they receded. In another account, Zeus sent two ravens out from the ends of the earth to find its center, and their beaks touched over the omphalos. The stone is presently kept in a museum.

The centerpiece of Delphi was the Temple of Apollo, built with donations from every Greek city-state and from abroad. The base of the temple still stands, with half a dozen of the original columns. On the outside of the base are over 700 inscriptions, most announcing the emancipation of slaves, which was considered a special act of piety to be performed at Delphi. At the far end of the Temple is the altar, originally decorated with memorials, ex-votos, statues, and offerings.

The myths said that during the winter, when Apollo went to his other shrine at Delos, the slopes of Mount Parnassus became the playground of the god Pan, patron of fertility. Above and away from the shrine of Delphi is a grove that is difficult to reach, at the end of an ancient cobblestone trail called the Kalkí Skála, or "evil stairway." Nearby are two pinnacles from which those convicted of sacrilege against the gods were thrown to their deaths. Also in the area is the Corycian Cave, sacred to Pan, and here each November ancient worship rituals involving drinking and sexual orgies took place. The contrast with the Delphic shrine on the lower slopes is striking, and perhaps out of embarrassment, no attempt has been made either to publicize the place or to make it easy to visit. Pan's image in art—

half-man, half-goat with horns—was adopted in the Christian era as the image of the Devil.

Above the Temple of Apollo is an outdoor theater with 33 tiers of stone seats that held about 5,000 people. A stadium seating 7,000 nearby was used for the Phythian Games, held every four years to celebrate the victory of Athens over the Phocians, who had attacked Delphi and tried to seize its treasures. Several centuries later, when Rome conquered Greece and Athenian protection collapsed, the Emperor Nero looted 500 statues from the shrine. In the fourth century CE, Julian the Apostate, a Christian emperor who returned to paganism, ordered Delphi's restoration as part of his campaign to restore the ancient gods, but in an eerie scene, the oracle wailed but refused to prophesy. That event was considered a sign of the end, and in 390 CE the shrine was closed by the Christian Emperor Theodosius. Soon after, the temple was razed.

See also Delos

References Flavio Conti, *Centers of Belief.* Boston, HBJ Press, 1978, 41–56. Joseph Fontenrose, *The Delphic Oracle.* Berkeley, University of California Press, 1978. Neville Lewis, *Delphi and the Sacred Way.* London, Michael Haag, 1987.

DILWARA, India

Dilwara, on the slopes of Mount Abu, is the chief mountain shrine of the Jain faith. It is considered the finest example of Jain architecture, and its carvings are among the outstanding marble sculptures in the world.

The Jains follow a religion of nonviolence and revere mountains as the sites of major events in the lives of their 24 *Tirthankaras,* or savior teachers. Jains reject the idea of god, although most revere the popular gods of the Hindus. The word *Jain* means "conqueror" and refers to Jainism's

demanding asceticism. Their founder, Mahavira ("Great Hero"), began preaching shortly before the Buddha (500 BCE) and shared his experience of rigorous self-discipline.

The Jain ideal is the Tirthankaras ("crossing makers"), of whom Mahavira was the last and greatest. These men conquered their desires and thereby attained perfect wisdom; their title means that they have made the passage from the material world to the spiritual, from interior slavery to freedom. This passage is accomplished through the training called the Three Jewels: right faith, right knowledge, and right conduct. The great sins are falsehood, theft, lust, greed, and violence, and the last is the most evil. A true Jain lives by *ahimsa,* reverence for all life, and casts out any thought or action that might hurt another living being. Jains are strict vegetarians. Their most austere sect, the "sky clad," never wear clothing, as a sign of their contempt for material things.

The Jain temples on Mount Abu are a cluster of buildings rather than a single shrine. Of the five temples there, only two are of importance architecturally or devotionally. The oldest temple, Vimal Vasahi, was built in 1031 CE to honor the first Tirthankar and features a statue of him in its central courtyard. Around the temple courtyard are 52 cells, each containing a cross-legged, seated statue. Leading up to Vimal Vasahi is the House of Elephants, which contains a processional row of stone elephants going to the temple. In the Tejpal Temple (1230 CE) are the finest temple carvings. To say that they are intricate or detailed does not begin to describe them. Every surface above the floors—columns, walls, and ceilings—is covered with traceries so fine that they seem light despite their massiveness. Nothing appears in relief. Instead, the carvers pierced the stone to

Intricately carved dancers circle a column of the Dilwara temple that was built by the Jains in the thirteenth century. The central shrine of the Jain faith, Dilwara consists of five temples located on Mount Abu in Rajasthan, India.

make all their work stand away from its base. The effect is lace-like, when it might have been overwhelming or confusing. In some places, the carving is so fine that light shines through the marble.

References Michael Carrithers and Caroline Humphrey, *The Assembly of Listeners.* Cambridge, UK, Cambridge University, 1991. Paul Dundas, *The Jains.* New York, Routledge, 1992. O.P. Tandon, *Jaina Shrines in India.* New Delhi, Indian Ministry of Information, 1986.

DJENNE, Mali

A cultural center and African crossroads during the Middle Ages, Djenné's importance is linked to its role as a religious and missionary center. For centuries it has been an outpost of Islam in the harsh country of southern Mali.

The city can be traced to at least 850 CE. Until the development of shipping by the Portuguese in the 1400s, Djenné was on the rich, busy caravan routes that carried gold and salt across the vast African deserts. Along with trade goods, the caravans also brought Islam to West Africa. Djenné forms one of the frontiers between Islam and animism, and it was from here that Islam went forth into the region.

Djenné is now difficult to get to. Timbuktu lies to the north, and Mopti, a market town where camel caravans still bring slabs of salt to trade, is 56 miles away. A handful of travelers pass through on their way to the Dogon Cliffs, spending a few moments at the famous mosque and then continuing their journeys. The town itself is not only old, but has never been modernized. The narrow alleys and mud walls lend a biblical atmosphere.

The often-photographed Grand Mosque is the largest adobe structure in the world and the finest example of Sudanese mud architecture. Completed in 1907, it rests on a platform in a great open plaza, facing Mecca. Three towers, some ten stories high, rise to conical points. Its uniform brown color blends with the soil from which it came and creates a sense of unity with the surrounding landscape. From a distance, the Grand Mosque looks like a huge sand castle bristling with protruding timbers. These are used as perches by workers, who replaster the outside walls each year after the rainy season. The long walls, perhaps six stories high, are studded with smaller cones. Despite its mud walls, the mosque looks airy and light rising from the flat plain. It is the center of local activity, and the plaza livens for the Monday market.

West Africa's oldest city, Jenné-Jeno, lies two miles from Djenné. It dates from about 250 BCE but has been abandoned since 1400, when the Muslim leadership of Djenné made a concerted effort to undermine its remaining paganism. The ruins washed away with the rains centuries ago, and it has been largely looted of its artifacts.

See also Dogon Cliffs.

References Carolyn Fluehr-Lobban, *Islamic Society in Practice.* Gainesville, University of Florida, 1994. Philip Koslow, *Mali: The Land of Gold.* Philadelphia, Ingram, 1995 (juvenile). Susan McIntosh, *Excavations at Jenne-Jeno, Hambarketolo, and Kaniana.* Berkeley, University of California, 1995.

DOGON CLIFFS, Mali

One of the most inaccessible parts of the world is the Bandiagara Cliff of Mali, home of the Dogon people. It can be reached only by four-wheel-drive vehicle after a river launch trip of several days. Here the Dogon, who have resisted Christianity and Islam, continue their traditional religion with its elaborate cult of the ancestors.

The escarpment rises 600 feet above a broad plain. Dogon settlements cling to the sides and hide in the folds of rock. The highest of many caves in the cliff, the Tellem caves, are used for burial. The Dogon make ropes of baobab fiber to hoist the dead to the caves, where they join very ancient burials left from an earlier people, the Tellem. The Tellem caves are thought to have great magic, but none is used for religious rituals, and people are forbidden to visit them except when taking a body there.

The Dogon worship a supreme creator named Amma. After making the sun and moon from clay, Amma brought them together with earth and produced humankind. Dogon villages are laid out in an oval shape representing the unity of male and female in the body of Amma. At the head is the men's meeting house; at the feet, the altars. Village homes form the chest, and the two women's meeting houses, the hands. One of the women's houses is for everyday use; the other, guarded by the sacred serpent-god Lébé, is where women must stay during their menstrual periods. Between the family houses and the altars is the village altar, a pillar representing the male sex organ. Nearby is a stone, used for oil crushing, that represents the female genitals. Each family residence is laid out with similar generativity symbolism.

The Dogon do not separate religion from life, and social order is organized around four cults that descend from the four mythical male ancestors of the people. Each clan is headed by a priest, each with different functions: one is a prophet, another the liaison between Amma and his people, a third administers justice, and the last is responsible for funerals. Diviners plot out grids in the sand where they leave small offerings of food. At night, foxes (sacred to the Dogon) take the bait, and the diviner interprets the paw prints within the grid to answer questions posed by villagers.

Funerals are major cultic events, celebrated by the mask society. Every boy is inducted after his circumcision; each carves his own mask and dances with it during funerals. Men are thus associated with death, and women may not get near the masks because women are associated with fertility and life. The mask society, and hence all males, are taught to speak a secret language not known to females. One dance, the *dama,* may be performed before women, and this dance is often done for foreign tourists. Wearing long masks and dancing on 12-foot stilts, the men celebrate the spirits of the ancestors.

Every 60 years the mask society dances the *sigi,* a sumptuous and elaborate resurrection dance ceremony lasting some days. The next sigi will be around 2030. It marks the renewal of the generations (60 being the average lifespan) and the rebirth of a white dwarf star near Sirius. The Dogon have danced to honor this star for centuries, even though western scientists only discovered it in 1928 and first photographed it in 1970. Dogon tradition taught that their sacred star orbited Sirius every 50 years; astronomers have determined that they were two weeks off!

References Caroline Haardt, "The Dogon: Mali's People of the Cliffs," *UNESCO Courier* 1991:5, 42–46 (May 1991). Pascal Imperato, *Dogon Cliff Dwellers: The Art of Mali's Mountain People.* New York, African Arts, 1978. David Roberts, "Mali's Dogon People," *National Geographic* 178:4, 100–127 (October 1990).

EIGHTY-EIGHT TEMPLES PILGRIMAGE, Japan

One of the longest pilgrimages in the world is that undertaken by the Japanese Buddhists. They visit 88 temples in a great clockwise circle around Shikoku, the smallest of the major islands of Japan. The pathway is over 700 miles long and takes up to eight weeks to cover, although many people today take package bus tours that compress the pilgrimage into two weeks. The pilgrimage was begun by Kobo Daishi (714–835 CE), who founded an important Buddhist sect and is revered as Japan's greatest saint. When Kobo Daishi began the pilgrimage, it was the only unrestricted travel permitted in the kingdom.

According to Buddhist belief, the pilgrim who prays at all 88 temples is released from the cycle of rebirth and reincarnation and raised to complete fulfillment. Many make the trek on behalf of the spirits of their dead, hoping for the same deliverance for them. The pilgrimage is also made to atone for sins or to mark a departure point in one's life. It is a popular undertaking for those just reaching retirement, and until World War II, people dying of cancer or other fatal diseases would make the circuit until they died, to be buried by the side of the road. Called "The Trail of Tears," the 88 temple pilgrimage is often made in response to a personal crisis—a lost job, serious illness, or family problems.

The pilgrim, known as *henro,* dresses in white, the color of dead souls on their way to heaven. He or she carries a walking stick, which symbolizes Kobo Daishi, who in this way symbolically accompanies every pilgrim. Traditionally, local residents offer food and water to pilgrims as they trudge along. The pilgrim carries a book in which he records his arrival at each temple and adds the temple stamp. Also at each of the 88 temples, the pilgrim recites a special Buddhist text appropriate to that place and puts his name and address into a box. In themselves, none of the 88 temples is particularly significant artistically or as a religious center; their importance is in being part of the total temple circuit.

References Buddhism: The Land of the Disappearing Buddha—Japan. Richmond, VA, Time-Life, 1978. Oliver Statler, *Japanese Pilgrimage.* New York, Morrow, 1983. Hiroshi Tanaka, *Pilgrim Places: A Study of the Eighty-Eight Sacred Precincts of the Shikoku Pilgrimage.* Ann Arbor, MI, University Microfilms, 1975.

EINSIEDELN, Switzerland

Set in one of Europe's most beautiful baroque churches, in the foothills of the Alps south of Zürich, the shrine of the Black Madonna of Einsiedeln has drawn pilgrims since the Middle Ages. The site was established when an early hermit, St. Meinrad, built a cabin there in 828 *(Einsiedeln* means "hermitage"). In 861 he was murdered by two bandits, and according to legend, the two crows that lived with Meinrad pursued the killers to Zürich, where the killers were captured. Meinrad was recognized as a holy man and martyr, and in 934 a monastery was built incorporating the cabin.

Throughout the Middle Ages, the monastery prospered and received royal grants and gifts. Monks were chosen from the upper classes, and the monastery became a center for learning and the arts, producing outstanding hand-lettered illuminated manuscripts of the Bible. In the eleventh century the monastery took the leadership in the reform of other monasteries in the region and in 1526 began admitting monks from all social classes. In 1602, Einsiedeln became the center for the Swiss Benedictine congregation, which built monasteries in a number of countries, including the United States. The present monastery at Einsiedeln was completed in 1780, although it was suppressed and empty for several years during the turmoil following the French Revolution. In 1801 it was reestablished without its feudal rights, and it has grown and prospered since. The monastery today has over 120 monks, who direct the shrine and two schools—a high school and an agricultural school.

All this would be only of historical interest if not for the shrine of the Black Madonna. Legend has it that Jesus himself appeared in 948 to consecrate a chapel on the site of Meinrad's hut, a tradition that is celebrated by a torchlight procession on the feast of the Miraculous Consecration (September 14). At first the chapel itself attracted the pilgrims, and many reported cures from the water in its sacred spring. Later, the object of reverence became the statue of Mary holding the Child Jesus, mentioned in written records from 1286. The statue is still regarded as miraculous by the faithful, and the spring has now been channeled into Our Lady's Well, the purification well and fountain that stands on the paved square in front of the monastery.

The monastery itself is massive and sits on a low hill above the town. Pilgrims approach across the open plaza where the spring is located. Many wash their hands there as an act of purification. The church itself is a baroque splendor: white walls and pillars lead the eye up to complex paintings and frescoes in the vaults of the ceiling. The most popular of these, the Christmas Cupola, presents a scene of the nativity of Jesus. Elaborate gold-painted stucco work adorns the walls. The effect is richness and light. The interior decoration was done by the Asam brothers, Cosmas and Egid, regarded as the finest decorative artists of eighteenth-century baroque.

The Lady Chapel is near the entrance, and in striking contrast, is built of black marble. It is built over the place where Meinrad's cabin stood. The present shrine was built in 1816, replacing one destroyed by French troops in 1798. The shrine draws several hundred thousand each year. The pilgrimages are subdued in comparison with those at other Marian shrines. The high point here is the singing of Vespers, the ancient prayer of psalms and scripture readings, followed by the *Salve Regina*, a plainchant tribute to Mary. The style of Alpine Catholicism is reserved and includes little external pietistic expression. The monastery maintains a high level of sacred music, and besides the daily use of chant, masses with full orchestras are celebrated on important feasts. Since 1924, the medieval tradition of holding morality plays has been revived at Einsiedeln. *The Great Theatre of the World* will next be offered in 2002 (it is performed every five years). It involves 600 participants and lasts several hours.

The statue, under the title of Our Lady of Hermits, is probably south German and replaces the 1286 statue destroyed by fire in 1465. Dressed in a long red gown, the Black

Madonna carries a naked Christ Child in her left arm. She and the child are totally black, probably the result of centuries of smoke from votive lamps burnt in the chapel, although some disagree. The visitor cannot see the full statue, however, since it has been dressed in a heavy brocade gown adapted from Spanish court style since 1600.

See also Marian Apparitions.

References Ean Begg, *The Cult of the Black Virgin.* Boston, Arkana, 1985. Ludwig Raeber, *The Abbey of Einsiedeln.* Einsiedeln, Benziger, 1975. Gerard Sherry, *The Catholic Shrines of Europe.* Huntington, IN, Our Sunday Visitor, 1986.

ELLORA CAVES, India

About 200 miles east of Bombay lie the Ellora Caves, 34 religious caves noted for their fine sculpture. One of them, Kailasa, was built over a period of 100 years during the eighth century. It is considered the greatest cave temple in India.

Built on a site where prehistoric cults performed blood sacrifices, Ellora is sacred not only to Buddhists but also to Jains and Hindus. Twelve of the caves are Buddhist, five Jain, and seventeen Hindu. Constructed after the completion of Ajanta, a similar group of religious caves just 50 miles away, Ellora is thought to be the work of the same builders. But unlike Ajanta with its steep cliff face, Ellora's hillside slopes gently, allowing entrance halls and easier access to the cave temples. The carved fronts and great arched entries are as elaborate as any western cathedral. By far the most important artistically are the Hindu caves with their intricate carvings of gods victorious over demons and their traditional scenes, such as the god Shiva with his beloved consort Parvati.

Some sculptures are violent, such as one of Shiva baring fangs like an angry baboon while spearing one victim with a trident and holding another down with his foot. He rattles a drum and catches his prey's blood to drink, while Parvati holds out a bowl to catch some blood for herself as well. Until the 1700s, the Thugs, a Hindu cult that practiced ritual murder, regarded Ellora as a source of the mysteries of their gory rites.

The greatest cave temple in India is the Kailasa (Shiva's Paradise), a Hindu cave carved not horizontally but vertically into the living rock. Great trenches over 100 feet deep were cut along the lines that would become the edges of the temple, and 200,000 tons of stone were removed. The temple was then hewn from the massive block bordered by the trenches, leaving a free-standing solid stone temple below ground level. The main walls of the trenches were then removed to leave the temple open. In this respect the Kailasa resembles Lalibela in Ethiopia. Although Kailasa is counted as one of the Ellora Caves (#16), it really is not a cave at all but an enormous rock sculpture.

The Kailasa, which honors Shiva, is huge. The courtyard entryway alone is 240 by 150 feet, and 100 feet high. It is named for Mount Kailas in the Himalayas, the great Hindu pilgrimage site and Shiva's traditional home. Around the temple are a number of chapels and monks' cells cut into the rock. From a wide porch, the visitor enters the portico and a large room with a shrine to Nandi, the bull of Shiva, flanked by two columns over 50 feet high. The porch, the Nandi shrine, and the inner shrine are connected by flying bridges, cut directly from the stone, 25 feet above the floor. Relief carvings of dancers recall Shiva's role as Lord of the Dance. In the inner shrine the sacred lingam, Shiva's sex organ, was worshipped, surrounded by

ŚIVA DANCING: KATISAMA
नृत्यत्शिव कटिसम्

Relief carvings of dancers, such as this carving of Shiva, cover the walls of the Kailasa temple. The temple honors Shiva, "Lord of the Dance," and was built in the eighth century.

flowers and candles. Hindu faithful still worship at this shrine.

See also Ajanta.

References James Burgers and James Fergusson, *The Cave Temples of India.* Philadelphia, Coronet, 2d ed., 1969. Trilok Majupuria and Indra Majupuria, *Holy Places of Buddhism in Nepal and India.* Bangkok, Tecpress, 2d ed., 1993. Satcheverell Sitwell, *Great Temples of the East.* New York, Ivan Obolensky, 1963.

EMEI SHAN, China

Emei Shan, "the lofty eyebrow mountain," is one of the four sacred mountains of Buddhist China. At its greatest, in the fifteenth century, the mountainside contained 150 monasteries. Today, even after decades of Communism and extensive damage during the Cultural Revolution (1966–1969), 20 monasteries remain. They are used as rest houses by pilgrims undertaking the trek up the 10,000-foot mountain.

The visitor to the top of Emei climbs through groves of pines up thousands of stairs that are draped by flowering bushes in the spring and covered treacherously by snow and ice in the winter. As a concession to religious tourism, buses and a cable car have been installed to replace the climb. Both of the two walking routes begin at the Baogua Temple, which can be traced to the sixth century. The easier path is 27 miles long; the 40-mile path is not only long but also rugged and challenging. Buses usually take pilgrims to a starting point about two days' walk from the summit. Both paths pass by caves and temples that serve as stations along the route, with names like Crouching Tiger and Myriad Ages temples and the Nine Immortals Cave. Here the devout pray and burn votive papers with sacred texts written on them. The two paths converge at the Elephant Bathing Pond, where purification rites take place.

The patron of Emei Shan is the Bodhisattva Puxian, who is represented in art riding an elephant. (A bodhisattva is a Buddhist saint who forgoes entry into complete bliss in order to devote himself to the spiritual needs of lesser persons.) A 1,000-year-old bronze statue of Puxian stands at the point where most pilgrimages begin. The final ascent brings the pilgrim to the Golden Summit and the view of Buddha's Halo, an effect of light refracted from water crystals suspended in the cold air at the summit. Although there are numerous Buddha shrines along the mountainside, the preeminent one is Huazang Temple on the summit, rebuilt in 1989 after it had been destroyed by a 1972 fire.

See also Mountains, Sacred; T'ai Shan.

References H.G. Creel, *Chinese Thought from Confucius to Mao Tse-tung.* Chicago, University of Chicago, 1953. Mary Mullikan and Anna Hotchkis, *The Nine Sacred Mountains of China.* Hong Kong, Vetch & Lee, 1973. Robert Orr, *Religion in China.* New York, Friendship Press, 1980.

EMERALD BUDDHA, Thailand

Adjoining the Royal Palace in Bangkok is the Wat Phra Keo, or the Temple of the Emerald Buddha, the royal chapel where the king of Thailand performs his official religious duties. Its gilded spires and pavilions, rising between the Chao Phrang River and one of the many canals that crisscross the city, are among the unforgettable sights of Bangkok. Wat Phra Keo has been made sacred because of its official standing and because it houses the national religious treasure, the Emerald Buddha.

Built by King Rama I in 1782 as a setting for the Emerald Buddha, Wat Phra Keo has expanded into a complex of buildings, each seemingly more wondrous than the next. The walls surrounding the shrine are painted with 178 murals telling the story of the Ramayana, the Hindu epic, in a Thai version called the *Ramakien*. Pilgrims walk around the compound, following the ancient tale. The monkey-god Hanuman is the hero who defeats the forces of corruption in the *Ramakien*, one of the great myths of the battle between good and evil.

The numerous reliquary spires, both rounded (*chedi*) and pointed (*prang*), are covered with mirrored tiles, mosaics of bright-colored glass, and gold leaf. The tallest and most striking of these spires is the Golden Chedi, covered completely in gold. It rests on a marble platform that it shares with the library (*Mondop*) and the Royal Pavilion. The Golden Chedi contains a major relic of the Buddha. In the Mondop the visitor will find a cabinet containing Buddhist scriptures and a number of statues of the Buddha and of sacred white elephants. The Royal Pavilion, which serves as the monarch's private chapel, contains a model of the famous temple at Angkor Wat, so influential in Thai religious architecture. In front of the buildings and in the courtyards stand statues of mythical creatures: the *nagas* (protective cobras), *yakshas* (short, fierce, fanged warriors who keep away evil spirits), and the Thai national symbol, the *garuda* (a great bird with the lower body of a man).

The Emerald Buddha, the most sacred object in Thailand, is about 30 inches tall. It sits in a meditation pose on a 40-foot-high altar of intricate goldwork, flanked by crystal balls representing the sun and moon. A nine-tiered umbrella rises above it, a sign of great honor. Among the religious functions of the king is to change the robes of the Emerald Buddha three times a year to indi-

cate the beginning of each new season. There are three gold robes: a robe with blue highlights for the rainy season, an enameled robe for the cool season, and a robe with diamonds for the hot season. The Emerald Buddha was found in 1436 inside a chedi where it had apparently been hidden. It was plastered over and gilt, probably to disguise it from bandits or invaders. But when it was cleaned, its jade body was revealed. It was stolen at one point, then taken as booty of war, and finally came into the hands of Rama I in a battle in 1778.

The sanctuary, roofed in iridescent blue tile, rests on a marble base, guarded by garudas holding nagas in their claws. Several sets of murals in the shrine present the life of the Buddha. Before entering the sanctuary, pilgrims remove their shoes; they usually prostrate themselves and make offerings of flowers or incense. The atmosphere is one of deep reverence, with none of the chatting and play that goes on throughout the rest of the compound. Around the sanctuary are 12 pavilions.

On Chakri Day (April 6), which celebrates the founding of the Chakri Dynasty (of which the present king is ninth), people take flowers and incense to the Temple in honor of past Chakri kings. The Pantheon houses the statues of each king and is open to the public only on this day.

See also Wat Po.

References Karen Schur Narula, *Voyage of the Emerald Buddha*. New York, Oxford University Press, 1994. Alistair Shearer, *Thailand: The Lotus Kingdom*. London, John Murray, 1989. Sacheverell Sitwell, *Great Temples of the East*. New York, Ivan Obolensky, 1963.

EPHESUS, Turkey

The city of Ephesus (Efes in modern Turkey) was an important religious center,

The Library of Celcus is one of the many ancient buildings still standing in Ephesus. Ephesus was a hotbed for the new Christian religion, and St. Paul and Apostle John are said to have preached the gospel in the city.

not only for the Greeks and Romans but also for Christians. It was the center of worship of Diana, goddess of the hunt, and St. Paul established a Christian community there, to which he later addressed one of his epistles. At one point, 17 gods and goddesses were worshiped in Ephesus.

In the first century CE, Ephesus was the center of the cult of Artemis, or Diana. Its religious life centered on her shrine, the largest Greek temple in antiquity and one of the Seven Wonders of the ancient world. The cult of Diana was organized on the principle of the beehive. Diana, the queen, was surrounded by priests and priestesses, musicians, dancers, and acrobats. The temple had its own mounted police, and the economy of the city benefited greatly from the silver statues and ex-votos produced for her worship. Unfortunately, the magnificent temple of Diana is now only an outline on the earth, its archaeological remains removed to the British Museum. In its day, though, the annual festival of Diana stopped work for a month while huge numbers of pilgrims arrived in the city and celebrations erupted on every corner. The ruins of the city reveal some parts of the cult of Diana, such as the Sacred Way that led to the temple. Remnants of some of the other temples also survive.

When Christianity arrived, Ephesus was the largest port in the Middle East, so important to trade that distances were measured from it. There was also a large Jewish community, but little evidence of it remains.

St. Paul spent his longest missionary tour in Ephesus (Acts 18–20). In the midst of the maelstrom of the festival, Paul decided to preach the Gospel. The silversmiths fomented a riot against him, and the excited crowd chanted, "Great is Diana of the Ephesians!" The mob would have lynched him if they could have found him. But Paul was persuaded to depart for Greece. The Great Theater, where the riot occurred, still stands.

There is no biblical evidence that the Apostle John lived in Ephesus, but Christian literature from the second century on attests that he did. John was exiled from Ephesus to Patmos, where he wrote his Epistles and the Book of Revelation. Tradition says that he wrote his Gospel in Ephesus, and his tomb is a major shrine there. The present church is a heavily restored version of the shrine built by the Emperor Justinian in the 500s.

Pious tradition has also associated Ephesus with the Virgin Mary, because at the time of his death, Jesus consigned her to the care of John (John 19:26–27). It is her presence that attracts most pilgrims. In 1841, a book by a German mystic, Anna Katerina Emmerich, was published, recounting visions of Mary living in Ephesus. Following her descriptions, a house was discovered that was proclaimed to be Mary's. It is known as the Panaya Kapula ("Doorway to the Virgin"). Since 1892 it has been an official pilgrimage site, and Pope Paul VI visited it in 1967. On 15 August, Orthodox and Muslim clergy conduct a service together at the shrine, one of the rare occasions this happens anywhere.

Near Ephesus is the Grotto of the Seven Sleepers, a cave where seven Christian youth were walled up during the Roman persecutions. An earthquake supposedly freed them two centuries later, and they arose as if from sleep. It is a popular shrine with the Greek Orthodox.

References Ronald Brownrigg, *Pauline Places*. London, Hodder & Staughton, 1989. Steven Friesen, "Ephesus—Key to the Vision in Revelation," *Biblical Archaeology Review* 19:3, 24–37 (May-June 1993). Sharon Gritz, *Paul, Women, and the*

Mother Goddess at Ephesus. Lanham, MD, University Press of America, 1991.

ERAWAN SHRINE, Thailand

The shrine at Bangkok's Erawan Hotel is one of the most elaborate spirit shrines in Thailand. It honors the Hindu spirit Thao Maha Brahma (the Four-Faced) who, along with the spirits of the place, guards against bad luck. The shrine was built in 1956 during construction of the hotel, after several accidents had occurred among the workers. The hotel was completed, then torn down and replaced without further injuries. Thus the shrine gained a reputation for protection and good fortune. It is now one of the most frequently visited shrines in Thailand, and a plaza has been built around it to handle the flow of suppliants.

Alongside Buddhism, the main religion of Thailand, belief in a spirit world persists. The Thais refer to spirits as *phi* and believe that they outnumber the human race. Many *phi* engage in mischievous behavior, tempting people or tricking them, and one bothersome *phi* is known to trick women into taking off their clothes in public. Throughout the country, the Thais build spirit houses near homes, farms, and public buildings. These small structures, often no larger than a birdhouse, provide a resting spot for the spirit of the place, and Thais often leave small offerings—flowers and incense sticks—before them. The location of the spirit house is chosen after calculating the astrological signs. Usually it is situated so that the shadow of the building does not fall on it—which takes careful calculations in Bangkok because land values are high and plots small. Spirit houses in public buildings—hotels, schools, and shopping malls—are usually larger and more elaborate than those found near homes and farms. Where spirit houses are found along major streets

in city centers, stands sell freshly made flower garlands, small carved elephants, and other offerings. At Erawan, the spikes on the fence along the periphery of the shrine are always topped with garlands of flowers.

Thai teenagers sporting the latest fashions drop by Erawan from the fashionable Rajadamri Arcade to leave offerings before examinations. They mix easily with the elderly and the visiting peasants and workers. In thanks for favors, petitioners can arrange to have a classical Thai dance performed, but this practice is much less common at Erawan than at Lakmuang Shrine. By custom, women danced naked before the shrine in thanksgiving, but the shrine's location on a busy street has made this sort of thanksgiving impractical. The ingenious solution has been to allow playing of sexually explicit videos, although the shrine guardians confine the practice to the late night. The Erawan shrine seems to have an affinity for matters of love and sex. Popular petitions are for a good mate, a happy marriage, or the birth of a son. Prostitutes from the red-light district often ask for generous clients.

References Trilock Majupuria, *Erawan Shrine and Brahma Worship in Thailand.* Bangkok, Tecpress, 1993. Ormond McGill, *Religious Mysteries of the Orient.* South Brunswick, NJ, Barnes, 1976. Rudolph Wurlitzer, *Hard Travel to Sacred Places.* Boston, Shambhala, 1995.

EXTERNSTEINE, Germany

This outcropping of five enormous limestone pillars near Detmold in northern Germany has been a sanctuary and place of mystic power since prehistoric times. A network of hermitages, chapels, Celtic stones, and sacred sites are bound together by a series of straight lines called *Heilige Linien* (holy lines), adding to the mystery of the place.

Offerings are heaped before the Erawan shrine, one of the most popular and frequented shrines in Thailand.

Little is known of the activities that took place at Externsteine in the early Christian period: holes were carefully drilled for no apparent reason, stairs lead to dead ends, platforms seem to serve no purpose, and a large space faces the midsummer sunrise. This last element has led many analysts to assume that Externsteine was a solar observatory, or that this was part of its cultic use. In other such rock sanctuaries, the apparently aimless holes and structures symbolize multiple entry-points into the earth to release its energies. One thing is certain, however: one large room was used to initiate the priests of an ancient, pre-Christian cult.

Externsteine was a pagan cultic center until 782 CE, when Charlemagne, as part of a campaign against Saxon paganism, forbade its use for ceremonies. Shortly thereafter, hermit monks settled into caves in the base of the rocks to Christianize the spot and drive out its evil powers. Beautifully preserved carved reliefs date from this period. Their purpose—to show the triumph of Christianity over paganism—is shown most strongly in the twelfth-century wall sculpture of the Tree of Life. It is an extraordinary bas relief carving of the traditional northern European *Irminsul*, a pagan representation of earth power, bowing down in adoration as the body of Jesus is taken from the Cross. Nicodemus, who is described in the Gospels as helping remove the body of Jesus from the Cross (John 19:39–40), is shown lowering the body, stepping on the pagan tree symbolizing the backbone of the universe, which curves obediently under his weight. The sun and moon—important pagan fertility images of masculine and feminine—are weeping. The ancient tree of pagan knowledge submits to the Tree of the Cross. The snake symbol of the earth energies is pushed down into the earth beneath the feet of the disciples. (In Jewish and Christian mythology, the serpent is the symbol of the Devil, the Evil One.) This bas relief, carved from the living rock, is the only example of German sculpture showing a Byzantine influence.

Atop one of the pillars, accessible only by a metal footbridge, is a chapel with a tiny pillar altar cut out of the living rock. A 20-inch window is directed at the midsummer sunrise and the most northerly rising of the moon. During the Middle Ages, hermits prayed in the chapel. Scholars think that the monks demolished an observatory which they built over the chapel to drive out the pagan influences. Some investigation shows that the chapel may have been part of a zodiac orientation, in which the rays of the sun are thrown in such a way as to tell time (as in a sundial) or to indicate its path through the zodiac. Since astrology—prophecy through the study of the stars—was universal before modern science, this explanation is not unreasonable. The position of the chapel allows the first rays of the summer solstice to cut an arc of light in the center of the wall behind the altar. Perhaps the light beam originally was cast on some ex-voto or sacred object placed upon the altar.

Today, Externsteine is no longer a Christian shrine, but it does draw many devotees. Most follow various New Age beliefs and are attracted to Externsteine by its astrological aspects. They gather in summer and winter to celebrate the solstices. Neopagans are also drawn to Externsteine. Some of them are motivated by extreme nationalism, even neo-Nazism. A few miles away is *Hermann's Denkmal*, a shrine glorifying German nationalism.

References Paul Devereux, *Secrets of Ancient and Sacred Places*. London, Blandford, 1992. Einhard and Notker the Stammerer, *Two Lives of Charlemagne.*

New York, Penguin, 1969. Walter Matthes, *Corvey und die Externsteine.* Stuttgart, Urachhaus, 1982.

EX-VOTOS

Ex-votos, sometimes called votive offerings, are gifts presented to a shrine as a sign of the pilgrim's devotion.

The Latin root of the word *votive*—*votum* (vow)—reveals that the gifts originally symbolized pilgrims' promises to fulfill some pledge if they received the help for which they prayed. Through the offering, the givers dedicated themselves to the god or saint. Pilgrims who pray for some blessing—a healing, success in exams, or the conversion of a loved one—are making a promise to persist in prayer themselves.

An ex-voto may be a simple gift or souvenir of a person's visit to a holy place. Pilgrims often leave some token of their visit, a gift that represents themselves. This might be money, a donation of work, or a symbolic offering. (Money is sometimes given in ways not always appreciated by shrine staff, such as pinning currency to the gowns of statues or tossing coins into sacred waters.) Some religions believe that the deities will use the offerings; thus it is common to see cigars, uncooked rice, and rum before the shrines of Santería saints in Cuba.

Besides tangible gifts, many give their services or talents. A popular American Christmas song, "The Drummer Boy," tells the tale of a poor crippled boy who played for the Christ Child as a way of giving his gift of self. Lourdes in France is famous for its *brancardiers*, stretcher-bearing pilgrims who offer days or weeks of service to the sick and handicapped, carrying them to services or the clinics and seeing to their needs. At Walsingham in England, the annual pilgrimage for the severely retarded depends on large numbers of volunteers.

In France, marble plaques with the word *Merci* (thanks) etched in gold are common, usually with a comment written on the back. The most elaborate form of thank-offering is a votive painting commissioned by the pilgrim showing the cure or deliverance, usually with the holy protector hovering in the heavens above. Some of these are pictures of ships being torpedoed in war, or cars in accidents, to show the disaster from which the grateful pilgrim was delivered safely. In the cathedral of Turin, Italy, are several paintings showing people who have been saved from near-fatal falls during mountain climbing.

Another common form of thank-offering is the *milagro,* a tiny image stamped in tin of an ear, hand, or eye, giving thanks for the cure of that part of the body. At Catholic shrines in Portugal and Spain, milagros are also found in molded wax, but in ancient Greek pagan shrines like Delphi and Delos, they were cast in bronze or terra cotta. Military veterans leave their medals as thanks for safe delivery from battle. Lech Walesa, first president of Poland after the collapse of Communism there, presented his 1983 Nobel Prize Medal to the shrine of Our Lady of Czestochowa at Jasna Góra in thanks for his preservation from Communist persecution. At the Peace Shrine at Hiroshima, thank-offerings take the form of tens of thousands of strands of folded paper cranes, symbols of new life in Japanese culture.

Most common, however, are the votive offerings that simply testify to the pilgrim's presence and are understood to prolong that presence. Candles, incense, and flowers are the most universal forms of this type of ex-voto. Some pilgrims leave graffiti or put their names on rocks near a shrine. In Japan, pilgrims paint their names on smooth stones that are then tossed into ponds. In Turkey, on the tombs of Muslim holy men *(türbes),* visitors commonly leave a strip torn from their clothing. In Tibet and India, tree branches flutter with pilgrims' small, personally inscribed banners. Like the "rag offerings," they remain until they rot away. The most dramatic of this type of ex-voto is the presentation of a woman's hair, a custom that goes back to pre-Christian Rome but is still seen in modern Italy. The contemporary forms of this ex-voto of presence are photographs and the visitor's book, where pilgrims sign their names and comment about the experience for the edification of those who follow.

Votive offerings are also found at cemeteries, where some cultures leave food and drink for the dead. In Africa, people pour out a libation (beer or a soft drink) for their ancestors on important occasions.

One shrine, the Hill of Crosses in Siauliai, Lithuania, is composed entirely of ex-votos: tens of thousands of crosses of all sizes and shapes cover the hillside as a striking testimonial of faith.

References Martha Egan, *Milagros: Votive Offerings from the Americas.* Santa Fe, Museum of New Mexico, 1991. Mary Lee and Sidney Nolan, *Christian Pilgrimage in Modern Western Europe.* Chapel Hill, University of North Carolina, 1989. William Rouse, *Greek Votive Offerings.* New York, Arno, 1975.

the vision only brought mockery and derision, but 60 people came to the second vision in June. Only the children saw the Lady, who again told them to pray the rosary. She told them to learn to read and predicted the deaths of the younger two. As she left, the small crowd could see a cloud rising and tree branches bowing toward it.

After the apparition, authorities put great pressure on the three children to deny what they had seen. Nevertheless, they returned to Cova da Iria on July 13. Lucia asked the Lady for a sign and was promised that in October she would reveal her name and give a sign for all. She also gave the children three secrets: the first was a vision of hell "like a sea of fire," the second was a prophecy that Russia would be converted if people prayed (this occurred several months before the Communists took power there). The third secret has never been revealed.

Eighteen thousand people came for the August apparition, but the children were kept in detention for three days by an antireligious local official. He threatened them to no avail. On the nineteenth, the Lady appeared, expressing displeasure at the cancelled meeting. Thirty thousand people crammed the area for the fifth apparition in September, and the children had difficulty getting through. By this time, the press was covering the apparitions, and all Europe had heard of them. A few people believed they saw a globe of light as the children spoke to the Lady, and when Lucia asked for healings, the Lady promised to cure some of those present.

The October apparition drew 70,000 people. Mary announced that she was Our Lady of the Rosary and asked that this prayer be offered for an end to World War I, and that a church be built in her honor. She

FATIMA, Portugal

A rural village in central Portugal was the site of one of the best-known visions of the Virgin Mary, which has become a main pilgrimage center.

On the thirteenth of the months from May to October 1917, three illiterate children said they had visions of the Virgin Mary. The visions were vivid and the Virgin's messages pointed, involving prophecies concerning world events about which the children were completely ignorant. The alleged vision immediately became part of conflicts between the Church and the anticlerical government, which accused Church authorities of trying to mobilize the peasants. The visions of Fátima soon moved beyond Portuguese politics, however, and became a worldwide phenomenon. Our Lady of Fátima became a symbol of resistance to Communism, and the shrine became among the most popular Catholic pilgrimage destinations in the world.

The first apparition came to Lucia and her cousins, Jacinta and Francisco, as they tended sheep in an isolated ravine called Cova da Iria. Suddenly they saw a woman in white, "more brilliant than the sun, shedding rays of light." She told them that she came from heaven and promised that they would suffer much, but said that they should continue to pray the rosary. News of

JACINTA   FRANCISCO   LUCIA

The three visionaries of Fátima, pictured here in 1917, claimed to see apparitions of the Virgin Mary, Joseph, and the Christ child. The children's visions received international media attention and drew thousands of people hoping to see the visions themselves.

then disappeared in a blaze of light, to be replaced by several visions of Mary, Joseph, and the Christ Child. All of this was seen only by the children. The crowd had patiently stood throughout, drenched by a heavy rain, when Lucia cried out, "Look at the sun!" It seemed to dance in the sky, whirling toward the earth and then back. After the spinning of the sun, the crowd found its clothing completely dry. This was the sign that the Lady had promised, and it was experienced by all those present.

Francisco and Jacinta both died during the worldwide influenza epidemic of 1918–1920, and Lucia, constantly harassed by the curious, became a nun in 1926 and moved to Spain. Four years later, the apparitions of Fátima were approved by the Church. In 1948 Lucia entered a cloistered convent and has rarely left it since. She has visited the shrine only five times since the church was built.

The third secret has been the cause of much speculation. Lucia wrote it down in 1944 with instructions that the envelope be opened in 1960. It was sent to the Vatican in 1957, but if it has been read, its contents have never been revealed. Due to its connections with anti-Communism, Fátima has lost popularity since the fall of the Soviets, though it still draws over four million visitors each year.

The town of Fátima was desperately poor in 1917. Though it has expanded to accommodate pilgrim hostels and commercial development, much of it remains simple and even austere. The sanctuary, completed in 1953, is a massive white colonnaded structure. Pilgrims go first to the tomb of Francisco, around whom a cult has developed, and many devotees are promoting his recognition as a saint. An open chapel has been built on the site of the apparitions, and Mass is celebrated there continually from dawn to dusk. Worked into the crown of the statue of Our Lady of Fátima at the chapel is the bullet removed from Pope John Paul II after the assassination attempt on him in 1981.

To the east of the sanctuary, a path winds through stony farm fields to Aljestrel, the hamlet where the three seers lived. The path is lined with 14 Stations of the Cross commemorating the Passion and death of Jesus, erected by refugees who fled Hungary in 1956. A fifteenth station, of the Resurrection, was built after Hungary's liberation from Communism. Along the way is the tree of Mary's fourth apparition (August 19, 1917), the only vision that did not take place at the Cova da Iria. At dusk, local residents often come here to sing a haunting chant in the local dialect in honor of the Virgin. Years later, Lucia revealed that the children had seen three visions of angels in 1916. Near the Way of the Cross is the spot of the first and third of these. The second is at the well in the backyard of Lucia's home in the village.

See also Marian Apparitions.

References Frederick Miller (ed.), *Exploring Fatima*. Washington, DC, Ave Maria Institute, 1989. *Miracles of Lourdes, Fatima, Guadelupe and Knock*. Stafford, VA, CDR Communications, 1988 (video). Sandra Zimdars-Schwartz, *Encountering Mary*. Princeton, NJ, Princeton University, 1991.

fountain with miraculous waters. Major festivals are held on May 8 and September 29, the Feast of St. Michael. Very early Christian documents suggest that the building of this shrine on Gárgano was the occasion for establishing this feast day, which is observed throughout the world.

The ancient pilgrim route wound through a river valley, past a number of shrines. Ironically, the first village on the route, which now draws one million international visitors each year, became famous only recently. *San Giovanni Rotondo* originally was known for its venerable statue of Our Lady of Grace, but modern pilgrims come to visit the tomb of a famous mystic, Padre Pio (+1968). During his lifetime, he advised a constant stream of people who believed that he had the gift of reading hearts. In his hands he bore the stigmata, the bleeding nail wounds of Christ, which caused him to lose a cup of blood a day. Reputedly, he was also able to be in two places at once, and several cardinals in the Vatican were shocked to have him appear to them while he was asleep back in San Giovanni Rotondo. When asked about his alleged bilocations, Padre Pio only answered enigmatically, "I am where I am."

Padre Pio's prophecies are also striking. He is said to have predicted that a young Polish theology student in Rome, Karol Wojtyla, would one day be pope. Wojtyla has become Pope John Paul II. Because of the saint's reputation for healings, American devotees have built a hospital in San Giovanni Rotondo, named after Fiorello LaGuardia, the first Italian-American mayor of New York. Ironically, LaGuardia was a Protestant, but the cult of Padre Pio has become worldwide and is especially strong in the United States. Even so, the case for

THE GARGANO MASSIF, Italy

In southern Italy along the Adriatic Sea lies the Gárgano Massif, a breathtakingly beautiful mountainous area that is the site of Italy's oldest pilgrimage route and its newest shrine. Even the names of the mountains tell of the region's spiritual traditions: Monte Sacro, Monte Salvatore, Monte Sant' Angelo, and Monte degli Angeli.

Monte Sant'Angelo is named for St. Michael the Archangel, invoked in the Middle Ages as the chief protector against the power of the Devil. Michael's cult was widespread throughout Europe, and Michael was traditionally honored on high places. According to local legend, St. Michael appeared at a grotto to several shepherds around 490 CE, leaving a red cloak as a testimonial. Immediately Christians undertook pilgrimages to the site, which previously had been a pagan holy place. In the eighth century, a monk named Aubert took a piece of the cloak to France, where he built Mont-Saint-Michel to shelter the relic. Throughout the thirteenth and fourteenth centuries, when crusaders sailed from nearby Manfredónia, they would visit the shrine to ask the blessing of Michael, patron of warriors. The present sanctuary church dates from this period. A magnificent Byzantine bronze door opens to the cave where Michael was alleged to have appeared. Inside the grotto is a church and a

Padre Pio's sainthood has moved slowly. Even when mystical phenomena are deemed authentic, they are not regarded by the Catholic church as a sign of sanctity. The Vatican regards Padre Pio's growing cult with suspicion and has proceeded slowly.

References *A Celebration of Padre Pio.* Harrison, NY, Ignatius Press, (n.d. video). Ted Harrison, *Stigmata: A Medieval Mystery in a Modern Age.* New York, Viking, 1996. C. Bernard Ruffin, *Padre Pio: The True Story.* Huntington, IN, Our Sunday Visitor, 1982.

GENEVA, Switzerland

Geneva, the largest city in French-speaking Switzerland, is one of the earliest and greatest centers of Protestantism. Here John Calvin (1509–1564) developed the major alternative to Lutheranism, and from here his doctrine spread to France (where Calvinism remains the main expression of Protestantism), the Netherlands, and Scotland. Known as the Presbyterian Church in the English-speaking world, Calvinism is also prominent as far afield as Korea, where it is the largest Christian faith. A number of sites in Geneva evoke the spirit of Calvin and his message, but because of Calvinist disapproval of shrines and pilgrimages, these places are seen as memorials, sources of inspiration and reaffirmation of faith.

Geneva was governed as a city-state by prince-bishops from the twelfth century. Thus, when Calvin arrived in 1536 and Geneva accepted Protestantism, it was easily transformed into a republic with a religious leader. Calvin ruled unchallenged for a quarter-century, leaving his mark on the spirit of the city and making Calvinism its universal faith. Refugee Protestants fled to Geneva, sparking a revival of the economy. Calvin preached the morality of capitalism, and in a sense, prosperous Geneva is a monument to his social doctrine. Another monument to Calvinism is the International Red Cross, founded in Geneva in 1864 and inspired directly by a Calvinist sense of calling to service. For the same reason, the city has become a beacon for peace-making and arms-reduction efforts as well as truce negotiations. Often called the "Protestant Rome," Geneva is also headquarters of the World Council of Churches. Ironically, the city today is half Catholic.

St. Peter's Cathedral, recently restored, contains the pulpit from which Calvin preached for 28 years. Originally built between 1150 and 1225, the cathedral shows the effects of the Reformation, which sought to eliminate those Catholic devotions that came between the individual and God. Not only statues, but also stained-glass windows, church music, and tabernacles were removed. The interior of St. Peter's is notable for its simplicity. It contains the tomb of the Duc de Rohan, an early head of the Reformed Church in France.

The Reformers' Wall, over 100 yards long, is a carved granite and quartz monument to the leaders of the Reformation. Its ten statues, with the main Calvinists at the center, include a statue of Roger Williams, the Pilgrim who founded Rhode Island. There are also plaques dedicated to Martin Luther and to Ulrich Zwingli, the other major personality in Swiss Protestantism.

The major celebration in the city is Escalade Day, December 12. It commemorates the Catholic attack on the city in 1602 and the brave resistance that saved it. Processions and scenes are performed in period costumes, including a scene where the defenders, running out of rocks, poured their rations—cauldrons of boiling soup—from the tops of the walls on the attackers.

References William Bousma, *John Calvin: A Sixteenth Century Portrait.* New York,

Oxford University Press, 1987. Alister McGrath, *A Life of John Calvin.* Cambridge, England, Basil Blackwell, 1990. E. William Monter, *Calvin's Geneva.* New York, Wiley, 1967. *The Presbyterians.* Nashville, TN, EcuFilm, n.d. (video).

GGANTIJA, Malta

Ġgantija is the site of a collection of prehistoric shrines located on Gozo, the second-largest island in Malta. One temple is believed to be the oldest free-standing stone structure in the world, several hundred years older than Stonehenge or the Egyptian pyramids.

Prehistoric shrines are rare in Europe, but the small island nation of Malta has remnants of over 40 of them. The earliest Maltese shrines were burial caves. Later temples were used for animal sacrifices to appease the powers of the sea. The most complete complex, estimated to have been built between 3600 and 3000 BCE, is found at Ġgantija. The site actually consists of two temples surrounded by a common wall and sharing a common forecourt. The temples are massive. The two sanctuaries cover 10,000 square feet, with lobed chambers off each. The outer wall reaches up to 17 feet, and the stones that form the many niches and altars weigh several tons. The question of how early peoples were able to quarry and move the stones remains unsettled, although the slabs may have been rolled in place on stones. A number of these stone "rollers"—about the size of cannon balls—have been found.

The two sanctuaries suggest the shape of

Archaeological findings indicate that the oldest Ġgantija temple was built between 3600 and 3000 BCE, making it the oldest free-standing stone structure in the world.

the body of the Earth Mother, with broad hips and full breasts. Much of the temple interior, which was roofed in ancient times, was painted red, the color of life. Carvings of snakes (a fertility symbol) can still be found. The ritual rooms themselves are round, suggesting that the cult priestess entered as if into her mother's womb, to return reborn. At dawn of the spring equinox, the first rays of the rising sun fall on the main altar stone. Ġgantija is the oldest example of architecture in the world, and it delights in rounded, curved forms, reflecting a mother goddess who is powerful, massive, and full-figured. An ancient legend has it that the temple walls were built in one night and one day by a female giant named Sunsuna, nursing a baby while carrying the rocks on her head. *Ġgantija* is the Maltese word for "giant's grotto."

The temples were part of the cult of the Great Earth Mother, a goddess of fertility, and Ġgantija was probably used to pray for healing. Evidence indicates that there was an oracle, a consecrated woman who prophesied while in a trance, possessed by the spirit of the goddess. The few artifacts that have been found have been placed in the national museum. They include a small clay figure of a sleeping goddess and another of a seated one. Both have the corpulent, full-breasted form of a fertility goddess. The sleeping figure was found in an egg-shaped chamber, another symbol of fecundity.

The temple seems to have been a place of pilgrimage for the island population and even attracted worshippers from the North African coast and Sicily. Though the religious cult was not the only major cultural activity of this ancient people, it does seem to have taken up much of their time and energies.

References J.D. Evans, *Malta*. New York, Praeger, 1959. Marija Gimbutas, *The Civilization of the Goddess.* San Francisco, Harper San Francisco, 1991. Merlin Stone, *When God Was a Woman.* New York, Harcourt Brace Jovanovich, 1976. Peg Streep, *Sanctuaries of the Goddess.* Boston, Little, Brown, 1994.

GLENDALOUGH, Ireland

Glendalough (glen of the two lakes), resting in the Wicklow Hills south of Dublin, is one of the best-preserved Irish monastic settlements. It was settled by the hermit St. Kevin in 622 as a place to escape the temptations of young women. Legend has it that when one determined colleen found his hiding place, he threw her into a lake. A more charming tale recounts that Kevin discovered an abandoned baby and raised it, and a doe came each day to give milk for the child. He is said to have worn animal skins and slept outside in the winter, and he often prayed while up to his waist in icy water. Myth and fact blend hopelessly in the legends of St. Kevin, but all the stories illustrate his goodness. As Kevin's reputation for holiness spread, disciples were attracted to him, and he abandoned his life as a hermit to found the monastic village of Glendalough.

At its height, Glendalough had a renowned school and a population of 4,000, of whom 1,000 were monks. The largest group of residents was the students. Some residents were criminals who were safe from arrest under the law of sanctuary as long as they remained within the walls and committed no further crimes. Besides the residents, a steady flow of pilgrims visited the settlement.

The present buildings at Glendalough date from throughout the long period of Celtic monasticism, stretching from the fifth to eleventh centuries. Buildings from Kevin's time still stand, as does the cathedral built in the seventh century. A bishop-abbot governed here until the thirteenth century, when the bishopric was transferred to Dublin. Glendalough was also the burial place of the O'Tooles and the kings of Leinster.

The cathedral is noted for several massive stone crosses, one dedicated to St. Kevin, the others erected in remembrance of now-forgotten Irish chieftains. A small oratory called St. Kevin's House or St. Kevin's Kitchen is often thought to be the saint's hut, but in fact, he lived across one of the lakes in "St. Kevin's bed," a pagan burial cave barely four by seven feet and four feet high. What strikes the visitor to Glendalough is the 100-foot-high tower, 50 feet around. This structure provided the monks with a refuge from bandits and Viking raiders by means of an entrance ten feet above the ground, accessible only by ladder. Once they were safely inside, the monks pulled the ladder after them.

Glendalough was abandoned in 1398 after an attack by the English, but pilgrimages continued long after Glendalough was abandoned and were finally suppressed in 1862 because of rowdiness and fights. Families saved grudges until the St. Kevin's pilgrimage on June 3, then settled them with brutal contests by chosen champions. Although the pilgrimage is being restored as an ecumenical event for Catholics and Anglicans, Glendalough is now primarily a tourist destination whose 500,000 visitors overwhelm the few hundred religious pilgrims. Monastic community life has been restored recently by a small band of Canadian Benedictines, and a hermit has taken up residence.

References John Dunne, *Shrines of Ireland*. Dublin, Veritas, 1989. *A Guide to Celtic Monasteries*. Dublin, Irish Visions and Sounds, 1995 (video). Robert Van der Weyer (ed.), *Celtic Fire*. New York, Doubleday, 1990.

GOLDEN TEMPLE, India

Located in Amritsar, a city founded by Sikhs, the Golden Temple is the holiest Sikh shrine.

Guru Nanak (1469–1539) saw an essential unity between Hindu and Islamic teachings. In preaching this unity, he founded the Sikh religion, which was expanded and developed by his successors. The fifth of these men, Guru Arjun (+1606), began building the Golden Temple. By this time, the writings and hymns of Guru Nanak had become recognized as the religion's scriptures, the *Granth Sahib* (Book of the Lord). However, the Sikhs were attacked from the beginning (Arjun was martyred), and they became militant in response. Sikh men all carry a small dagger in their belts as testimony of their commitment to defend their faith. They are also bearded and never cut their hair, which is worn under a turban.

The Golden Temple, which sits over a reflecting pool at the end of a marble causeway, is the centerpiece of Amritsar. The building is a simple two-story square topped by a dome representing an inverted lotus blossom, pointing down to show Sikh concern with the everyday concerns of the world. The first story is marble with floral patterns inlaid in mother-of-pearl and semiprecious stone; the second story is covered with gold leaf. Sikhs are monotheists and do not use images, so the shrine contains no statues or pictures, only the sacred scriptures. The Granth Sahib is enshrined in the inner sanctum each morning in a solemn procession, and all day long a reading from the Granth is broadcast by loudspeaker. Nanak's hymns are also sung continuously throughout the day. The Golden Temple has numerous small shrines, including one, *Akal Takht* ("Throne of the Ever-Living God"), that holds the arms of warrior gurus.

The holiest Sikh shrine, the Golden Temple, sits atop a reflecting pool and is connected to the mainland by a 200-foot-long marble causeway. The two-storied structure, the first level constructed of marble and the second covered with gold leaf, contains only the sacred scriptures.

The temple is open to both Sikhs and other visitors, but it must be approached with head covered and feet bare. On arriving, pilgrims give sweet bread to the attendants, who redistribute it to visitors as they leave the temple. The compound surrounding the reflecting pool contains sleeping ac-

commodations, and meals are served daily to the thousands of pilgrims, all without charge.

During the Punjab unrest in the 1980s, the Golden Temple was taken over by extremists demanding an independent Sikh state. They were driven out by the Indian army in 1984 at a cost of several thousand lives, mostly innocent pilgrims. Most Sikhs do not approve of the extremists, but all regard the bloody eviction as a sacrilege. Later that year, Prime Minister Indira Gandhi was assassinated by her Sikh guards, and the resulting tension between the Sikhs and the government has never been resolved.

References *Sikh Religion*. Detroit, Sikh Missionary Center, 1990. W. Owen Cole, *A Popular Dictionary of Sikhism*. Glen Dale, MD, Curzon, 1990. Mark Tully and Satish Jacob, *Amritsar: Mrs. Gandhi's Last Battle*. London, Jonathan Cape, 1985.

GOREE ISLAND, Senegal

The most famous of all African slave trade centers, Gorée Island lies two miles off the port of Dakar, Senegal's modern capital. Its peacefulness belies its bloody history. The main purpose of its 1,000 residents today is to preserve the memory of its slave depot and of the antislavery movement.

The House of Slaves was built by the Dutch in 1776 as a place of detention before captives from the interior were shipped off to the Americas to be sold. After being kidnapped or captured inland by slavers, the men and women were force-marched to Dakar and taken out to Gorée. There they were inspected, weighed, and priced like animals. Those under 130 pounds were sent to a feeding room to gain weight. Others were crammed naked and chained into tiny pens—20 men in a 7-by-8-foot room—where they stayed for an average of three months before a slave ship arrived for a new cargo. For children there was a separate tiny dungeon.

Conditions were inhuman. The captives were given little food so that they were forced to fight for it; in this way they were kept divided and unable to organize against their captors. Seawater was pumped into the cells so that the slaves stood or lay constantly in water. Women were routinely raped by their captors, and virgins were kept in a special cell to be available to officers. Many slaves died. Those who survived were branded before being shipped off. Resisters were chained to the walls, and those who tried to escape were thrown out the exit to their deaths in the sea. This was the notorious "door of no return," an opening at the end of a stone corridor; through this door Africans were led to ships taking them into slavery. Close to five million slaves were shipped through Gorée. The House of Slaves was restored in 1990 and is listed on UNESCO's World Heritage List.

Since the publication of Alex Haley's book *Roots*, and the television series based on it, the House of Slaves has become a place of pilgrimage for many black people from the worldwide diaspora. About 30,000 African Americans retrace the journey of their ancestors each year. Many write in the visitors' book of "coming home to Mother Africa." They often invoke the spirits of their ancestors, pray with them and offer ex-votos, such as candles or flowers. African-American groups have placed a number of plaques and monuments near the House of Slaves. The former director-general of UNESCO called it "a place for meditation . . . where those most aware of the tragedies of history gain a better sense of justice and brotherhood."

Besides being the site of the House of Slaves, Gorée was the home of many prominent people. Free people of mixed race who were not descended from slaves settled on the island, and many became prosperous traders. The home of Anne-Marie Javouhey, a progressive nineteenth-century French nun who fought for the emancipation and education of Africans, is maintained as an antislavery memorial. There is also a museum in a nearby fort.

See also Slave Depots.

References *Gorée: Door of No Return,* Princeton,NJ, Films for the Humanities, 1992 (video). Caroline Haardt, "Goree, Island of Slaves," *UNESCO Courier* 48:3, 48–50 (October 1992). Alex Haley, *Roots.* Garden City, NY, Doubleday, 1976.

GUADALUPE, Mexico

Site of the oldest recorded miracles in the New World and the shrine of Our Lady of Guadalupe, Patroness of the Americas, Guadalupe is also a rallying place for Mexicans and Chicanos.

On a cold December day in 1531, just ten years after the Spanish conquest of the Aztec Empire, a recent Christian convert named Juan Diego (*Quauhtlatoatzin* or "Talking Eagle" in Nahuatl, his native tongue) was walking past a hill called Tepeyac on the outskirts of Mexico City. Usually he avoided this hill, because it belonged to the Aztec mother goddess Tonantzin. But when he passed the hill this time, he heard a sound like flocks of birds singing. Suddenly a woman appeared and spoke to him in Nahuatl, a language forbidden by the Spaniards. She addressed him as "my littlest son" and called herself "the ever-virgin Mary, Mother of the Living God, for whom we live."

She asked that a chapel be built on Tepeyac and sent him to the bishop, the imposing and powerful Fray Juan de Zumárraga, who treated him indulgently and sent him away. Juan Diego returned to Tepeyac to report his dismissal, addressing Mary as an old man would:"Lady, the smallest of my daughters, my child." He begged her to send someone important, saying, "I am no-body." But she sent him back, saying, "There are many I could send, but it is you whom I have chosen." The attendants made him wait for hours before admitting him to see the bishop, who this time asked for a sign—some proof that this was the Lady of Heaven. The Lady promised a sign the next day, but instead of visiting the hill, Diego went in search of a priest to anoint his uncle, Juan Bernardino, whom he found ill and close to death. When he skirted Tepeyac to escape Mary, she stopped him and assured him that his uncle was cured. At that moment, Mary appeared to Juan Bernardino and he was cured—the first of the miracles of Tepeyac. In this simple and trusting way, the legend of Guadalupe begins, the oldest tale of the colonial New World.

For the promised sign, Mary sent Juan Diego to the top of the hill to gather flowers, even though Tepeyac was craggy and bare and the temperature was below freezing. When he returned, he had many kinds of flowers in his *tilma,* a mantle made of cactus fiber. He went to see the bishop and was again admitted, but only after harassment from the attendants. He opened his tilma and everyone gasped as the flowers fell to the floor. The bishop went to his knees, for on the tilma was an image of Mary as a dark Aztec princess, wearing the garb of a pregnant woman. They then went to see Juan Bernardino, who told them that the woman's name was "the Virgin who crushes the head of the serpent." In Nahuatl, this is *Tequatlaxopeuh,* which the Spaniards could not pronounce. In memory of the shrine of the Conquistadors in Spain, however, they named the shrine Guadalupe. Juan Diego and Juan Bernardino lived as caretakers near the sanctuary that was built in 1533. Juan Diego died in 1548, aged 74, and was beatified in 1990.

The tilma has been investigated by infrared spectrographs and computer enhancement, but the nature of the image cannot be determined. Ordinarily, cactus fabric should have disintegrated in about 20 years, but after 465 years it remains sturdy and the image has not cracked or faded. A great basilica was dedicated in 1709, but it became too small to handle the crowds and was damaged by earthquakes, so another was built in 1976. About twelve million people come each year to see the image, which has become a symbol of Mexican identity and of the new *mestizo* race created by the intermarriage of Spaniards and Indians. In 1555, the apparitions were officially approved, and Our Lady of Guadalupe was proclaimed Patroness of the Americas in 1945.

See also Guadalupe, Spain; Marian Apparitions.

References *Our Lady of Guadalupe.* Middletown, NJ, Keepsake Video, 1994 (video). Jeanette Rodriquez, *Our Lady of Guadalupe: Faith and Empowerment among Mexican-American Women.* Austin, University of Texas Press, 1994. Jody Smith, *The Image of Guadalupe: Myth or Miracle?* Garden City, NY, Doubleday, 1983.

GUADALUPE, Spain

One of the major sanctuaries of Spain, the Royal Monastery of Guadalupe perches on the high cliffs of the Altamira Range in Extramadura, the frontier province from which the conquistadors came to the Americas. Rivaling El Pilar, Guadalupe is famous for its thirteenth-century image of the Virgin. Despite the shrine's remoteness 1,000–2,000 pilgrims visit it every day—in good weather. In the winter, the narrow mountain roads make access difficult.

The shrine began as a small chapel, but a monastery was established by royal de-crees in 1347 to celebrate a victory over the Muslims. In 1389 the monastery came under the care of the Order of St. Jerome, or Hieronymites, who were scholarly aristocrats with strong ties to the Jewish financial community. In their monastery, hermits and monks lived monastic life together, and Hieronymite spirituality had a strongly mystical bent. The Hieronymite period was one of great expansion, and the present church and monastery were built and decorated in lavish style. The monastery sponsored a choir school, a medical center, and other charities. St. John of God, the founder of the first hospital order, studied here for two years before beginning his work. The Hieronymites continued in the monastery until 1835, when religious orders were disbanded in Spain. Today, the Hieronymite order, once large, has only two monasteries.

The shrine derived its importance from its central role in Extramaduran faith. Extramadura produced large numbers of knights and fighting men for the *Reconquista*, the centuries-long crusade to drive the Muslims from Spain. Christians freed from Moorish slavery saw the Virgin as their patroness and brought their chains to the shrine, where they were forged into the massive ironwork found throughout the church. Kings of Spain came to the shrine to pay homage and pray for victory, and foreign expeditions, including Columbus's voyages to the New World, were commissioned from the shrine. The defeat of the Muslims took place in 1492, and the conquistadors soon followed Columbus, conquering the Aztec and Incan empires. When the Virgin appeared in Mexico, she was given the name the Virgin of Guadalupe.

The statue of the Virgin is covered with rich robes in Spanish style, so that her face and right hand are seen. She holds the

Child Jesus, who raises his hand in blessing. The statue is garlanded with jewels—one dress is covered with 150,000 pearls—and both figures are crowned. Legend has it that the statue was made by St. Luke the Evangelist and made its way to Spain around 600. Hidden during the Moorish occupation, it was supposedly rediscovered around 1300 by means of a miracle. It is kept in a separate chapel on a turntable above the main altar so that it can be turned to face the congregation during services. The chapel is small but sumptuously decorated in baroque style.

From 1835 to 1908, the shrine operated as a parish church, and that year the Franciscan friars took charge, with instructions to restore the complex to its former glory. In 1928 the statue of the Virgin was crowned as Queen of All the Spains, a name that was intended to include Latin America as well as Spain itself. During the Spanish Civil War (1936–1939), the extensive lands of the monastery were taken and distributed to their peasant workers.

The monastery is in Mudéjar style with Gothic and baroque sections, all blending together into a harmonious architectural statement. The art collection is outstanding, especially the collected works of Zurbarán, who had a great affection for the Hieronymites and did a series of paintings of the abbots. A variety of museums house collections of miniatures, manuscripts, and fabrics and embroideries. The monastery also maintains a pilgrim hotel, where the superior presides daily over the main meal.

Across from the monastery and shrine is a government *parador*, or travelers' hotel, in the buildings of a fifteenth-century pilgrim hostel and a choir school once sponsored by the monastery.

See also Guadalupe, Mexico; Marian Apparitions.

References Arturo Alvarez, *Guadalupe: arte, historia y devocion mariana.* Madrid, Ediciones Studium, 1964. W.A. Christian, *Apparitions in Late Medieval and Renaissance Spain.* Princeton, NJ, Princeton University, 1981. René Laurentin, *Pilgrimages, Sanctuaries, Icons, and Apparitions.* Milford, OH, Faith, 1994.

GUNUNG AGUNG, Bali, Indonesia

Mountains on the island of Bali are the abodes of the gods, who have the power to reward good and punish evil. The most important of these is the volcano Gunung Agung.

Gunung Agung means "great mountain." According to legend, it is a piece of the mythical Mount Meru, the cosmic mountain where, in the Hindu tradition, humans first encountered the supreme God. Favoring Bali, the gods plucked a peak from Meru and used it to anchor Bali in the sea. The Balinese also call Gunung Agung "the navel of the world," and their everyday lives are oriented toward it. The devout situate their beds so that their heads lie pointing toward the mountain, while the dead are laid out facing the sea, the home of evil spirits and the powers of death. At 10,308 feet, Gunung Agung towers above the island, a smoldering volcano of terrifying power. Lines of people struggle through the lava fields to bring offerings of food and flowers to the high god of the mountain. The demons, who live in the sea and the jungles, are placated with food offerings.

Balinese religion is an artful blending of two traditions. The ancient animist religion worshipped the gods of rice, sea, sky, and mountain. Hinduism and its pantheon of gods and goddesses arrived later and became the primary religion of the island—without removing the reverence for the ancient deities. In Bali, the Hindu gods are worshipped but their statues are rarely seen. Over the Hindu trinity of Brahma the creator, Vishnu the preserver, and Shiva the destroyer, the Balinese place a high god of purely local origin, Sanghyang Widhi Wasa. Balinese Hinduism seeks a middle way that brings the favor of good spirits and neutralizes the powers of the evil ones. It is intensely communal and enforces common values through collective responsibility. Contact with death, menstruation, and recent sexual activity are believed to make one spiritually unclean and unworthy to enter a temple. These and other local traditions and religious customs make Balinese Hinduism unrecognizable to a Hindu from India.

Throughout Bali one finds little *merus*, shrines dedicated to Gunung Agung and its god, in every temple except Pura Besakih, the Balinese "mother temple." Built in the eleventh century, it was a state temple until 500 years ago, with every Balinese god represented there. It is a huge compound with over 30 buildings—pagodas, shrines, housing, and courtyards—and sits on the flank of Gunung Agung itself. At its center is the main shrine with three altars, one for each manifestation of the high god Sanghyang Widhi Wasa—as Brahma, Vishnu, and Shiva.

Periodically, the priests of the temple perform the Eka Dasa Rudra ceremonies, a festival that brings the Balinese people to the shrine over a three-month period. In this ceremony, Sanghyang Widhi Wasa, in his incarnation as Shiva, drives out battalions of evil spirits in response to animal sacrifices. The purpose of the ceremony is to right the imbalance of evil and good in the world, driving out sinful forces and restoring harmony in the universe. In 1963, in the midst of a national upheaval, the Eka Dasa Rudra ceremonies were conducted outside their usual schedule, and Gunung Agung erupted, killing several thousand people and devastating huge tracts of farm land. The most recent ceremonies, on schedule, were held in 1979, attracting over a million people, half the population of Bali.

See also Mountains, Sacred.

References Edwin Bernbaum, *Sacred Mountains of the World*. San Francisco, Sierra Club, 1990. David Fox, *Once a Century: Pura Besakih and the Eka Dasa Rudra Festival*. Jakarta, Penerbit Citra, 1982. Eric Oey, *Bali, the Emerald Isle*. Chicago, Passport Books, 1990.

HAGIA SOPHIA, Turkey

For centuries the most important church in Eastern Orthodoxy, Hagia Sophia ("Holy Wisdom") in Constantinople (today's Istanbul), was a symbol of the greatness of the Byzantine Empire. The first church was built by the Emperor Constantine two years after his conversion in 322 CE. Two centuries later the Emperor Justinian commissioned the present basilica to celebrate his victory over the Nika revolt, which he put down brutally by slaughtering 30,000 rebels. Tradition has it that when Justinian rode into sight of Hagia Sophia on the day of its dedication in 537, he exclaimed, "Solomon, I have surpassed you!"

Magnificent in scope and an engineering feat of mammoth proportions, Hagia Sophia is the only true domed basilica in Christian architecture. The architects added to the Byzantine style, which is characterized by a vast central space for worshippers, by building a Western-style processional aisle. The dome itself is over 100 feet in diameter, and at its base the walls are pierced by 40 windows. The effect is one of lightness and buoyancy, not massiveness or heaviness. Slim marble columns—104 in all—bear the weight of the dome and walls. To make it possible for such slender pillars to support the tremendous mass, the columns are bound with metal rings. The tops of the columns are decorated in acanthus leaves, a Greek motif; but because the Byzantines had already invented the drill, the decorations are open and lacy, creating an impression of delicacy and lightness. Galleries circle the second level, providing segregated areas for men and women worshippers.

Hagia Sophia is intended to inspire awe. Its vast central space is open. The altar (long ago removed) was gold encrusted with jewels, and the sanctuary around it was inlaid with 20 tons of silver, with the most majestic of the mosaics covering the apex of the dome. This triumphal assertion of imperial wealth and power is underlined everywhere in the basilica. Emperors and their consorts are presented in mosaics as saints, or shown by the side of Christ, and even the religious themes reflect imperial power. The Christ shown is never the suffering Savior but the creator and universal ruler. Justinian and his successors presided here over religious ceremonies of great splendor. Robed and bejeweled, surrounded on feast days by courtiers costumed as the 12 Apostles, the emperor sat on a throne across from that of the patriarch and presided over church synods

Because of its riches, Hagia Sophia was a target whenever the city was attacked. The worst damage was suffered in the sack of 1204, when Crusaders stripped it of its treasures. Catholic troops defiled the basilica, stabling their horses under the dome and installing a prostitute on the throne of the head of the Byzantine Church—all the while carrying on a drunken orgy and burning precious manuscripts and relics. This blasphemy was one of the causes of the break between Eastern and Western Christianity.

In 1453 the Turks captured the city, and the sultan went in procession to Hagia Sophia to give thanks to Allah for his victory. Shortly after, the church was turned

The only true domed basilica in Christian architecture, the Hagia Sophia, built 322–537 CE, was converted to an Islamic mosque in 1453 and later became a museum following World War I.

into a mosque and the mosaics were whitewashed, since Islam does not permit images. When Kemal Attaturk, the father of modern Turkey, secularized the state after World War I, he turned Hagia Sophia into a museum and had the mosaics restored. The restored mosaics now share space with the Islamic decorations—Arabic calligraphy—that had replaced them. Outside, four minarets (prayer towers) were added during the Islamic period, as well as fountains for the cleansing rituals required of Muslims before entering a mosque. Today the only prayer services held in the Hagia Sophia are Islamic; they take place in a small corner of the building.

See also Istanbul Mosques.
References Heinz Kahler, *Hagia Sophia*. New York, Praeger, 1967. Mark Robert, *The Hagia Sophia from the Age of Justinian to the Present*. New York, Cambridge University, 1992. Merle Severy, "The Byzantine Empire: Rome of the East," *National Geographic* 164:6, 709–730 (December 1983).

HAJJ, Saudi Arabia

Each year, millions of Muslims converge on the holy cities of Mecca and Medina in the largest single pilgrimage in the world, called the Hajj.

Mecca is the spiritual home of Islam.

Here Abraham built the first house of God on the spot where, according to legend, Adam first erected a place of worship and where the Prophet Mohammed received the revelation of the Qur'an directly from God. One of the basic teachings of Islam is that every able-bodied Muslim must make a pilgrimage to the holy places at least once during his or her lifetime.

Muslim tradition recounts that the Prophet Abraham, patriarch of the Jewish people, left his wife Hagar and his son Ishmael in the Arabian desert at the command of God. When their water ran out, Hagar ran to and fro across a narrow valley, pleading for God's mercy, which was granted her when a spring (the Well of Zamzam) was revealed by the Angel Gabriel. Abraham returned years later with a vision commanding him to sacrifice Ishmael, but his son was miraculously replaced by a ram, which Abraham sacrificed instead. Hagar had been buried under a mound that turned out to be the ruins of Adam's temple, and it was there that Abraham built his House of God. At the end of the construction, God brought forth a black stone to finish the work, one he had given to Adam. Today this Black Stone is imbedded in the wall of the Ka'bah. It is the most sacred emblem in the most sacred place in Islam. Legend has it that the stone was originally white but became black as it absorbed the sins of the world. Abraham and Ishmael circled the shrine seven times and began to preach a pilgrimage of salvation. All these events told in the Qur'an figure in the devotions of the hajj, the pilgrimage of purification.

With time, the Ka'bah became a den of idolatry filled with pagan statues. Only a few worshippers remained true to the One God, Allah. Among them was a prophetic figure, Mohammed, who would lay the foundations of Islam and be proclaimed by Allah as the last and greatest of his prophets. To Muslims, Mohammed is known simply as the Prophet. He received his revelations in a long series that he dictated to his first followers. Together they form the Qur'an, the divinely revealed sacred scripture of Islam. For ten years Mohammed preached to disbelieving crowds until he was welcomed into Medina. His migration there in 622 CE, the Hegira, marks the beginning of the Muslim calendar. Gathering strength, Mohammed's forces crossed Arabia, entering Mecca triumphantly in 632. Mohammed reclaimed the Ka'bah by touching each of the 360 idols, which smashed themselves to the ground before his authority.

The pilgrimage today is made mostly by air, but in the past, pilgrims faced daunting and exhausting treks to achieve their goal. Because of the numbers involved, the Saudi Arabian government, whose royal family are the Guardians of the Holy Places, manages the hajj in detail. Quotas are assigned to every Islamic community at a rate of 1,000 pilgrims per million Muslims. The government provides security, especially in the light of tensions between Iran and other Islamic countries in recent years. Saudia Arabia also provides basic necessities, but the hajj is not luxurious or even comfortable for most. Pilgrims camp out, cooking in the streets over charcoal fires and often sleeping in the fields. Only the wealthy can afford to stay in modern hotels.

About 2 million pilgrims make the hajj each year during the month of Dhu al-Hijjah in the Muslim calendar. At any time of year, the *'umrah,* or "lesser pilgrimage," may be made, visiting the same places but with fewer rites involved. Women may come to either only in the company of their husbands or a male relative. The pilgrimage takes place within the precincts of the *haram,* a sacred area 6 miles wide and 20 miles long, stretching from the Sacred Mosque, which contains the Ka'bah, to the Plains of Arafat.

Each man must follow a purification ritual during the hajj in order to enter the state of *ihram* or consecration. He must trim his facial hair (many also shave their heads) and remove all body hair before donning a pair of sandals and a garment made of two unsewn pieces of white cloth. No other dress is permitted for men. As a symbol of how believers will appear as they meet Allah on Judgment Day, many hajji (pilgrims) keep this dress to use as a burial shroud.

Most men perform both the main pilgrimage and the 'umrah during the hajj. The 'umrah consists of the seven circuits around the Ka'bah and running back and forth across the valley in imitation of Hagar's plea for mercy. The focus of the pilgrimage is the Sacred Mosque, rebuilt and enlarged a number of times. Entered by a magnificent gateway flanked by two minarets, it has a capacity of 500,000 during the prostrations at midday prayers. As the pilgrim enters, he says a set prayer asking for Allah's blessing and mercy. Then men begin the circuits around the Ka'bah, each begun by kissing or touching the Black Stone, encased in silver and set into the southeast corner of the Ka'bah. Muslims do not believe that the stone has magical power, but they kiss or revere it because the Prophet did. Women perform these rites separately. The circuits provide one of the most awesome sights in the hajj—circling masses of humanity united in prayer.

After completing the rotations, the pilgrims pray at the Station of Abraham, where the prophet prayed. In a golden cage is the stone that Abraham reputedly stood on as he built the Ka'bah; it bears the imprint of his foot. Pilgrims make three prostrations at the Station of Abraham while reading or reciting from the Qur'an, and then rest for a moment at the Well of Zamzam. Despite the extraordinary demands upon it, the well never fails to provide refreshment for the multitudes of pilgrims. Then the hajji move to the two small hills where Hagar ran back and forth and reenact her desperate run, praying for the mercy of Allah. This is done in a long arcade that juts out from the Sacred Mosque and crosses the streets of the city, providing shade from the sun. To avoid accidents, pilgrims run in wide, one-way galleries in the colonnade.

On the seventh day of the month of pilgrimage, the king of Saudi Arabia arrives to wash the Ka'bah and bedeck it with a new black cloth, embroidered in gold with Qur'anic verses. The cloth is handwoven on wooden looms by 100 men who spend a year on its creation; it weighs two tons when completed. The ceremony is performed in the presence of representatives of Islamic nations and before thousands of pilgrims.

The pilgrims have now purified themselves in humble devotion to Allah. Dressed alike with no distinction between poor and rich, powerful and unimportant, Arab, African, and Asian, they have humbly entered into purity of heart and worshipped the one true God. The moment has come to reaffirm the pilgrims' faith and solidarity with other Muslims. It is the thirteenth and second-to-last day of the hajj, and all those in attendance come together in a last act of veneration, the Standing at Arafat. A stream of pilgrims moves toward Mount Arafat, Jabal-al-Ramah, the Mount of Mercy, site of Mohammed's farewell address. Here he told his followers, "This day have I perfected your religion for you and chosen Islam for you as your religion" (Qur'an 5:3). He also received his last revelation here and taught of the brotherhood of Muslims and their commitment to Islam. The hajj ends at this spot with a rededication to Islam. Legend has it that it was to the Plains of Arafat that Adam and Eve came after the Fall and began the human race. Thus its consecration to Allah closes a circle of physical and spiritual birth. The hours at Arafat are usually the most profound experience of the hajj.

On the Plains of Arafat, the pilgrim gathers either 49 or 70 small stones. Leaving Arafat, he proceeds to the town of Mina, a short walk back toward Mecca, where three pillars stand, symbols of the devils who tempted Abraham. The pilgrims stone the pillars in several rituals over two days, as a sign of rejection of evil in their lives. After throwing the first seven stones, men shave their heads. If a hajji misses his target, he must repeat the ceremony.

The hajj is closed by the great feast of Idd al-Adha, in which sheep, camels, and goats are slaughtered in memory of Abraham's sacrifice. United with the hajji, Muslims all over the world slaughter animals on this feast. Most of the meat is given to the poor. So many herds are killed and dressed in Saudi Arabia during the feast that the government arranges a fleet of refrigerated ships to carry the excess to other countries for distribution.

One aspect of the pilgrimage remains optional but still compelling to most Muslims. Islam's second-holiest city, Medina, lies 275 miles north of Mecca. Many pilgrims go to Medina for a few days, before returning to Mecca for the trek to Mount Arafat, the stoning of the pillars, and Idd al-Adha. On the way to Medina pilgrims usually stop at Badr, the site of the Battle of al-Farquan, the first decisive clash with the infidels that gave Islam its first martyrs. Mosques have been built at various places where the Prophet was welcomed after his rejection in Mecca, and pilgrims visit them on their journey. The high point of the visit to Medina is the Mosque of the Prophet, his burial place. He is buried under a large green dome built in 1860. Nearby is the tomb of Abu Bakr, Mohammed's closest friend and leading disciple. Other mosques in the city recall various revelations to Mohammed. Their interior decorations feature inlaid colored marbles, intricate carving, and brasswork. Praying before the gorgeously adorned spot where the Prophet himself led his followers in prayer is a high point in a pilgrimage that has been a lifetime goal of most of its participants.

See also Pilgrimage.

References Mohamed Amin, *Pilgrimage to Mecca.* London, Macdonald & Jane's, 1978. Flavio Conti, *Architecture as Environment.* Boston, HBJ Press, 1978. F.P. Peters, *The Hajj.* Princeton, NJ, Princeton University Press, 1994.

HASEDERA TEMPLE, Japan

Hasedera Temple, which stands atop a hill with lovely views of Sagami Bay, near both Tokyo and Yokohama, is known for both its importance to the cult of the Hase Kannon and its garden where women pray for the souls of aborted children.

The main shrine in Hasedera is that of Kannon, the Goddess of Mercy. Her statue is an immense and powerful presence, gilt and majestic. Carved in 721 CE, it is 30 feet high with an eleven-faced crown. The faces look in all directions as a sign of Kannon's ability to see and hear the pleas of all and to save them. In a nearby building is a prayer wheel over 20 feet tall containing Buddhist scriptures; it is sometimes called "the revolving bookcase." Pilgrims believe that when they spin the wheel, the texts inscribed on it are continually recited.

Important though the cult of Kannon is, the shrine to Kannon is not what attracts most visitors. In the beautifully tended gardens covering the hill are thousands of small grey statues of *Jizobosatsu*, the God of Travelers and of Children. They are dedicated to the souls of aborted children. Small toys have been placed before many of them, and some have been dressed in tiny bibs and baby clothes. The women who have purchased them to honor their lost children come to pray, make offerings, and write little notes to their children on the backs of the statues.

Abortion does not stir the religious controversy in Japan that it does in the West, but it does cause a deep sense of loss. Many women believe that the spirits of their unborn live at the temple and need to be mourned. The gardens contain a wide variety of ex-votos: statuettes, banners, plaques, candles, smooth stones with mothers' names on them, and lucky ¥5 coins. Landscaped pools, streams, and waterfalls, along with a quiet cave and lush trails provide places for reflection and meditation. The two shrines to the unborn in the temple gardens are festooned with colorful garlands of folded paper cranes, a symbol of life. From time to time, a Buddhist priestess conducts ceremonies of purification here for doctors with abortion practices.

A few minutes' walk away is the Great Buddha (*Daibutsu*) at the Kotokuin Temple, a 42-foot, 850-ton seated image cast in 1252. It once sat in a vast hall, but a tidal wave washed the building away in 1495, leaving the statue in the open air. It is the main Buddha shrine of several Japanese sects popular for teaching a simple and personal doctrine of salvation. Pilgrims usually visit both the Great Buddha and the Hase Kannon. There are also 70 other lesser shrines and temples in Hasedera.

References *Buddhism: The Land of the Disappearing Buddha—Japan*. Richmond, VA, Time-Life, 1978 (video). Joseph Kitagawa, *On Understanding Japanese Religion*. Princeton, NJ, Princeton University, 1987. Peter Popham, *Wooden Temples of Japan*. London, Tauris Parke, 1990.

HEARTH OF BUDDHISM, India/Nepal

The major sites of the life of the Buddha form a pilgrimage way known as the Hearth of Buddhism, sacred to Buddhists. These sites mark the places of the Buddha's birth, his enlightenment, his first sermon, and his death. The Buddha himself is said to have asked his disciples to observe the custom of visiting these places, and visitors come from all over the world. Organized pilgrimages are especially popular among Buddhists from Japan and Southeast Asia.

Siddhartha Gautama, who would become the Buddha, the Enlightened One, was born in *Lumbini*, in west-central Nepal near the Indian border, around 540 BCE. Lumbini is not easy to get to, and the numbers who come here are small, mostly from Southeast Asia, Japan, and Tibet. No Buddhists live in the area, which is completely Hindu. The site is a garden with a grove of pipal trees. Legend has it that his mother, Queen Mayadevi, rested here as she traveled to her parents' palace to give birth. A bas-relief shows the Buddha standing on a lotus leaf, his mother above him, holding onto a branch of the tree, the pose she took as he came from her side. Buddha is said to have announced, "This is my final rebirth," a reference to the Buddhist belief that individuals are reborn or reincarnated after death in a cycle until they reach perfection. The legend of the Buddha includes a number of nativity stories. He stood and walked immediately after his birth and took seven steps, under each of which a lotus flower bloomed.

The garden was lost until 1895, when a German archeologist came upon an ancient pillar set up by the Emperor Ashoka in 249 BCE with the inscription, "Buddha, the blessed one, was born here." A number of monasteries and temples were erected here up to the ninth century CE. But after the arrival of Islam (and later, of Hinduism), Buddhism declined, and only a sculpture remained, revered by local women as a fertility symbol. A temple was later uncovered and named the Maya Devi after Buddha's mother. Its fragile sandstone sculptures have been removed to the National Museum in Kathmandu for protection. Little was done to protect the shrine until 1977, when a design for its development was advanced by a Japanese architect. It has been developed very slowly, and at present, the area is largely park land. Besides the Ashoka pillar, the main feature is the Mayadevi sacred pond, where the queen bathed and where the newborn was washed by two dragons. Next to the pond is the ancient temple housing the bas-relief.

The remaining places associated with the life of the Buddha lie in northern India. *Bodh Gaya* marks the site of Buddha's enlightenment. He had tried to achieve holiness through fasting and asceticism, without success. He meditated for six years, according to legend, eating one grain of rice a day at first, and then nothing. He became so emaciated that when he touched his stomach he could feel his backbone. Voices told him that mortification would not bring enlightenment, so he began meditating under a banyan (*bodhi*) tree until he reached enlightenment.

Of the Hearth of Buddhism centers, Bodh Gaya is the most important. The others are archeological sites, but Bodh Gaya is alive with activity. Buddhist communities from eight Asian countries have already built monasteries here, and several other monasteries are being constructed. The Dalai Lama, spiritual head of Tibetan Buddhism, often spends the month of December at Bodh Gaya, as do many Tibetan pilgrims. The spire of the main temple, Mahabodhi, reaches 160 feet into the sky. The temple houses a statue of the seated Buddha, his hand touching the earth as a sign of enlightenment. There is a bodhi tree, raised from a sapling taken from the original, on which the faithful tie scarves, flags, and banners as ex-votos. The place where the Buddha meditated is marked by a stone platform. Bodh Gaya is managed by a joint Hindu-Buddhist council, since Hindus revere the Buddha as a reincarnation of Vishnu. The Hindus have insisted on the right to erect their own shrines and have even placed a Shiva lingam pillar before the Buddha statue, which has angered Buddhists and caused incidents of violence.

Sarnath, where the Buddha first taught and gave his first sermon, is near Varanasi, Hinduism's holiest city. The Buddha, having achieved enlightenment, came here to a deer park to begin his mission of spreading the message of the Four Noble Truths: that human existence is comprised of sorrow and suffering; that this suffering is caused by human desire; that desire can be overcome; and that desire is overcome by following the Eight-Fold Path. The Eight-Fold Path, the basis of Buddhist philosophy, consists of

1. Right Understanding (know the Four Noble Truths)
2. Right Aspiration (choose the true path)
3. Right Speech (speak truth in charity)
4. Right Behavior (do not kill, steal, lie, be unchaste, or use stimulants)
5. Right Living (take up work that fosters liberation of spirit)

6. Right Discipline (persevere in the daily effort for improvement)
7. Right Mindfulness (be self-aware and conscious of every action)
8. Right Contemplation (meditate deeply on the reality of life)

In the fifth century CE, Sarnath had 1,500 priests and a number of monasteries, a great stupa (a conical shrine containing relics), and the prominent stone pillar erected by Ashoka, the great Buddhist emperor. Sarnath went into decline when Muslim invaders destroyed the city, and it remained deserted for 1,000 years until 1836, when the British began its restoration. The spot where Buddha is said to have preached his first sermon is marked by a 100-foot stupa dating from 200 BCE. The main shrine (actually only the foundation of a destroyed sanctuary) indicates where the Buddha meditated. A seventh-century writer described it as 200 feet high, with 100 niches along each outside wall, each containing a Buddha carving. A life-sized statue shows the Buddha turning the wheel of the law. Near the statue are the remains of the Ashoka Pillar, with some interesting carvings on the base. The pillar was broken during excavation, and its superb capital, as well as many statues and carvings, are kept in a museum for their protection. Six national temples have been built by various Asian Buddhist communities, and the deer park is maintained as a kind of open animal park.

The Buddha died at *Kushinagar*, supposedly by mistakenly eating poisoned mushrooms. His last words were, "Decay is part of all conditioned beings." In a sense, Kushinagar is testimony to the impermanence of life that Buddha's last words describe, since little remains there today. The Buddha's disciples berated him for dying "in this miserable little town." It has never become more than a poor village, so far off the beaten track that it is the destination of only the most dedicated pilgrims. There is a Buddhist Center here and a temple with a large reclining Buddha statue intended to show him dying. The main pilgrimage attraction is the brick stupa where the Buddha was cremated. Conflict over the Buddha's relics broke out into the War of the Relics in India, and the eight Buddhist kingdoms finally divided them and took them to their respective countries to be enshrined. There are none at Kushinagar.

References Heinz Bechert and Richard Gombrich (eds.), *The World of Buddhism*. London, Thames & Hudson, 1984. Trilok Majupuria and Indra Majupuria, *Holy Places of Buddhism in Nepal and India*. Bangkok, Craftsman Press, rev. ed., 1993. George Michell, *Penguin Guide to the Monuments of India, Volume I*. London, Viking, 1989.

HEBRON, Palestinian Authority

A sacred site for both Jews and Muslims, the city of Hebron is the site of the tombs of Abraham, father of the Jewish and Islamic faiths, and his wife Sarah. Located in the Palestinian Authority in the West Bank, not far from Bethlehem, the atmosphere in Hebron is hostile and tense today.

The Patriarch Abraham is one of the towering figures of the Hebrew Scriptures, a nomadic chieftain who, around 2000 BCE, led his clan across the Near East to Israel. Abraham purchased a cave called Machpelah in Hebron as a burial place. Here also were buried Isaac and Rebekah and Jacob and Leah. Because Abraham had no settled home, Hebron became the focus for his family.

After the Jewish commander Joshua conquered Hebron, it became a town of refuge. David made Hebron his capital and reigned there as king of Judah for seven years before moving to Jerusalem. David's son Absalom used it as his headquarters when he plotted against his father. Herod the Great built the existing enclosure around the Cave of Machpelah. Because of this history, Hebron is a sacred site for both Jews and Muslims.

The *Ibrahim Mosque* attracts Muslims, the *Cave of the Patriarchs* Jews, and the shrine at Machpelah attracts people from both groups. During the Byzantine period, a Christian church was built over the caves. The enclosure of the shrine, with its log-like stones (the largest of which is over 24 feet long), is architecturally notable. The shrine itself, which is massive, shows patch-work signs of its history—a Crusader church and the later mosques and syna-gogues. The base, with three-foot thick walls, dates from King Herod's reign. Sev-eral synagogues have been erected on the site and remain today, one containing sym-bolic empty tombs for Abraham and Sarah. The two mosques (one for men and one for women) are ornate, their floors covered in gorgeous Persian carpets. The cave, 50 feet below ground, is thought to be the lo-cation of the remains of Abraham and Sarah. From the mosque above, pilgrims can peer down into the darkness through a grating. The entry to the cave was ce-mented over after a group of Jews went down the shaft leading to the tombs in 1979. Only a few others have ever pene-trated to the caves in the past 500 years.

Many legends surround the Hebron shrines. Jewish tradition holds that Abraham chose this site because Adam and Eve are buried here; Muslims have erected a marker for the patriarch Joseph, who they believe was buried on this hill. In the women's mosque is a small stone impressed, accord-ing to myth, by the footprint of Adam, who landed on it when he was cast out of the Garden of Eden. A mile west of Hebron is the Oak of Mamre, where Abraham pitched his tent and entertained the three angels who foretold the birth of Isaac. A Russian Orthodox monastery has been built around the oak, which has been much damaged by relic and souvenir hunters.

Hebron today is disputed ground, a place of bitter controversy between Jews and Arabs. Due to tensions, foreign tourists are discouraged from visiting, and Arab Christian pilgrims are rare. Jews and Mus-lims once lived together in the city, but in 1929 Arabs attacked the Jewish quarter, killing 67 Jews and driving the others out. In 1994 a Jewish settler opened fire with an automatic weapon, killing 29 Muslim wor-shippers at the mosque and wounding 125 during the predawn prayer of Ramadan, the holiest month of the Muslim calendar. Dr. Baruch Goldstein, the American re-sponsible for the slaughter, is buried at nearby Qiryat Arba, a large settler enclave. His grave, with a small shrine, has become a place of prayer for militant Jewish settlers who oppose the Israeli-Palestinian peace process. Security at the Cave of the Patri-archs is strict. All weapons are prohibited, and the two groups are kept apart. The Isaac Hall is reserved for Muslims, and two smaller halls, named for Abraham and Jacob, are set aside for Jews. Metal detectors, steel gates, and video surveillance equip-ment have been installed. Entry is restricted to 300 from each group, and on ten annual holy days for each faith, no one from the other group is allowed to be present.

References Frederick Bruce, *Abraham and David: Places They Knew.* Nashville, TN, Thomas Nelson, 1984. John Van Seters, *Abraham in History and Tradition.* New Haven, CT, Yale University, 1975. Amy

Wilentz, "Battling over Abraham," *The New Yorker* 72:27, 46–50 (16 September 1996).

HILL OF CROSSES, Lithuania

Kryziu kalnas, the Hill of Crosses, is the Lithuanian national pilgrimage center, combining Christian devotion with Lithuanian national identity. It lies outside Silauliai, a small city near the northern border of Lithuania.

The custom of planting crosses on the hill began in the 1300s, probably as an expression of Lithuanian defiance of the Teutonic Order, which attempted to control the area and subjugate it. Silauliai is the center of the last province in Europe to convert to Christianity, finally doing so through union with Poland in 1413. Since this medieval period, the Hill of Crosses has represented the passive resistance of Lithuanian Catholicism to oppression. Under Soviet occupation (1940–1990), the hill was leveled three times, once with the removal of 5,000 crosses. The Soviets covered the hill with waste and sewage. Yet each time it was destroyed, the hill reappeared, covered with crosses. It remained one of the few avenues of protest during the period of Soviet occupation, when 36,000 Lithuanian national leaders were executed or deported.

The twin-ridged hill is covered with tens of thousands of crosses, some tiny and simple, others large and ornate, including masterpieces of folk carving. Rosaries hang from some of them, tinkling gently in the wind. Attached to a few crosses are pictures of Jesus or saints; others memorialize a loved one with a photograph. For many years the photos of exiles predominated. Crosses have also been added as memorials to patriots, especially following uprisings against occupying Russians in the nineteenth century. Since independence in 1991, the number of crosses has increased; the current estimate is 40,000. Paths and stairs lead pilgrims into the forest of crosses. Though visitors arrive in small numbers daily—and add to the thicket of crosses—the main pilgrimage occurs at Easter. The Hill of Crosses has never had a religious association with the sufferings of Jesus, but with the triumph of the cross over evil—more a symbol of Resurrection than of suffering.

References Michael Bordeau, *Land of Crosses: The Struggle for Religious Freedom in Lithuania, 1939–1978*. Chumleigh, UK, Augustine, 1979. Antanas Stavinskas, *Lietuviu Liaudies Menas*. Vilnius, Lithuania, Vagos, 1992. Saulius Suziedelis, *The Sword and the Cross: A History of the Church in Lithuania*. Huntington, IN, Our Sunday Visitor, 1988.

HIROSHIMA PEACE MEMORIAL, Japan

Hiroshima, the western Japanese city that was the target of the first atomic bomb, is now the site of a moving memorial to the hundreds of thousands of civilians who died in the blast.

The bomb was dropped by an American plane on 6 August 1945. The effect was horrendous. The center of the city was vaporized by 12,632° heat, leaving behind a ghost scene. More than 75,000 people died instantly. For some, a shadow burned into stone is the only evidence that a person once stood there. About 200,000 died later of the effects of nuclear radiation, especially cancers and leukemia. The epicenter of the blast was downtown, at a spot where a unique T-shaped bridge connects two sides of the river and an island. The blast center is marked by the steel skeleton of the Atomic Bomb Dome, at the time of the bombing the Industrial Promotion Hall. The heat of the blast burned away the concrete cover-

The steel skeletal dome of the Hiroshima Peace Memorial marks the blast center of the first atomic bomb, which fell on 6 August 1945.

ing of the dome, leaving the skeletal outline, which has become the city's symbol.

The rebirth of Hiroshima as an "international city of peace" began soon after the bomb fell. After the war, a Peace Memorial Park was built on the island as a monument to the commitment to work for world peace. Every August 6 a solemn festival is held here, with paper lanterns floated on the river for the repose of the souls of the dead. A Peace Museum shows photos of the devastation, although it also includes exhibits on the causes of the war and Japan's aggression. A Peace Flame burns in the park and will continue to burn until the last atomic bomb has been eliminated. The Cenotaph for A-Bomb Victims, a large vault shaped like the clay figurine saddles found in ancient tombs, contains a chest with the ashes of those killed by the bomb. On it are engraved the words "Rest in peace, for the error will not be repeated." The main memorials are placed in the gardens in such a way that a visitor standing in front of the Cenotaph can see the Peace Flame and the Atomic Dome in a direct line.

The park includes many quiet areas for rest or reflection, even though it is busy throughout the day, especially with school groups. Traditionally, Japanese students make long strings of folded-paper (*origami*) cranes, a symbol of life, and lay them at the various memorials. At any time, millions of colorful crane leis decorate the park. Besides religious shrines, many small memorials honor special groups: schoolchildren who were killed; members of unions; construction and office workers; residents of nearby neighborhoods. One popular memorial honors the Mobilized Students, a team of high-school youth who were doing community service in the area when the bomb fell. Perhaps the most visited memorial is the A-Bombed Children's Statue, a vaulted concrete dome with a statue of a 12-year-old girl, Sadako, holding out a crane. Sadako believed that if she made 1,000 paper cranes she would be cured of leukemia, but she died after making 644. Schoolchildren often bring the other 356 to the memorial in memory of the 356 her classmates made so she could be buried with 1,000 cranes.

References Eleanor Coerr, *Sadako and the Thousand Paper Cranes*. New York, Put-nam, 1977 (juvenile). Ted Gap, "Hiroshima," *National Geographic* 188:2, 78–101 (August 1995). John Hersey, *Hiroshima*. New York, Knopf, rev. ed., 1985.

HOLOCAUST SITES

The mass extermination of European Jews by the Nazis during World War II—known as the Holocaust—was the worst instance of genocide in modern times.

The Nazis, who came to power in Germany after its defeat in World War I, in 1941 decreed the murder of every person with Jewish ancestry, regardless of age or sex. At first, Jews were selectively executed. But when the war began in 1939, every German military drive included a special unit whose task was to seize the Jews in each town and gun down groups of them. Soon even this procedure proved inefficient, though, and the Nazis turned to a calculated plan of systematic extermination called the "Final Solution." Jews were gathered together into concentration camps as slave labor under conditions that hastened their death from malnutrition and exhaustion. Then, after 1942, death camps were set up to which Jews were shipped in large numbers. The only purpose of these camps was mass executions.

Detained Jews were herded onto sealed cattle cars, forced to stand for days with little water or food and no toilet facilities. Along the way, a few stops would be made to remove the bodies of the dead. On arrival, two lines would be formed: one of the weak, elderly, and children, the other of the able-bodied. The first group was immediately taken to the gas chambers and executed. The second was put to work in slave labor factories. Any sign of weakness was cause for a beating or death, which any guard could inflict without answering to superior officers.

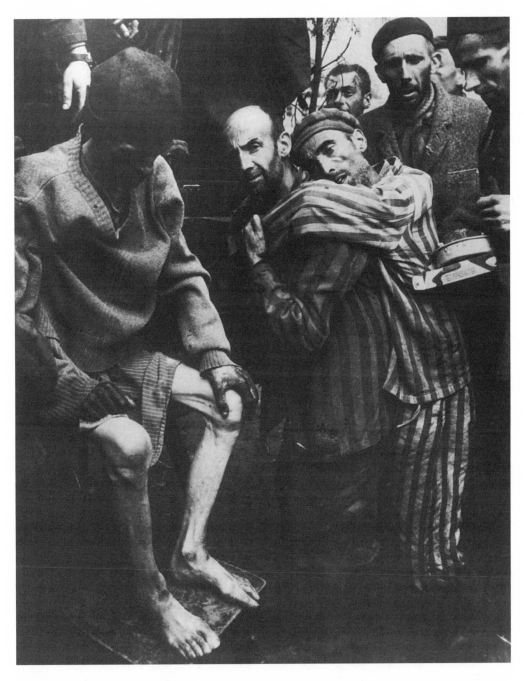

Liberated Wobbelin concentration camp prisoners, emaciated and ill, are taken to a German hospital, 4 May 1945.

Living conditions were unspeakably harsh. People slept in rows, crammed onto ledges with a few inches' clearance, in dormitories that had no sanitary facilities beyond a few slop buckets. Disease spread rapidly under these conditions, and prisoners died in large numbers of typhus and dysentery. Food consisted of a little bread, often made with sawdust, and some weak soup with rotten vegetables. Whippings were given for the least infraction of the rules, such as hiding a carrot or beet in one's pallet to eat later. For such "crimes" as smuggling out a letter or hiding money, an entire barracks could be ordered to march for up to ten hours a day, regardless of weather. Groups of prisoners were distinguished by cloth triangles sewn onto their clothing: red for political prisoners, yellow for Jews, black for Gypsies, green for criminals, and pink for homosexuals.

The work camps were critically important for the German war effort, producing armaments, building roads, and draining marshes to provide increased farm land. Some work camps were large enough to have their own barracks, but when a prisoner was too exhausted to work, he was returned to the main camp to be disposed of. At the gate to each camp was the cynical slogan *Arbeit Macht Frei,* "Work makes one free."

The most frequently visited Holocaust sites—visited by many in order to pray for the dead or to reaffirm a commitment that such evil must never happen again—are listed below. They include *Bergen-Belsen* in Germany, the first concentration camp to be liberated by the Allies. Although Bergen-Belsen never had gas chambers or crematoria, 50,000 people (30,000 Jews) died there, an appalling 36,000 of them in the last six weeks before the liberation. One of these was Anne Frank, deported from

Amsterdam. These figures do not include over 50,000 Russians who perished uncounted. The camp was demolished in 1950. Today only two memorials mark its existence: an obelisk with a memorial wall and a monument to the Jews. Ironically, it served as a displaced-persons' camp after the war and had a lively Jewish cultural life, Zionist groups, and Yiddish newspapers.

Chelmno, Poland, was the first camp designed for mass executions (1941). There 320,000 people were killed—loaded into two sealed vans into which carbon monoxide gas was pumped as they drove to the burial pits. The camp was destroyed by the Nazis in 1945. After the war, 11 Chelmno camp officers were executed for war crimes committed there. The town, one of the few in Poland that is completely walled, was a medieval stronghold of the Teutonic Knights.

Jasenovac, Croatia, was an Ustaša death camp at the center of a complex of internment camps, including one for women. The Ustaša were Croatian fascists who established a puppet state under Nazi patronage, using the opportunity to slaughter both Jews and Serbs. The Ustaša guards were cruel sadists; the most notorious was a former priest who delighted in killing prisoners with his own hands. Over 600,000 perished at Jasenovac, of whom 25,000 were Jews. (Most Croatian Jews were deported to Auschwitz.) The camp was destroyed in 1945 before partisans could liberate it.

The city of *Kraków,* Poland, has one of the few living Jewish communities left in East Europe. Nazi wartime activities there are widely known mainly from the film *Schindler's List,* an account of the German businessman who saved wartime Jews assigned to his factory as slave labor. Tour groups can follow the path of events from the movie. Oskar Schindler's factory still stands, operating today under another owner. The site of the Psaszów concentration camp is marked only by a memorial, though the camp built for the film, including a copy of the infamous street paved with Jewish gravestones, is visited on the tour. This camp is a leading example of attempts to educate people about the Holocaust.

Majdenek, Poland, outside Lublin, is one of the best-preserved death camps, including guard towers, barbed wire, barracks, and crematoria. It is an immense complex, where 360,000 people met their deaths, about 80 percent of them Jews. A memorial has been erected there, and a domed mausoleum holds the ashes of the dead.

Mauthausen, Austria, was a slave labor camp at a quarry near Linz, Hitler's birthplace. It began operating in 1938, shortly after the Nazi occupation of Austria. The camp population was mixed; it included Germans, Spaniards, Soviet prisoners of war, Jews, and political prisoners from every occupied country in Europe. Its 34 satellite camps varied in size from small camps that held a few hundred prisoners to those that held over 10,000. Prisoners dug underground bunkers for hidden munitions factories or worked in the infamous quarry, where they carried blocks of stone up 186 steps to the surface. Those who hesitated or fell under blows were instantly killed. Few endured more than a few months. Starvation and disease accounted for 95 percent of the deaths. In the last months of the war, the occupants of the satellite camps were brought to Mauthausen and conditions became utterly inhuman. So many were killed that the crematorium could not handle the corpses, and incidents of cannibalism occurred. Two hundred thousand people passed through Mauthausen; 119,000 died, of whom 38,000 were Jews.

Paneriai, Lithuania, was a Nazi death camp where 100,000 Lithuanians perished, including 70,000 Jews from nearby Vilnius. A memorial has been erected at the site, along with a small but powerful Museum of Genocide. Trails lead to large hollows, pits, and trenches where the mass executions took place and where the victims' remains were burned. Under Communism, no mention was made of the Jews executed here, but since the end of Soviet rule, Jews are specifically mentioned at the memorial.

Ravensbrück, 56 miles north of Berlin, was opened as a women's camp in 1939. The hub of a labor-camp complex with 34 satellites at arms factories, Ravensbrück itself housed 27,000 prisoners, primarily political prisoners (15 percent Jews). Many prisoners were suspected members of the anti-Nazi underground.

Sachsenhausen, established in 1936, lies near Berlin in the town of Oranienburg in the former East Germany. Much of the camp is preserved as it was, including the cell block with its torture chambers and the block where medical experiments were performed on live prisoners as well as on corpses. Sachsenhausen was a labor camp that held, at its height, 48,000 prisoners. About 30,000 prisoners perished there, along with 18,000 captured Russian troops who were brought there for execution.

Sobibór, Poland, was a death camp that the Germans ran with Ukrainian guards. Arriving prisoners were stripped and all their valuables were taken; women's hair was cut off. The Jews were then herded naked along a fenced path ("the tube") to the gas chambers, which were disguised as showers. About 1,200 people could be gassed at one time. Carbon monoxide was used, and the process took about 30 minutes. The bodies were then thrown into large burial pits. Those who were too weak to walk to the gas chambers were taken directly to the pits and buried alive. In all, about 250,000 people perished at Sobibór. As the numbers increased, the Nazis resorted to burning bodies rather than burying them. The camp was closed after an uprising in which several hundred escaped after killing 11 SS troops. All traces of the camp have been removed. Today only a memorial remains.

Theresienstadt in the Czech Republic was a ghetto camp. The Nazis took over an eighteenth-century town and deported Jews to it, mostly from Germany and occupied Czechoslovakia. At its height, it had 53,000 internees. It was guarded by local police and governed by a Jewish council, which was responsible for food distribution, work assignments, and the dreaded deportation lists.

The Nazis planned Theresienstadt as a model Jewish community that they could show to the Red Cross and other international rights groups. At the same time, they were quietly shipping residents to extermination camps, where most perished in the gas chambers. The relative freedom of Theresienstadt, despite harsh living conditions, allowed Zionist groups to form there, and a lively program of cultural activities emerged. In 1944 the Red Cross made a formal investigation. Dummy shops were set up, a school opened, and the Jews were forced to act as if they led normal lives. The Nazis even made a film of the event to show the "good" circumstances under which Jews lived. After the visit, all those in the film, including children, were sent to Auschwitz for extermination. One hundred forty-thousand Jews were sent to Theresienstadt; 33,000 died there, 88,000 died in death camps, and 19,000 survived.

Treblinka, Poland, was an extermination camp destroyed by the Germans in 1944 after an attempted uprising. It was constructed and operated very much like Sobibór but heavily camouflaged. By 1944, the Nazis' murderous efficiency meant that they could "process" 2,000 victims in 90 minutes from arrival to burial, using the camp's 13 gas chambers. There 870,000 Jews were gassed and burned. The monument at Treblinka is striking: a tall obelisk, rent in two by a vertical cleft, stands surrounded by 17,000 granite stones of uneven size.

Before 1939, *Warsaw,* Poland, was home to Europe's largest Jewish community. The Nazis set up a ghetto there where 500,000 people were walled in before being shipped to death camps. In 1943 a heroic uprising took place, and after it was defeated, the Nazis razed the ghetto. Today parts of the ghetto wall can be found and there are many memorials in the area. The best-known memorial is the Rapoport memorial, a large sculptured monument depicting the deportations and the ghetto uprising.

Yad Vashem in Jerusalem is one of the world's great Holocaust memorials. Both a shrine and a museum, it tells the story of the mass deaths but also draws the visitor into the experience of a prayer of remembrance. Yad Vashem is discussed more fully in the article on Jerusalem, Jewish Sites.

See also Anne Frank House; Auschwitz-Birkenau; Babi Yar; Buchenwald; Dachau.

References Israel Gutman (ed.), *Encyclopedia of the Holocaust.* 4 vols. New York, Macmillan, 1990. Michael Marrus, *The Holocaust in History.* Hanover, NH, University Press of New England, 1987. Adolf Rieth, *Monuments to the Victims of Tyranny.* New York, Praeger, 1968. *Shoah.* Los Angeles, Simon Wiesenthal Center, 1985 (video).

HOLY BLOOD, Belgium

A procession of medieval pageantry and splendor takes place each year in Brugge, Belgium, on Ascension Day, 40 days after Easter. Ranks of costumed trumpeters, groups carrying the banners of every province of Belgium, floats with scenes from the Passion of Jesus, all precede a mounted couple representing the Count of Flanders and his wife. At the end comes the most sacred relic in the country, a vial reputed to contain a drop of the blood of Christ, carried in a magnificent gold reliquary by a group of bishops. The dress of the participants comes from the golden age of Brugge, but the pageant is much older. Principal episodes of the Bible, from the fall of Adam and Eve to the mission of the apostles of Jesus, are either presented in tableaux, acted, sung, or performed in mime during the procession.

The object of this veneration is a vial kept in its own chapel on the town square. The chapel was built in the twelfth century for the Count of Flanders and dedicated to St. Basil. At various times it served as the chapel of the candlemakers' and stone masons' guilds. The building is a small, two-story structure, and the upper chapel houses the sacred relic. It is a vial containing lamb's wool supposedly used to clean the wounds of Jesus before his burial. It is saturated with dried blood. Each Friday, the relic is exposed for veneration in the upper chapel.

According to tradition, the relic was a gift from the patriarch of Jerusalem to Count Derrick of Alsace for his bravery during the Second Crusade in 1150. Research has revealed, however, that it came from Constantinople in the early 1200s. It soon became the totem of the city, and oaths of loyalty were sworn on it. From time to time, it was presented to the populace for veneration, and from this custom the procession developed. The magistrates and guilds of Brugge took the lead in developing the procession, and the relic and its chapel are still owned by the city. The property has been managed since 1405 by the Confraternity of the Precious Blood, made up of the most prominent men of the town's elite families. The present shrine dates from 1617 and is a masterwork of the goldsmith Jan Crabbe.

The relic has never been without its critics. St. Thomas Aquinas, the medieval theologian, openly doubted its authenticity. When the matter was debated in 1463 in the presence of Pope Pius V, the jury of cardinals adjourned without making a decision. The Confraternity has refused to have the relic tested scientifically.

References Joan Cruz, *Relics.* Huntington, IN, Our Sunday Visitor, 1984. David Sox, *Relics and Shrines.* London, George Allen & Unwin, 1985.

INFANT JESUS OF PRAGUE, Czech Republic

A worldwide and popular Catholic devotion has developed from this simple parish church, center of the cult of the Infant Jesus. The church was built in 1613 by Lutherans, the first baroque church in the city. After the Battle of the White Mountain (1620), in which the Protestant forces were defeated by the Austrian emperor, the victorious Catholics presented the church to the Carmelite Friars, who renamed it the Church of Our Lady Triumphant in honor of the battle.

In 1628, Polyxena de Lobkowitz, a member of the Spanish nobility, donated the small (18-inch) wax statue of the Child Jesus. Over time it became known as a source of special blessings and miraculous favors, and its devotion spread internationally. It is especially revered in the Philippines, where a version of the statue arrived about the same time as in Prague. It is credited with helping to Christianize the islands and unite them with a sense of national consciousness. The devotion to the Infant Jesus of Prague is also strong in Latin America. In all cases, the devotion is presumed to have originated in Spain.

The statue, kept on a side altar, wears a gold crown and one of over seventy outfits that are changed regularly, depending on the seasons of the church year and feast days. The child is shown with his right hand raised in blessing, with the left holding a golden orb, the royal symbol of kingship. The statue was probably made in the fifteenth century and has been documented from the 1550s. Devotion to the humanity of Christ was strong in Spain at that time, and the cult of the Infant Jesus was part of a new emphasis on Jesus' incarnation in a human body. It, along with other influences, resulted in the development of the celebration of Christmas, with its focus on the Infant Jesus.

During the Thirty Years' War (1618–1648), the Saxons pillaged the church, and the statue was thrown onto a trash heap behind the altar. Around 1640 it was discovered, repaired, and enthroned. After a Swedish siege was lifted following special prayers before the statue, the statue became a national symbol. In 1784 the Emperor Joseph II expelled the Carmelites and entrusted the church to the Knights of Malta. Under Communism during the cold war, all religious orders were suppressed, and the parish was taken under the care of the diocesan clergy. But the church was never closed, and pilgrims continued to visit. Worldwide, the Carmelite Order continued to publicize the devotion to the Infant Jesus. In 1993, after the restoration of religious orders in Czechoslovakia following the fall of Communism, the Carmelites were invited back to take charge of the church.

References *The Holy Infant of Prague.* Prague, Kostel Prazského Jesulátka, n.d. Ludvik Nemec, *Infant Jesus of Prague.* Totowa, NJ, Catholic Books, 1978.

IONA, Scotland

A storm-swept island about a mile off the northern Scots coast, Iona has been a place of Christian pilgrimage and a center of

Scots religious culture since the sixth century. Its history can be divided into three distinct but related eras: Celtic monasticism, Benedictine monasticism, and the Iona Community.

Its first development began with the foundation of a monastery by St. Columba in 563 CE. Columba was a powerful figure in Irish politics. Some think he may have founded the monastery as penance for a civil war he instigated in 561, for which he was reputedly exiled with instructions to convert as many souls as had been lost in battle. Until the seventh century Iona was the most important center of Irish monasticism. It was ruled by priest-abbots, many of them kinsmen of Columba. Iona governed 42 parishes in Ireland and 57 in Scotland until the ninth century.

Like other Celtic monasteries, Iona had a central church surrounded by beehive huts for the monks. There was probably a more permanent house for the abbot, a library, and a resthouse for travelers. However, the buildings were built of earth and timber and thatched with reeds; thus nothing remains except a splendid carved high cross. The monks at Iona supported themselves by farming, and not even the abbot was exempt from this duty. The Irish monks were literate—unusual for that era—and devoted themselves to studying the Scriptures. Iona produced several fine writers of Gaelic, as well as those accomplished in Latin, Greek, and Hebrew. From their school came several prominent English churchmen, including three abbots of Lindisfarne.

Iona remained Celtic in its religious practices even after Roman ways were introduced into Britain, but the raids of the Danes in the following centuries weakened it. In 806, 68 monks died in a massacre, and in 814 the headship of Iona was transferred to Kells in Ireland. In 825 another mass martyrdom occurred, and by 1204 the monastery was empty. The original graveyard is regarded as the holiest ground in Scotland, the resting place for both martyrs and 48 Scots kings, including Macbeth.

The pope sent the Benedictines to Iona to found a new monastery. They introduced the second period of Iona's history and built the medieval stone buildings that remain at the site. The Benedictine period ended when the monastery was broken up during the Protestant Reformation. Another martyrdom closed this period, when 400 monks were thrown into the sea by the Protestants.

Shortly before his death Columba prophesied, "Before the world comes to an end, Iona shall be as she was." He was right. Slowly, people began to return to Iona. At first it was tourists seeking the pleasant charm of the island, but in 1899 the Duke of Argyll restored the church there. The third era of spiritual renewal came to Iona in the form of George Macleod.

Born into the wealth and privilege of the aristocracy, Macleod became the Presbyterian pastor of the poorest church of Glasgow, then a grim and filthy industrial city. A passionate preacher in an unbroken 550-year line of Scots churchmen, he was also a poet, a mystic, and a much-decorated war hero of World War I. His war experience made him a pacifist, a devoted socialist, and a crusader for nuclear disarmament. Through the 1930s he worked to raise the money to restore Iona's monastic ruins, which haunted him, and in 1938 he left his industrial mission to found a community at Iona. He rebuilt the abbey for living quarters for his companions and sent missionaries into Scotland as Columba had fourteen centuries before. Macleod, who combined a burning crusade for justice for the poor and oppressed with a delicate sense of liturgy and worship, is regarded as one of the greatest leaders of public worship in modern Scotland.

Iona is not a monastic community but a missionary one. It originally attracted those marginalized by society: ex-prisoners, troubled youth, the disabled, those whose lives were collapsing. At the same time, "Iona men" became apostles in the public housing settlements, factories, and mean streets of the industrial north. Members of the community commit themselves to sharing the life of labor and worship while they are on the island, but most do not live there. They have jobs and careers and are engaged in religious work elsewhere. Membership in the community requires four disciplines: a daily period of meditation and Bible study; a simple lifestyle and regular giving to help meet the needs of developing countries; a similar donation of time; and a commitment to work for peace. All the members gather for a week and for three shorter meetings each year. The community runs summer youth camps, including one for boys from detention homes.

Macleod refused his father's title in 1934 but was named to the House of Lords in 1966, the only Presbyterian minister there. Macleod staunchly maintained the necessary connection between religion and politics, spirituality and justice, and the Iona Community became a center for international church conferences. A large Centre for Reconciliation was built to accommodate visitors. Macleod was elected moderator of the general assembly of the Presbyterian Church in 1957, which helped to silence his many critics. He remained leader of the community until 1967, and the community has remained vital even after his death in 1991. John Smith, leader of Britain's Labour Party, was a devout member of the community and was buried there in 1994.

References John Dunbar and Ian Fisher, *Iona*. Edinburgh, HMSO, 1983. Shiela Hobden, *George Macleod and the Iona Community*. London, SCM Press, 1973 (young adult). F. Marian McNeill, *Iona: A History of the Island*. Glasgow, Blackie, 1959.

ISE, Japan

Ise, on a peninsula in southern Honshu, is the holiest shrine of Shinto, the Japanese national religion. During the fifteenth century, shrine clerics traveled throughout Japan gathering donations and promising blessings to those who came to Ise. Thus the tradition was established that all devout followers of Shinto should make the pilgrimage to Ise at least once in their lives. Associations (kō) were formed to organize pilgrimages, and on New Year's Day, a million people visit Ise. Each year 8.5 million Japanese pilgrims come, making Ise the leading pilgrimage site in Japan.

What makes Ise the holiest shrine of Shinto is its role as resting place for the spirit of Amaterasu, the Sun Goddess and highest deity of the Shinto pantheon. Amaterasu is the mythical ancestor of the imperial family and the grounds for considering the family divine. The myth of Amaterasu tells of her birth from the creators who brought her forth after first creating the islands of Japan. When her brother insulted and shamed her, she withdrew into a cave, causing total darkness to fall on the earth. Another goddess lured her forth by dancing lewdly before the cave to remind her of her duty to foster life and fertility. Amaterasu gave her son three sacred treasures—a mirror used in the dance, a sword, and jewels—and sent him to rule Japan. The present emperor of Japan is the 124th in

A ceremonial gateway, or torii, in Ise, Japan.

that line, and the treasures are tokens of his divine right to rule.

The Outer Shrine at Ise, dating from 478, honors the Goddess of Grain and Agriculture, who served Amaterasu. The shrine's wide approach is flanked by stately cedar trees. Its main hall is made of un-painted Japanese cypress, which quickly weathers to a deep hue that gives the impression of great age. It is surrounded by four fences, so visitors may only glimpse the buildings through a white silk curtain that decorates the main gate.

The Inner Shrine, where Amaterasu resides, is several miles away. It is built in a special style forbidden to other shrines, and its holiest relic is the mirror that is one of the three sacred treasures of the imperial family. Except for the years of militaristic Shinto

(1868–1946), a princess of the royal family has served as high priestess of the Inner Shrine, and certain rites are performed there and nowhere else. In October, the emperor comes to the Inner Shrine for the dedication of the new rice; other cere-monies are held to pray for a rich harvest. The rice used in the shrine rites is raised in a special rice paddy, and sake (rice wine) is made from it according to an ancient for-mula. Food offerings, later destroyed, are made to the goddess. Over 100 priests serve at Ise, along with shrine maidens who offer sacred dances for festal occasions. One dance, performed by a single male, is per-mitted only at Ise and in the imperial household.

Every 20 years the entire complex, with over 200 buildings and shrines, is completely rebuilt. In a special ceremony, the spirit of Amaterasu is moved to her new quarters. The most recent renewal of the shrines—the sixty-first—occurred in 1993, at a cost of ¥5 billion ($59 million). In the "thanksgiving years" immediately following a rebuilding, pilgrimages intensify.

Ise and the other Grand Shrines are devoted to the imperial cult. Only the emperor may enter the Inner Shrine at Ise or pass its four entryways. Outside the shrine park is the Shinto university, Kogakkan, closed by the Americans after World War II and reopened after the occupation. Its 20,000 students focus their studies on *nihonjinron*, the essence of what is Japanese. Traditional Japanese military values are taught along with the doctrine of the superiority of the Japanese race and culture.

See also Shinto Shrines.

References Joseph Kitagawa, *Religion in Japanese History*. New York, Columbia University, 1966. ———, *On Understanding Japanese Religion*. Princeton, NJ, Princeton University, 1987. Peter Popham, *Wooden Temples of Japan*. London, Tauris Parke, 1990.

ISTANBUL MOSQUES

After conquering Constantinople (today's Istanbul) in 1453, the Ottoman Turks ruled a vast empire from the city for 500 years. In the process, they embellished the city. At first the Ottomans Muslims made do with remodeled Christian churches, but within a few years they were spending huge sums of money to construct a network of mosques that rivaled those in any Muslim city in the world.

Although the *Hagia Sophia* was made into a mosque in 1453 by Mehmet the Conqueror, for some years it has been operated as a museum by the government. Across the park from it is the *Blue Mosque*,

an Islamic architectural wonder facing the Christian one. Properly called the *Sultan Ahmet Mosque*, the popular name comes from its blue interior tilework. It was the last imperial mosque built (1609–1617) and the only one with six minarets. If the Blue Mosque was an attempt to rival Hagia Sophia, it was a failure. Although it is large and well proportioned, its interior is gloomy and unattractive. The poor lighting reduces the effect of the tiles, and the effect is cavernous rather than awesome. The Blue Mosque is still in use for prayers, although the crush of tourists often makes this impractical.

The *Fatih Mosque* served as Mehmet's personal royal mosque (*fatih* means "conqueror"), and consequently it was surrounded by signs of his generosity—religious schools, a soup kitchen to serve the poor, a Turkish bath, and a clinic. Mehmet was not pleased, however, when the original dome was not higher than Hagia Sophia's, and the luckless architect was maimed and then executed.

The *Süleymaniye*, one of the largest mosques in the world, was built to replace the Hagia Sophia as the chief mosque of the sultan. The greatest of the Ottoman sultans, Süleyman the Magnificent (1520–1566), commissioned it, and it was completed in 1557. Crowning a hill with a commanding view, it backs up to the gardens of the Istanbul University. Beautifully proportioned, with four minarets, it overlooks the Golden Horn, the inlet of the Bosphorus that divides the ancient city and the new.

Hemmed in by the city, Süleymaniye and its courtyard are enclosed by a stone wall. A row of seats and water taps provides for the required ritual washings before entering. Visually balancing the courtyard behind the mosque is the royal graveyard. At the center of this is Süleyman's *türbe*, or mausoleum, inside a small octagonal building, topped by a royal turban and covered with green cloth. The tomb is often reverenced by Islamic visitors. Green, the sacred color of Islam, is used throughout, starting with the green marble of the entrance and the padded drape that guards the interior. The design is so lovely and harmonious, and the mosque such a part of Turkish culture, that the architect's portrait is featured on Turkish currency. For special occasions—and even for Friday prayers—the assembly at Süleymaniye is so large that *mihrabs* (decorated niches facing Mecca) are placed on the outside walls for the overflow crowds. Inside, the immense floor is covered in a sea of red carpets. The dome (85 feet in diameter and 175 high) is decorated in gold calligraphy. The great height is made less awesome by a number of chandeliers, which provide the main light.

Yeni Mosque was commissioned in 1597 for the *valide* or Queen Mother, but after its architect was executed two years later, it sat unfinished for 50 years until another queen mother completed it. The valide was often the sultan's chief advisor. She determined which of his wives had access to him (and thus could bear children) and was a powerful figure with her own court. The Yeni Camii is lined in blue tiles and is the last mosque to retain the custom of stringing sacred sayings in lights between its minarets.

See also Hagia Sophia.

References *Living Islam*. New York, BBC, 1993 (video). Merle Severy, "Süleyman the Magnificent," *National Geographic* 172:5, 552–601 (November 1987). Paul Underwood, *The Kariye Djami*. New York, Bollingen Foundation, 1966.

IZUMO TAISHA SHRINE, Japan

Among Shinto shrines, Izumo Taisha is second only to the sacred shrines of Ise. It lies on the northern coast of Honshu Island, far from any major Japanese city. The oldest continuing shrine in Japan, it is dedicated to Okuninushi, the deity credited with introducing medicine, silkworms, and agriculture into the world.

Okuninushi is also the spirit god of marriage. In Shinto shrines generally, one approaches the shrine, bows, and then claps twice to summon the spirit god—or some would say, to attract his attention. At Izumo Taisha, however, petitioners clap four times, twice for themselves and twice for their spouses or future spouses. Okuninushi is represented in the form of Daikoku, a smiling corpulent man carrying a sack and standing by several bales of rice. Since most marriages in Japan are solemnized by the exchange of vows before a Shinto spirit hall, Izumo Taisha is a very popular place for weddings. At the entrance to the main hall, the largest in Japan, hangs a huge straw rope (*shimenewa*). It is over 30 yards long and weighs 3,300 pounds. Those hoping for a happy marriage throw ¥45 into the offering box before the shrine, since the Japanese for "45 yen" is *shiju-goen,* which also means "constant chances for romance." Young people write the names of their sweethearts on scraps of paper and attach them to trees in the shrine compound, thus placing them "in the laps of the gods." By extension of the shrine's dedication to relationships, it has also become popular in recent years as a place to pray for successful business mergers.

The ritual before entering the inner shrine, which towers seven stories high, is one of purification. The visitor dons a white coat and then washes his hands in flowing water. A Shinto priest, waving a wand streaming with streamers of paper slips emblazoned with symbols, brings the visitor to the shrine. There the pilgrim claps four times and then receives a cup of rice wine, which is drunk in honor of the gods.

The shrine dates from at least the seventh century, probably earlier. But following Shinto custom, the buildings are replaced periodically. Most of the present structures date from the nineteenth century; and the present main shrine was constructed in 1744. The entrance is a giant torii arch. From there the visitor walks for a quarter of an hour along a pine-shaded path to the shrine. The hall is representative of the oldest characteristics of shrine architecture, with a compressed bark roof that slants from front to back rather than from side to side. Another distinctive feature is two long open shelters that serve as havens for Shinto's deities—and there are some eight million of them—when they come to Izumo Taisha for their annual gathering in the lunar month of October. In Izumo, October is called *Kamiarizuki,* or the "Month with Gods," while throughout the rest of Japan it is *Kannazuki,* the "Month without Gods."

Izumo is also revered as the birthplace of kabuki, the uniquely Japanese formal style of theater. It was created in the seventeenth century by Izumo Okuni, a woman dancer and, some say, a priestess of the Izumo Taisha Shrine. Her tomb is near the shrine and is visited by many kabuki actors, who also perform here each year. Izumo Taisha has some 200 satellite shrines, several of which have been targets of arsonists. They are presumed to be radical socialists who oppose both Shinto and the imperial family.

See also Shinto Shrines.

References Lafcadio Hearn, *Glimpses of Unfamiliar Japan.* Boston, Houghton Mifflin, 1894. Yasutada Watanabe, *Shinto Art: Ise and Izumo Shrines.* New York, Weatherhill, n.d.

JANAKPUR, Nepal

The city of Janakpur in Nepal is the mythical birthplace of Sita, consort of Rama. Rama is the hero of the Hindu epic, the Ramayana.

The city has large numbers of shrines and over a thousand ghats, or sacred bathing places, where pilgrims purify themselves before reverencing the gods at the many temples. The purification rites take many forms, from washing clothing and bathing oneself to scrubbing down water buffalos. The *puja*, or ritual offerings and prayers, are not all solemn. Pilgrims swim and frolic in the ponds and pools, and the pilgrimage is often a joyous outing, accompanied by eating and even shopping.

Tradition has it that Sita was born when King Janak, her father, was blessing the fields to make them fertile. When she came of age, her hand was offered to the suitor who could bend the bow of the god Shiva, and fresh from the defeat of a group of demons, Rama came in disguise to claim her. King Janak built the ghats to refresh the gods who traveled to the nuptials from faraway Mount Kailas. One of the temples is on the site of this sacred marriage, and an annual celebration in early December brings hundreds of thousands of pilgrims to the city. The marriage is reenacted in a massive procession.

The Ramayana recounts how Rama was later sent into exile. An evil king took advantage of Rama's absence to try to seduce Sita, but she remained faithful and rejected all his advances. The monkey-god, Hanuman, discovered her and brought Rama to her side. Rama triumphed over the king, and this battle of good and evil is also reenacted every March in Janakpur by throngs of the ardent faithful. Newlyweds of both Hindu and Buddhist traditions come to Janakpur to dedicate their marriages to the ideal couple, Rama and Sita. Their main shrine is Janaki Mandir, where at dawn and dust, believers join the temple priests in puja rites before an image of the sacred couple. The wedding scene is presented in a tableau at the Ram Janaki Vivek Mandap, a temple nearby.

References David Kinsley, *Hindu Goddesses.* Berkeley, University of California, 1986. Ormond McGill, *Religious Mysteries of the Orient.* South Brunswick, NJ, Barnes, 1976. *Nepal: Land of the Gods.* New York, Mystic Fire, 1976 (video).

JASNA GORA, Poland

As the national shrine of Poland, Jasna Góra in the city of Czestochowa attracts a regular flow of delegations from all elements of society. Parliament and government leaders visit regularly, and student groups, war veterans, miners, actors, former Stalinist prisoners, and factory workers arrive in a regular stream of organized pilgrimages. It is estimated to be the fifth-largest pilgrimage center in the world, after Varanasi, Mecca (the Hajj), Lourdes, and Rome. The focus of these pilgrims is the chapel of the Black Madonna. It is on the side of the large baroque monastery church that dominates the hilltop. The icon shows Mary holding Jesus on her left arm; the Christ Child holds a Bible in his hands. The

The chapel of the Black Madonna houses an icon of Mary and the Christ Child holding the Holy Scriptures. Jasna Góra is one of the largest pilgrimage centers in the world, drawing thousands of people who come to honor the icon.

image is in a gold frame decorated with hundreds of gems.

Many shrines to the Virgin Mary claim to have a painting of Mary done by Luke the Evangelist. The one at Jasna Góra is alleged to have been painted on a tabletop built by the carpenter Jesus. The legend also relates that the painting, a beautiful icon, was discovered by St. Helena, the mother of Emperor Constantine and an avid collector of sacred relics.

It is historically certain that the icon arrived in Poland in 1382 with a Polish army fleeing the Tartars, who had struck it with an arrow. A monastery was established in Czestochowa to care for the icon, but it was again attacked in 1430, when Protestant Hussite invaders slashed the face with a sword. The arrow mark and the two sword gashes remain clearly visible today.

In 1655, the monks held out against invading Swedes for a 40-day siege, inspiring a popular Polish uprising that led to the liberation of the country within a year. After that event, the shrine of Czestochowa became a symbol of Polish national identity, and the icon was crowned Queen of Poland. Considering its violent history, it is no surprise that Jasna Góra is built as a walled fortress, with its shrines and chapels well protected inside.

The main avenue of Czestochowa has a broad park-like median lined with trees, and every day from early until late, groups march to the shrine along this route, separated by a few hundred feet so that they do not disturb the groups before and behind them. As groups walk along, praying the rosary and singing hymns, young men carry battery packs and push speakers on wheels to lead the singing. The rhythm of song and prayer from group after group moves along the street in waves of sound. Pilgrims wear badges with the name of their town and a number showing how many times they have come to the shrine. Many have come annually for 30 years or more.

Jasna Góra receives pilgrims daily in a constant stream, but Marian feast days bring throngs, especially on Assumption Day (August 15), when up to a half million people crowd the city. Since 1711, a walking pilgrimage has left Warsaw and 32 other towns and walked in procession for up to 21 days; today it numbers from 50,000 to 100,000 pilgrims converging on the city. After venerating the icon, pilgrims usually pin their badges to the walls of the chapel as an ex-voto. There are four other national pilgrimages: May 3 (Mary, Queen of Poland), August 26 (Our Lady of Czestochowa), September 8 (Nativity of Mary) and December 8 (Immaculate Conception). In 1991 Pope John Paul II held his Sixth World Youth Day at Czestochowa with some 350,000 young people from all over Europe.

Two museums display the many gifts given the Virgin. Princes have presented their swords and scepters to her along with the spoils of victory, including Turkish guns and the great battle tents of the sultan captured at the siege of Vienna in 1683. Among the treasures is the Nobel Peace Prize medal awarded Lech Walesa in 1983 and rosaries made of dried bread by Nazi concentration camp survivors. There are tear-gas cylinders used against the Solidarity protesters by the Communists in the 1980s, since Jasna Góra was a center of anti-Communist resistance during the Cold War.

See also Marian Apparitions.

References Zbigiew Bania et al., *Jasna Góra*. Wroclaw, Poland, Interpress, 1986. Caroline Peters, *The Black Madonna*. Paterson, NJ, St. Anthony Guild, 1962. Gerard Sherry, *The Catholic Shrines of Europe*. Huntington, IN, Our Sunday Visitor, 1986.

JERUSALEM, CHRISTIAN SITES

In 325 CE the Empress Helena, mother of Constantine and one of the most powerful women of her day, went to Jerusalem to identify the places associated with the life of Jesus. She found that they were not as difficult to trace as might be imagined, since the local Christians had kept track of some, while the Roman emperors had been unintentionally helpful by erecting pagan idols over others as markers of Roman triumph.

When excavators found a cross and spears in a dig in Jerusalem, Helena regarded it as a miraculous revelation of the True Cross. Legend has it that only an innocent boy could lift it. Helena ordered a basilica built over the site of the burial of Jesus. This was the first *Church of the Holy Sepulchre*, destroyed by the Persians in 614, restored and demolished again in 1009, and then rebuilt by the Crusaders. Their basilica was expanded to bring the nearby rock-cut tomb of Jesus and the site of Calvary under one roof. It is this Crusader church that exists today in the Christian Quarter of the Old City of Jerusalem. Because Jesus' burial place was described as outside the walls of the city, the Church of the Holy Sepulchre has been disputed, but recent scholarship supports it as the most likely site; in Jesus' time it was outside the old walls. The Garden Tomb located on the Mount of Olives, favored by some Protestants, has been disproved.

The Holy Sepulchre is a carefully controlled shrine. In 1757, Turkish rulers attempted to deal with the bitter rivalries of Christian groups by dividing it into spheres of control. Roman (Latin) Catholics have the largest share, followed by the Greek Orthodox, Armenians, Syrians, and Copts. The Ethiopians have been relegated to the roof of one of the chapels. Only Latin Catholics and Greek and Armenian Orthodox may celebrate Mass in the church, hold processions, or use incense. Each group is jealous of the others' space and eager to claim rights to it, so that even simple repairs can cause years of negotiation. Consequently, the Holy Sepulchre has serious maintenance problems.

The *Mount of Olives* is the site of Jesus' night vigil before his crucifixion. It is a serene setting. There are several "Gardens of Gethsemane" alongside the *Chapel of the Ascension,* which most Christians accept as the spot from which Jesus is believed to have ascended into heaven. At the foot of the hill is *Dominus Flevit* ("the Lord wept"), a tear-shaped church on the spot where Jesus wept for Jerusalem.

Mount Zion, the mountain of the Lord that has come to symbolize Jerusalem itself, figures in the messianic hopes of Christians. On one of the peaks of Zion, Jesus fulfilled his destiny by becoming the sacrifice of the New Law, making Mount Zion the New Jerusalem. Many evangelicals identify Mount Zion as the actual place upon which Jesus will return in his second coming, to proclaim the end of time and the fulfillment of all sacred history. Since this can happen only when Judaism has been restored to the Holy Land, many evangelicals give strong support to modern Israel and its religious claims to Palestine. Mount Zion, David's original city, is the site of the Cenacle, the probable location of the Last Supper. The space is undecorated and unremarkable.

The *Via Dolorosa* is a narrow street along which Jesus supposedly carried his cross to his death. It is marked by stations, places where certain events took place. These are reproduced in Catholic churches around the world by small plaques (Stations of the Cross) showing the various scenes. Some locations are biblical and others legendary, but the devotional pattern is traditional. The Way of the Cross is conducted twice daily for pilgrims, with Fridays especially popular. A few people carry large wooden crosses along the Way as a penance for their sins.

Station I (the place of Jesus' condemnation by Pilate) is at either the Lion's Gate or the Jaffa Gate. II (Jesus receives the cross) is on the pavement of the Roman fortress, now a convent. III (Jesus falls) and IV (Jesus meets his mother) are near the Armenian Church of Our Lady of the Spasm. V (Simon carries Jesus' cross) is by a small Franciscan chapel, and VI (Veronica wipes Jesus' face) is in a small Crusader monastery. Legend has it that when a woman wiped Jesus' face, his image miraculously appeared on the cloth. This relic is now in St. Peter's in Rome. VII (Jesus falls again) is where the Via crosses a market. VIII (Jesus speaks to the women of Jerusalem) is nearby and recalls when some women wept for him, and he told them to lament for themselves and their children. IX (Jesus falls a third time) is by an Ethiopian monastery. X–XIV (Jesus is stripped, nailed to the cross, dies, is taken from the cross, and laid in the tomb) are all within the Church of the Holy Sepulchre, the final station. It is a marble chapel built in the center of the rotunda on the ground floor of the church. The site of the burial place of Jesus is marked with lamps and candles. Nearby is the Chapel of Mary Magdalene, where Jesus was first seen after the Resurrection.

Along the Via Dolorosa is the Crusader Church of St. Anne, commemorating the birthplace of the Virgin Mary. It is one of the best-preserved Crusader churches in the Holy Land, but its most interesting feature is in its gardens: the *Pool of Bethesda*, where sheep were brought to be washed before being sacrificed at the Temple and where Jesus cured a paralytic. A healing pool in biblical times, it does not have that reputation today.

See also Jerusalem, Islamic Sites; Jerusalem, Jewish Sites.

References W. Joseph Clark, *The Holy Land*. Huntington, IN, Our Sunday Visitor, 1986. Alan Mairson, "The Three Faces of Jerusalem," *National Geographic* 189:4, 2–31 (April 1996). Hershel Shanks, *Jerusalem: An Archeological Biography*. New York, Random House, 1995.

JERUSALEM, ISLAMIC SITES

Mount Zion, the holy city of Jerusalem, ranks second in importance as an Islamic pilgrimage site, after Mecca and Medina, the places of the Hajj. To Muslims the city is known simply as Al Quds, "The Holy." It contains numerous sites associated with the prophets who preceded Mohammed—Abraham, David, Solomon, and Jesus.

The *Dome of the Rock* stands over the site of Solomon's Temple at the peak of the Temple Mount. Here Abraham offered his son for sacrifice, and here the Prophet Mohammed went into the sky on a winged steed—Al-Burak, "the Lightning"—in his night journey to Paradise (*Qur'an*, Sura 17), accompanied by the Archangel Gabriel. The name refers to a large rock that bears the imprint of Mohammed's horse as it leapt into the sky, carrying him off to the delights of heaven. From ancient times the rock had been in the center of Solomon's Temple. Muslim tradition holds that an angel of Allah will come to the Dome of the Rock to sound the trumpet call of the Last Judgment to mark the end of the world. The Dome of the Rock has become a symbol of Jerusalem because of its magnificent golden dome (actually aluminum with gold leaf) set above a lovely blue-tiled octagonal building. The interior is decorated by bands

Its gold dome rising above Jerusalem, the Dome of the Rock, located at the peak of the Temple Mount, is revered by Muslims, Jews, and Christians. The dome contains a large rock from which the prophet Mohammed soared heavenward, his horse leaving an imprint.

of Qur'anic inscriptions and panels of bright tiles. The rock is surrounded by a carved wooden screen, and the stained-glass and mosaics in the shrine are among the finest in the world. A small reliquary holds some hairs from Mohammed's beard. Next to the Dome of the Rock is a smaller copy of it, the *Dome of the Chain,* where a legendary chain once hung, to be grasped only by the righteous.

The *al-Aqsa Mosque* at the south end of the Temple Mount commemorates the fact that Muslims once prayed toward Jerusalem instead of Mecca. Al-Aqsa has an intricately carved mihrab, the niche in the wall indicating the direction of Mecca for prayer, and a priceless set of oriental carpets. The minbar, or pulpit, was commissioned by Saladin around 1190 and towers over a

story high. The Temple Mount is closed to non-Muslims on Fridays.

Since Jews, Muslims, and Christians all venerate Mount Zion, it has been a source of conflict and tension. History records bloody clashes and constant exchanges of jurisdiction as different groups asserted control over the city. The Jewish temples were systematically destroyed by their enemies, the first by the Persians in 586 BCE, the second by the Romans in 70 CE. A triumphant Islam built the Dome of the Rock in 691 CE on the ruins of the temple. When the Crusaders defeated the Muslims, they established their headquarters on the Temple Mount in 1099, only to be dislodged by the Muslims in 1187. At the time of foundation of the Israeli state in 1948, the city was divided, but Israel seized all of it in the

1967 Six-Day War. The status of Jerusalem remains the thorniest issue between the Palestinians and Israel, both of whom claim it as their capital. Most countries (including the United States) avoid recognizing it as the capital of Israel, and the Vatican has called for it to be an international city.

See also Jerusalem, Christian Sites; Jerusalem, Jewish Sites.

References Kenneth Cragg, *The Dome and the Rock*. Cairo, S.P.C.K., 1964. Christopher Hollis and Robert Brownrigg, *Holy Places*. New York, Praeger, 1969. Jerry Landay, *Dome of the Rock*. Pleasantville, NY, Reader's Digest, 1972. Francis Peters, *The Distant Shrine*. New York, AMS, 1993.

JERUSALEM, JEWISH SITES

All of Jerusalem is a holy city for Jews, the embodiment of *eretz Isra'el*, the promised land that is the birthright of every Jew. The most sacred ceremonies of Judaism, the Day of Atonement and the seder meal on the eve of Passover, conclude with the words "Next year in Jerusalem!" Jerusalem means true worship, fidelity to the Torah, and a messianic future. It is a symbol of Jewish unity, and its restoration has been both a religious hope and a political goal. But the Israeli position demanding an undivided Jerusalem has resulted in bitter debate in negotiations with the Palestinian Authority, which wants Jerusalem as the capital of a Palestinian state.

For Jews, the most important site of pilgrimage and veneration has always been the high place on which the Temple was built. Jerusalem itself is often referred to as "the Holy Mountain," and the two became identified with one another. To "go up to Jerusalem" meant going to the Lord as Moses had gone up to Sinai to meet God. *Mount Moriah*, traditionally the place where

Abraham bound Isaac, was the site of Solomon's temple, chosen by King David. The Ark of the Covenant containing the tablets given to Moses on Mount Sinai was brought to the temple, symbolically sealing the union of the two high places.

Jews were barred from Jerusalem when Herod's Temple was destroyed by the Romans in 70 CE. Only the *Western Wall* (popularly called the Wailing Wall) remained; it became the principal place of pilgrimage for Jews. The wall is part of the western base of the Temple Mount; its nickname comes from the Jewish use of the site to mourn the loss of the temple and the keening sound of their prayers. It is faced by an open plaza. Men and women are separated by a low wooden fence, and even gentile men are required to wear a hat or yarmulke, a small skull cap. The scene at the wall reveals the wide cultural base of Judaism—European and American Jews in Western dress topped by a prayer shawl, Chassidic men in hats and black suits, Yemenis in colorful garb, and Russians in heavy coats and fur hats. Some lean against the stones, praying; others insert notes with petitions and prayers into the cracks between the massive blocks. Men pray before a veiled Torah, the scroll of the first five books of the Hebrew Scriptures. Young Jews are brought from around the world to celebrate their Bar Mitzvah or Bat Mitzvah, the ceremonial presentation of a son or daughter of the Covenant as an adult in the Jewish community. Devout groups dancing and singing with the Torah are a common sight. Photography is barred on the Sabbath, but on other days tourists abound.

The Wailing Wall is unadorned, stark and austere. Jews believe that even though the temple was torn down, the divine presence still hovers over the remnant. In 637 CE, after the Muslim conquest, Jews were al-

The Wailing Wall is the only structure left standing after the Romans destroyed Herod's Temple in 70 CE. People of the Jewish faith believe the divine spirit still presides over the remaining wall.

lowed to return to the city. However, the Muslims incorporated the wall into the Dome of the Rock, which commemorates the night that Mohammed was drawn up to heaven from that spot (*see* the entry for Jerusalem, Islamic Sites). Throughout the era of the Crusades, Ottoman and British occupations, and the division of the city after Israeli independence, the wall remained the site of Jewish hopes for a new temple. Many people assume that the wall is the last remaining part of Herod's Temple; it is, in fact, a remnant of a much later retaining wall of the Temple Mount rather than the temple itself.

In 1995, Jerusalem celebrated 3,000 years of Jewish history, beginning from the approximate date that King David conquered the city. Just inside the Jaffa Gate to the Old City is the massive Citadel of David. Its highest point is the Tower of David, built by Herod. According to the Bible, Jerusalem was the last Canaanite city conquered by David and the site of his new capital, which was shrewdly placed between Israel and Judah and belonged to neither.

The *Mount of Olives* lies east of the Old City. In Jewish tradition, the Messiah will come down from the Mount of Olives, raising the dead, healing the sick, judging all souls, and establishing the kingdom of God on earth. Those buried there will be the first to greet the Messiah, and many Jews have chosen to be entombed on its slopes. Jewish pilgrims come to the *Common Grave* of those who died defending the Jewish Quarter during the 1948 war. The nearby *Jewish Graveyard* is the largest in the world. Mourners place a small pebble on the graves of those for whom they pray as an ex-voto. Just below the cemetery are the *Tombs of the Prophets,* tunnels with burial alcoves supposedly containing the remains of

the prophets Haggai, Malachi, Zachariah, and others.

A visit to *Yad Vashem*, the Holocaust memorial in Jerusalem, is a deeply moving experience. One enters by the *Avenue of the Righteous,* a grove of 26,000 trees, each with the name of a gentile who saved Jews during the Holocaust. Another grove is the *Garden of the Children of the Holocaust,* and nearby is a *Memorial to the Destroyed Communities*, commemorating Jewish villages and ghettos in Eastern Europe that were razed during the Holocaust. In Yad Vashem the visitor will find a museum that traces the rise of Nazi Germany and the brutality of the Holocaust, along with documentation and education centers. Most moving, however, are the perpetual memorials. In The Hall of Remembrance, a simple room with the names of the 22 main Nazi concentration camps inlaid in the floor, an Eternal Light burns in a broken bronze cup in front of a vault containing ashes of the dead from each of the camps. A rabbi constantly intones *kaddish*, the prayer for the dead. In another room, pilgrims walk through a dark room lit only by candles, one for each of the 1.5 million children who died in the infamous camps; the only sound is a voice endlessly reciting their names.

See also Holocaust Sites; Jerusalem, Christian Sites; Jerusalem, Islamic Sites; Mount Sinai.

References Abraham Millgram, *Jerusalem Curiosities*. Philadelphia, Jewish Publications Society, 1990. Leen Ritmeyer, "The Ark of the Covenant: Where It Stood in Solomon's Temple," *Biblical Archaeology Review* 22:1, 45–55, 70–73 (January-February 1996). Hershel Shanks, *The City of David*. Washington, DC, Biblical Archaeology Society, 1975. ———, *Jerusalem: An Archeological Biography*. New York, Random House, 1995.

JOKHANG TEMPLE, Tibet, China

The spiritual center of Tibetan Buddhism, the Jokhang Temple attracts thousands of pilgrims, many from the far corners of the country. They come on foot under conditions of great hardship to do penance and pay homage to the temple and its guardian spirits.

According to tradition, in the seventh century King Songtsen Gampo's consort brought a valuable statue of the Buddha from China. To determine where to build a temple to house it, the king threw his ring into the air so the spirits would determine the site. The ring fell into a lake, from which a miraculous stupa emerged, and the lake was filled in to form the base for the temple. The Jokhang Temple sits in the middle of Lhasa, fronted by a large plaza and an open porch. Both are usually filled with pilgrims, bowing or lying fully prostrate on the ground in reverence toward the inner sanctum of the shrine. It is not uncommon for the devout to approach the Jokhang crawling on their bellies from considerable distances. A popular route circles the temple for about five miles.

The Jokhang has been added to many times through the centuries. The main cloister, which leads to the shrine, is ringed with numerous large prayer wheels, which are kept turning to the hum of pilgrim prayers. Inside the temple are many small chapels dedicated to various gods and bodhisattvas (perfected beings who have voluntarily renounced enlightenment in order to help humans on earth). In Tibet, the most important bodhisattva is Avalokiteshvara, "hearer of the cries of the world" and patron of the country. Tibetan Buddhism was reformed in the fourteenth century by a prince believed to be a reincarnation of this bodhisattva. The chapels surround the main shrine containing the statue of the Jowo Sakyamuni Buddha, over 1,300 years old. The pilgrims work their way through the complex, circumambulating the main shrine, often on their hands and knees, and sometimes on their bellies as a sign of complete submission. They bring white scarves to the gods and add small gifts of yak butter to the votive lamps that are the light source inside the temple.

The cloister is frescoed, and on a floor above the shrine is another cloister with more beautiful wall paintings. The painted statues, murals, and decorations represent the peak achievement of Tibetan religious art—with one exception: Many of the paintings on the entry floor have been removed by the Chinese authorities since the military occupation of Tibet and replaced with cheap murals. The focus of the pilgrims is not the frescoes, however, but the statue of the Sakyamuni Buddha. In religious art, the posture and the placement of the Buddha's hands indicate stages of his life, and many of these versions line the walls of the shrine. The Sakyamuni Buddha is often regarded as the "historical" Buddha, although there are no known representations of Gautama Buddha himself. The statue presents him sitting in the lotus position, cross-legged, on a three-tiered lotus throne. It shows him at age 12, with his left hand lying on his lap, palm upturned, and his right hand touching the earth. He is thus seen to be open to receive blessings from heaven (the upturned palms) and to bestow them on the earth. The statue is gilded and adorned with a riot of jewels, gemstones, and elaborate carvings.

Tibetan Buddhism is based on Mahayana, which emphasizes the Buddha's compassionate nature, joy, and sensitivity to the needs of his people. There are some twenty branches of Buddhism in Tibet, but the dominant one is the Yellow Hat sect, to

Pilgrims, such as the one pictured here, travel on foot from all corners of Tibet to the Jokhang Temple, the spiritual center of Tibetan Buddhism.

which the Dalai Lama belongs. Tibetan Buddhism is often called Lamaism because of the important role of the lamas, or spiritual masters. The Dalai Lama and his council ruled Tibet until the Chinese Communist occupation in 1951. He and 80,000 disciples fled to India in 1959, and he was awarded the Nobel Peace Prize in 1989. The Chinese have embarked on a repressive program of cultural genocide during which the Jokhang Temple has been the focus of resistance and has taken on a political role. Ethnic Chinese have colonized the country until they constitute more than half the population and control all government posts. Tibetan casualties over the years total in the tens of thousands. During China's Cultural Revolution (1966–1976) more than 5,000 monasteries were closed, and part of the Jokhang was converted into a pigsty. Another section was used to billet soldiers, after the troops spent five days burning the Temple's ancient Tibetan scriptures.

Jokhang's monks are kept under close surveillance, since they have often led demonstrations and are the heart of Tibetan resistance. People have been killed in Jokhang protests, and all monasteries are restricted or closed. Jokhang has a government quota of 100 monks, and presently has close to that number. Some 800 police are reputed to be kept in the area, and it is not safe for Jokhang monks to speak with foreigners. Still, the pilgrims throng the shrine, laying their bodies before it, using prayer as their gesture of resistance.

References John Avedon, *In Exile from the Land of Snows*. New York, Michael Joseph, 1984. Thubten Jigme Norbu and Colin Turnbull, *Tibet: Its History, Religion, and People*. New York, Penguin Books, 1983. *Tibet: The Survival of the Spirit*. New York, Mystic Fire, 1991 (video).

Nothing remains of the original 670 CE mosque. But the *Great Mosque,* which dates from 863, is still one of the leading holy sites of Islam. It is approached through a large marble-paved courtyard where the devout, having removed their shoes, ritually wash to purify themselves before entering the mosque. The colonnade surrounding the courtyard is supported by 400 pillars plundered from many local sources, and pagan Roman, Byzantine, and Latin Christian symbols are scattered about incongruously. The massive wooden doors leading into the prayer hall are beautifully carved in detailed inlaid marquetry. The main aisle leads to the *mihrab,* a large tiled niche that shows the direction of Mecca so that prayers may be offered facing the holy places. The mosque may be entered through several entryways, and it contains the tombs of local saints. Nearby is a cemetery restricted to descendants of the family of the Prophet Mohammed. The minaret, or prayer tower used by the muezzin for the daily calls to prayer, is 115 feet high, a landmark in the city.

KAIROUAN, Tunisia

The Great Mosque at Kairouan is the oldest Islamic place of prayer in North Africa and popularly regarded as the fourth holiest in Islam, after Mecca, Jerusalem, and Medina. For many Muslims for whom the hajj (the pilgrimage to to the holy places of Mecca and Medina) was an impossible dream, Kairouan served as a substitute. Local Islamic tradition taught that seven trips to Kairouan equal the hajj.

The name *Kairouan* means "the caravan," which indicates the city's origins as a settlement where desert trade caravans stopped. It is well watered and thus became an early Arab outpost during the invasions of the seventh century, when it was proclaimed that Kairouan would survive until Judgment Day. A military outpost by 670, it was resettled in 694 as an Islamic religious center, cut off from the surrounding Christian and Jewish populations, which had not yet begun to die out. Only Muslims were allowed entrance inside the walls until modern times, and the city has always been an orthodox Islamic enclave standing against heretical forms of Islam as well as infidels. In the ninth century it was also a major endpoint of the lucrative trans-Sahara trade routes, and it became wealthy and powerful, especially from the slave trade until the mid-nineteenth century. Part of its economic base, however, was the pilgrimages to the holy places.

Although the Great Mosque is the primary goal of the pilgrims, there are other shrines of importance in Kairouan, and it is customary for pilgrims to make the rounds of them. The *Three Gates Mosque* was a center for one of the Muslim religious societies, or brotherhoods, that have dominated Islam in Tunisia. At the center of the old town is the Bir Barouta, an ancient well that is pumped by a blindfolded camel trudging in circles. Legend has it that its water comes directly from Mecca. The desert Bedouins eagerly seek the well in order to sip holy water from the holy land. Across the market from the Great Mosque is the Martyrs' Gate, built to commemorate a group of tenth-century Qur'anic teachers murdered by a Shiite ruler for their orthodoxy.

The city is also known for several *zaouia*, or mosques containing the tombs of important saints. The first of these is the *Zaouia of Sidi Amor Abbada*, an eccentric prophet whose revelations are inscribed on huge tablets around his tomb, itself massive and impressive. Sidi Amor Abbada was a blacksmith, and on display in the zaouia is a huge anchor, created to keep Kairouan from drifting out to sea—quite a vision, since the city is inland. The most important tomb, however, is the *Zaouia of Sidi Sahbi*, which draws more pilgrims than even the Great Mosque itself. A *sidi sahbi* was a companion of the Prophet, and this zaouia is the burial place of Abu Zama Balawi, who wore a locket containing the precious relic of three hairs from the beard of the Prophet. For this reason, it is popularly known as the "Mosque of the Barber." The zaouia dates from the fourteenth century and is decorated with tiles that cover the courtyard walls. Pilgrims leave scarves as ex-votos on the tomb, and by tradition, babies are brought to the tomb to be anointed.

The holiest times for visiting Kairouan are Ramadan, the month of fasting and self-discipline, and the feast of Mouloud al Nabi, which has a special following in Kairouan. This is the birthday of the Prophet and is celebrated with feasting and dancing.

See also Touba.

References Carolyn Fluehr-Lobban, *Islamic Society in Practice*. Gainesville, University of Florida, 1994. Nikki Keddie (ed.), *Scholars, Saints, and Sufis*. Berkeley, University of California, 1972. *Living Islam*. New York, BBC, 1993 (video).

KEK LOK SI, Malaysia

Kek Lok Si, set on a hill above the island city of Penang, is the largest Buddhist complex in Southeast Asia. Begun in 1890, it took 20 years to complete. It is a seven-story pagoda, 92 feet high, in the suburban village of Air Itam. Its three-level structure reflects the cultural mix of Buddhism on the island: its octagonal base is Chinese in form, the middle tiers of the pagoda are done in Thai style, and the round stupa-like spiral dome that tops it all is characteristically Burmese. Curiously harmonious and attractive, Kek Lok Si reflects the harmonious relations between the various groups it represents.

To reach the temple a visitor must climb along winding, arcaded steps hemmed by hawkers and souvenir sellers, push through hanging T-shirts, and clamber over stacks of gewgaws. The loud rock music and the smells of food add to the market atmosphere—the Chinese Buddhist way of bringing together the commercial and the religious.

Once the visitor reaches the top of the stairs, he or she emerges into a series of small plazas or squares leading to the shrines and temples. Although Kek Lok Si is a major pilgrimage site with a constant stream of visitors, no shrine predominates among the worship halls. The first open space, forming a frontier between the vendors' stalls and the last stairs to the complex, contains a gaudy tableau of the Buddha's first sermon in the deer park at Sarnath (Varanasi). Several temples with seated Buddhas draw devotees. The central statues are usually surrounded by numerous small Buddhas as well as formal statues of famous Buddhist teachers—all identical to indicate surrender of personality. Unlike most other Buddhist temples, there are no niches at Kek Lok Si for the ashes of saints or benefactors. Services are rare at the temples; not even the birthday of the Buddha—Wesak Day, a national holiday—is celebrated at the

The Kek Lok Si temple, located in Penang, Malaysia, reflects the cultural mix of Buddhism in its three distinctly styled levels—the octagonal base is Chinese, the middle tiers of the pagoda are Thai, and the spiral dome on top is Burmese.

temple but by a nighttime procession in the city of Penang.

Penang is a religious melting pot in a predominantly Muslim country, and Malay Buddhists of every extraction join in celebrating one another's feasts. Pilgrims worship in a variety of ways, offering incense or burning paper money, using prayer beads, or bowing and clapping (to attract the attention of the spirits); the diverse forms are characteristic of the different ethnic groups. Kek Lok Si also attracts large numbers of Overseas Chinese from Singapore, Hong Kong, and the Philippines.

On a hill above the complex, which includes a monastery for the monks who administer it, is a huge statue of Kuan Yin, the Goddess of Mercy, which can be seen from miles around. She is also featured in several shrines, and pilgrims can buy paper money to burn before her statues. Here, she is invoked by women for fertility.

References Heinz Bechert and Richard Gombrich (eds.), *The World of Buddhism.* London, Thames & Hudson, 1984. Fong Pheng Khuan, *Penang.* Boston, Houghton Mifflin, 1994. Leon Komber, *Chinese Ancestor Worship in Malaya.* Singapore, D. Moore, 1954.

KIBEHO, Rwanda

In late 1981, a 16-year-old boarder at a Catholic school in Kibeho, in central Rwanda, had what she realized was a vision of the Virgin Mary. Although the genocide of 1994 left only destruction in its wake and no shrine has been built at the site, Kibeho remains the only approved Marian apparition in Africa. It is becoming a symbol of hope for unity and forgiveness in a devastated nation.

Alphonsine Mumureke heard a voice call her as she was serving lunch in the cafeteria and saw a barefoot woman dressed in a white robe and veil. When asked who she was, the woman replied, "Ndi Nyina wa Jambo," which is translated as "I am the mother of the Word." Alphonsine's fellow students began to mock her, convinced that the vision of the Virgin Mary she had was the result of evil spirits, but soon other students also began receiving visions.

A year later, an illiterate pagan shepherd named Segatashya, living in the bush and unknown in Kibeho, heard a voice: "My child, if someone gives you a mission, would you be capable of carrying it out?" He spontaneously answered, "Yes." Segatashya claims to have received a nonverbal message that sent him on his way. Arriving at a village, he realized that he was naked. Segatashya heard a voice say, "Tell them that the Son of Man has come on the earth and one has to cast off his clothes. If you continue to carry out my message, you will be reclothed." Segatashya looked up to see an African man wearing a loin-cloth, surrounded by a brilliant light. His family took Segatashya away, calling him crazy, but two days later, Jesus appeared again, this time in the family compound. He taught Segatashya how to say the Lord's Prayer and the Rosary while the family looked on. Emmanuel, the name chosen for him by Jesus as he prepared for baptism, continued to have visions of Christ and later of the Virgin.

This series of apparitions created tremendous excitement among the Rwandese people. About 15,000 came to the college to see the visionaries in ecstasy. The local bishop set up an international investigating commission made up of physicians and theologians, a psychiatrist, and an anthropologist. They determined that the seers were mentally healthy and that there seemed to be no evidence of delusion. The crowds swelled to 20,000 at later apparitions but remained orderly and calm. The bishop was disposed to believe the visionaries, but a number of fake seers went to the media, even traveling about in neighboring countries seeking publicity. As a result, it took several years to discern who the true visionaries were, and after seven were officially acknowledged, worship at the site was approved. By this time, foreign pilgrims had begun to arrive, and a video of the visionaries in ecstasy was made in the United States and circulated widely.

The effect of the apparitions on the people of the area was profound. Spiritual renewal and conversion abounded, and there was a widespread return to prayer. Few physical cures were reported, however; Kibeho is concerned with spiritual revival rather than physical manifestations.

The message of the Virgin was one of repentance and prayer and return to Christ, common themes in apparitions. Emmanuel received messages for the clergy from Jesus calling for fidelity and care for the sick and poor. He reproached them and called the priests to conversion: "Look at yourself and correct yourselves!" The seers often blessed the crowd and sprinkled onlookers' rosaries with holy water. When the sick were presented to them, they gently laid the Bible on their heads. The seven showed several signs of mystical states, several of them being carried off on what they jokingly called "weekends with the Virgin," in which they seemed to go into deep coma. Emmanuel once fasted for 18 days, seven of which were without water.

Despite their drama, not all the messages were revealed to the public during the 1981–1989 period of the visions. One vision, which lasted eight hours, prophesied a hideous slaughter, with scenes of rivers of blood, a tree in flames, and fields of headless corpses. It was revealed only after the genocide of 1994–1995, in which nearly a mil-

lion persons were killed in a wanton slaughter. Meticulously planned down to the village and block level, an atrocity unparalleled in African history took place, in which Hutu militia and raging mobs killed most of the Tutsi population. Kibeho became a refuge for fleeing citizens, and the church was the scene of a horrific slaughter. These events have further convinced many of the truth of the apparitions. In the resulting confusion, the visionaries shared the fate of their people: Emmanuel was murdered, several fled into exile, and only one remains in Rwanda.

See also Marian Apparitions.
References *Kibeho, Africa: Apparitions of the Blessed Virgin.* Lima, PA, Marian Video, 1989. Gabriel Maindron, *Des apparitions à Kibeho.* Paris, OEIL, 1984. *Marian Apparitions of the Twentieth Century.* Lima, PA, Marian Video, 1991.

KILAUEA, Hawaii

Pele, the Hawaiian goddess of fire, has her traditional home atop Mount Kilauea, the world's most active volcano. The worship of Pele was introduced to the islands in the twelfth century by Tahitian conquerors, who also established human sacrifice and reorganized Hawaiian society into a new hierarchical order enforced by elaborate taboos. Pele was a protectress of the Hawaiian nation, and she joined the great King Kamehamea in battle against a rival trying to prevent him from uniting the islands. Kilauea exploded during that battle—its only recorded explosive eruption—driving off the enemy warriors.

Pele is believed to appear just before a new lava flow, to enable people to come to the volcano to observe and make sacrifice. She usually appears as an old witch or a beautiful woman. Since the lava flows are not explosive, they can be approached to the very edge, and devotees leave votive offerings to be consumed by the flames. Pele herself lives in the caldera, or central firepit, of the volcano, which until 1924 held a lake of molten lava. Smaller lava lakes formed briefly in 1967 and 1982, but the caldera can now be safely crossed. Ongoing eruptions began in 1983 and continue with regularity. The outpouring of the volcano has created a shoreline of black cinder and green sands alongside the white beaches.

It is customary for a pilgrim to leave an offering of 'ohelo berries from the 'ohi'alehua tree, which has fire-red blossoms. In Hawaiian myths, a young lover once rejected Pele, and in a fury she turned him into this tree. It is sacred to Pele, and leis made of the blossoms are worn in hula dances in Pele's honor. The hula is a gift of Pele, who ordered her younger sister Laka to create dance. Hula was a sacred art taught in temple schools, in which the dancers, accompanied by songs that come from the gods, seek to become united with the deity of that dance. Today there are attempts to revive the hula, which has become debased as a tourist entertainment.

In 1824, Chief Kapiolani, a recent convert to Christianity, went to the crater rim where she mockingly ate 'ohelo berries instead of offering them, and then cast stones into the lava and prayed to Jesus. When nothing happened to her, the event became a turning point in the Christianization of the islands. Nevertheless, Pele is the only Hawaiian deity to have survived the advent of Christianity, and many Hawaiians keep up a quiet reverence to her.

A food offering or a bottle of gin is an acceptable substitute offering for a lei or berries, since Pele likes a drink. Of the food offerings, roast pig is considered the best, since there was a taboo on women eating pork and only Pele had that privilege.

Human sacrifices were never offered to Pele, although the molten lava was used in the past for the cremation of bodies.

Although followers of New Age religions often make offerings, the Hawaiians believe that only indigenous people have that right, and they have protested the appropriation of the worship of Pele by others. Native Hawaiians are also battling the development of a geothermal plant on the slopes of the volcano as a profanation of sacred ground. Visitors are warned never to take souvenir rocks from the side of Kilauea because they bring misfortune. Every day, National Park rangers receive rocks returned by mail, with stories of bad luck that have befallen the senders

See also Mountains, Sacred.

References Martha Beckwith, *Hawaiian Mythology*. New Haven, CT, Yale University Press, 1940. Katherine Luomala, "Hawaiian Religion," in Mircea Eliade (ed.), *Encyclopedia of Religion*, vol. 6. New York, Macmillan, 1984. Leinani Melville, *Children of the Rainbow*. Wheaton, IL, Theosophical, 1990.

KONYA, Turkey

Konya's glory is that it was the home of Mevlâna (Our Guide) Jalalu'd-Din Rumi (1207–1273), one of the world's greatest religious mystics, philosophers, and poets. The most famous of his works is the *Spiritual Mathnawi*, ethical teachings presented in 40,000 double-rhymed verses written in Persian. The Mevlâna taught that love is the path to spiritual insight and practiced a broad toleration: "Come, whoever you are—fire-worshipper, idolaters, pagans—all who enter will be welcome here."

High on the central plateau of Turkey, an oasis of green in a dry area, Konya is an ancient city. It was called Iconium when St. Paul visited it, and because of its central location, it continued to thrive during the Byzantine period. (No evidence of Paul's visit remains, however). Today, Konya remains a holy city with a devout Islamic population.

The building that brings visitors to Konya is the former Tekke (monastery) of the Whirling Dervishes, now a government "museum," though the term is somewhat misleading. Even though the Dervishes have been banned, the Tekke is really a shrine, and its main room is the *türbe*, or tomb, of the Mevlåna. It is covered with a great velvet pall embroidered in gold. Beside him is his father, whose sarcophagus stands upright, for legend has it that when Rumi was buried, his father's tomb "rose and bowed in reverence." In the museum are vestments and musical instruments from the monastery, as well as a sacred relic, a hair from the beard of the Prophet Mohammed. Next door is the mosque of Selim II. It is considered part of the pilgrimages and attracts over a million Muslims every year. In addition to the Mevlevi complex, mosques and other Muslim monuments abound in Konya.

Among the Sufis—Muslims who practice a mystical form of Islam—religious life focuses on the Muslim Brotherhoods. These are religious fraternities inspired by great Muslim holy men who taught spiritual ways (*tariq*) to attain ecstasy, a state of trance where one comes into communion with Allah. There are a variety of techniques, including chanting the Ninety-Nine Names of Allah or meditation on some expression from the Qur'an. For the Dervishes, the technique is a sacred dance. Dressed in long pleated gowns and wearing high, cone-shaped hats, the Dervishes dance with arms outstretched, their right hands turned up to receive blessing from heaven, their left hands turned down to bestow it to the earth. They form a circle, each turning with the rhythm of the accompanying music as the circle itself moves around, a dignified circular dance that begins slowly and picks up tempo until all collapse in spiritual exaltation. The long white robes represent burial shrouds, and the hats a tombstone, symbolizing death to self, as the ecstasy is an entry into divine life. This was the way of the Mevlåna, and the tradition is still found in Egypt and Syria.

The secularization of Turkey after World War I was the policy of the great national hero, Kemal Attaturk. During the Ottoman period, the Dervishes had acquired power in the sultan's palace, so the Brotherhoods were regarded as reactionary and dangerous to the new republic. They were banned in 1925 and their properties confiscated, though a few members struggled on in secret until the dances were again allowed in 1953. At Konya, the Dervishes are permitted only at two annual festivals. Although they are officially only a cultural association, the Dervishes continue their tradition, recruiting new members and passing on the traditions of the order. Today, when the Brotherhoods throughout Islam are the vehicle of fundamentalism, the Dervishes are again on the rise in Turkey and are still regarded as a challenge to democratic government.

See also Kairouan; Touba.

References Shems Friedlander, *The Whirling Dervishes.* Albany, SUNY, 2d ed., 1991. David Hadland, *Rumi: The Persian Mystic.* Chicago, Kazi, 1985. Annemarie Schimmel, *I Am Wind, You Are Fire: The Life and Work of Rumi.* Boston, Shambhala Publishers, 1992.

KOREAN MARTYRS' SHRINES

Korea's first Christian was a young man who was converted after reading the Bible and some books he obtained from Jesuits at the court of the emperor of China. Returning home, he converted several prominent families to Christianity, which began to spread through study groups. These small communities were begun by Koreans without missionaries. When one of those converts, Yun Chi-Chung, refused to allow the ancestor cult at his mother's funeral in 1791, he was denounced and decapitated, setting off a widespread persecution. Four others followed in 1801, 1839, 1846, and 1866.

The first Korean Catholic priest, Kim Dae-gon, was martyred in 1846, but the main persecution came in 1866, when eight French missionaries were beheaded, followed by 8,000 of the 15,000 Korean Catholics. Sixty-four shrines, chapels, and tombs scattered throughout Korea commemorate this sacrifice. They vary from majestic churches to the simplest unmarked burial mounds. What is striking is the numbers of people who visit them consistently, even those in out-of-the-way places far from major cities. All are tended carefully by the faithful. In 1984, 103 Korean Martyrs were recognized as saints by Pope John Paul II.

Saenamt'o is a church built in pure Korean style on the site of the old execution spot for criminals. It was built by a Korean religious order, the Brothers of the Martyrs, in 1987, and its tiled and gabled roofs stand out in Seoul. Here various martyrs were killed throughout the nineteenth century, including St. Kim.

A public park near the Seoul rail station holds a modern memorial, again on an old execution site. Forty-four of the 103 recognized martyrs died here, including Lee Sung-Hoon, the first Korean Christian. The shrine is a narrow marble pyramid, flanked by a smaller one, both marked with bronze plaques depicting scenes of the martyrdoms.

Choldu-san (the name means "beheading hill") is a rocky promontory overlooking the Han River in Seoul. During the 1866 persecution, thousands of Christians were beheaded on the bluff and their bodies thrown over the cliff into the river. Since no public records were kept, only 31 are known by name. At the centenary in 1966, a shrine was built on the cliff, including a church, a museum, and a cemetery for 28 of the martyrs. There are also memorials for a number of other Koreans who died for their faith, including a life-sized statue of St. Kim Dae-gon Andrew, one of three Koreans who died in Japan, and another honoring several members of the same family who died together. The formal park setting attracts a regular stream of pilgrims and visitors. Kim himself is buried alongside his mother and eight unknown martyrs in a tiny chapel in Mirinae, a country village some distance from Seoul.

For the Koreans, martyrdom is not a past event, and the persecution of 1950–1953 in North Korea, in which several hundred clergy and many laity were killed or died in prison, is a fresh memory. A cycle of prayer on behalf of North Korean Christians is kept going constantly.

See also Martyrs' Hill.

References Donald Clark, *Christianity in Modern Korea.* Lanham, MD, University Press of America, 1986. James Grayson, *Korea: A Religious History.* Oxford, Clarendon Press, 1989. Earl Phillips and Eui-Yong Yu, *Religions in Korea.* Los Angeles, California State University, 1982.

KUMBH MELA SITES, India

The Kumbh Mela is perhaps the world's largest religious gathering. Hindu legend has it that a pitcher (*kumbha*) containing the nectar of immortality emerged from chaos when, at the creation, gods and demons stirred the ageless deeps. Before the gods won and drank the liquor of eternal life, they fought the demons over the pitcher. Four times the precious fluid spilled; these became the four sites of the Kumbh Mela festival: at *Allahabad* on the Ganges, *Nasik* on the Godavari, *Ujjain* on the Kshipra, and finally, *Hardwar* at the point where the Ganges emerges from the Himalayan Mountains. In that order, a festival is held every three years, and every 12 years a "great mela" is held, usually in Allahabad. The last (in 1989) drew 15 million people, while the intermediate melas attract between 3.5 and 10 million. The festival lasts up to two months, its length determined by astrological signs. The Kumbh Mela pilgrimages have been recorded from the thirteenth century and are certainly older.

The Kumbh Mela is known not only for its holiness but also for its violence, which Hindus accept as a sign that the gods and demons are still in conflict. Every few years there are incidents when hundreds of people are crushed in stampedes to get to the water at the times announced as most favorable by the astrologers. In the eighteenth century, warfare between sects was common, and in one festival, rival monks led armies into a battle where 18,000 died. Besides epidemics that break out because several million people are gathered under unsanitary conditions, murders and rapes always occur. The Thugs, an extremist sect that practices ritual murder to satisfy the blood-lust of the goddess Kali, finds victims on the steps of the bathing ghats.

The devout Hindu believes that the waters of sacred rivers, especially the Ganges, have the power to wash away sin back to the eighty-eighth generation of one's ancestors. These waters have themselves been washed by the drink of eternal life. Therefore, at the festival times, people throng the waters where broad stairs have been built leading into the rivers from temples and shrines. These ghats, or bathing platforms, are also used to wash away the ashes of those who have been cremated. Two of the main duties of the Hindu—worship and cremation of the dead—are therefore satisfied on the sacred rivers. The elderly sometimes come to the sacred cities for their last days, knowing that they will be cremated at the riverside and sent into the next life on the waters of the holy river. Offerings of candles or flowers are made to the rivers, placed on little leaf boats and floated down the streams. At night, the tiny flames mirror the starry skies in a lovely display.

The Kumbh Mela is the occasion for gatherings of holy men and ascetics for a kind of "Parliament" for religious and spiritual debates, since Hinduism has no teaching authority or hierarchy. There is a procession of naked *sadhus* (holy men), whose nudity is a sign they are detached from every worldly need. To gaze upon one of these men is to be instantly cleansed of sin. Various Hindu cults and sects also use the Kumbh Mela for initiation rites and ceremonies.

References Surinder Bhardwaj, *Hindu Places of Pilgrimage in India.* Berkeley, University of California, 1973. Steven Darian, *The Ganges in Myth and History.* Honolulu, University of Hawai'i Press, 1978. Tony Heiderer, "Sacred Space, Sacred Time: India's Maha Kumbh Mela," *National Geographic* 177:5, 106–117 (May 1990).

KYOTO, Japan

Kyoto is a city of 2,000 shrines and temples, and despite modernization, retains much of its spiritual sense. Since the ninth century it has been the imperial capital of Japan, which it continued to be long after Tokyo had become the government center. Rising to the northeast is a sacred mountain, Hiei, which became the center for the politically

Popularly known as the Golden Temple, the Kinkakuji Temple extends over a lake, its reflection giving it an appearance of being suspended between heaven and earth. The temple, originally built in 1397, had to be rebuilt in 1950 after a fanatic monk set fire to the temple.

powerful Tendai sect of Buddhism in 805 CE, whose *Enryakuji Monastery* once had 3,000 buildings and a standing army. Now a small fraction of that size, it remains, its continuity symbolized by three lamps that have burned ceaselessly for 1,200 years. The monastery, which is a pilgrimage center, conducts regular prayer rituals for the preservation of the Japanese state.

The *Ryoanji Temple* is known best for its sand garden, representing the sea. As a sign of the sea's restless, ever-changing nature, the garden is raked into a new design each day around 15 rocks that seem to float in this austere setting, surrounded by an earthen wall that anchors its perimeter. In Buddhism, 15 is the number of fullness, so from the viewing veranda, only 14 rocks can be seen at one time. Move slightly and the hidden rock appears, but another disappears. All 15 cannot be seen at once, demonstrating the human inability to grasp completeness.

Ginkakuji Temple is best approached by the lovely and meditative *Path of Philosophy*, which follows a small stream lined with cherry, willow, and maple trees. Originally the home of a powerful local ruler, Ginkakuji was converted to a temple around 1500. The name means "silver pavilion," in contrast to the "golden pavilion" (Kinkakuji) across the city, although the plans to cover it with silver foil never materialized. A statue of Kannon, Goddess of Mercy, is enshrined on the second story, and on the first are 1,000 statues of Jizo, guardian god of children. It was at Ginkakuji that the elaborate Japanese tea ceremony was first raised to a high art, and the original tea ceremony room is preserved. Ginkakuji has a sand garden featuring high cones symbolizing mountains; because it sparkles in the moonlight it is called the "Sea of Silver Sand."

Kinkakuji Temple, known as the Golden Temple, was first built in 1397, but in 1950 a fanatic monk burnt it to the ground. The present buildings are exact replicas of the first temple. The temple is covered with gold leaf and juts out over a lake, itself an exquisite creation that seems a different place from every angle, with rocks and tiny islets placed to attract the eye. The Kinkakuji is reflected in the water so that the temple seems suspended between heaven and earth. It is the image of the power and magnificence of the ruler who built it, but it is serene in its setting. Kinkakuji presents one of the most-photographed scenes in Japan.

References Diane Durston, *Kyoto: Seven Paths to the Heart of the City.* New York, Weatherhill, 1992. Charles McCarry and George Mobley, "Kyoto and Nara: Keepers of Japan's Past," *National Geographic* 149:6, 636–658 (June 1976). Peter Popham, *Wooden Temples of Japan.* London, Tauris Parke, 1990.

L

LAKMUANG SHRINE, Thailand

In the center of Bangkok, a small brick temple called Lakmuang Shrine honors the guardian god of the city, represented by a slender red stone idol. *Lak Muang* means "strength of the city," and the pillar, set there by King Rama I at the foundation of Bangkok in 1782, is the official place from which all distances in the country are measured. Its similarity to the Hindu *lingam*, which represents the sex organ of the god Shiva, has made it a fertility shrine as well, and many women come to pray either for pregnancy or an easy delivery.

The scene at Lakmuang is a busy one reminiscent of a medieval fair. People buy incense sticks and necklaces of flowers to be laid before the idol or hung on the fences around the shrine. Because the deity is also considered an oracle, a number of Chinese, who believe in fortune-telling, also come to Lakmuang. The deity is thought to bring good fortune, especially in the national lottery, and lottery ticket sellers throng the shrine precincts. Fortune tellers and horoscope readers do an active business in the courtyard.

When a devotee has received a favor from the guardian spirit of the shrine, he or she often expresses thanks by commissioning a sacred dance. There is a small theater on the grounds for this purpose, where a professional troupe performs traditional dances and songs. Not all are serious. Indeed, some skits are broad comedy or farce, with stage antics reminiscent of vaudeville. They draw laughter and cheers from the audience members, who are, through the act of enjoyment, earning merit. Strolling musicians and freelance entertainers roam the precincts offering Buddhist legends set to music; the most common instruments are gongs and drums.

The Thai understanding of virtue allows the devout to earn merit by any good deed, and the most meritorious will be reincarnated in the next life at a more advanced stage. Prayers, offerings, and good deeds combine to benefit both the seeker after merit and anyone who joins in—even one who shares in the enjoyment of a play or musical offered for the god. One can buy a caged bird from a stall and set it free to earn merit or engage in a number of other activities.

See also Erawan Shrine.

References Ormond McGill, *Religious Mysteries of the Orient.* South Brunswick, NJ, Barnes, 1976. Alistair Shearer, *Thailand: The Lotus Kingdom.* London, John Murray, 1989. Rudolph Wurlitzer, *Hard Travel to Sacred Places.* Boston, Shambhala, 1995.

LALIBELA, Ethiopia

A series of thirteen churches were carved into a sandstone cliff in the northern mountains of Ethiopia about 1,000 years ago by King Lalibela. According to legend, when the king began the prodigious task of carving a series of churches from living rock, angels came at night to continue where the workmen left off at the end of the day. The historical facts are more prosaic. King Lalibela was of the line of the

The church of Saint George, one of thirteen churches that are connected by a series of tunnels, was constructed 40 feet beneath ground level and has been in continuous use since the twelfth century.

Zagwe dynasty, which seized the throne around 1000 CE. When his rivals increased in power, he looked around for some way to gain the favor of the powerful Ethiopian Church and undertook the construction of thirteen churches at his capital, a small town named after him. The result was unexpected in two ways: it created a place of unparalleled religious beauty, and it brought about King Lalibela's conversion. After laboring for 20 years, he abdicated the throne to become a hermit, living on roots and vegetables. Ethiopian Christians regard him as one of their greatest saints.

The king's intention was to create a New Jerusalem for those who were unable to make a pilgrimage to the Holy Land. He made no attempt to copy the holy places and Lalibela is unique. Its setting is stunning: wild crags a mile and a half high, with hanging cliffs. The thirteen churches there were not constructed, but excavated. Each church was cut from the living bedrock and is a single solid piece, painstakingly hollowed out. Each is surrounded by trenches into which hermits' cells have been cut out. The largest church has walls 35 feet high. The roofs are level with the ground and can be reached through stairs descending into narrow trenches. They have been in continuous use since they were built in the twelfth century. Bet Giorgis (St. George's), perhaps the most spectacular of the churches, is cut 40 feet down. Its exterior was carved first; then it was painstakingly hollowed out. Fragile windows are sculpted in many forms of crosses, swastikas (an ancient Eastern motif), and even Muslim traceries. Several churches also have wall paintings. In Bet Maryam is a pillar on which King Lalibela wrote the secrets of the buildings. It is covered with drapes and only the priests may look on it.

The churches are connected by tunnels and walkways that stretch across sheer drops. Pilgrims believe that if they pass over these three times they will be saved; if they fall, they will go to hell. The interior pillars of the churches have been worn smooth by the hands of supplicating worshippers. On feast days, the priests bring out the *tabots*, the carved tablets kept by every Ethiopian church that are copies of the Tablets of the Law believed to rest in Axum. They are covered by beautiful fabrics and are taken outside to tents, where they are kept during an overnight prayer vigil before being triumphantly returned to the churches in procession.

Lalibela has 7,000 people; 1,000 of them are priests. The Ethiopian Church retains many ancient Jewish customs, including circumcision and a form of kosher food regulation. Extensive fasts are held. Liturgies are often conducted with crowds of singing and dancing priests, and the church teaches that the original Ark of the Covenant is in Axum. All these elements contribute to the sense of place that is biblical—timeless and serene, largely untouched by modern life.

See also Axum; Debra Libanos.

References Graham Hancock, *The Sign and the Seal*. New York, Crown, 1992. Marilyn Heldman et al., *African Zion*. New Haven, CT, Yale University, 1994. Angela Schuster, "Hidden Sanctuaries of Ethiopia," *Archaeology* 47:1, 28–35 (January 1994).

LINDISFARNE, England

One of England's oldest missionary centers, Lindisfarne is on Holy Island in the North Sea. The site, on Britain's east coast, is remote and can be visited only at low tide, when enough sand is exposed to make it possible to cross from the mainland.

In the seventh century a Benedictine abbey was built at Lindisfarne by St. Aidan. He was succeeded by Cuthbert (+687), who was both abbot and bishop there and was credited with bringing the Christian faith to northern England. After his death, St. Cuthbert was recognized as the apostle of the north. His popularity is based on his efforts for the poor, caring for those struck by the plague and working miraculous cures.

Holy Island's location was its downfall. Directly across from Denmark, it was an easy target for marauding Viking raiders, who pillaged and burned villages and abbeys. The abbeys were particularly easy marks, because the monks were completely nonviolent and refused even to defend themselves. In the ninth century it was decided to remove the treasures of the monastery inland to protect them from raids. Cuthbert's body, which was already

Partial walls are all that remains of the Lindisfarne priory, which was built in 1093.

attracting pilgrims, was taken to Durham Cathedral, where his shrine became a prominent medieval pilgrimage site. When Henry VIII's agents came to loot the treasure of the shrine, the body was found incorrupt, causing the shrine to be saved.

Little remains of the monastic settlement on Holy Island—only some walls of the 1093 priory and a few ruins of monastic buildings. Pilgrims visit these ruins, the thirteenth-century parish church, and the empty tombs of St. Cuthbert and St. Aidan. The medieval Pilgrim Route is posted with wooden poles, which disappear under the tide. The island also functions as a nature sanctuary and continues to attract 50,000 visitors annually, including pilgrims. It is privately owned, but access is not restricted.

References Christopher Bamford, *Celtic Christianity.* Hudson, NY, Lindisfarne Press, 1987. Brendan Lehane, *The Quest of Three Abbots.* Hudson, NY, Lindisfarne Press, 1994. *The Lindisfarne Gospels.* Rohnert Park, CA, Pomegranate Artbooks, 1995. Magnus Magnusson, *Lindisfarne, the Cradle Island.* Boston, Oriel Press, 1984.

LISIEUX, France

The Sanctuary of the Little Flower, known by the nickname given to Sainte-Thérèse of Lisieux, one of the most popular saints of the twentieth century, stands in Lisieux, a small town in Normandy. It is neither attractive nor the site of any miraculous events or visions. Indeed, the basilica is ugly and garish, in total contrast with the simplicity of the woman whose remains are enshrined in it. Even so, large numbers of pilgrims are attracted by the inspiration of a woman who taught a deep yet simple spirituality known as "the little way."

In 1888, at only 15, Thérèse Martin entered the cloistered Carmelite convent in Lisieux after much opposition from Church authorities, who gave in after she appealed personally to the pope. She died there of tuberculosis in 1897 after writing a remarkable autobiography, *The Story of a Soul*, at the request of her prioress. Published after her death, it was translated into 50 languages and remains popular today. Her message is straightforward, offering a path to holiness in everyday life. Thérèse had no visions and performed no miracles in her lifetime; her spirituality is based on the banal routines of life, transformed by God's merciful love. The positive tone of her teaching is the book's greatest attraction, along with the delightful, wry anecdotes with which she illustrates her life story.

Despite her seclusion, Thérèse was intensely interested in foreign missions and petitioned to be sent to a convent in the Third World. She corresponded with a number of French missionaries in Vietnam and is regarded as patroness of foreign missions. Consequently, many missionaries visit her shrine on their way to their new assignments. In the crypt of the basilica are the tombs of members of her family, but Thérèse is buried simply in the sisters' cemetery at the convent next to the basilica.

References Alain Cavalier, *Thérèse*. Des Moines, IA, Ingram International, 1986 (video). Dorothy Day, *Therese*. Springfield, IL, Templegate, 1979. Ronald Knox (ed.), *Therese of Lisieux: The Story of a Soul*. San Francisco, Harper SF, 1991.

LOPPIANO, Italy

Outside Florence lies Loppiano, a small town that is the center of a worldwide community dedicated to principles of love and unity—the Focolare. Founded by an Italian woman, Chiara Lubich, the Focolare has expanded from its Catholic roots to embrace an ecumenical Christian membership. Loppiano, with some 800 Focolarini living there, is the most important of the movement's 40 "cities of faith."

The Focolare arose from the ashes of World War II. Gathered in an air-raid shelter in 1943, Chiara Lubich and a small circle of friends began to tend to the needs of those confined with them. It seemed that when all their personal hopes and plans for the future were stripped away by the war, only love made sense. They pledged themselves to seek a way that would allow them to spread this experience. *Focolare* means "gathered around the hearth," and its spirit includes a strong family element. Its primary religious practice features regular periods of Scripture sharing using a Gospel text chosen for a month of meditation and reflection. The emphasis is always on the lived and experienced Gospel and its power to create and build community among its members. Chiara Lubich is a powerful but not domineering personality. In 1977 her work of building bridges among Christians was recognized with the Templeton Prize, often regarded as the "Nobel Prize for Religion."

The Focolare has fostered a number of associated ecumenical movements, all of which welcome Muslims, Buddhists, and Jews as well as Christians, and have attracted 87,000 members to its various expressions. It is best known for its development of youth gatherings called Genfests—"people's festivals"—that draw thousands of young people to experience unity in celebration, sharing, and prayer. Each summer, over 100 encampments come together, with some 100,000 young people in attendance. These festivals have developed into more permanent Focolare towns modeled on Loppiano.

Anyone is welcome to the monthly sharing sessions at any Focolare community around the world, and the members may be from any situation in life—married, single, or divorced, of any age or class. At the heart of the community, however, are the Focolarini, a grouping of dedicated members who live in common, share their goods, and are celibate. They exhibit most of the characteristics of a religious order without many of its structures and are regarded as a lay movement in the Catholic church. The Focolare does not sponsor schools or hospitals; the members work at whatever professions and jobs their talents allow. The emphasis is on living together in a harmonious community of faith and sharing that gift with others. Its most notable Catholic tradition is a strong devotion to Mary, the mother of Jesus, and Loppiano is officially called Mariopolis, the "city of Mary."

Loppiano was founded in 1964 on a property inherited by four sisters and brothers who were members of the Focolare. Its primary purpose is to be a "city of the spirit," a place where all expressions of the Focolare may come together from every continent and every race to experience and witness to unity and to refresh themselves at the wellspring of the movement. Loppiano has all the services of a normal town, including a school for residents' children. A woodworking shop makes craft items for sale, while others make clothing for the residents, produce artwork, and take in contract work in a small assembly plant. Loppiano also serves as the training center for aspiring Focolarini, who come to the town for a period of two years as part of their candidacy. These young people live in small communities scattered around the town in residential neighborhoods, where Focolare families live in private homes. The focus of Loppiano's day of work, shared prayer, and common meals is a Mass celebrated for all at noon. Though there is no mistaking the Catholic atmosphere and spirit of the place, Loppiano also accepts and involves a variety of visitors, who flow through it for periods of a few days or weeks. Many of these are merely curious, but others are eager seekers for spiritual truth. All share in the common work while in Loppiano.

References Focolare Movement, *Unity Our Adventure.* Hyde Park, NY, New City, 1987. Chiara Lubich, *May They All Be One.* New York, New City, 1984. Franca Zambonini, *Chiara Lubich: A Life for Unity.* London, New City, 1992.

LORETO, Italy

One of the stranger shrines and relics in Christianity is the Holy House of Loreto, in the town of that name in central Italy. It is alleged to be the house where an angel told Mary that she would be the mother of Jesus. The Holy House first appears in history when St. Helena, the mother of the Emperor Constantine, heard of its discovery in the Holy Land and protected it by building a church around it. Thus it remained through the Arab occupation and the Crusader period, until the Muslims again began to invade Palestine.

Miraculously, according to legend, it was transported to Dalmatia in modern Croatia in 1291, to a field where there had been no house before. A vision revealed that it was Mary's house, which had disappeared from the Holy Land shortly before the Muslims seized the area. Three years later, angels again carried it across the Adriatic Sea in advance of another Muslim invasion, this time to the town of Loreto in Italy. The myth of the Holy House says that the trees bowed down in respect as it was lowered into place. Archaeological evidence attests, more prosaically, that the house was shipped by sea. It is made of limestone and cedar, neither of which are available in the region of Loreto. The walls of the structure are the originals, and the materials match the foundation of the supposed Holy House in Nazareth. As one authority has written, Loreto has received "the ridicule of one half of the world and the devotion of the other."

The Holy House itself is quite small, a single room with a small altar, a black Madonna statue, and a blue ceiling with gold stars. To protect it, a large church was built around it in 1500, and it was approved for pilgrimages in 1510. Its most popular devotion, the Litany of Loreto, is a series of invocations of Mary addressing her by many of her medieval titles: Ark of the Covenant, Mystical Rose, Seat of Wisdom. This devotion is popular throughout the Catholic world.

Because of the legend of the "flying house," Our Lady of Loreto is patroness of aviators. A Loreto statuette went along with Charles Lindbergh on the first solo flight across the Atlantic, and a Loreto medallion accompanied *Apollo 9* on its trip to the moon.

References Floriano Grimaldi, *La historia della Chiesa di Santa Maria de Loreto*, Loreto, Italy, Casa di resparmio di Loretto, 1993. Kenneth MacGowan, *An Illustrated History of the House of Loreto*. Loreto, Italy, Santa Casa, 1976.

LOUGH DERG, Ireland

Tiny Station Island (Lough Derg means the "red lake," which is located on the island) is the site of one of Ireland's great penitential pilgrimages. It is surrounded by legends, including one that contends that a cave there is the entrance to Purgatory, and that the voices of the dead can be heard speaking from its depths. Its association with penance comes from the tradition that St. Patrick once spent the 40 days of Lent in prayer and fasting on the island; during his stay, he drove the evil spirits from the cave and received a vision of Purgatory—hence the island's popular nickname, "St. Patrick's Purgatory." Whatever the tales, the island has been a place of pilgrimage since the eighth century, and the ruins of six hermits' cells—"the penitential beds"—attest to ancient use. Today the island is completely covered with buildings, including a large basilica church famed for its stained-glass windows of the Stations of the Cross.

Lough Derg was known throughout Europe in the Middle Ages, when pilgrimages were harsh and demanding. From 1100 to 1500, noblemen came to do penance for their sins, especially for the atrocities of war. The penitent spent 15 days on the island for the prescribed spiritual exercises, ending with being locked up in the cave without food or water for 24 hours as a symbol of Purgatory. To prepare for this day, penitents spent the first two weeks fasting on bread and water, with total abstinence from food or drink on the day before entering the cave. They lay on the ground as a sign of passing through death, and the full Office of the Dead was chanted over them by monks. When they emerged, the penitents plunged themselves into the Lough Derg three times as a sign of being cleansed.

In 1632, during the Reformation, the pilgrimages were banned by the Puritans and the statues and relics smashed. Despite this and, after 1704, the fines that were levied against them, pilgrims continued to come to the island. After the Catholic Emancipation in 1829, which permitted Catholics full liberty to practice their religion, the number of visitors increased. During the terrible famine year of 1846, 30,000 pilgrims visited the island.

The pilgrimage season is from June 1 to August 15, and about 25,000 come each year; the minimum age is 17. Today, the spiritual regimen at Lough Derg is three days, not counting a day of fasting before arrival. The first night is spent in an all-night vigil of prayer. One daily meal is served on the island—black tea and bread. The penitents remain barefoot and keep total silence at all times, except for group prayers. Pilgrims make their ways around nine stations, or shrines, including crosses that honor St. Patrick and St. Brigid, patrons of Ireland. There are 1,449 prescribed prayers; one, for example, requires pilgrims to stand facing away from St. Brigid's Cross, intoning, "I renounce the World, the Flesh, and the Devil." They also circle the basilica and the penitential beds several times, an ancient Irish pilgrim custom. One night is spent in vigil inside the locked basilica, its closing doors a reminder of the medieval enclosure in the cave. The cave itself has been sealed since 1780.

See also Croagh Patrick.

References John Dunne, *Shrines of Ireland*. Dublin, Veritas, 1989. Marie de France, *St. Patrick's Purgatory*. Binghamton, NY, Medieval and Renaissance Texts, 1993. Peter Harbison, *Pilgrimage in Ireland*. Syracuse, NY, Syracuse University, 1991.

LOURDES, France

A small city framed by mountains in the south of France, Lourdes is the site of the most famous series of apparitions of the Virgin Mary. An endless stream of pilgrims comes here to find healing, both physical and spiritual.

The story begins simply with a 14-year-old peasant girl named Bernadette Soubirous. One cold February day in 1858,

as she was gathering firewood, she saw a mysterious Lady. Bernadette was not overly religious, and indeed, had been held back from receiving her first Communion because she did not know her catechism. The vision emerged from a small grotto across the millstream from where Bernadette stood, and she said later that all fear left her in the Lady's presence. It was the first of 19 apparitions of the Virgin Mary that Bernadette would experience.

During the ninth apparition, Mary revealed a small spring, which soon became known for the miraculous cures associated with it. Mary later asked that a chapel be built on the spot, and finally, Bernadette asked her name. She had to insist three times, and at last the Lady said, "I am the Immaculate Conception." The Catholic tradition that Mary had been conceived without original sin so that she might be worthy to be the mother of God had only been formally defined as official Church doctrine in 1854; the theological expression would have meant nothing to the simple peasant girl.

Bernadette's parish priest became convinced of her sincerity, but government authorities were less approving and fenced off the grotto, arresting and fining people who crossed over to pray. It took an order from Emperor Napoleon III to open the area to pilgrims. Even then, the local bishop undertook an exhaustive (and to the frail girl, exhausting) investigation, and Bernadette was quizzed, questioned, prodded, and harassed by theologians, physicians, and psychologists. She never altered her account: "I do not ask you to believe; I only told you what I had seen." The bishop accepted the apparitions and approved the shrine in 1862. In 1866, Bernadette entered a convent hundreds of miles north, but she still suffered from the incessant curiosity of tourists. She never showed interest in the miraculous healings and never sought one. She died of tuberculosis in 1879 and was recognized as a saint by the Catholic church in 1933.

The railroad to Lourdes was completed the same year Bernadette entered the convent, which made Lourdes the first shrine to benefit from modern transportation. The number of pilgrims quickly began to expand. Today pilgrims come from all over the world by bus, chartered plane, and special trains, most as part of an organized pilgrimage with its own chaplain. The spirit of Lourdes is bourgeois, and the streets leading to the shrine are lined with shops selling every religious trinket imaginable, some reverential and others merely tacky and tasteless. Glow-in-the-dark rosaries, water jugs in the shape of the Virgin Mary, automobile pendants, and Marian refrigerator magnets all compete for the tourist's attention. The shrine area, however, turns its back on the commercial vulgarity of the town. In a peaceful park with no commercial outlets, it accommodates the large crowds in an atmosphere of dignity and recollection. Pilgrims feel that they have left a tawdry world and entered a place of prayer.

The focus of the pilgrims is an area known as the grotto, where the miraculous spring has been channeled into a long row of spigots where visitors may collect "Lourdes water" and take it home. People bring votive candles up to several feet in height to set against the grotto wall, and even on a day when the shrine is not crowded, these number in the thousands. It is possible to attend Mass at the grotto in a variety of languages. The local anthem, the Lourdes Hymn, has been translated into most languages in the world and is known by Catholics worldwide. To hear it sung simultaneously in German, English, Italian, Tagalog, and Polish—not an unusual combination—is to experience an affirmation of the universality of faith.

The daily processions—especially the Rosary procession held by torchlight each evening—are moving, but the entire shrine area is active throughout the day and evening with various services, processions, and blessings of the sick. The basilica of the apparitions rises in three tiers with ramps arching out to allow access by wheelchair to all levels. Another smaller sanctuary sits across the stream from the grotto, and a cavernous underground church seats 20,000.

In Lourdes are a small hospital and a number of hostels to serve the needs of the infirm and seriously ill, for Lourdes is a place where one comes seeking a miraculous cure. The first cure took place after the thirteenth apparition, restoring the sight of a blind stonecutter after his eyes were bathed in Lourdes water. Since then, thousands of physical cures of the most astounding sort have taken place. Baths were set up, and in 1882 a medical bureau was established to test the validity of the cures.

Lourdes is the world's most prominent center for the application of scientific analysis to alleged miraculous cures. A permanent staff documents the cures in collaboration with an international committee that includes physicians from every important medical specialty. The committee is open to medical professionals of any faith (or none) who wish to examine pilgrims claiming cures, and its archives are available to medical professionals for research. The person claiming a miraculous cure must have come to Lourdes with medical testimony that he suffers from an incurable condition. Without this, or if the record is too vague, no medical investigation will be conducted. When an investigation occurs, the conclusion is placed in one of four possible categories: (1) there has been no cure;

(2) a partial cure has taken place; (3) there has been a cure, but there are medical or psychological reasons for it; or (4) there has been a cure for which there is no natural or scientific explanation. The pilgrim must then return after a year for further examination.

The medical bureau never pronounces a cure to be a miracle, which would be beyond its scientific scope. Nor does the Church have any process for certifying a miracle. People are left free to believe or disbelieve as they wish. By 1910 there were over 4,000 "category four" cures, and they continue at a rate of about 15 a year.

See also Marian Apparitions.

References G. Bertin, *Lourdes: A History of Its Apparitions and Cures.* New York, Gordon, 1973. Ruth Cranston, *The Miracle of Lourdes.* New York, Doubleday, Medical Bureau Edition, 1988. Patrick Marnham, *Lourdes: A Modern Pilgrimage.* London, Heinemann, 1980. Franz Werfel, *The Song of Bernadette.* New York, Viking, 1942.

LUTHER CIRCLE, Germany

Martin Luther (1483–1546), the man who brought the simmering religious discontent of the sixteenth century to the boiling point and sparked the Protestant Reformation, lived and died within a small area in eastern Germany. The circle of towns associated with his life has become a pilgrimage route.

Luther was born in *Eisleben,* where he also died while on a return visit. His birthday and his baptism are jointly observed there on November 10–11 by Catholics and Lutherans, who celebrate together the feast of St. Martin of Tours, after whom Luther was named. The "birth house," as it is known locally, has been a museum for over 300 years and is the logical first stop on the Luther Circle. The "death house" contains the winding sheet placed on Luther's body after his death; this is revered by many Lutherans as a holy relic. In the town are two churches associated with Luther: Ss. Peter and Paul, where he was baptized, and St. Andrew's, where he preached his last sermon two days before his death. In the nearby village of *Mansfield* is the substantial Luther home where Martin was raised.

A law student, the son of a miner turned prosperous merchant, Luther had a conversion experience when he was knocked down by lightning and made a vow to become a monk. At *Erfurt,* Luther studied as a young Augustinian friar and was ordained a priest. The monastery cloister where Luther lived is used today as a Lutheran school. Several books on display there have notes in Luther's handwriting, and a cell in which he slept has been preserved.

Wittenberg, where he lived for 36 years, is the city most associated with Luther and the first place to accept his teachings. Tradition says that it was here, in 1517, that Luther, a professor of scripture at the university, nailed 95 propositions for debate to the door of the Castle Church, setting off the arguments that ended with the establishment of Protestantism. The church contains the tombs of Luther, his disciple Melancthon, and the Elector Frederick the Wise. Its interesting decorations include statues and fine stained-glass windows, installed in 1983, depicting the 12 leading European reformers. In 1989, the tradition of protest against authoritarianism was renewed; the Castle Church pulpit was a leading one in the movement that opposed and eventually brought down Communism.

Besides the Castle Church on the main square, there is the Town Church where Luther preached, with a magnificent altarpiece done by Lucas Cranach the Elder,

Luther's friend and the first Protestant artist. The lower panels of the altarpiece show the Lutheran religious system: Melancthon performing a baptism, the Communion of the people, public confession, and Luther preaching from the open Bible. Here the first Mass was celebrated in German (1522) and the Communion cup was first given to the people, causing the Town Church to call itself the "Mother Church of the Reformation." Luther baptized his six children in its baptismal font. One of Cranach's paintings depicts Judas, the traitor, as a contemporary Jew, and a carved relief outside the church is offensively anti-Semitic, with a blasphemous inscription, revealing something of the dark side of Luther's culture.

One gains the best sense of Luther as a person, however, from the Luther Hall, the priory where Luther lived as an Augustinian friar and which the town gave him after the friary was dissolved. Here he lived with his family and a few students. His wife's wedding ring, other personal effects, a Gutenberg Bible, his pulpit, and several of Cranach's paintings, all bring the visitor closer to the great reformer. Cranach's house is nearby, as is that of Luther's great friend, the theologian Philip Melancthon, whom Luther called "Germany's teacher." This house is still as Melancthon left it; it was both his home and a school in the 1520s.

After Luther's denunciation for heresy in 1521, he was spirited away for safekeeping to *Eisenach*, where he lived at the Wartburg Castle high above the town, writing and translating the New Testament into German. At one point, legend says, Luther was tempted by Satan, and he dismissed the Evil One by throwing an inkwell at the Devil. The wall has been carved away by the faithful seeking mementoes of that legendary event. Eisenach attracts Lutheran pilgrims from around the world.

References Roland Bainton, *Here I Stand: A Life of Martin Luther.* New York, New American Library, 1989. Merle Severy, "The World of Martin Luther," *National Geographic* 164:4, 418–463 (October 1983). *Where Luther Walked.* Burnsville, MN, Charthouse International, 1983 (video).

MACHU PICCHU, Peru

The mysterious Inca city and ceremonial center of Machu Picchu lies high in the Peruvian Andes, 50 miles northwest of Cuzco, capital of the Inca Empire. Its existence was unknown until 1911; it is not mentioned in accounts of the Incas from the time of the Spanish conquest. Machu Picchu ("old peak") is not the city's Inca name, which is unknown.

The Incas worshipped the features of the earth, especially high mountains. The mountains were perceived to be the source of water and weather and had to be appeased with human sacrifices. (In late 1995 a fifteenth-century ceremonial center was discovered on a mountain that included several well-preserved bodies of sacrificial maidens.) The mountain gods, in particular, were worshipped at Machu Picchu, which straddles a ridge between their two most sacred mountains—both over 20,000 feet high. A sacred river runs in a horseshoe around the base of the mountain. From it, Machu Picchu rises in terraces, laboriously farmed to provide food for the nobles and residents. Machu Picchu was occupied from 1476 to 1534 CE, and it sits on a steep hill guarding a pass to the Amazon River Valley. The ruins are substantial and extensive, including houses, a temple plaza, and granaries.

The Sacred Plaza, reached by thousands of granite stairs, was the scene of most ceremonies. At one end of the plaza is a large temple with an altar stone cut from a single, 14-foot piece of granite, evidently modeled on the Temple of the Sun at Cuzco. The temple priests conducted rites to "tie" the sun to the altar of the god Inti at the winter solstice, so that the sun would return and not fade away. Since the emperor himself (called the Inca) was considered the descendant of the sun, these rites were critical for the continuance of the nation. Second only to the Inca himself were the sacred Virgins of the Sun, its mystical brides, who served the temple. The altar, the *Intihuatana* ("hitching-post of the sun"), was also used as a solar observatory and for divination, which involved examining the entrails of slaughtered llamas for signs from the gods.

The mountain city was also used for ritual burials, and in 1912 a burial cave was found with 173 skeletons, 150 of which were women, who had the richest graves. It is speculated that these are the remains of the Virgins of the Sun. Other graves of important women have been found in the city itself.

No one knows the cause of Machu Picchu's decline. Clearly a royal center, it was a well-protected refuge that the Spaniards never discovered. Perhaps the populace fled during a plague. Or perhaps the residents were ritually slaughtered—the punishment for any town where one of the Virgins of the Sun was defiled by having sex. The answer has remained a mystery.

Along the southern Peruvian coast stretch a long series of lines, animal figures, and designs that are observable only from the air. The Nazca Lines, as they are called after a prehistoric people who inhabited the area, date from the third century BCE. They point toward sacred mountains and may

Atop the Andes mountains lies the ruins of the city Machu Picchu, which were not discovered until 1911. Built at the height of Inca power in the fifteenth century, the ancient city served as a refuge from the conquering Spaniards, who never discovered it.

have been used to invoke the blessings of rain.

See also Cuzco; Nazca Lines.

References John Bierhorst, *Black Rainbow: Legends of the Incas and Myths of Ancient Peru*. New York, Farrar, Straus and Giroux, 1976. Evan Hadingham, *Lines to the Mountain Gods: Nazca and the Mysteries of Peru*. New York, Random House, 1987. John Hemming, *Machu Picchu*. New York, Newsweek Books, 1981. Pablo Neruda, *The Heights of Machu Picchu*. London, Jonathan Cape, 1966.

MARIAN APPARITIONS

Large numbers of shrines around the world are connected with apparitions of the Virgin Mary. In both Catholic and Orthodox traditions, the authority for approving apparitions rests with the local bishop, not with the pope or the patriarch. The criteria for approval are straightforward: (1) The visionaries must be honest, psychologically balanced, morally upright, and respectful of Church authority; (2) those responding to the message should experience healthy religious devotion and not collective hysteria; (3) the revelations should be free of doctrinal and moral error; (4) making money should not be a motive for the visionaries; (5) the facts of the case should be free from error and studied objectively by experts, usually including a psychiatrist.

In recent years alleged apparitions have increased notably—over 100 in the United States alone since 1980. Because Marian apparitions lend themselves to superstition and credulity, bishops have been universally slow to approve them until they have been tested. Over 90 percent have been rejected as based on unbalanced delusions or erroneous doctrine. Most of these have lost their followings soon after, but a few have created their own cults, such as the apparitions of Garabandal (described below) and those of Bayside, New York (1975–present). Among other eccentric teachings at Bayside is Mary's reputed allegation that the pope is a satanic agent, an imposter created by a plastic surgeon. Not surprisingly, the revelations from Bayside include anti-Semitic statements.

Protestant traditions have historically disapproved of apparitions, most especially those involving Mary. They consider any mediator between God and his people—other than Jesus Christ—unnecessary. All Christian traditions agree, however, that God's revelation to humanity ended with the biblical period. Any further inspiration or revelation is strictly private and unable to add anything to basic Christian teaching.

Apparitions usually result in the creation of a shrine. These are numerous; the account of Marian shrines in Spain alone fills three volumes. In addition to those listed at the end of this article, the following are a cross-section of Marian apparitions of modern times:

Akita, Japan, 1973. Sister Katsuko Sasagawa was totally deaf when she first saw a white light coming from the tabernacle (the small metal safe used for storing the Eucharist) of the chapel of her convent in northern Japan. A few weeks later, a wound shaped like a cross appeared on her left palm, and when she prayed before a statue of Our Lady of All Nations that had been carved by a Buddhist sculptor, she heard a voice address her as "my daughter." The

next day a wound like Sister Katsuko's appeared on the hand of the statue, oozing blood. During this time, Sister Katsuko experienced visits from her guardian angel, who joined her in prayer, and Mary spoke again to her, asking for repentance from sin. In two weeks, her wound was cured. The statue, however, continued to exhibit dramatic manifestations. Over a hundred times in the following years it was seen to weep, and in 1982 Sister Katsuko was instantly cured of her deafness. In response to this and other cures, and after investigations, in 1984 the bishop of Niigata proclaimed the visions to be valid.

Banneux, Belgium, 1933. When Mariette Beco, 11, saw a beautiful Lady in the garden, she immediately recognized her as the Virgin Mary. Mariette and her family were poor prospects for visionaries; they had stopped attending Mass and Mariette had dropped her catechism classes. Her mother, who could see only a vague outline, declared the vision to be a witch and forbade her daughter to go out. A second appearance took place a few days later when the Lady led Mariette to a place where she uncovered a spring. Mary brought Mariette to the spring several more times, saying, "I am come to relieve suffering." She called herself the Virgin of the Poor. The spring became an important curative shrine, and in 1949, after an exhaustive study, the bishop proclaimed the authenticity of the apparitions. The grounds, in a pine forest, include a number of chapels and small shrines and a 320-bed hostel for the sick and elderly who come on pilgrimage.

Garabandal, Spain, 1961–1965. Garabandal is typical of the majority of Marian apparitions that have been declared invalid by church authorities, but it continues to draw a devoted following. It began with a superstitious group of girls who heard a clap of thunder after raiding an apple orchard. Believing that the Devil had discovered their theft, they began throwing stones over their left shoulders. They then saw a young man radiant in light, whom they took to be an angel. They ran off to tell the villagers and returned often to meet the angel. During one of these apparitions, they were promised a vision of Mary, who appeared to them the next day with the Archangel Michael. There was also a large eye, which the girls took to be the presence of God. The girls soon demonstrated extraordinary physical powers, racing backwards at full speed, bending backwards until their heads touched their waists, and running on their knees. Many devout Christians considered their powers demonic.

The girls claimed that the Virgin appeared to them more than 2,000 times over the following four years. The messages were those of many other apparitions: people must do penance for their sins, pray, and reform their lives or God would bring down punishment on the world. Twice, they were shown the punishment, which the girls found terrifying but would not describe. During the visions, the girls entered a trance in which they had no feelings, as attested to by doctors who touched them and stuck them with needles. Once Conchita, the leader, fell to her knees and a Communion bread appeared on her tongue, placed there, she said, by an angel. A great miracle was later promised on a secret date known only to Conchita. If the world rejected this miracle, God's wrath would follow. Mary also predicted that the girls would renounce the apparitions, and indeed, all four recanted in 1966. Several church commissions have investigated the events at Garabandal, and the local bishop has denied the validity of the apparitions.

Knock, Ireland, 1879. When the parish housekeeper saw three figures outside the church, she thought the priest had bought some new statues. A passerby thought the same and complained about "another collection" to pay for them. Only in the evening did someone realize that the figures—Mary, St. Joseph, and St. John—were hovering several feet above the ground. Fourteen people saw the silent apparition that night. Experts tried to reproduce the sight with lights to no avail. In 1882, the archbishop of Hobart, Tasmania, was cured of blindness when he visited the shrine. The miraculous cures continued, and now a million pilgrims come to Knock each year. It has the distinction of being the only shrine with its own international airport.

La Salette, France, 1846. In an inaccessible meadow high in the French Alps, two young shepherds named Melanie and Maximin were surprised by a vision of the Virgin Mary. She was seated on a rock with her head in her hands, weeping. She spoke to them, recounting her sorrow at the neglect of faith in France, and prophesying that her son Jesus was about to strike down sinners. She condemned cursing and secular observance of Sundays, and warned of a famine. Mary then held out a promise that if people repented, "the rocks will become piles of wheat and the potatoes will sow themselves." After intense interrogations during which the children held to their story, they were taken back to the site. When a man broke off a bit of the rock, a spring gushed forth, and later a woman was cured after drinking the water. On the first anniversary of the vision, 50,000 people came to the hillside, and in 1851 the apparition was approved by Church authorities. Despite this, La Salette has always had its critics. Both the seers led aimless and troubled lives after their experience. Melanie drifted into superstition and wrote a book about her visions and revelations that was banned by the Church.

Miraculous Medal Shrine, Paris, 1830. In the middle of the night, a young woman living as a candidate in the convent of the Sisters of Charity in Paris was awakened by an angel who led her to the chapel. There Catherine Labouré saw a Lady surrounded with light who told her she had been chosen for a special mission. A few months later, Mary appeared again standing on a white globe, crushing a serpent with her foot. Mary told Catherine to have a medal struck with this image, and as she departed, the tableau turned to show a reverse side, a large M surmounted by a cross, and with the hearts of Jesus and Mary below. Catherine was tested by her confessor, who was skeptical of her visions, but the medal was finally struck with the approval of the archbishop of Paris. It soon became known as the Miraculous Medal from the many cures attributed to it, and two million copies were distributed. Catherine's connection to the medal was kept secret, and she lived an ordinary life tending the elderly until her death at 69 in 1876. She was recognized as a saint in 1947. The chapel remains a popular center of prayer in the midst of a busy shopping district in Paris.

Pontmain, France, 1871. In a town near the battlefront during the Franco-Prussian War, five children saw Mary crowned with three bright stars. Soon the entire village had assembled and began to pray and sing hymns as signs appeared in the sky: "Pray, my children," and "My Son has been touched." The adults could see the stars, but not the Virgin's image. The first miracle attributed to Mary was halting the German army and the ceasefire signed ten days later. The apparitions were approved in 1872.

Zeitoun, Egypt, 1968–1971. The first to see the Virgin on top of a Coptic Orthodox church north of Cairo was a Muslim who thought she was a woman about to commit suicide. Soon crowds assembled to watch the vision, statue-like, rising into the air above the church dome. Cures and conversions were reported in the following weeks, and the patriarch, head of the Coptic Church, declared the visions "not false or hallucinations, but real." The visions continued, accompanied by flights of white doves and the odor of incense. Mary never spoke. Zeitoun has attracted a middle-class and educated following of both Christian Copts and Muslims, who also revere Mary. She is praised in Sura 37 of the Qur'an.

The shrine of *Lourdes*, France, is perhaps the most famous Marian apparition, and its visionary, Saint Bernadette, is one of the few who has been recognized as a saint. The apparitions took place in 1858 and were immediately popular. Two years later, Bernadette moved into a local hospice because of persistent poor health, and in 1866 she entered the Sisters of Charity in Nevers. She patiently suffered indignities under a superior who felt that Bernadette needed to learn humility. In 1879, 35 years old, she died after a long illness, and she was proclaimed a saint in 1933, not because of her visions, but because of "her total commitment in simplicity, integrity and trust." Her incorrupt body lies in state in the chapel of the convent, and many pilgrims to Lourdes visit there.

See also Fátima; Guadalupe, Mexico; Kibeho; Lourdes; Medjugorje; El Pilar; Tinos; Walsingham.

References Michael Durham, *Miracles of Mary.* San Francisco, Harper San Francisco, 1995. René Laurentin, *The Apparitions of the Blessed Virgin Mary Today.* Dublin, Veritas, 1990. Sandra Zimdars-Schwartz, *Encountering Mary.* Princeton, NJ, Princeton University, 1991. *Marian*

Apparitions of the 20th Century. Lima, PA, Marian Video, 1991.

MARTYRS' HILL, Japan

The city of Nagasaki contains Martyrs' Hill, the foremost Christian shrine in Japan. Nagasaki developed as a Christian center with a small village of several hundred families, two hospitals for lepers, and a church. In 1587, Regent Hideyoshi ordered an end to Christian evangelism, which had been increasingly successful, but local Catholic rulers protected the missionaries and Japanese clergy. Ten years later, whipped up against the Christians by a hostile provincial governor, Hideyoshi ordered the arrest of the leading Christian figures. But the resulting raids also caught a number of simple workers and several children in its dragnet. Hideyoshi ordered that 20 Japanese, 4 Spaniards, an Indian, and a Mexican be crucified on a hill above Nagasaki. But first the victims' left ears were cut off, and they were marched to Nagasaki from neighboring Urakami, about two miles away, leaving a trail of blood. The way is now followed as a pilgrimage route by Christian pilgrims.

The group ranged in age from 12 to 64 and included clergy, church workers, and laymen. On their crosses, they sang and chanted psalms and verses from the Bible. Paul Miki, a Jesuit seminarian, delivered a brief sermon that impressed even the soldiers. The martyrs' lives were ended in the traditional Japanese manner, with two lances simultaneously thrust through their bodies from either side. The corpses were left for the vultures but went untouched for eight months until they were removed by the local Christians. The following year, the last remains were removed on the petition of Philippine authorities, and the crosses were taken down. The local Christians planted an evergreen tree in each post hole as a memorial. During a period of renewed persecution from 1616 to 1632, thousands of other Christians died for their faith, many crucified or burned alive on Martyrs' Hill.

In 1862, the martyrs were declared saints by the pope, and the first church in modern Japan was named for them. In 1865 a group of Japanese women timidly approached a priest there and revealed that there were tens of thousands of secret Christians who had maintained a clandestine faith during the centuries of persecution. The return of these people to Catholicism marked the first surge of Christianity in Japan in modern times.

Martyrs' Hill became a place of pilgrimage, and in 1962 a shrine was built. It includes a long granite wall with bronze bas-reliefs of each of the martyrs, by A. Y. Funakoshi. The other side of the monument, by Kenji Imai, is inlaid stone, symbolizing the arduous march from Urakami to Nagasaki. A large museum includes historical artifacts and striking mosaics. The shrine church is constructed in an art nouveau style, and the complex is completed by the Nagai Student Center, named for a prominent Catholic physician and victim of the Nagasaki atomic bombing.

See also Korean Martyrs' Shrines.

References Neil Fujita, *Japan's Encounter with Christianity.* New York, Paulist, 1991. *Spirit of the Rising Sun: Christians in Japan.* Nashville, EcuFilm, 1990 (video). Diego Yuki, SJ, *The Martyrs' Hill, Nagasaki.* Nagasaki, 26 Martyrs' Museum, 1979.

MASADA, Israel

On a butte protected by a sheer drop of 1,300 feet to the Dead Sea rests the rock fortress of Masada, site of a mass suicide that is one of the great episodes of Jewish history.

The last free Jewish kingdom, that of the Maccabees, was overthrown by the Romans in 64 BCE. But despite the appointment of a ruler whose family were converts to Judaism (Herod the Great), the Roman occupation forces faced constant resistance for nearly a century. But in 66 CE the last resistance campaign collapsed. The Romans destroyed Jerusalem and demolished the Temple, leaving only its Western Wall. The Jews were expelled and forbidden to live in Israel. Only Masada continued as a center of resistance.

There had been fortified buildings on Masada for many years, but around 30 BCE, Herod the Great expanded this complex into a major military bastion with watchtowers, a wall, barracks, and an ingenious water collection system. Intended as a royal refuge, it included two palaces. Masada was seized by Jewish zealots in 66 CE, shortly after the rebellion began, and remained the last resistance center of the war. The Roman army surrounded Masada in 72 CE. After a protracted siege, the army broke through the walls—a massive undertaking that included building a six-foot wall all around the plateau, with twelve towers and eight camps, and an earthen ramp to the top. The clear intention was not only to capture the heights but to destroy the Masada defenders. Rather than surrender to a life of slavery, 960 Jewish men, women, and children took their own lives, the men slaying their families and then themselves.

In the fifth and sixth centuries a small colony of Byzantine hermits lived on the butte, but otherwise it was left abandoned. Between 1963 and 1965, the site was excavated by an Israeli archeological team. The earthen siege ramp built by the Romans is the main approach, although a cable car was installed in 1971. Arduous work by archaeologists has revealed some of the treasures of Masada. Mosaic floors and wall paintings in Herod's palace have come to light, as well as his Roman baths. Here were found the skeletons of a Masada warrior with his wife and child; they evidently died together. Many everyday items—pottery and oil lamps, sandals, and cosmetic cases—also have been found, along with several hordes of coins made for the Jewish revolt. Some of the greatest finds were the parchment scrolls of biblical passages and other Jewish writings. The ruins of the synagogue and *mikvah* (ritual bath) are particularly important for pilgrims. About 25 skeletons of Masada defenders were discovered in a cave on one of the wall faces. One of the mysterious and awesome finds is of 11 potsherds with names on them. Since the historian Josephus records that the defenders chose lots to determine the ten who would execute the others, these are revered as the possible means of that fatal lottery.

Masada has become a major tourist site despite the difficulty of getting there. The first pilgrims were members of Israeli youth groups who began trekking to Masada as part of the enthusiastic flowering of Jewish identity that followed the establishment of the state of Israel. Today, not only pilgrims and tourists come to Masada, but also the young recruits of the Israel Armored Corps, who come to the heights each year to swear their oaths of allegiance to Israel with the cry, "Masada shall not fall again!"

References Flavius Josephus, *The Jewish War.* New York, Viking Penguin, 1984. *Masada: A Story of Heroism.* Teaneck, NJ, Ergo, 1987 (video). Ehud Netzer, "The Last Days and Hours at Masada," *Biblical Archaeology Review* 17:6, 20–32 (November-December 1991). Yigael Yadin, *Masada.* New York, Random House, 1966.

MASJID AL-BADAWI, Egypt

A large mosque built over the tomb of Ahmad al-Badawi, founder of one of the largest Sufi brotherhoods in Egypt, the Ah-madiya. The cult has always attracted primarily the poor and uneducated, and it soon spread from its place of origin in the Nile Delta into the emerging city of Cairo to the south, where it attracted the urban masses.

Although revering saints is not taught in the Qur'an, it is practiced among Muslims and is an important part of Sufi devotional life. The Sufis are members of religious brotherhoods who practice various spiritual disciplines in order to attain communion with Allah. Best known are the dervishes, who worship by means of ecstatic dancing, but each brotherhood has its own *tariq*, or way of entering into contact with the divine. Most Islamic saints come from the Sufi tradition and are renowned holy men who founded brotherhoods. It is believed that they had special spiritual powers and are able to dispense divine blessing (*berakah*). In death, their tombs became centers of popular worship where the saint's blessing and intercession before Allah is believed possible.

Ahmad al-Badawi was born in Morocco in 1199 and raised in the holy city of Mecca. As a young man, he went to Iran to place himself under Sufi masters. During his training he received a vision commanding him to move to Tanta, in the broad delta where the Nile River enters the Mediterranean Sea. Soon al-Badawi attracted many followers by his miraculous powers and founded the Ahmadiya brotherhood. As a warrior, he took part in the defense against the Crusades, including the campaign that defeated King Louis IX of France at the mouth of the Nile.

When al-Badawi died in 1276, his followers came to Tanta to pledge their covenant to his successor as head of the brotherhood, the Kahlif Abd-al-Al. This gathering has been repeated annually as a *mawlid*, or anniversary pilgrimage. Abd-al-Al erected a building over al-Badawi's tomb and built a large mosque, and this compound is known as the Masjid al-Badawi.

The shrine holds al-Badawi's tomb in the usual Islamic style: the saint is buried below ground, with a cloth-covered wooden frame above it, surmounted by a wood plaque draped in green cloth. This symbolizes the saint's divine power. Islamic teaching allows no statues or pictures of the saint in the shrine. Encircling the shrine is an ambulatory, or circular walkway, used by pilgrims in walking around the shrine a number of times while pleading for blessings. There are also processions around the ambulatory, accompanied by a cacophony of cries, clapping, cheers, and pleas for blessings. A black stone has been placed in this corridor, reminiscent of the Ka'bah in Mecca, a prominent object of devotion. On it are two footprints said to be those of the Prophet Mohammed, and it is considered a blessing to touch this. This practice is especially popular among the poorest, and making the mawlid to al-Badawi's shrine several times is considered almost as good as the hajj, the pilgrimage to Mecca. The mawlid is not made on the saint's birthday or even the anniversary of the pledge taken to Kahlif Abd-al-Al, but after the harvest, so that the delta peasants, his original devotees, can come in large numbers. The mawlid has the spirit of a fair, with food stalls, games, and shows. It has become a national observance in Egypt, although it is not an official holiday.

The main goal of the pilgrimage is the performance of *dhikr*, a remembrance ritual that is characteristic of Sufi spirituality. It can take many forms, and at the Mawlid al-Badawi various Sufi brotherhoods set up tents to conduct rituals. The most common is the chanting of the Ninety-Nine Names of God, a litany of praise to Allah. The chief dhikr at Masjid al-Badawi, however, is rubbing the stone imprinted with the footprints of the Prophet. Many orthodox Muslims, however, condemn such practices as superstitions.

See also Kairouan; Touba.

References Carolyn Fluehr-Lobban, *Islamic Society in Practice.* Gainesville, University of Florida, 1994. Nikki Keddie (ed.), *Scholars, Saints, and Sufis.* Berkeley, University of California, 1972. *Living Islam.* New York, BBC, 1993 (video).

MEDICINE WHEELS, USA

Throughout the Great Plains of North America lie a number of medicine wheels, sacred places outlined by a circle of stones, constructed by the Plains Indians. Designed for predicting both seasons and the lunar month, they were probably also used for special councils and worship, including sacred dances. All of those found have been at high altitudes, usually on mountains, and are challenging to get to. A few are still in use, and ruins of a number can be identified.

Medicine wheels (Amerindians use the term "medicine" to mean supernatural power) are laid out as large circles of rocks around a central cairn, or rock pile. Rows of stones radiate out from the cairn to the rim, following solstice lines. Some have interpreted this design as a symbol of the sun. Before the arrival of Europeans a class of astrologer shamans interpreted signs from the medicine wheels.

Although medicine wheels have been in use by a number of Amerindian tribes for centuries, evidence suggests that they began to be used before Amerindians entered the West. Medicine wheels share the same pattern as Plains Indian medicine lodges, which has caused some scholars to propose an Amerindian origin for them, but it is as likely that there is a common ancestry from unknown tribes that predated the arrival of the modern Plains Indians. *Majorville Wheel* in Alberta, for example, has been dated as 4,000 to 5,000 years old. The number of spokes radiating from its center is the same as the number of poles of a medicine lodge or a Sun Dance ground among the Sioux, Crow, and Cheyenne. Because the edges of tepees were held down by rocks, some speculated that medicine wheels are tepee rings, but this theory has been disproved.

According to Crow tradition, the medicine wheels were built by the "little people," a race that went before them. The "little people" are dedicated to impish devilment and will confuse and distract those who come to the medicine wheel without proper reverence. The dignity of the wheels must be respected, therefore, and this insistence has caused clashes with the U.S. Forest Service, which often owns the lands where medicine wheels are found. Amerindians have fought attempts to set up viewing stands so tourists could watch them at prayer and are attempting to maintain a two-mile tourist-free radius around Bighorn Medicine Wheel in Wyoming.

Moose Mountain Medicine Wheel in Saskatchewan is the most notable of a number in western Canada. It consists of a central cairn and four smaller ones on the rim. The rim cairns align exactly with the solstice sunrise and sunset and with the morning stars. Moose Mountain Medicine Wheel, which is about 1,700 years old, seems to have the same alignments as the Bighorn Medicine Wheel in Wyoming, but Moose Mountain has only 5 spokes, while Bighorn has 28.

A few miles from Saskatoon, Saskatchewan, is *Wanuskewin*, where one finds many tepee rings, a number of prehistoric archeological sites, and a medicine wheel. As a prayer center, it was a place of neutrality among the Plains peoples; the name means "being in harmony" in Cree. The wheel is protected by a national park, and access is restricted. Sweat lodges are still in use here.

Sedona, Arizona, in the heart of the Navajo nation, has one of the few complete medicine wheels in the American Southwest. Simply built of stones without cairns, it overlooks Long Canyon and is set amidst red rock cliffs and tablelands.

Because of their connection with the sun and their alignments, medicine wheels have interested adherents of New Age religious groups. Prayer and offering sessions have been devised using medicine wheels built for that purpose. After establishing a rim of stones with a center, the four directions are carefully determined. Spiritual traits—wisdom, feelings, change, spirit—are attributed to the four directions, which are used for meditation, homage, or offering. These rituals, however, have no roots in Amerindian culture, either recent or ancient, and are a cause of tension between Amerindians and New Agers.

See also Bighorn Medicine Wheel; Black Hills; Native American Sacred Places.

References John Eddy, "Probing the Mysteries of the Medicine Wheels," *National Geographic* 151:1, 140–146 (January 1977). Courtney Milne, *Sacred Places in North America*. New York, Stewart, Tabori & Chang, 1994. Ruth Underhill, *Red Man's Religion*. Chicago, University of Chicago, 1965.

MEDJUGORJE, Bosnia and Herzegovina

From 1981 to the present, the Virgin Mary is alleged to have appeared at Medjugorje, a small town in Bosnia, beginning when it was part of Communist Yugoslavia and continuing to the present day, despite the devastating civil war that intervened. Popular response has been tremendous. Organized pilgrimages have come from all parts of the world, even during the worst of the war, and Medjugorje has been transformed from a small village to a booming shrine town with shops, tourist motels, and restaurants. After Guadalupe in Mexico, Lourdes in France, and Fátima in Portugal, it is the most important Marian shrine in the world.

When Mary first appeared to the six young Croatians, they ranged in age from 10 to 17. On the third day of her appearances, Mary said that she was "Gospa," the Mother of God. The crowds that began gathering immediately made the Communist authorities extremely wary. They had doctors examine the children and tried to keep them away from the hill where they said Mary had appeared. After a week, the police came to arrest them, but the pastor, a Franciscan friar who had once seen Mary when the visionaries did, hid them in the parish church. He was later arrested, held and tortured for 18 months, and forbidden ever to return to Medjugorje. Still, the apparitions continued almost daily, in a variety of places, and the Lady gave herself another name: "the Queen of Peace." Others began to see visions as well. Several times hundreds claimed to see the sun spin on its axis and the word "peace" in Croatian appear in the sky.

The Virgin promised ten secrets to each visionary and said that a permanent sign would appear on the mountain, but "those who wait for the sign will have waited too long." Since the Virgin called for prayer and fasting, most followers fast completely one day a week, taking only water.

Since 1981, the visionaries have become adults, married, and begun families. (One of the young men briefly attended a seminary but decided not to continue studies for the priesthood.) Three of them still receive daily visions, the others a few times a year. One has moved to Italy, from which she faxes accounts of her visions back to Medjugorje. One visionary came to the United States for an eye operation, and afterwards toured the country. During her tour, her visions took place at the same time each day, including once while she visited Disney World!

The relationship of the apparitions to Croatian nationalism, as well as the callous way many in the area have exploited the war and its refugees, has cast doubt on the truth of Medjugorje. Some critics see the hand of the Franciscans, who have long been in conflict with the diocesan authorities, in the promotion of the apparitions. The bishop of Mostar, who has jurisdiction in the matter, has called the visions "collective hallucination." Both he and the Vatican have forbidden organized pilgrimages, a ruling that bishops from Europe and the United States routinely ignore. Two commissions of theologians, psychologists, and scientists have repudiated the visions, but the distinguished Marian scholar and critic, René Laurentin, perhaps the world's leading authority on visions and apparitions, supports the visionaries.

Despite the debates, believers come by the tens of thousands, seeking out the visionaries, sharing lengthy and fervent prayer vigils, fasting, and confessing their sins. Even the devastating war has only reduced, not eliminated, the flow of pilgrims. Each year, a million communion wafers are used at Medjugorje's Masses. A typical pilgrimage is made with a group organized by speciality tour companies, some of which sponsor trips only to Medjugorje. Pilgrims are housed either in small hotels or with local families. Every day Masses are held and the Rosary is recited. Processions to the appari-

tion sites also occur daily, and a visit with one of the visionaries is always included on the tour.

See also Marian Apparitions.

References Rene Laurentin, *Medjugorje: Fifteen Years Later*. Milford, OH, Faith, 1996. *The Madonna of Medjugorje*. London, BBC, 1987 (video). Elizabeth Rubin, "Souvenir Miracles," *Harper's Magazine* 289:1737, 65 ff. (February 1995).

MEENAKSHI TEMPLE, India

Near the southern tip of the Indian subcontinent is a Hindu temple dedicated to Meenakshi, consort of Lord Shiva. Its 1,000-pillared hall fills for the many festivals that attract the devout from across India, but even on an ordinary day, up to 10,000 pilgrims visit. Shiva, destroyer and reproducer god, takes many forms: he is the Great Yogi meditating on Mount Kailas (where Meenakshi met him), the god of the dance who so shook the cosmos that he frightened off ignorance and created the world, and the seed of life whose lingam (phallic statue) is worshipped. Meenakshi is pure energy. In her generous form she is Parvati the beautiful, and in her terrifying form she is Kali or Durga, who demands sacrifice.

The Meenakshi Temple has roots 2,000 years old, but the present structure was built from 1623 to 1655. It covers almost 15 acres and has four entrances and 16 towers; each tower is a multistoried structure in its own right, covered with tens of thousands of stone figures of animals, gods, and demons painted in bright hues. Inside, over 30,000 statues compete for the pilgrim's attention, although the major ones are Shiva's mount (a bull named Nandi) and his lingam at the center of the courtyard. The temple has a number of extra features, including a large pool or bathing tank for purification (the

The Hindu Meenakshi Temple is a massive structure that covers nearly 15 acres and has 16 towers.

Tank of the Golden Lily), markets, a museum, and a music hall, in addition to dozens of minor shrines. The museum has a fine exhibit on the Hindu pantheon of gods and goddesses, who are so numerous as to be confusing sometimes even to Hindus.

The shrine to Kali features a coal-black statue of the goddess, 10 feet high, her four arms frozen in a frenetic dance of fury. She wears a necklace of skulls, and pilgrims honor her by throwing balls of cold butter onto the statue to cool her anger. Many pilgrims come to Meenakshi Temple to fulfill a vow or atone for sins; traditionally, they abstain from meat and sex for 48 days beforehand and must sleep only on a hard pallet. They make the pilgrimage clad only in a black loin cloth.

The legend of Meenakshi says that she was born a princess, but with three breasts.

A holy man told her she would lose the third breast when she met her husband, which she did on a pilgrimage to Mount Kailas. He was Lord Shiva, and for 1,300 years, every evening before closing the temple, a raucous ritual procession led by drummers and a brass ensemble carries an image of Shiva to Meenakshi/Parvati's bedroom to consummate their union. Each shrine on the way is honored before Shiva spends the night, to be taken back to his day setting the next morning at dawn. Their marriage is celebrated each year by a festival in which Meenakshi and Shiva, mounted on a golden bull, are carried through the city on carved temple chariots.

References Elizabeth Harding, *Kali.* York Beach, ME, Nicolas-Hays, 1993. *The Hindu World.* Columbus, OH, Coronet, 1963 (video). David Kinsley, *Hindu*

Goddesses. Berkeley, University of California, 1986.

METEORA MONASTERIES, Greece

The monasteries of Meteora, perched on pinnacles of rock high above the surrounding plains, are almost totally inaccessible. Until the sixteenth century, 24 monasteries clung precariously to these rock spires, but today only six are occupied, four for monks and two for nuns. These are the monasteries of *Great Meteoron, Agia Trias, Varlaam,* and *Agios Nikolaos,* and the convents of *Agios Stefanos* and *Agia Barbara.* Roads now lead to all of them, but in former times, only ladders or rickety basket lifts brought supplies or visitors.

Meteora is part of an ancient volcanic upthrust that left enormous masses of stone and the gigantic pillars that attracted the Orthodox monks seeking solitude. Hermits preceded them as early as the ninth century, and a few small cloisters were set up. But around 1360, Athanasius, a notably holy recluse, attracted disciples for whom he founded the Great Meteoron and wrote a rule that all the pinnacle monasteries still follow. It forbade all contact with women and required an oath of silence and a life of great austerity. Besides the monasteries, numbers of hermits nested in caves and tiny huts on the sides of the rock faces.

Because they were unreachable, the monasteries became places of refuge where Byzantine culture and art were preserved during the centuries of Ottoman Turkish occupation. All the monasteries retain priceless icons, wall paintings, and frescoes, and each monastery keeps a small museum of its treasures. Perhaps the best artwork is Varlaam's chapel frescoes of the Last Judgment and the life of St. John the Baptist, and Agios Nikolaos's marvelous sixteenth-century frescoes by the Cretan master Theophanes, whose work is also found at Mount Athos. Great Meteoron's Chapel of the Transfiguration is a gem of Byzantine art, although some find the grisly martyrdom scenes a bit extreme.

All of the monasteries may be visited today by both men and women, and several are regular stops on tours. Some visitors complain at rarely seeing a monk, but in general, the areas open during visitors' hours are shunned by the monks, who attempt to maintain their solitude. The tiny garden plots, made from soil carried to the pinnacles in baskets, no longer serve to raise enough vegetables for the inhabitants, and the monasteries today are supported by entrance fees. But somehow, around the distraction of tourism, they preserve the spirit of prayer.

See also Mount Athos.

References Anonymous, *The Lives of the Monastery Builders of Meteora.* Buena Vista, CO, Holy Apostles Convent, 1991. Demetrius Constantelos, *Understanding the Greek Orthodox Church.* New York, Seabury, 1982. Merle Severy, "The Byzantine Empire: Rome of the East," *National Geographic* 164:6, 709–730 (December 1983).

THE MEZQUITA, Spain

Once the third-ranking Islamic pilgrimage site in the world (after Mecca and Jerusalem), the Mezquita (mosque) of Córdoba in southern Spain is one of the most beautiful mosques ever built. Still the third-largest mosque in the world, it is also one of the oddest, because it contains a Christian cathedral built within it after the expulsion of the Moors in 1236. The lovely Moorish architecture combined with the triumphant baroque cathedral memorialize in stone the conflict between Christianity and Islam that racked Spain for 700 years. The mosque was constructed in 785 and enlarged four times during the following 200 years; the cathedral was added in the sixteenth century.

The main entry is through the Gate of Pardon, which leads into the Patio de los Naranjos (Court of the Orange Trees), a formal garden where hundreds of orange trees grow, as well as cypresses and olive trees. Before entering the mosque, a Muslim pilgrim purifies himself at the fountain, supplied with water by a large tank built beneath the patio. Entering the interior of the Mezquita, the visitor is struck by the sight of aisles of columns topped with candy-striped arches that alternate white bands with red, yellow, and green. In the dim light, the impression is not garish or distracting, but of long, inviting corridors. They lead the eye to the walls, along which are chapels with mosaics and tiles in intricate combinations, contrasting with the elegant austerity of the columned aisles. The jewels of these small rooms are the two *mihrabs*. A mihrab is usually an arched indentation in the wall to show the direction of Mecca so that worshippers may face the Ka'bah, the central holy place of Islam. At the Mezquita, the two mihrabs are small chapel rooms, superbly decorated even though they were never intended to be entered. Jewel-like tiles sparkle in the reflected sunshine from small skylights. Because the Mezquita was built on the foundations of an earlier Christian church, however, its mihrabs face south rather than southeast as they should.

The glory of the Mezquita is its decoration. The eastern gate, for instance, is a scalloped arch flanked by smaller arches. The lattice-work and intricately carved niches contrast with the tiles of the interior. Since Islam does not permit statues, pictures, or other representations, Islamic art has perfected decorative styles using bas-reliefs, floral designs, and elaborate Arabic calligraphy.

Covering 8 of the Mezquita's 19 aisles is the cathedral, itself a marvelous place of worship but a clash with the unity of the Mezquita. The first church was built shortly after the recapture of the city by the Spaniards, but the present cathedral was constructed between 1523 and 1600 over the protests of the cathedral council and the townspeople. The Emperor Charles V said in dismay, "You have destroyed something unique to build something commonplace!" Indeed, the cathedral, completely contained within the Mezquita, is a collection of styles: a Gothic transept and apse, a Renaissance dome and decorations, and a baroque high altar. From the outside, the whole massive cathedral structure seems to erupt from the low roof of the Mezquita as if exploding from beneath. The bell tower encloses the original minaret from which the muezzins called the Muslim faithful to prayer. Despite the obvious intrusion, the cathedral is so overwhelmed by the sheer size of the Mezquita (the square footage of three football fields) that its styles interact with the Islamic, which itself included some pre-Islamic elements from the earlier Christian Visigothic culture. The cathedral's decorative work, especially the baroque ceilings and altar, are magnificent and allow for comparisons with the equally gorgeous Moorish style of adornment.

Although it has been centuries since Muslims have been able to use the Mezquita regularly for prayer, Arabs still come to Córdoba in such numbers that the local tourist office must print its literature in Arabic as well as the usual western languages.

References Thomas Abercrombie, "When the Moors Ruled Spain," 174 *National Geographic* 174:1, 86–119 (July 1988). Michael Brett and Werner Forman, *The Moors*. London, Orbis, 1980. Enrique Sordo, *Moorish Spain*. London, Elek, 1963.

MONTE CASSINO, Italy

Saint Benedict, the patron saint of Europe, and his twin sister, Saint Scholastica, are closely associated with two places in central Italy—Subiaco and Monte Cassino. Subiaco has never attracted many pilgrims, while Monte Cassino, where the saints' tombs are, has become a place of pilgrimage. Historically, the two are prominent as the founders of monastic life in the West. Benedict's monasteries and his *Rule of Life* became the standard for monasticism throughout the Middle Ages and remain vigorous even today.

At first, though, Benedict had no such elaborate plans. He was a hermit, living in a small cave 50 miles from Rome—the place that became Subiaco. Benedict's cave at Subiaco is preserved, and two Benedictine monasteries have been built there. Disciples were attracted to him, though, and he soon realized that he had been called to lead a community rather than be a hermit. Benedict moved to Monte Cassino in 528, where he wrote his *Rule*, a model of common sense. From this spot Benedictinism radiated out and became the major force for converting the barbarian tribes that thrust into Europe during the Dark Ages. The monks also provided havens of stability during troubled times and helped preserve the ancient learning that was being lost during the barbarian onslaught.

For several centuries after Benedict's time, Monte Cassino was the center of his movement, and the men's and women's monasteries still crown the mount there, although almost nothing of the originals remains. Beautiful frescoes show scenes from his and Scholastica's lives, including one showing their last meal together and another of the vision Benedict had of his sister's death, with her soul ascending to heaven as a dove. In 543, 33 years after Benedict's death, Monte Cassino was sacked by the barbarians. It was rebuilt, though, and by the eleventh century was the wealthiest monastery in the world. Despite repeated attacks and pillage, the monastery still contains magnificent manuscripts, illuminated Bibles, and other examples of medieval art.

Monte Cassino rises on a steep hill. Its modern history is engraved in the memories of many as the site of a terrible battle of World War II, one that continues to be controversial. Heavily fortified by Nazi forces, the hill was the target of assault after assault by Allied troops until the fortification was destroyed by air bombardment. The hill was finally captured at fearful cost by the Polish Army. A large Polish war cemetery covers a hillside across the valley, facing that of Monte Cassino. Although the monastery was destroyed, the crypt with the tombs of the saints was not damaged.

The monastery buildings were last rebuilt after the 1944 bombings, using the old plans. A museum recounts the history of monasticism, but the object of pilgrims' visits is the monastic church, where an urn under the high altar contains the relics of Benedict and Scholastica. The basilica is richly decorated in stucco and mosaics.

References David Knowles, OSB, *Christian Monasticism*. New York, McGraw-Hill, 1969. *Life of St. Benedict*. Fairfield, NJ, Keep the Faith, 1975 (video). Janusz Piekalkiewicz, *The Battle for Cassino*. New York, Macmillan, 1980.

MONT-SAINT-MICHEL, France

One of the most spectacular sights in Europe is the approach to Mont-Saint-Michel, a vast monastic structure on top of

Originally built on the shoreline, Mont-Saint-Michel came to sit on an island after an unusual riptide separated it from land in 709.

an island mountain that emerges from the sea as if straining to escape its bonds. The island is bound by fifteenth-century walls and topped by a massive thirteenth-century abbey, *La Merveille* (The Marvel). The pinnacle of its highest tower is 500 feet above the sea, crowned by a statue of the Archangel Michael in the act of striking down the devil in the form of a dragon. The monastery buildings seem part of the rocky island, which is attached to the shoreline at the base of the Normandy peninsula by a narrow causeway, formerly covered at high tide. At the full moon, the waves of the tide are among the most dramatic scenes along the Atlantic Coast.

Mont-Saint-Michel has been a shrine since the dawn of history. The Celts worshipped their god Belenus on the mountain, and the Romans built a shrine there to Jove. Early Christian hermits took posses-sion in the fifth century, but Mont-Saint-Michel's real history begins in 708, when Bishop Aubert of Avranches received an inspiration in a dream to build a shrine to St. Michael on the mount. Up to this time, the hill was along the shoreline, but the following year a freak riptide scoured a channel between it and the forests, and Mont-Saint-Michel became an island. Thus it also became a bastion against Viking raiders and English invaders—a place of refuge. In the Middle Ages the mount was fortified, and in 1425 its 120 knights held off 8,000 English troops. Mont-Saint-Michel was never taken in battle. For several centuries the abbey was wealthy and owned land in several countries, but by the sixteenth century it was in decline. Its monks went through cycles of fervor and disorder, and several times all the monks were dismissed to be replaced by new ones from more faithful monasteries.

After the French Revolution, the abbey was secularized and the island used as a prison until 1863. When restoration began, much of the statuary was found destroyed. Through the centuries portions of the walls have collapsed and been replaced.

After entering the narrow gate from the causeway, the traveler walks up a long street, no more than a widened alley. Pretentiously named Le Grand Rue, it is lined with tawdry souvenir shops, overpriced eateries, and shoddy displays masquerading as museums. The senses are assaulted on all sides by a cacophony of sounds and odors and the jostling of boisterous crowds. The impact is claustrophobic and overwhelming, but it is exactly the way Mont-Saint-Michel has been experienced for centuries. The medieval pilgrim, too, was part of a noisy, commercialized and raucous crowd, pushing and shoving toward the summit of the island. The contrast between the awesome and solemn sight of the mount as it is approached and the herded confinement within its walls is part of the pilgrim experience. Mont-Saint-Michel is the second-most-visited site in France. To get the full flavor of its popularity, a visitor should brave the dense crowds on the feast of St. Michael, the last Sunday in September.

Halfway to the abbey lies the parish church of St. Michael, a tiny chapel built to serve the workers and residents. On either side of the statue of the archangel are boards with ex-votos attached—badges and petitions, symbols of cures, and even military medals presented in thanks for returning home safely after combat. The church remains an active parish for those who live on the island. In 1966, for the thousandth anniversary of the monastery, the French government permitted the restoration of monastic life on Mont-Saint-Michel, and a group of monks, nuns, and lay oblates inhabit part of the abbey, where they give tours and provide services to pilgrims. The abbey church, where Mass is still celebrated daily for pilgrims, is a soaring triumph of light and elegance. The lightness of the stone and windows shows the best of the Flamboyant Gothic style. The interiors are stark, since the revolutionaries of 1789 looted the tapestries and art and took down the blue and gold ceiling in the monks' refectory.

References Henry Adams, *Mont-Saint-Michel and Chartres*. Boston, Houghton Mifflin, 1963. Wolfgang Braunfels, *Monasteries of Western Europe: The Architecture of the Orders*. New York, Thames and Hudson, 1972. *Mont-St-Michel*. Port Washington, NY, Applause, 1991 (video).

MONTSERRAT, Spain

The monastic shrine of Montserrat perches on the side of a 4,054-foot mountain, an hour northwest of the Catalonian capital of Barcelona. It is surrounded by serrated sandstone peaks that give its approach a moonscape appearance, especially for those who arrive by the aerial tramway that swings across the yawning gorges. Since 1025, this shrine has been a sanctuary of the Virgin and the center of Catalan national identity. By 1500 the monastery had the first printing press in the region and began a long tradition of publishing in Catalan. Montserrat has been closed briefly several times, most recently during the Spanish Civil War of 1936–1939. Though its influence abroad was extensive during the sixteenth century, when it had daughter houses in Portugal, Austria, Mexico, and Peru, today it is simply the shrine of the Black Virgin honored as the patroness of Catalonia.

During the Spanish Civil War, Catalonia was a hotbed of patriotic fervor for the left-wing government and the last area to fall to the Fascist forces of Generalissimo Fran-

Precariously perched on the side of a 4,054-foot mountain, Montserrat is the center of Catalan national identity.

cisco Franco. Persecution of the Church was extreme, and large numbers of priests, nuns, and prominent laity were tortured and murdered. The monks of Montserrat disbursed, but 23 lost their lives; their bodies are buried in the crypt of the basilica. During Franco's dictatorship (1939–1975), the public use of the Catalan language was banned and publications in the language were prohibited. Even so, the monastery continued to print secretly in Catalan.

The renowned statue, gilded polychrome wood, shows the seated Black Virgin holding Jesus in her lap. The color has caused her devotees affectionately to nickname her *Moreneta*—"Brownie." It sits in a special "holy room," richly decorated, above the main basilica, a huge vaulted eighteenth-century church. In typically Benedictine tradition, the liturgy is the focus of

the services in the basilica, and every service is conducted with solemnity and dignity. Each day, the boys' choir (the monastery maintains a choir school) sings a special litany honoring the Virgin of Montserrat, the *Virolai,* considered a gem of Catalan poetry. The basilica is decorated with chapels and paintings from all periods up to the present. The art is not lavish or bejewelled, but it does include excellent examples of the work of each generation.

Although the Black Virgin is what many pilgrims come to see, they can choose between several pilgrimage paths. One, which leads through the surrounding forests to life-size Stations of the Cross, ends at a chapel, Our Lady of Solitude. Above this chapel is a medieval hermitage and another chapel, one of 13 mountain hermitages that can be visited. An alternate path follows the theme of Mary's biblical song of praise (Luke 1:46–55); it is marked by lovely ceramics set into the rock faces along the way. At the foot of the mountain is the Holy Grotto, where the image of the Virgin was supposedly found in the ninth century. According to legend, the statue fled from Jerusalem to escape the Muslims and ended up in the mountains above Barcelona. The various combinations of shrines, chapels, and hermitages there make up eight "itineraries," and there are two simple pilgrim hostels and a hotel on the mountain.

References R. Berleant, *Montserrat.* Santa Barbara, CA, ABC-CLIO, 1991. Maur Boix, *What Is Montserrat?* Barcelona, Abidia de Montserrat, 1974. Justino Bruguera, *Montserrat.* Barcelona, Planeta, 1964.

MORADAS, New Mexico and Colorado, USA

Moradas, simple prayer and meeting rooms found only in New Mexico and southern Colorado, are built of La Santa Madre Tierra, Holy Mother Earth, made into adobe. They are built by members of the Penitente Brotherhood, many of whom are descendants of those brought to the frontier from New Spain (Mexico) in the eighteenth century to counterbalance the licentious, drunken settlers and soldiers. The ancestors of other brotherhood members were Spanish captives freed from slavery to the Navajos or Apaches. Properly, the Penitentes are known as *La Fraternidad Piadosa de Nuestro Padre Jesús Nazareno,* the Pious Society of Our Father Jesus the Nazarene. It is strictly a lay fraternity and not a religious order, and its ties to the Catholic church are informal. It began sometime around 1800 to provide spiritual support for Hispanics during a period when the Church had few priests. Members witnessed marriages, buried the dead, and cared for widows and orphans. Their piety is based on the Passion, death, and Resurrection of Jesus. Under colonial bishops they were driven underground, but since 1947 the Catholic church has recognized them.

A morada is small, barely enough for a dozen men to squat around in a circle. It has no windows and is made of adobe, sun-baked bricks mixed from soil, water, and a little straw. Some are plastered. A few moradas have stone bases, but characteristically a morada's architecture and spirit are one with the surrounding landscape—they are made of the earth and will eventually return to it. Moradas are considered outstanding examples of southwestern folk structures. Primarily, though, they are regarded as holy places and are used as chapter houses, where the members of brotherhood meet to pray and make decisions. They offer informal prayers, sing, and invoke favorite saints or ancestors. The brotherhood's more organized rituals are secret, which has given rise to fanciful accounts of exaggerated penances. In the nineteenth century, some Penitentes circulated stories of bloody scourgings and even crucifixions to frighten people away and help maintain seclusion. The stories had the opposite effect, attracting the curious and causing the false accounts to become even more lurid.

References Angelico Chavez, OFM, *My Penitente Land: Reflections on Spanish New Mexico.* Albuquerque, University of New Mexico, 1974. Jay Dolan and Allan Figueroa Deck (eds.), *Hispanic Catholic Culture in the U.S.* Notre Dame, IN, University of Notre Dame, 1994. Michael Wallis and Craig Varjabedian, *En Divina Luz: The Penitente Moradas of New Mexico.* Albuquerque, University of New Mexico, 1994.

MORIJA, South Africa

The pilgrimage and healing center of one of the most important African religion movements is located in the north of South Africa, in the Province of the Transvaal, at the religious settlement of Morija. In the early twentieth century, a religious movement called Zionism sprang up in southern Africa. Although it had roots in Protestant mission churches, it brought together Christian beliefs and African traditions in a new way, creating indigenous African Christian churches.

With over a million members, the Zion Christian Church (ZCC) is one of the taproots of the Zionist movements. It was founded in South Africa around 1910 by Ignatius Lekganyane, later led by his son Edward and his grandson Barnabas. Their authority came in part from their founding role, but mostly from their healing power. Through prayer, laying on of hands, and blessing with water or ashes, they cured the faithful and drove out evil spirits. The Lekganyanes proclaimed Jesus Christ the cornerstone of their work, but they were also personally exalted as prophets and divinely sent messengers. Later, some of their disciples, while acknowledging their descent from the Lekganyanes, founded independent Zionist churches in other African countries.

Although Zionism developed a considerable following in the cities of South Africa, its spiritual homeland was in the rural areas, in what were then called the Native Reserves. In the Zionist churches, the reserves were regarded as a kind of Promised Land. Here the sick were healed, here were the holy places where the Spirit could be encountered. Ignatius Lekganyane baptized his disciples in a river he called the Jordan, a short distance outside Pretoria. Sacred hilltops were dubbed "Jerusalem" by

the various sects, and it was on one of these that Lekganyane purchased 50 acres. He named it Morija, after Mount Moriah, a biblical name for Jerusalem.

Part of ZCC theology includes a spiritual geography that identifies Morija with the Mount Moriah on which Solomon's Temple was built. It is thus a "New Jerusalem" for the ZCC. Morija is 25 miles from Pietersburg in the Transvaal, where South African blacks maintain much of their original traditions. It is also considered a place that stands apart from and contrasts with the political power of nearby Pretoria, the nation's capital, and the economic power of Johannesburg. In the African townships around both of these cities, many ZCC faithful live under squalid conditions, but they travel in pilgrimage to Morija to find a sacred place of spiritual liberation. They come on regular occasions for pilgrimages, scores of thousands at a time, to witness to the power of the spirit. Morija has successful farms and businesses, and the bishop of the church maintains a fleet of expensive cars. Edward had 45, including several Rolls-Royces. Material possessions are considered signs of God's blessings.

Of the three major pilgrimages, the largest and most important is held at Easter. During each pilgrimage there is common worship, healing, and celebration. Clergy are ordained and sent back to continue the healing ministry. Members line up to throw donations into 10-gallon drums and then join dance circles. Dance is used in worship, and at Morija a dance group called the Soldiers of Zion, dressed in khaki uniforms, does a stomp dance wearing large white boots. It is similar to the "gum-boot" dances performed in the miners' slums in South Africa, where the stamping of feet is a form of percussion. In ZCC ritual, the boot dancers are stomping evil underfoot;

sometimes this symbolic action takes concrete form, as when pilgrims throw cigarettes beneath their feet.

The Zionists emphasize manifestations of the Holy Spirit, including speaking in tongues. They believe that the second coming of Christ is near, and they practice baptism by immersion. Their moral code is strict. At first they forbade having more than one wife, but after some years this policy was softened in the face of African reality. Now plural wives are accepted, a change that has attracted many converts from Western Christian churches. The code of moral purity forbids eating pork and the use of alcohol or tobacco. ZCC members also refuse all use of medicine, either that of witch doctors or modern medicine. To identify themselves, and so that others may hold them up to their strict code, ZCC members wear a cloth badge embroidered with "ZCC." They are known for nonviolence and obedience to authority. During the apartheid era in South Africa, they accepted the social policy of the government and refused to engage in the resistance movement. In 1985, President P. W. Botha was invited to speak at the Easter pilgrimage at Morija.

See also Cao Dai Temple.

References Davis Chidester, *Religions of South Africa*. New York, Routledge, 1992. Adrian Hastings, *A History of African Christianity, 1950–1975*. Cambridge, UK, Cambridge University, 1979. A. F. Walls and Wilbert Shenk, *Exploring New Religious Movements*. Elkhart, IN, Mission Focus, 1990.

MORMON TEMPLE, Utah, USA

The Mormon Temple in Salt Lake City, Utah, is the center of Mormonism, one of the few religions founded in the United States and one of the world's fastest-growing faiths. Today its missionaries, mostly youth who give 18 months of their lives to the church, are found across the globe. As a force in American society, Mormonism has long stood for solid family values, the sacredness of marriage, and cooperative effort, as well as generally conservative stances on the moral and political issues of the day. Until 1890, the church permitted a man to have several wives, but under intense U.S. government pressure, the head of the church, who is believed to receive direct teachings from God, proclaimed a revelation forbidding the practice.

The religious practice of Mormonism is based on revelations given Joseph Smith in the 1820s, capped by the apparition of the Angel Moroni, bearing golden tablets on which were engraved the scriptures of the new faith, the Book of Mormon. After Smith's martyrdom, the faithful were led west to Utah in 1847 by Brigham Young. As they arrived at the unsettled desert land, Smith was inspired to say, "This is the place." Salt Lake City was developed as a Mormon holy place, and the temple is its spiritual and cultural heart. The temple is central to 42 others around the world, and the secret rituals of Mormonism may be solemnized at any of them.

Brigham Young designed Salt Lake City on a grid pattern with Temple Square at its center. It covers ten acres, and all buildings there are open to visitors except the temple itself. Atop one of its three towers is a golden statue of the Angel Moroni, a symbol of the city. An elaborate visitors' center presents the history and beliefs of the Church of Christ of Latter-Day Saints, as the Mormons are formally known. Mormons teach that Native American Indians are descended from Hebrews who arrived from Jerusalem in 600 BCE, and that Jesus visited America after his resurrection from the dead. These events are pictured in large murals at the visitors' center. Most guests also visit the Mormon Tabernacle, built in 1867 and the home of the famed Mormon Tabernacle Choir. It is one of the most acoustically perfect structures ever built, and a coin dropped at one end can be heard 175 feet away. The choir is accompanied by a magnificent organ with 11,623 pipes. Also on Temple Square is the Museum of Church History and Art, and nearby is Brigham Young's home, the Beehive House, which gives a fascinating insight into early Mormon life in polygamous households.

The temple is reserved for Mormon rituals and open only to members of the church. Although such Christian practices as baptism and the Lord's Supper are part of Mormon practice, two customs are unique to Mormonism: baptism for the dead and sealing in marriage for eternity. Mormons believe that a merciful God cannot condemn those who die without hearing the message of the scriptures. Therefore, with a living Mormon witness standing in for them, the names of the dead are baptized into salvation. This practice has resulted in the gathering of the world's largest genealogical archive for this purpose, and its computerized index is available on Temple Square to anyone wanting to trace their ancestors.

Although civil marriage is permitted, the highest salvation is reserved for those sealed together for eternity. At the wedding ceremony, men and women are seated separately and clothed in white ritual dress. Several men take the roles of God, Jesus, and the Archangel Michael, dramatizing the Creation. The bride puts on a green apron symbolizing the fig leaf of modesty and proceeds to another room, where accounts are presented of the attempts of Satan to deceive the prophets and the people. It ends with a statement that those who do not live up to the covenant will perish. With Satan driven out, the couple is taught the ritual handshakes used in various temple services. They first use these when they are led to a floor-length veil with slits, through which they embrace as a sign that their union will be what brings them through this life to heaven. Each is given a new name—the groom's kept secret, the bride's confided only to him. Then the couple goes through the veil to the Celestial Room, where they are greeted by their families. The temple sealing ceremony is followed by a wedding, which is simple. In 1990, elements of the ceremonies deemed offensive to women of non-Mormon faiths were removed.

References *The Book of Mormon.* Salt Lake City, Herald House, 1973. Deborah Laake, *Secret Ceremonies.* New York, William Morrow, 1993 (controversial). Matthew Naythons, *The Mission.* New York, Warner Books, 1995.

MOUND-BUILDERS, USA

Three ancient cultures in North America that preceded the Native American Indians built ceremonial earthwork mounds. These were the Adena and Hopewell peoples, centered in the Ohio River Valley, and the Mississippians, who lived along the Mississippi River and in the Southeast. Today, hundreds of mounds, in various states of preservation, are found scattered across the central and southern parts of the United States, with concentrations in Ohio, Wisconsin, Illinois, Alabama, Mississippi, and Oklahoma.

The Adena culture flourished from approximately 1000 BCE to 700 CE and left a number of burial mounds. Adena society was matrilinear—that is, inheritance descended through the female line, and women chose their own husbands. A class of priests and rulers dominated the Adena, who were hunters and traders, dealing their

Serpent Mound, pictured here, is believed to have been built by the Adena, one of three cultures in North America between 1000 BCE and 700 CE.

lovely jewelry and furs as far as the Gulf of Mexico and into the Southwest. Their burial mounds contain a number of wealth objects from which the extent of Adena trade can be judged. The jewelry uses turquoise, mica, sharks' teeth, quartz, and obsidian, as well as pearls. Besides the burial mounds, the Adena built several effigy mounds, evidently for religious purposes, in the shapes of animals. The most important of these is Serpent Mound in Ohio. Hundreds of the various types of mounds are scattered throughout the Midwest.

The Hopewell people overlapped the time period of the Adena but survived until about 1000 CE. Although burial mounds were built by both Adena and Hopewell

peoples, the two groups intersect, and the mounds are often commonly referred to as Adena. The trademark mounds of the third group, the Mississippians, were temple mounds, flat-topped pyramids sometimes grouped around an open court to create a huge ceremonial ground. The best example of their work is at Cahokia Mounds Historic Site in Illinois.

Besides their obvious relation to the religion of the ancient peoples, the mounds have taken on new religious meaning in the last twenty years as New Age devotees have interested themselves in places where ancient peoples gathered for worship. New Age practitioners have begun to compare effigy mounds, for example, to the constellations to see if certain star groups are represented in the structures of the mounds. Serpent Mound, it has been suggested, is patterned on the Little Dipper. If this is so, it would indicate a sacred energy flow between heaven and earth. Many mound sites have been analyzed for ley lines, which conduct energy flows between sacred sites in ancient religions, according to New Age thought. New Age followers often use the mounds for solstice celebrations, as do occasional witches' covens. Because of the gathered spiritual energy present at the mounds, according to believers, focused human energy can trigger emanations of peace and higher consciousness.

Effigy Mounds, near Marquette, Iowa, contains almost 200 mounds, 29 of them effigy figures of birds and animals, covering fifteen hundred acres. Certainly the most striking is a series of ten bears in a file—the "marching bears"—with three eagles hovering nearby.

Lizard Mound, near West Bend, Wisconsin, with its 31 effigy mounds, is the greatest concentration of effigy mounds in the United States. Each is three to four feet high, and there are both animal and geometric shapes. Many of the effigy mounds are graves. The bodies are buried either at the place of the animal's vital organs or (in the case of birds) in the wings. It is thought that the dead were buried in an effigy of their totem, or sacred creature. If this theory is correct, the place would have been the burial and ceremonial site of several clans, who perhaps gathered there from time to time for religious and funeral purposes. A second theory holds that totem animals appeared in dreams during a vision quest, perhaps to the founder of a clan. In addition to the Lizard Mound, for which the site is named, there are seven panther effigies ranging from 73 to 211 feet in length.

Mound City, near Chillicothe, Ohio, is one of the best-preserved Hopewell sites, built around 200 BCE. A low earthen wall surrounds thirteen acres of land with 23 mounds. They have been excavated and rebuilt, yielding a ceremonial death mask that was evidently used in funerals, fragments of teeth and bones from prehistoric animals, and other effects. There are no effigy mounds here.

Newark Earthworks, near Newark, Ohio, were once an extensive development of earthworks, including effigy mounds, burial mounds, and other earthworks in geometric designs. All of this covered about four square miles and is associated with the Hopewell people. The major structure remaining today is the Octagon, which encloses 8 acres of mounds within several parallel walls. Another enclosure, Mound Builders' Memorial, is a large circle with walls up to 14 feet high, containing 26 acres. There is also a museum of Hopewell artifacts.

Serpent Mound, near Peebles, Ohio, is an effigy mound of an uncoiling snake about to swallow an oval, usually interpreted as an egg. It is a quarter-mile long and rises to between four and five feet in height. It was never used as a burial mound. In the 1880s, the site was purchased by Harvard University to save it from developers. It was later given to the state of Ohio. Stretched along a hilltop, the serpent clearly had some religious meaning and purpose. Until recently, it was thought to have been built by the Adena about 2,000 years ago. Carbon testing done in 1995 on pieces of charcoal, however, has dated the construction around 1070 CE, meaning that it belongs with the much later Fort Ancient culture (1000–1500 CE). One suspicion is that the charcoal might be related to the 1066 appearance of Halley's Comet. There is no certain conclusion as to Serpent Mound's use, but today it is a favorite place for New Age individuals and groups, for meditation and occasionally, for rituals.

See also Cahokia Mounds.

References Maureen Korp, *The Mound Builders: Mysteries of the Ancient Americas.* Pleasantville, NY, Reader's Digest, 1986. Robert Silverberg, *Mound Builders of Ancient America.* New York, Graphic Society, 1968. Susan Woodward and Jerry McDonald, *Indian Mounds of the Middle Ohio Valley.* Blacksburg, VA, McDonald and Woodward, 1986.

MOUNTAINS, SACRED

The perception that the sacred is associated with high places, that mountains point to a heaven above and beyond the earth, is deeply ingrained in human consciousness. Mountains have been seen as the homes of the gods (Kilauea, Mount Olympus), as places of revelation (Mount Sinai, Mount Shasta), as places to discover spiritual insight (Mount Athos, the Black Hills), and as deities themselves (Mount Fuji, T'ai Shan). Forbidding and difficult to climb, with wooded slopes, barren rock faces and summits of rock or snow, mountains have a harsh beauty not part of the everyday life of most people and, according to Edwin Bernbaum, "extraordinary power to awaken the sense of the sacred." Religious pilgrims accept the physical challenges of the climb in order to experience the spiritual ascent that goes with it.

Mount Olympus in Greece is the best-known example of a mountain that served as the home of the gods. According to Greek mythology, Zeus, king of the gods, was born in a mountain cave on Crete, where his mother had fled to protect him from a wrathful father bent on destroying his sons and rivals. Zeus was raised on another Cretan sacred mountain, Ida, from which he returned to Olympus to overthrow his father and claim his kingship. From there, as god of storms and thunder, he hurled lightning bolts to earth to demonstrate his power. On Olympus he lived with the other eleven Olympians, the chief gods of the Greek pantheon. Though Olympus was their principal home, each also had another sacred mountain—Apollo at Delphi, for example. When they gathered at rugged Olympus, they lived in perfect comfort, untouched by wind or snow, feasting and constantly entertained by music and dancing.

Olympus is the highest mountain in Greece (9,570 feet). Bare and stark on its upper reaches, inhospitable to humans, it emanates power and authority. No shrines were ever built on the sides of this mountain; instead, such secondary places as Delos or Delphi became the sites of shrines and temples.

Mount Kilimanjaro, the highest mountain in Africa (19,340 feet), has three peaks, and the climate zones on its sides range from rainforest to meadows to glaciers. The Chagga people regard the mountain as an abode of the great god Ruwa, but it is also their tribal home. A wide band around the lower flanks of Kilimanjaro is settled, and the Chagga consider those who reside on the surrounding plains as inferior peoples. Above the settled area is the holy ground, and only males who have passed through initiation may go there. People are honored in reference to Kibo, the highest peak: it is respectful, for example, when passing someone to allow them the side toward Kibo. The dead are buried facing the mountain, and people sleep with their beds in the same direction.

Some mountains have meaning because they embody the spiritual manifestations of nature. T'ai Shan, for example, draws its importance from being the sacred mount that first receives the life-giving rays of the sun. Traditional Korean religion believes that energy flows along the mountains that form the spine of the country, influencing and shaping the people and their national character. As part of Japan's attempt at cultural genocide during the colonial period (1905–1945), huge spikes were driven into the mountain ridges to remind the Korean people of their subjugation. Only today are these being removed by the Korean government.

Christian tradition associates many mountains and high places with Jesus, who was born in Bethlehem, a high place, preached a "Sermon on the Mount," revealed himself transfigured on Mount Tabor, and made his supreme sacrifice on the Mount of Calvary. The Catholic and Orthodox traditions record many examples of appearances of saints or of the Virgin Mary on mountains or in mountain ranges such as Medjugorje, Einsiedeln, and Jasna Góra. The tradition of high places as locations for revelation are also embedded in Jewish experience; Yahweh spoke to Moses on Mount Sinai and is worshipped on *Mount Zion*.

Mountains also serve as places of refuge, contemplation, and holiness. Christian mystics and saints are often associated with mountains or seek high places for their spiritual quest. St. Benedict began Western monasticism at Subiaco, settling on Monte Cassino; Carmelite hermits went to *Mount Carmel* in Israel. Meteora, *St. Catherine's*, and Mount Athos are cradles of Orthodox monasticism; monks consider themselves blessed for being able to live in the vestibule of heaven.

See also Black Hills, Croagh Patrick; Dilwara; Emei Shan; Gunung Agung; Kilauea; Machu Picchu; Monte Cassino; Montserrat; Mount Athos; Mount Brandon; Mount Fuji; Mount Kailas; Mount Kenya; Mount Shasta; Mount Sinai; T'ai Shan; Uluru and Kata Tjuta.

References Edwin Bernbaum, *Sacred Mountains of the World*. San Francisco, Sierra Club, 1990. Ronald Clark, *Men, Myths and Mountains*. New York, Crowell, 1976. Michael Tobias and Harold Drasdo, *The Mountain Spirit*. Woodstock, NY, Overlook Press, 1979.

MOUNT ATHOS, Greece

Politically, culturally, and socially, Mount Athos is an anomaly. Perched above the sea on a closed peninsula jutting forth from northern Greece, it is a semi-autonomous monastic theocracy ruled by monks. The mountain rises 6,670 feet above the sea near the end of the peninsula, and its marble cliffs make perfect perches for the monastic dwellings. Life on Mount Athos moves to their rhythms in the atmosphere of their severe austerities. Visitors are screened, after presenting letters of reference and registering with the Greek police, and only 10 non-Orthodox men are admitted each day. A visa is stamped in the visitor's passport. Not only a refuge from the world, Mount Athos is a world unto itself.

The legend of Mount Athos says that Mary, the mother of Jesus, was shipwrecked here on her way to join the apostles in their mission of preaching the Gospel. A statue of Apollo declared itself a false god in her presence, and the pagan idols threw themselves at her feet and were shattered. From that time, the Virgin Mary is the only woman allowed on Mount Athos. No female of any species may enter the confines of the Holy Mountain—no woman, cow, or hen. Twice in the Middle Ages, when empresses attempted to visit, they were met by visions of the Virgin commanding them to go no further. The first monk, Peter the Athonite, received his call in a vision of the Virgin, and in her name he drove out the demons who inhabited the caves on the side of the mountain. These were soon filled by hermits and holy men.

History records that the first monks on Mount Athos were Eastern Orthodox hermits, penitential men given to extreme austerities. The most illustrious of these began to attract disciples, and by the ninth century several monastic communities had been established. From the first, the Great Lavra (963 CE), to the most recent, Stavronikita (1540), over 20 monasteries have been founded. The larger monasteries were constructed as monastic villages. The Great Lavra, for example, has 15 chapels built around a central courtyard. Each monastery has a keep, a tower—often fortified against pirates—that houses the monastery treasury and library. The keep of Vatopedi has 634 Greek manuscripts, 150 ancient musical scores, and many valuable books. There is also a well at each monastery, used for blessed water and symbolic of baptism. At its height in the Middle Ages, 10,000 monks inhabited Mount Athos, and to preserve a sense of solitude in the bustling monasteries of that time, many monks moved into small communities (*sketes*) or reopened hermitages on the mountain sides.

These monasteries are centers of meditation and penance. There are no monastic schools, not even a seminary. The sense of separation from the world begins with the monastic day, which starts at sunset—12 o'clock by Athonite calculation. (Only one monastery uses modern time rather than this ancient Byzantine method.) The Bible is prayed rather than studied, to avoid the temptation of argument and confusion. Mount Athos has been a center for the spread of Christian mantric prayer, where one chants the name of Jesus as a way of entering into ecstasy. The monasteries preserve some important religious art, but it is of little importance to the monks and is rarely displayed, except for those pieces regarded as wonder-working icons. Mount Athos preserves more icons that survived eighth-century iconoclasm than anywhere else. In this Christian controversy, which split church communities and lined up powerful people on either side, some enemies of images of Christ and the saints destroyed most of the icons created before 800 CE.

Once there were 300 monasteries on Mount Athos; today, 20 self-governing monasteries remain. Their abbots form a coordinating council on common matters. Though the majority are Greek, there are also Serbian, Russian, and Bulgarian Orthodox monasteries on the mountain. In recent years, the Greek government has refused entry permits to many non-Greek candidates, and a recent conflict over authority between the council and the Greek patriarch has disturbed the usual monastic calm of the Holy Mountain. Eleven monasteries follow the Rule of St. Basil, which requires communal living and common meals. These are always vegetarian and frugal, and taken either in silence or while one of the brothers reads from a religious book. The monks occupy themselves in tending gardens and orchards and in the tasks necessary for maintaining the monasteries. Some "write" (paint) icons for distribution to Orthodox churches around the world, where they are highly prized. As in every Christian monastic tradition, work keeps the monk anchored in God's creation even as his soul reaches to attain unity with the Divine.

See also Meteora Monasteries.

References Flavio Conti, *The Closed Faith.* Boston, HBJ Press, 1979, 9–40. Philip Sherrard, *Athos: The Holy Mountain.*

Woodstock, NY, Overlook Press, 1985. James Stanfield, "Mount Athos," *National Geographic* 164:6, 739–747 (December 1983).

MOUNT BRANDON, Ireland

Mount Brandon, at 3,127 feet, dominates the Dingle Peninsula in southwest Ireland. It is a center of pilgrimage in memory of St. Brendan the Navigator and has been so since Celtic times. It is said that Brendan built the trail to the summit himself, where he left an oratory as a sign of the triumph of Christianity.

Brendan is the legendary sailor who first reached "the Heavenly Isles" or the "Promised Land of the Saints," where food was found in abundance, gems and gold were strewn on the ground, and Christ was said to reign in light. The account of Brendan's voyage is one of the important tales of the Middle Ages, and from it Brendan became the patron of pilgrims.

In pagan times, Mount Brandon was one of two sites (the other was Croagh Patrick) for the Lughnasa, a harvest festival in honor of the Celtic god, Lug. It was held on the mountaintops at the end of July, now the time of the St. Brendan Festival with its boat races.

The great pilgrimage day is the last Sunday in July, clearly a Christian replacement for the pagan festival. For centuries people have come to this combination pilgrimage and fair from as far away as Britain and Scotland, most of them by sea. When they arrived, they found beehive-shaped stone huts for their use; several hundred still exist on the slopes of the mountain, and there were many more in former times. The huts are corbelled, that is, made of stones fitted closely together without mortar and gradually sloping to a point. After a thousand years, most are still waterproof. Pilgrims might stay for a few days or up to several weeks until the clouds lifted and allowed a safe ascent of the mountain. Along the way, they stopped for prayers at various stations. Several of these were crosses or markers in honor of other pilgrim saints, such as St. Colman. There was even a litany invoking the pilgrim saints for their blessing along the journey.

The pilgrimage has had its ups and downs. In the eighteenth century it was suppressed by the Church because of the gambling, dancing, and faction fights that became attached to it. (The fights were a way for clans to settle scores by choosing champions to challenge one another in bloody contests.) At various times the pilgrimage has even died out, only to revive, and today it involves a week-long series of visits to shrines and holy places along the way to the mountain. A revival of the harvest festival has also taken place, although a soccer match has replaced the faction fights. Local pagan customs have persisted, including one involving the capture of a wild goat on the mountain. The goat is crowned "king of all Ireland" for the three days of the festival. Regard for the ancient pagan god Lug remained until 1993, when his stone head, kept near a local church, was stolen. People kissed the stone in the superstitious belief that to do so would prevent or cure toothaches.

See also Mountains, Sacred.

References Peter Harbison, *Pilgrimage in Ireland.* Syracuse, Syracuse University, 1992. Steve MacDonagh, *A Visitor's Guide to the Dingle Peninsula.* Dingle, n.p., 1985. Máire MacNeill, *The Festival of Lughnasa.* London, Oxford, 1962.

MOUNT FUJI, Japan

Following the sweeping lines of an inverted fan, in perfect patterns of snow and light, dark woods and iridescent blue sky, Japanese

Shrines dating from the ninth century line the base and rim of Mount Fuji and honor the deity Konohana Sakuya Hime. From July to August over 400,000 people visit the shrines as they climb to the crest of the mountain.

artists have never tired of portraying Mount Fuji as the embodiment of the nation's spirit. An inactive but not dormant volcano, Mount Fuji floats 12,385 feet above the surrounding landscape of fields, lakes, and sea, the symmetry of its form arresting in its simplicity. Japanese myth asserts that the mountain was created in a single night by the ancient gods.

Because of its earlier volcanic activity, Mount Fuji was first seen as the abode of a fire god, and in the ninth century several shrines were built along its slopes for rituals to placate the deity and keep the mountain quiet. In time, the fire god was replaced by the Shinto goddess of flowering trees, Konohana Sakuya Hime, who is the primary deity honored in the shrines along the rim of the crater and at the base of the mountain. She is worshipped by the use of fire, especially at the annual festival that marks the end of the climbing season. At that time, a group of men carry a lacquered model of the mountain, weighing well over a ton, while boys carry a smaller model. At a shrine at the base of Mount Fuji, priests lead a procession of people, who carry straw replicas of the mountain that they have built. These are then lighted. Although Mount Fuji's last eruption was in 1707, hot spots remain on the rim, a reminder of the volcano's power. The bonfires imitate the lava flow of the volcano, and the sparks dance above the flames like the gods dancing at the summit.

Both Shinto and Buddhism surround their beliefs with legendary tales of the origin of the sacred mountain and the powers that dwell there. Buddhists regard Mount Fuji as the home of a deity who is the presence of spiritual wisdom. In the early centuries, they considered climbing the mountain sacrilegious, but in the twelfth century, a Buddhist priest made the first docu-mented ascent to build a temple and then climbed the mountain over 200 times to worship there. The word for "the summit," *zenjo*, is the word for "perfect concentration," and Fuji's crest is an ideal place for contemplation, raised above the cares and distractions of the world below. Buddhists have identified Mount Fuji as a sacred circle or mandala, pointing out details along the crater rim as manifestations of the lotus petals on which the Buddha rests.

A pilgrim route had been established to the summit of Mount Fuji by the fourteenth century. Several centuries later, devotional associations began organized climbing. In the seventeenth century, a number of cults were founded, based on visions received by prophetic hermits settled in caves on the flanks of the mountain. Gradually Mount Fuji became the preeminent mountain in all Japan. The Japanese had always worshipped sacred mountains, but messianic movements raised Fuji to the first rank, the supreme mountain whose worship transcended all other religions, including Buddhism. It became not only the abode of the gods, but a god itself. Most influential of these cults was Fuji-ko, whose charismatic founder starved himself to death on the mountain in 1733 as a sacrifice to implore the gods to deliver Japan from a famine. The movement spread, and Mount Fuji became a symbol of stability and strength during a time when Japan was racked by civil wars and economic collapse. Identified with the emerging cult of the emperor, Fuji became the foundation of the nation as well as the womb from which Japan was reborn. The Shinto cult of Mount Fuji was tied to nationalism, and many Japanese felt betrayed by the mountain after the defeat in World War II. Both Shinto and the Fuji cult suffered as a result.

Two cultic acts are associated with Fuji:

fire rituals and climbing the mountain. The Fuji-ko perform fire ceremonies before any ascent of the mountain and burn straw replicas of Mount Fuji at home altars. More than 400,000 people make the climb during the official safe season, July and August. Cult groups climb alongside groups of people with only the vaguest religious motives. Customarily, pilgrims start at a shrine at the base of the mountain. Each of the routes has ten rest stations, maintained by descendants of the religious guides of earlier centuries. At each of these stations, a character is burned into the pilgrim's walking staff. These wooden staffs are much prized, even by the nonreligious. The most popular route has 99 switchbacks, and though arduous, can be accomplished by anyone in reasonable physical condition. Children and elders make the climb regularly. It is spiritually important that they be assisted if necessary, since the ascent is not an endurance test or an ascetical practice. It is important that all who make the attempt succeed, not just the strong or powerful. A focal point of the climb is the place where the founder of Fuji-ko fasted to death. The most auspicious time to arrive at the top is in time for dawn, but in all climbs the pilgrim ritually hikes around the crater rim.

See also Mountains, Sacred.

References H. Byron Earhart, *Religions of Japan.* San Francisco, Harper San Francisco, 1984. Kosuke Koyama, *Mount Fuji and Mount Sinai.* Maryknoll, NY, Orbis, 1984. Henry Smith, *Hokusai: One Hundred Views of Mt. Fuji.* New York, Brazillier, 1988.

MOUNT KAILAS, Tibet, China

At 22,027 feet, Mount Kailas rises like a huge bald dome from the surrounding highlands in the far western reaches of Tibet, near the borders of both Nepal and India. It is Tibet's most sacred mountain, now cut off from foreign visitors by Communist authorities because of its proximity to disputed border areas. Nevertheless, Kailas still receives pilgrims from the four faiths that regard it as holy. Under the best conditions, access to the holy mountain is extremely difficult, and the pilgrimage makes exhausting demands. The area is one of the most desolate and barren places in the world, four days' hard travel from the nearest entry point.

Mount Kailas is important as the source of the Indus, Ganges, Sutlej, and Brahmaputra Rivers, the last of which is Tibet's main waterway. The first two of these are among the most important sacred rivers on the Indian subcontinent, and the Kailas Range is regarded as a holy place by Hindus, Buddhists, Jains, and adherents of Tibet's primal religion, Bön. At the foot of the mountain is Lake Manasarovar, the highest body of fresh water in the world, fed by the Kailas glaciers.

For the Hindus, Mount Kailas is the home of Shiva, who lives there in paradise, with his long, dreadlocked hair falling about him. From one of these strands flows the mighty Ganges, holiest of rivers. The Buddhists regard Kailas as the center of the world. To them, the geographical features are heavy with symbolism: Kailas itself is the father principle, the means to enlightenment; Holy Manasarovar represents the mother-principle, transcendent consciousness. For the Jains, Kailas is the place where their first saint and founder, Rishabanatha, attained spiritual liberation. The Bön, holding to the Tibetan indigenous religion, merge national identity with the spiritual power of the mountain. Kailas symbolizes the continuity of the people and protects Tibet, the swastika-like gash on its southern flank an affirmation of that great power.

Among the shrines on the mountain was the Buddhist one to Yamantaka, one of the eight guardians of the faith. Many-armed and wearing a necklace of skulls, he stamps out laziness, stupidity, and cynicism. In the shrine he is shown locked in sexual embrace with his consort, symbolizing the mystic union of compassion and wisdom. Unfortunately, almost all of the religious establishments were destroyed in the Cultural Revolution (1966–1976) under Mao Tse-Tung. The 13 monasteries in the area were demolished, as well as the shrines that marked important spots on the pilgrim way. Pilgrims have placed rock cairns at the locations to mark them, but no shrines remain. Ten of the monasteries have been reopened under the strict quota system imposed by the Communist authorities to permit token monastic life, but each community has only a handful of monks.

Followed for over 1,000 years, the Kailas pilgrimage is one of the world's oldest continuing religious journeys. However, it would be the height of sacrilege to climb to the summit of the sacred mountain. Kailas has never been climbed. Instead, the main act of the pilgrimage is the *kora*, the 32-mile circuit of the mountain, which can be accomplished in a strenuous day's trek. Although one circuit is believed to be enough to erase a lifetime of sin, the goal of most pilgrims is to make the kora three times. The most determined seek a lifetime total of 108 circuits, which is said to ensure enlightenment to the pure-hearted. Some still make the 32-mile path fully prostrate, "measuring the holy way with their bodies."

At the approach to the mountain are four prostration stations where prayers are offered. Another important stop is the flagpole erected each year for the full moon nearest the anniversary of the Buddha's birth. There are also three monasteries on the way with small shrines. Four stations mark footprints of the Buddha along the trail. Mantras are chanted along the way, the ideal being to breathe in and out with the words until they merge with the self. Prayer flags, printed with prayers or symbols, are placed on cairns or hung on lines stretched between rocks; as they flutter in the wind, their blessings are released endlessly. At a number of places are *chortens*, a form of stupa. Simple brick monuments containing a few relics or sacred writings, they are decorated with prayer flags and *mani* stones engraved with the mantra, *Om mani padme hum*, "the jewel in the lotus." From station to station, the kora leads around the sacred mountain, increasing merit and inducing purification, leading to liberation. On arriving at each station, *gompa*, or chorten, the pilgrim usually circles it three times.

The kora around Mount Kailas is considered a pilgrimage through a complete cycle of life and death. Circles within the great circle symbolize the suffering of life, death, and rebirth, and the arduousness of the pilgrimage earns merit for liberation from the drudgery of life. At the highest pass, which symbolizes the passage from death to new life, pilgrims leave articles of clothing as to symbolize leaving behind their old ways. On this spot, death ceremonies are often conducted to drive out evil spirits and make the soul available to rebirth. The high point, both literally and in faith, is the Dolma Stone, the Hill of Salvation at the crest of the pathway. After prayers and prostrations, a celebration is held with sharing of food.

The Ramayana, sacred scripture of the Hindus, praises Lake Manasarovar, "its waters like pearls." Bathing in it ensures entry to paradise; drinking from it releases the soul from the sins of a hundred births. Hindus circuit the shoreline and take ritual baths in its waters, although no ghats are built there. At 64 miles, this trek is twice as long as the one around the mountain. It is also made clockwise.

See also Mountains, Sacred.

References Charles Allen, *A Mountain in Tibet*. London, Futura Macdonald, 1983. Russell Johnson and Kerry Moran, *The Sacred Mountain of Tibet*. Rochester, VT, Park Street Press, 1989. John Snelling, *The Sacred Mountain*. London, East-West Publications, 1983.

MOUNT KENYA, Kenya

Mount Kenya, a volcanic cone, is the second-highest mountain in Africa after Kilimanjaro, sacred to several peoples. Its three peaks—Lenana, Nelion, and Batian—range from 16,355 to 17,058 feet and are named after the three leading *laibons*, or prophet-healers, who ruled the Maasai people in the nineteenth century.

As part of the centuries-long great migrations across Africa, the Kikuyu, a Bantu people, arrived at Mount Kenya's base in the seventeenth century, where they came together with Hamitic and Nilotic tribes. The Maasai, Embu, Meru, and Kikuyu all worship the mountain as the home of their high god, Ngai, creator of the world. They permit no other temples to Ngai; away from the mountain, they worship under special trees that represent it. Some have incorporated worship of the mountain with Christianity, equating Ngai with the Creator God of the Bible. A cross sent by Pope Pius XI was placed at Point Lenana in 1933. Some climb Mount Kenya to commune with their god. A few Kikuyu mystics climb the mountain barefoot, despite the fact that the ascent is more difficult than any major Alpine peak.

The Kikuyu people of East Africa have always revered Mount Kenya, the "mountain of brightness," as the home of Ngai and the place where Ngai first created humanity. The Kikuyu creation myth recounts that Ngai took the first tribesman, named Gikuyu, to the top of Mount Kenya when he created the world and parceled it out among the peoples of the earth. Ngai pointed out a fig grove for Gikuyu, and there he found a wife, Mumbi, awaiting him. Together they had nine daughters, mothers of the nine clans of the Kikuyu tribe. Ngai has few relations with his people. Troubles, such as violation of taboos or failures in life, are not of interest to Ngai; a person must turn to the ancestors for solutions. Nor do individuals pray to Ngai; only a family seeking blessings together will be granted them. There are four sacred moments when a family raises its hands toward Mount Kenya to seek Ngai's blessings: birth, initiation, marriage, and death. Perhaps the most elaborate rituals are those of initiation, which may be at the time of circumcision (leaving childhood for adult status) or when becoming an elder. At circumcision the elders draw emblems on the initiates' bodies in chalk brought from Mount Kenya, a symbol of its eternal snow. At other special times, a red or black lamb is sacrificed to Ngai. The god is also beseeched for rain, and for blessings when holding a council or building a new house.

The mountain has continued to have special meaning in the life of the Kikuyu. During the Mau Mau rebellion against British colonialism in the 1950s, the guerrillas, mostly Kikuyu, took refuge in the forests of Mount Kenya, where they trusted Ngai to protect them. Before raids they offered sacrifices on the side of the mountain. Mount Kenya also represents freedom to the Kenyan people. On the eve of independence in 1963, Kenyan climbers raised the new flag on the summit at midnight to proclaim the new country.

See also Mountains, Sacred.

References Mohamed Amin, Duncan Willetts, and Brian Tetley, *On God's Mountain*. Nairobi, Kenya, Camerapix, 1991. Edwin Bernbaum, *Sacred Mountains of the World*. San Francisco, Sierra Club, 1990. Jomo Kenyatta, *Facing Mount Kenya*. New York, Random House, 1965.

MOUNT SHASTA, California, USA

Looming over the Cascade Range in northern California, Mount Shasta has long been sacred to the Native American Indians of northern California. The Shasta people believed that the Great Spirit created the mountain from above, cutting a hole in the sky and pushing down ice and snow until a mountain was formed that pierced the clouds. The Great Spirit then used the mountain to step onto the earth, creating trees and calling upon the sun to melt snow to provide rivers and streams. He breathed upon the leaves of the trees and created birds to nest in their branches. When he broke up small twigs and cast them into the streams, they became fish. He cast branches into the forest to become animals; large animals sprang up when he threw down logs. The largest of these was the grizzly bear. For the Shasta, the mountain was at the center of creation.

The Modoc people, who share this account, believe that the Great Spirit took up his abode on the mountain. His daughter, who fell from the mountain, was raised by grizzly bears and married one of their clan. Their children were the first humans. In punishment for violating his authority, the Great Spirit condemned the bear to walk on four legs and scattered their progeny all over the world. Modern cults, copying quasi-Indian myths, tell the story of Coyote, who took refuge on the mountain when a flood covered the earth. His fires attracted other animals, and from them, life was renewed on the planet.

Today, the Shasta people have largely disappeared, scattered or absorbed into other groups through intermarriage. Mount Shasta has taken on new religious meaning in recent years, becoming an important locale for New Age groups. Awed by its power as it sits atop a lava flow along a major fault line, many regard the mountain as a source of cosmic energy. It was one of the centers for the 1987 Harmonic Convergence, in which New Agers gathered at a number of "power points" in the hope that their united spiritual energy might avert world catastrophe and usher in an age of harmony and peace.

Mount Shasta's energy is said to be magnetic, drawing people toward it. Over a hundred sects and groups regard Shasta as a sacred place. It has been identified as a UFO landing spot, a source of magic crystals, the entry point to the fifth dimension, and one of the nine sacred mountains of the world. The reference to the fifth dimension is based on the New Age belief that beyond the third dimension of human experience lies a fourth—time—and a fifth—playful tenderness. Mount Shasta is experienced by New Agers as a great mother and is often described as a mother's breast, an experience of harmony and belonging. In 1932 the Rosicrucians popularized the claim that Shasta is home to a race of humanoid creatures, the Lemurians, who are so spiritually advanced that they are able to transform themselves from material to spiritual levels at will. They work their power through a great cache of crystals they brought with them from their original continent in the Pacific Ocean when it was destroyed in a volcanic eruption.

The most famous New Age association of Mount Shasta has been with the Ascended Master St. Germaine, who first appeared when Guy Ballard, the founder of the "I AM" movement, claims to have met him on the slopes of Mount Shasta in 1930. Ascended Masters are those who have integrated thought and feeling and manifest "the luminous essence of divine love." According to New Age tradition, they guard and assist human evolution. The great popularizer of both the ideas associated with St. Germaine and revelations on Mount Shasta is Elizabeth Clare Prophet, one of the most prominent New Age teachers. The town of Mount Shasta, at the foot of the mountain, has become headquarters for a number of New Age and spiritualist societies. At several study centers in the town, seekers can explore esoteric teachings.

In recent years, revived Native American religion has begun to celebrate Mount Shasta. Each year a sweat lodge ceremony is conducted halfway up the mountain. The Wintu, who have always venerated the mountain, invoke its spirit with ritual dances.

See also Mountains, Sacred; Native American Sacred Places; New Age.

References Arthus Eichorn, *The Mount Shasta Story*. Mount Shasta, CA, Mount Shasta Herald, 2d ed., 1971. William Hamilton, *Mount Shasta, Home of the Ancients*. Mokelumne Hill, CA, Health Research, 1986. Rosemary Holsinger, *Shasta Indian Tales*. Happy Camp, CA, Naturegraph, 1982.

MOUNT SINAI, Egypt

In the heart of the Sinai Desert, in an area with no natural attractions, a small mountain rises, marking one of the great holy places of three religions—Judaism, Christianity, and Islam. It was there, on Mount Sinai, that Moses met God and received the stone tablets of the Law.

Earlier, when Moses was grazing his flocks on the side of the mountain, he came upon a burning bush that was not consumed, from which Yahweh spoke, calling Moses to deliver the Jews from bondage. Much of the first half of the book of Exodus is the account of the people going to Sinai, where they camped in the wilderness. Here God spoke: "You have seen what I did to the Egyptians, and how I bore you up on eagles' wings and brought you to myself." Then God offered the Covenant by which the people became God's "possession among all the peoples." The people purified themselves for three days and then assembled at the foot of the mountain. Yahweh descended upon it in fire and it was wrapped in smoke and trembled. When Moses went up the mountain, God gave him the Ten Commandments. The glory of the Lord, "like a consuming fire on the top of the mountain," was visible to all the people. Even after the people built and worshipped a golden calf, God did not desert them but sent an angel to guide them from Mount Sinai to the other holy mountain, Mount Zion, identified with the Temple Mount in Jerusalem.

Because Yahweh came down from the mountain and journeyed with them, Mount Sinai never became an organized place of pilgrimage for Jews, although many come today as religious tourists. The mountain never became holy in its own right because God had gone from there, but the Covenant is holy, and the word of God remains. Sinai is invoked in synagogue services as a symbol of the Covenant.

Christians, on the other hand, revered Mount Sinai as the site of the scenes so vividly told in Exodus. The area is sere and awesome; the mountain rises 7,500 feet above a wilderness wasteland of sand, rock, and burning sun. It was the perfect isolation for early Christian hermits, who began to settle on Jebel Musa, the Mountain of Moses, now known as Mount Sinai. They began to attract pilgrims, despite the terrible conditions involved in making the trip. By 300 CE some of the hermits had banded together into monastic communities, partly to protect themselves from raids by desert bands who often murdered them or looted their simple possessions. In the sixth century, the Emperor Justinian built a fortified monastery on the site where the monks claimed to have found the burning bush. This became *Saint Catherine's Monastery*, which has continued as an Orthodox monastery to this day. Guaranteed the protection of the new Islamic rulers who occupied Egypt several centuries later, the monastery maintained a precarious but continuing existence, and it is the primary Christian presence in the Sinai Desert.

Muslims revere Moses as one of the prophets, but the mountain is mostly a Christian pilgrimage site. According to tradition, the body of St. Catherine, an Egyptian martyr, was carried by angels to a nearby mountain. There her relics were discovered and brought to the monastery at the base of Mount Sinai, which was then named in her honor. St. Catherine's also became the inspiration for a number of other monasteries throughout the world during the Middle Ages, and its fame spread. The monks are Greek Orthodox, under the jurisdiction of the patriarch of Constantinople. Down to only seven monks in 1970, the monastery has grown steadily in recent years and now numbers about 20. The compound is surrounded by granite walls and contains a principal church, many devotional chapels, a magnificent library of ancient manuscripts, and the monastery quarters. The church is on the site of the burning bush,

and the monks will show visitors the plant itself, which they believe to be thousands of years old. The monastery's collection of icons is one of the finest in the world. Its isolation kept them from being destroyed during the iconoclast conflict, when those who opposed depictions of Christ or the saints broke up and burned any icons they could find. Consequently, St. Catherine's collection includes the largest number of truly ancient icons in existence.

Pilgrims usually attend liturgy at the monastery and may stay in a small hostel there, although most are housed in modern motels in the area, built for tourism. The main attraction is the ascent of the mountain, up 3,000 steps cut into the mountainside. It is customary to make the climb during the night, both to avoid the heat of the day and to be on the summit for dawn. Close to the top is an arch where monks once heard confessions and refused entry onto the holy ground for those whose sinfulness or lack of faith made them unworthy and thus might cause God to strike them down. Near the peak is a stone hut marking the spot where the Prophet Elijah heard the voice of God in the breeze, telling him to anoint a new king in Israel. At the summit is a small chapel, and the view of the surrounding desert and mountains is powerful and moving. Mount Sinai presents itself as a huge altar of God, a place to worship his might.

See also Mountains, Sacred; Mount Athos.

References John Gayley, *Sinai and the Monastery of St. Catherine*. London, Chatto & Windus, 1980. Joseph Hobbs, *Mount Sinai*. Austin, University of Texas, 1995. Jill Kamil, *The Monastery of St. Catherine in Sinai*. Cairo, Egypt, American University Press, 1991.

pilgrimage involving, in normal times, tens of thousands. Devout Shi'a men keep a three-day growth of beard in perpetual mourning for Husayn. Karbala is a religious symbol for redemptive suffering that will lead to liberation from oppression, and many aged Shi'a come to die in Karbala because of their belief that the city is one of the gates to the Heavenly Paradise promised the faithful in the Holy Qur'an.

Sunni rulers have prohibited the Karbala pilgrimage several times and even destroyed the shrines, but they are always rebuilt. Because the Shi'a believe in an eventual messiah, the *mahdi,* who will establish a kingdom of peace and justice on earth, the cult is regarded as revolutionary and threatening. In recent years, Shi'ite association with the Iranian revolution under the Ayatollah Khomeini caused the Iraqi government to suppress the Shi'a, with frightful loss of life. In 1991, the shrines, which were richly endowed, were plundered of their valuables by the Iraqi army. Thirty-two mosques, 10 religious schools, and 66 prayer halls were destroyed in ruthless shelling and tank attacks to retake the city after it rebelled against the regime of Saddam Hussein.

Until the rise of the Saddam Hussein regime, Karbala was a place of sanctuary for religious dissidents from Iran and Iraq, but this role is no longer respected. Karbala was also a gathering place for pilgrim caravans to Najaf and Mecca. Besides the shrine of Husayn, a shrine in Karbala is dedicated to his half brother, al-Abas, who is invoked for miraculous cures.

Najaf is the location of the shrine of the first Shi'ite imam, Ali, son-in-law of Mohammed. Many Shi'a bring their dead to the shrine, carrying the coffin around the sarcophagus before taking it away to be

NAJAF AND KARBALA, Iraq

These two Persian cities, 50 miles apart, are centers of Shi'a teaching and devotion. After Mohammed's death in 632, Islam was divided between those who believed that leadership should fall on his descendants and those who believed that the community should choose its leaders independently. At Karbala, the Imam Husayn, grandson of the Prophet Mohammed, was martyred along with many followers in 680 CE during this conflict. With Husayn's martyrdom, the two traditions—Shi'a and Sunni—became permanently separated. The Shi'a believe that the Imams, though not prophets, have divine authority and inspiration. The Shi'ites revere their leaders and saints and have developed places to honor them. Husayn's shrine became a place of pilgrimage immediately after his murder, and the more extreme devotees argued that a pilgrimage to Karbala was equal to the Hajj.

The cult of Husayn is obsessed with his death, producing laments and dirges that are sung as part of the pilgrimage rites. The vast dome over Husayn's gold-and-silver tomb is covered with mosaics of mirrors, and pilgrims kissed the silver cover of the tomb (now looted). The annual period of mourning for Husayn is the time of an extended

197

buried. It is considered holy to be buried in Najaf near Ali. (However, his tomb may be only a symbolic resting place rather than his actual resting place.) Besides the traditional dome over the tomb, Najaf has cells for Sufi mystics who have formed convents there. Nearby are other shrines, including a mosque on the spot where Ali was martyred. Many Sh'ia are called Twelvers because they believe that the twelfth imam, who disappeared, will one day return as the messiah. According to legend, the Hidden Imam appears each Tuesday for sunset prayer at a certain Najaf mosque, which always draws crowds on that day.

For many years, Najaf was the center of Shi'a learning, but in the twentieth century this role has shifted to Qom in Iran. Najaf, which traditionally avoided all politics, took up the cause of the Iranian ayatollahs in the religious and political revolution of the 1970s. Ayatollah Khomeini lived in exile here from 1965 to 1978, leading opposition to the Iranian government of the Shah. Most of the Najaf shrines have also been despoiled by the Iraqi government, and many people believe that the stolen shrine gold and jewels personally enriched the family of President Hussein. In a somewhat cynical turnabout, Hussein has made a great show of repairing damage to the shrines caused when his army recaptured the city in 1991 after a rebellion against his regime.

References Hamid Algar, *Religion and State in Iran, 1785–1906.* Berkeley, University of California, 1969. *Living Islam.* New York, BBC, 1993 (video). Moojan Momen, *Introduction to Shi'a Islam.* New Haven, CT, Yale University, 1985.

NAN MADOL, Pohnpei

Between 500 and 1600 CE, a small island in the Caroline Islands near Guam was the social and religious center of a powerful Pacific island dynasty, the Saudeleurs, who ruled Pohnpei (Ponape) for 16 generations. The group took its name from a prominent sacred high priest, Sau Deleur, who ruled around 1000 CE and completed the construction of a unique sacred city. On the reef and tidal flats on the eastern shore of Pohnpei, the Saudeleurs built 92 artificial islands as their capital and cultic center. The islets are built close enough together that the surrounding water forms a series of canals, and the name *nan madol* means "between the spaces." One part of the area was set aside as a residence for the priests and rulers, and another was the administrative center that included temples, tombs, meeting houses, and such facilities as public baths and ponds for turtles and eels. The turtles were killed and offered to the sacred eels, who swam into their pond through an opening to the sea. Evidently, their arrival and acceptance of the offering was considered auspicious. The chief temple was dedicated to a crocodile spirit-god, and the sacred spirits were given offerings of cooked shellfish. The most important deities, who were seen as clans of gods, were protectors of seafaring and canoe-building. Tombs that indicate that ancestor worship was prominent in Nan Madol religion.

The city was built of huge slabs of basalt cut from the interior of the island, shaped and used like logs to construct imposing buildings. To a visitor arriving by sea, the sight of 30-foot-high black basalt walls made of log-like slabs that each weighed 25 to 50 tons is startling. The walls are filled with coral rubble to form strong structures. One islet has a seawall of monoliths similar to those of Easter Island. At its height, Nan Madol was home to 1,000 priests and elite of Pohnpei society. Around 1500 CE it was abandoned, and island oral tradition has it that a rival people overthrew the

Saudeleurs. Nan Madol had long ceased to be the headquarters of the rulers.

Nan Madol is one of the leading archaeological sites in the Pacific Ocean. Since 1979, it has been part of the Federated States of Micronesia; since 1986, in associate status with the United States. The local people, descendants of the kings who drove the Saudeleurs out, believe that their ancestors' spirits remain on Nan Madol, and they generally avoid the site, except to take tourists there.

See also Rapa Nui.

References William Ayres, "The Mystery Islets of Micronesia," *Archaeology* 43:1, 58–63. (January 1990). William Ballinger, *The Lost City of Stone.* New York, Simon & Schuster, 1978. Sherrill Miller, *The Sacred Earth.* Stillwater, MN, Voyageur, 1991, 103–107.

NARA, Japan

The city of Nara in northern Japan has been a Buddhist center and place of peace and pilgrimage since the eighth century. From 710 to 784, the town was the first capital of Japan. A great deal of Chinese culture was absorbed during this period, which is reflected in the artistic riches of the city's temples and shrines. Nara became the hub of Buddhism, but the resulting rise of a powerful Buddhist priesthood convinced the Emperor Kammu to move the capital to Kyoto. Thus bypassed by development, Nara has remained a quiet temple city. Paths in the forest surrounding the temple area are dotted with rustic Buddha shrines, including the popular Sunset Buddha, so named because the last rays of the sun light up its face. Most pilgrims visit the major temples.

Horyu-ji Temple, one of the oldest temple complexes in Japan, is set a distance from Nara City. Its collection of priceless Buddhist art in the Golden Hall dates from the seventh century, and throughout the buildings, the architectural details, statuary, and furniture are the finest examples of Buddhist artwork in Japan. The hall itself is the oldest wooden building in the world. But Horyu-ji is no mere tourist attraction; it is a living shrine. Devotees come daily in all seasons to worship in its serene atmosphere, a park-like setting with free-roaming deer, which are regarded as divine messengers.

In the sixth century, Horyu-ji was the focal point of the movement that brought Buddhism to Japan and raised it to dominance over Shinto, the traditional nature religion. Clan wars proliferated during this period until a Buddhist family overcame the last great Shinto clan, and Shotoku Taishi became prince-regent (593–622). He began constructing Horyu-ji in 607 and became an ardent promoter of Buddhism, translating major texts and spreading the religion. The Sacred Spirit Hall in the eastern section of the complex is dedicated to Prince Shotoku, built where his meditation chapel once stood. A century after Shotoku's death, Horyu-ji became the place where Buddhism and Shinto were reconciled; both retain their characteristic beliefs, but many elements are shared or blended. Above the Shaka (historic) Buddha in the Golden Hall are several delicate carvings of heavenly musicians, descending to earth with the Buddha to welcome the spirit of Shotoku. Nearby is the Yakushi (healing) Buddha.

Kasuga Taisha Shrine, founded in 768, is the main Shinto shrine in Nara and one of the three greatest in Japan. It is actually four shrines dedicated to different Shinto deities. The most distinctive features of Kasuga Taisha are 3,000 stone and bronze lanterns that line the approach to the shrine and are lit for lantern festivals in February and August, lending a dream-like atmosphere to the setting. The bright, vermilion-lacquered buildings contrast strikingly with the surrounding greenery. As is Shinto custom, the entire temple complex is rebuilt approximately every 20 years. The Treasure House, a modern building, contains artifacts for Shinto ceremonies.

The *Tōdai-ji Shrine,* which spreads over 60 serene blocks in the heart of the city, is a contrast to Horyu-ji, which is usually thronged with visitors. Its gate is supported by 19 pillars, and two huge guardian figures protect the entrance. The sense of triumph is reinforced by the Great Buddha Hall, advertised as the largest wooden structure in the world, 160 by 190 feet. The Great Buddha itself is a 550-ton bronze, 53 feet high, constructed in 749. Todai-ji was founded in 752, with a lavish dedication ceremony, to be the head temple of all Buddhist temples in Japan. The Great Buddha Hall has twice burned down and was last rebuilt (1708) at two-thirds the original size. Others of the many buildings contain priceless artwork: statues, wall paintings, and ceramics, all gifts to the shrine.

References Flavio Conti, *Splendor of the Gods.* Boston, HBJ Press, 1978. Charles McCarry and George Mobley, "Kyoto and Nara: Keepers of Japan's Past," *National Geographic* 149:6, 636–658 (June 1976). Peter Popham, *Wooden Temples of Japan.* London, Tauris Parke, 1990.

NATIVE AMERICAN
SACRED PLACES

Although many Native Amerindian traditions acknowledge special holy places, these are usually not shrines but sacred landscapes, especially mountains and rocks. Certain streams, because they are living water, are used by eastern tribes for purification rites, and the Cherokee, an agricultural people, conducted various rites in the fields,

using tobacco as incense and offering prayers for the harvest.

The major Native American sacred places are described in separate articles, but others of note include the following:

Onagazi, a mesa in the Dakota Badlands, is the site of the 1890 Ghost Dance held by Red Cloud and his disciples. The Ghost Dance was believed to bring back the souls of warrior ancestors, who would then join the living Indians in driving the white man from Indian land. It so infuriated and frightened government agents that it was forbidden, which led to the massacre at Wounded Knee later that year. The mesa is a high, windswept tableland, revered as a holy place but not used for pilgrimage or ceremonies.

Mato Tipi, or "Bear's Lodge," is known to whites as the Devil's Tower. It rises abruptly from the plain northwest of the Black Hills and is regarded as a sacred place by the Sioux. Each year the war chief Crazy Horse brought his clan here for the Sun Dance. In the Sun Dance, young braves demonstrate their willingness to endure suffering by having skewers inserted beneath the skin of their breasts. Thongs are tied to the skewers and also attached to a central pole. The dancers lean away from the pole, dancing and gazing into the sun, increasing their pain, until the skin rips free. They believe by enduring the Sun Dance they have suffered for their people and guaranteed the Great Spirit's blessings and protection. The warriors who pass out are considered to have entered into communion with the spirit world.

Canyon de Chelly, Arizona, contains an extensive collection of Anasazi ruins. The Anasazi—referred to as "the Ancient Ones" by their successors, the Hopi, Navajo, and Zuñi—flourished in the Southwest from about 500 to 1400 CE.

They left thousands of settlements, some of them multilevel buildings built on the sides of steep cliffs. When the Anasazi dispersed, they broke into smaller groups (perhaps clans) that evolved into the later Amerindian tribes. Canyon de Chelly (pronounced "de shay") reflects this unfolding with evidence of later occupation. The Anasazi ruins line the canyon, which stretches for 26 miles. Farming was conducted along the better-watered canyon floor, while hunting took place in the forested areas in the mountains. The Navajo later occupied the site, leaving wall paintings, and in 1863 they made their final stand here against Kit Carson. The area was returned to the Navajo in 1868 and is now managed by them in conjunction with the U.S. Park Service. Access is restricted to those with permits. In the dwellings, one may see kivas (worship rooms) and the characteristic hole in the main room, the *sipapu*, a symbolic entrance to the underworld from which the Anasazi believed they had come. There is also a burial cave, Mummy Cave, and several houses noted for their Navajo murals.

A parallel Anasazi development is found at *Mesa Verde* in Colorado, which at its height had 7,000 inhabitants. It was also abandoned around 1300 CE. It is listed on the UNESCO List of World Heritage Sites.

Amerindians often created temporary sacred spaces (and continue to do so), either for specific ceremonies or as places to seek wisdom and enlightenment. Prominent among them are the sweat lodges of the Plains Indians, built for purification, insight, and as part of a vision quest. Among the Apache, a special wikiup (a small tipi or hide-covered hut) was erected for a young girl's coming-of-age ceremony. It was used as a place for her to dance before the rituals conducted in the open. Though tipis were generally built for everyday use, special

ones were constructed for ceremonies, often with ritual elements like specially painted lodge poles. Ceremonial circles, some of them very elaborate, were used in many Native American traditions. All of these are examples of sacred spaces created for special events and then removed or allowed to decay and return to the earth. Many of these traditions continue.

Permanent religious shrines are uncommon in Native American cultures. One of the exceptions was the Cherokee Sacred Fire, kept burning in a national shrine until 1729, when it was allowed to die. When the tribe was force-marched to Oklahoma in the 1830s, ashes from the Sacred Fire were carried with them.

See also Bighorn Medicine Wheel; Black Hills; Cahokia Mounds; Chaco; Medicine Wheels; Mound-Builders; Sweat Lodge.

References George Cantor, *North American Indian Landmarks*. Detroit, Gale Research, 1993. Don Doll, SJ, *Vision Quest*. New York, Crown, 1994. Michael Durham, *Guide to Ancient Native American Sites*. Old Saybrook, CT, Globe Pequot Press, 1994. Arlene Hirschfelder and Paulette Molin, *The Encyclopedia of Native American Religions*. New York, Facts on File, 1992. Klara Kelley and Harris Francis, *Navajo Sacred Places*. Bloomington, Indiana University Press, 1994.

NAZARETH, Israel

Mary and Joseph's village in Galilee, northern Israel, was a hamlet of about 480 people when Jesus was a youth there. He left Nazareth to be baptized by his cousin John and begin his preaching. When he later returned to speak in the village synagogue, he was met with hostility. After the expulsion of the Jews from Jerusalem under the Emperor Hadrian, Nazareth was resettled by refugee priests from the temple. Jesus' family remained there, however, and in the third century, a Christian descendant named Conon, who had become a missionary, was martyred in Turkey.

The tiny Nazareth of Jesus' time contrasts with bustling, noisy Nazareth today. The chief shrine is the Church of the Annunciation, a double church completed in 1969 by the Franciscans. It is so large that it covers the entire area occupied by the village of Jesus' time. It is a beautiful structure, built with good taste and restraint, that blends harmoniously into its surroundings. It incorporates the sacred grotto where the angel Gabriel is believed to have appeared to Mary to tell her she had been chosen to be the mother of the Messiah. It also joins together the remnants of the Byzantine church (430 CE) and the medieval Crusader church. The art is outstanding, especially the stained-glass windows and mosaics from around the world. Wall paintings present the Annunciation as seen in different cultures, and magnificent bronze doors portray the life of Christ.

Beneath the Church of the Annunciation, excavations have revealed a small chapel facing toward Jerusalem, with a cross worked into its mosaic floor. It was probably a primitive Jewish Christian synagogue. (Early Jewish Christians observed all the Jewish prescriptions, but also celebrated the Lord's Supper.) A ritual bath from the second century was also located.

In or near the town are many other shrines and churches. Next to the Church of the Annunciation is St. Joseph's, built above what is thought to be Joseph's home, a single-roomed cottage used for both work and living space. The location of the synagogue where Jesus preached is now marked by the Greek Catholic Synagogue Church in the midst of the Arab market, a warren of unmarked alleys with shops and kiosks. Just north of Nazareth is Kafr Kana (Cana), regarded as the site of Jesus' first miracle. To the east is Mount Tabor, which St. Helena, the mother of Constantine, identified as the place of the Transfiguration; a large church marks the spot.

There was a Christian church in Nazareth by 350 CE, and in 570 a pilgrim wrote of visiting the synagogue where Jesus had preached and the house of Mary, which by that time was a basilica. After the Arab conquest in the eighth century, conditions deteriorated and the Christians had to pay an annual "ransom" as a tax for using the Church of the Annunciation. For most of the past hundred years, Nazareth has been an Arab Christian town, but pressure from the Israeli government has caused large numbers to emigrate to America and Europe.

See also Bethlehem.

References Chad Emmett, *Beyond the Basilica: Christians and Muslims in Nazareth*. Chicago, University of Chicago, 1995. Christopher Hollis and Ronald Brownrigg, *Holy Places*. New York, Praeger, 1969. M.J. Stiassny, *Nazareth*. Jerusalem, Jerusalem Publishing House, 1967.

NAZCA LINES, Peru

One of the great unsolved mysteries of the New World is the origin and purpose of the Nazca Lines of Peru, enigmatic scorings across the plateaus by which some ancient people drew the symbols of their faith. Created long before humans could fly, they can be seen only from the air. Perhaps they were intended to be seen only by the gods? The designs are also large: a 300-foot monkey, a 600-foot lizard, and a 200-foot hummingbird are typical of the desert drawings. They were made by removing the dark surface of the desert floor on a plateau in southern

Peru, revealing the underlying chalk that forms the drawings.

The Nazca people, about whom little is known, inhabited this barren area from about 1000 BCE to 700 CE, when they were absorbed into the rising Inca civilization. The lines are not the only relics of their civilization. They were skillful weavers, adept at dyeing in a wide range of colors. They also produced attractive polychrome pottery, where some of the same themes found on the desert floor (the hummingbird, for example) are repeated.

The lines are interspersed with spiral mazes, figures of animals, reptiles, birds, and flowers. They were unknown until 1927, when a Peruvian survey pilot discovered them on a routine flight. The lines radiate from hills or elevations, and special points are indicated by cairns (rock-pile markers). Spread across 200 miles of desert, the lines cut across valleys and hills without deviation. Similarities with the lines found at Cuzco lead some to speculate that the Nazca Lines preceded the Inca ones, or that the Inca learned them from the people they assimilated. Speculation further suggests that the lines were intended as "roads" for magical processions of the spirits of the ritual animals depicted in the drawings. Legends found among the peoples of the plateau when the Spaniards arrived in the late 1500s support this possibility.

Modern followers of New Age religions have interpreted the Nazca Lines as ley lines, straight alignments that are considered the paths of earth energy or some form of spiritual force. At Nazca the New Age students call them "ray centers," because they follow star patterns rather than running parallel. Despite the star shape, all attempts to connect them with sun or star sightings have proved fruitless.

See also Cuzco; New Age.

References Paul Devereux, *Secrets of Ancient and Sacred Places.* New York, Sterling, 1993. Richard Marshall, *Strange, Amazing and Mysterious Places.* San Francisco, Collins, 1993. Maria Reiche, *Mystery on the Desert.* n.p., Heinrich Fink, 1968.

NEW AGE

A large number of movements are gathered under the umbrella of the New Age movement. Although they are very diverse, common strands connect them: the goal of spiritual transformation, a tendency toward mystical experience, and reverence for the natural world and the forces of nature. New Agers share the values of environmentalists. There is no New Age authority and therefore no religious "doctrine," although common agreement can be found for a belief in a Higher Power, universal religion, and the desire for spiritual growth and fulfillment. Many accept reincarnation and pantheistic ideas of the spiritual powers of nature. The leading figures are often spiritual guides who lead groups of disciples.

New Age argues that Western philosophy and religion have separated humanity from nature, creating a dualism that is the source of alienation, loneliness, and anxiety. On a social level, this separation results in conflict, war, and racial and ethnic divisions. New Age argues that the exaltation of the intellectual and rational over the mythical and intuitive has resulted in a culture of dominance and competition rather than one of collaboration and mutuality. New Age rejects human superiority over the rest of nature as presented in the first chapters of Genesis in the Hebrew Bible. Only by reclaiming the primordial unity of all living beings can balance be restored.

New Age theorists incorporate many of the beliefs of primal peoples who worshipped the forces of nature and lived in harmony with it. Where traditional peoples continue to practice their ancestral religions, as with many American Indians, the appropriation of their religious practices by New Age devotees has caused friction and tensions.

Sacred sites hold a special place in New Age thought. Since the spiritual quest is focused on the reclaiming of an ancient heritage of unity with all matter, great emphasis is placed on search and pilgrimage. Sacred sites are seen as centers of earth energy where seekers experience recovery of what has been lost. The most powerful places are those that are naturally attuned or constructed to align themselves with sunlines, astral lines, meridians, or other channels of force and energy. These energy chains are cyclical and reflect the earth's magnetic fields or the circulating flow of the seasons. One form they take are ley lines, prehistoric paths connecting sacred places. A complex study of ley lines in the southwestern United States, the Nazca Plateau of Peru, and in southern England, as well as many other places, has resulted in a systematic theory of energy connection among sacred points.

When two or more energy meridians intersect, a psychic vortex results, and it is these natural "power spots" that the ancients recognized and used as places of worship. The comparison is often made with acupuncture points on the body, where oriental medicine believes energy flows center themselves in such a way that illness can be treated by manipulating these points to restore a natural flow of energy in the body. New Age believers usually agree that sacred sites, because they concentrate natural energy, are healing places. Because the mysteries of ancient wisdom are encoded and therefore unknowable to a modern mind clouded by rationality, only an elite can penetrate true knowledge. Consequently, there are important roles in New Age spirituality for persons with special gifts for deciphering the mysteries. These include gurus, spiritual guides, shamans, and wisdom figures. The images of pilgrimage, seeking, and spiritual search ("psychic venturing" or vision quest) are very strong elements of New Age thought.

Various followers of New Age conduct rituals at sacred sites, either to unlock the energy forces or to enter into deeper communion with nature and its mysteries. At the full moon in Aquarius in late summer, for example, the Night of the Shamans is celebrated on Mount Shasta, in which spiritual adepts gather to recharge their magical powers for another year. The numbers attracted to Stonehenge at the solstices have grown to such an extent that large security forces are needed for crowd control. In 1987, New Age devotees assembled at a number of sacred places believed to be power points to concentrate the forces of good against evil and thus avert a disaster predicted for the world. These gatherings, called the Harmonic Convergence, were a worldwide extension of smaller assemblies that are common in New Age.

Besides the movements with relationships to Wicca and various neopagan cults, New Age has influenced organized religion, emphasizing the values of closer experience of God and faith and the importance of spiritual growth. It shows itself in such forms as Cabbalistic mysticism among Jews and such cults as Our Lady of the Roses in Bayside, New York, among Catholics. Organized religion is generally hostile to New Age thought and practice, and recognized shrines are at pains to avoid association with it.

References Marilyn Bridges, *Markings: Aerial Views of Sacred Landscapes*. Oxford,

Phaidon, 1986. J. Gordon Melton, *New Age Encyclopedia*. Detroit, Gale Research, 1990. *The Shaman's Message*. Berkeley, Thinking Allowed (video).

NEWGRANGE, Ireland

Along the Boyne River north of Dublin lies the Brugh na Bóinne or Palace of the Boyne, the burial place of ancient tribal kings. The finest of the tombs is the passage grave at Newgrange, one of some 26 tombs in the valley. Its fame rests on the excellence of its workmanship and rock carvings, and its striking astronomical design. The tomb has been empty since 861 CE, when it was plundered by Viking raiders. By then the tombs were already ancient, since Newgrange has been dated to the Bronze Age, approximately 5,000 years ago, and it is not known for whom the tomb was built.

The Newgrange tomb covers an acre under an egg-shaped mound called a tumulus, rising from the meadow and surrounded by a stone curbing. Originally there were 38 pillar stones (12 remain) around the tomb, which is 250 feet across and 40 feet high. There are 97 curbstones carved with spirals, which followers of New Age religions interpret as symbolic of the journey to the next world. Scientific analysis suggests, however, that the stones were probably recycled from an earlier burial place and have no meaning at Newgrange. The facing around the perimeter of the tomb is several yards high and made of sparkling white quartz quarried 50 miles away. The bulk of the tumulus is made of 200,000 cantaloupe-sized stones brought in from 75 miles away. All of this is covered with soil to a depth of several yards. Clearly, a great effort went into the tomb's construction. The entrance is marked by the Threshold Stone, which is elaborately carved with spirals framed by concentric circles and diamond shapes.

Inside, a 60-foot passageway leads into a high-domed chamber with three side alcoves for burials. (The kings were cremated and only their ashes interred.) The inner room is made of layered stones forming a beehive vault, indicating that the builders had not yet discovered the arch. At the time of the midwinter solstice on December 21, the shortest day of the year, the passage to the interior tomb is pierced by a shaft of sunlight that touches a stone basin at the end of the passageway and lights up a series of spiral carvings whose meaning is unknown. This phenomenon lasts about 15 minutes.

The mysteries surrounding Newgrange have inspired a wide range of speculation and attracted spiritualists and modern druids. One theory even argues, based on its appearance, that Newgrange is a model of a flying saucer. Others consider it a solar temple built by a prehistoric race of supernatural people who lived in ancient Ireland before the Celts. It is known that the god of the pre-Christian period was Dagha, a sun idol. Scholars are generally agreed that Newgrange was both a tomb and a place for some sort of ceremonial and religious rites.

References Martin Brennan, *The Stars and the Stones*. London, Thames & Hudson, 1983. Peter Harbison, *Pre-Christian Ireland*. London, Thames & Hudson, 1988. Michael O'Kelly, *Newgrange*. New York, Thames & Hudson, 1994.

NIDAROS, Norway

Nidaros is the medieval name for the modern city of Trondheim along the central coast of Norway, a name that today is attached to Trondheim's great cathedral, Nidarosdomen, the resting place of St. Olav, apostle of Norway and heroic national figure.

As a young warrior, Olav Haraldson sailed forth to England a Viking and returned a Christian. In 1015 he was elected king of Norway by the parliament, which sat in Trondheim. Olav ruled for 13 years, evangelizing his people so zealously, especially attacking concubinage, that he made many enemies. He was dethroned by King St. Knut (Canute), a Danish ruler of England, and fled the country. Olav gathered his troops and returned in 1030. He died at the Battle of Stiklestad. Olav was buried at Trondheim, where his tomb began attracting pilgrims who regarded him as a martyr. The Christianity he tried so zealously to plant during his life began to take hold after his death.

Every year at Stiklestad, a short distance from Trondheim, the martyrdom is commemorated in the St. Olav Pageant on July 29. Over 350 participants perform before an audience of 20,000. The pageant recounts Olav's last days and gives an account of his life and faith. According to legend, one of the warriors who struck the king down saw a blind man cured after touching Olav's blood to his eyes. The knight went on pilgrimage to Jerusalem as a penance for his sin.

When Nidaros became the seat of an archbishop in 1152, there had been a basilica there for a century. But as the crush of pilgrims became greater, the church was expanded and decorated. The style is predominantly English Gothic, and Nidaros is Scandinavia's largest medieval building. The shrine of St. Olav became one of the most important pilgrimage places in the Middle Ages, despite the fact that Trondheim, halfway up Norway's coast, was difficult to get to by sea, and by land was at the end of a 20-day trek from Oslo. A series of pilgrim hostels was built across the country, and the devout from all over Europe flocked to Nidaros. The Norwegians were generous with hospitality and provided protection, and the way to Nidaros was reputed to be the safest pilgrimage route in Europe. It was marked by devotional crosses and curative springs associated with places visited by the saint. Approaching the cathedral, the pilgrim doffed his shoes and walked around it three times before entering. Some sought a cure, the release from a vow, or atonement for a crime.

Though much of the medieval splendor was destroyed by the Reformation, the fine stained-glass windows remain, along with a front entrance covered with stone carvings. The original shrine was so encrusted with gold and jewels that it took 60 men to carry it in the annual procession. At the time of the Reformation in 1537, the reliquary was taken and melted down (the receipt still exists), but Olav's body was returned to Nidaros in 1564. The grave was covered over a few years later, and its exact location in the cathedral is unknown.

See also Canterbury.

References Anonymous, *Great Sagas of Olaf Tryggvason and Olaf the Saint.* Copenhagen, Rosenkilde and Bagger, 1982. Dorothy Spicer, *Festivals of Western Europe.* New York, H.W. Wilson, 1958. Sigrid Undset, *Kristin Lavransdatter.* New York, Knopf, 1951 (fiction).

NIKKO, Japan

The city of Nikko began as a sacred place in the eighth century with the establishment of a Buddhist hermitage, and in time it became prominent for its training centers for Buddhist priests. Shrines and temples are clustered there. An old Japanese proverb says, "You have seen nothing splendid until you have seen Nikko."

Arching gracefully across the Daiya River and leading from the town to the

The Shinkyo, or sacred bridge of Nikko, arches across the Daiya River. Regarded as one of the most beautiful structures in Japan, the bridge was once used only by the emperor.

main shrines is the *Shinkyo* (sacred bridge), a red lacquered span that formerly only the emperor could use. The lacquered bridge at Nikko has long been considered one of the most beautiful structures in Japan, its simple elegance contrasting with the river gorge, the green hills, and the tumbling waters. Legend has it that the hermit who settled Nikko was carried across the river here by two serpents. From this spot, a road leads into the park, threading through 16,000 towering Japanese cedar trees that date from the seventeenth century.

Rinno-ji Temple, governed by a prince-abbot since 1300, is built on a hillside in a graceful and extensive meditation garden created in 1815, dotted with ponds and crisscrossed by paths leading amidst flowering azalea bushes. Its Three-Buddha Hall has many large lacquered statues, the most notable of which are the Thousand-Armed Kannon, Goddess of Mercy, and another Kannon with the head of a horse, protector of animals. Rinno-ji Temple was founded in 766 by the hermit who first settled the area, and a statue in his honor graces the park. At one time Rinno-ji had 500 subtemples under its rule.

The *Tosho-gu Shrine* is the centerpiece of Nikko. Its art either fills the visitor with awe or leaves him or her appalled at its vulgarity. It is dedicated to Ieyasu (+1616), who founded the Tokugawa Shogunate, a military dynasty that ruled Japan from 1603 to 1867. Ieyasu's burial at Nikko thrust it into national importance. Fifteen thousand artisans and craftsmen worked for two years, using 2.5 million sheets of gold leaf, to create a worthy shrine for the Tokugawa. The enshrinement of Ieyasu's spirit is reenacted twice a year in the Procession of the 1,000 Warriors.

Although it is a Shinto Shrine, Tosho-gu has several Buddhist elements. Next to the entrance gate is a five-story pagoda lacquered in red and gold. Beyond it is the formal entryway—a Buddhist-style Two Deva Kings (shrine guardians) Gate. It is followed by a granite water font for purification. Nearby is the Sacred Stable, where a white imperial horse is kept (a gift of New Zealand). It has become famous worldwide, because carved on its eaves are the original figures of the three monkeys "Hear no evil, Speak no evil, See no evil." A Buddhist "library" with over 7,000 scrolls of sacred texts is contained in a 20-foot revolving case; turning it is the equivalent of praying all those texts.

All the Tosho-gu buildings are noted for their intricate carvings and the splendor of their decoration. Unlike most Shinto shrines, which are well integrated into their natural settings and simple to the point of austerity, Tosho-gu is a riot of bright color and carving. Carved birds and flowers, dancing maidens, and sages follow one another around the buildings. The only exception to this mood of exuberance is Ieyasu's mausoleum itself, which is relatively simple. If the intention was to inspire awe and majesty rather than devotion, Tosho-gu succeeds. In 1868, at the end of the Tokugawa Era, Buddhism and Shinto were separated, and Rinno-ji became independent of the Tosho-gu Shrine.

Futara-san Shrine is the oldest building in the district, but it pales in comparison with Tosho-gu. It is consecrated to the mountain *kami*, a god and goddess couple and their god-child.

See also Nara; Shinto Shrines.

References *Buddhism: The Land of the Disappearing Buddha—Japan*. Richmond, VA, Time-Life, 1978 (video). H. Byron Earhart, *Religions of Japan*. San Francisco, Harper San Francisco, 1984. *Shinto: Nature, Gods and Man in Japan*. New York, Japan Society, 1977 (video).

The original script was rewritten in 1750, 1850, 1980, and 1984 to adjust to changing attitudes. The key changes in recent years have been in response to worldwide criticism that the text was anti-Semitic, leading to a boycott led by American Jews. A committee of American and German Catholics and Jews pressed for changes despite resistance from local people, who argued in favor of tradition, and who apparently did not see the anti-Semitism that was obvious to others. The final version made clear concessions, presenting Jesus as a Jew, fixing the blame for his death on the Roman authorities rather than the Jewish people, and redesigning costumes that had been stereotypes. Judas, for example, no longer wore yellow robes, the color assigned to Jews by Hitler, who had praised the play as a "convincing portrayal of the menace of Jewry." The curse on the Jews, "His blood be upon us and upon our children!" (Matthew 27:25), was no longer jeered by the total crowd but only by some of the Sanhedrin. An American priest called the changes "a magnificent turnaround," but many on the international committee hope to see further improvements.

References Lotte Eckener, *Oberammergau.* Westminster, MD. Newman Press, 1960. Vernon Heaton, *The Oberammergau Passion Play.* London, Hall, 1983. *Passion of Oberammergau.* Evanston, IL, Journal Films, 1990 (video). Leonard Swidler and Gerald Sloyan, *The Oberammergau Passionspiele Nineteen Eighty-Four.* New York, Anti-Defamation League, 1984.

OBERAMMERGAU, Germany

One of the most remarkable ex-votos in the world is the Passion play put on by the people of Oberammergau in Bavaria every ten years. A terrible plague stopped just short of the village in 1633, a blessing that the people regarded as a miracle. A vow was taken to enact Jesus' Passion and death as a thank offering, and it has been done ever since.

The next performance—the fortieth—is in 2000. Half the town takes part, over 1,100 as actors alone, and a year in advance men begin to grow long hair and beards to fit their parts. No outside help is involved; all props and costumes are made in the village. Over a half million people descend on the village for one of the 100 performances, and reservations two years in advance are recommended. Each presentation takes all day, with a break for lunch. In the first years, it was performed in the town cemetery on the graves of relatives who had died in the plague, but for several centuries it has been staged in an open-air theater.

There is competition for the major parts, and until 1990, the part of Mary was played only by a certified virgin under 35. That year a married mother of two shared the role after winning a court battle and enduring harassment and threats to herself and her children. Also for the first time in 1990, a Protestant was awarded a major part.

OLYMPIA, Greece

Olympia was the site of the greatest of the ancient games, held every fourth year after heralds traveled through ancient Greece proclaiming a sacred truce, thus making

An entranceway to the original Olympic stadium in Olympia, Greece. Inside the stadium, athletes competed in events such as chariot races, boxing, and wrestling. Three of the five-day games involved ceremonies to honor the gods; the last day was devoted to celebrating the winners.

travel safe. No war ever kept the ancient Greek Olympics from being held. Greek legends told of the foundation of the Olympics as part of the cult of the gods, and especially of Olympian Zeus, the high god in whose honor the games were held. They began in 776 BCE and lasted, unbroken, for 1,000 years. A series of four great games was held, one each year in rotation, always culminating in the greatest—Olympia.

The Olympic games lasted for five days. The first day was for sacrifices and offerings to the gods, followed by a day of chariot races, the pentathlon, and horse races. (In the horse and chariot races, the honor for winning did not go to the athlete, but to the owner.) The third day always fell on a full moon, and further religious ceremonies took place, closing with a great procession to the altar of Zeus for the sacrifice of 100 oxen, followed by a ceremonial feast. The boys' events (ages 12 to 17) were also held that day. The fourth day featured men's races, wrestling, boxing, and the *pankration*, a vicious fighting competition with almost no holds barred. Strangling, breaking fingers and blows to the genitals were all allowed, but not eye gouging. There was legal immunity for any unintended homicide.

The last day was the occasion for ceremonies and a feast in honor of the winners, further sacrifices, and the consecration of thank offerings, which were usually small statues of a runner or racer left at a shrine or in one of the many treasuries built by various city-states from across the Greek world.

Winners received only one prize—a wreath from a sacred olive tree. On returning home, however, victors were lavishly honored by their cities and were showered with gifts that could make them wealthy. Some were placed on pensions for life. Therefore, few participants were true amateurs.

The sacred precinct at Olympia contained many shrines, of which only fragmentary ruins remain. The main temples were dedicated to the goddess Hera and to Zeus, whose statue was an enormous three-story seated figure created by Phidias. He used over a ton of gold just for the drape the god wore, and the Greeks joked that Zeus had created elephants just to provide ivory for his statue. Around the statue was a shallow trench filled with olive oil, to reflect light on Zeus.

The race course and stadium were just outside the sacred precinct. Athletes were admitted after being tested and screened by priests in a month-long conditioning session. Those not in shape were flogged and expelled. Flogging was especially disgraceful, since it was otherwise reserved for slaves. The competitors took part in the nude, a symbol of ritual purity. The Greek cult of beautiful male bodies often caused spontaneous applause for particularly handsome athletes, and lesser games than Olympia included nude male beauty contests. In ancient Greek religion, piety, sport, and physical beauty were melded together. There were even funeral games that combined sport contests with mourning rites—the winner was rewarded with the dead hero's property.

Although thousands of spectators came to the games, adult women (but not small girls) were strictly prohibited, with the single exception of the priestess of Demeter. Women who were caught at the games were thrown over a cliff to their deaths. After one woman sneaked in disguised as her son's coach, even trainers were required to be naked during the games. As a concession for females, a footrace for girls and young women was held just before the men's games, evidently part of a religious coming-of-age ceremony for young women.

In 67 CE the Emperor Nero himself took part at Olympia, decreeing a special category of music and drama, which he won. He also took part in the chariot races and was awarded the winner's garland even though he fell off and failed to finish. When he died the next year, his bogus achievements were deleted from the records. In 393 CE the games were closed by the Christian Emperor Theodosius, who banned all pagan cults and sacrifices. Without the religious element, the Olympics could not survive. In the sixth century the area was devastated by earthquakes and was gradually abandoned and forgotten. It was rediscovered in the eighteenth century, giving inspiration to a modern revival of the games as an athletic contest, the first of which was held in Athens in 1896.

References Tessa Duder, *Journey to Olympia: The Story of the Ancient Olympics.* New York, Scholastic, 1992. Donald Kyle, "Winning at Olympia," *Archaeology* 49:4, 31–37 (July-August 1996). Judith Swadling, *The Ancient Olympic Games.* Austin, University of Texas, 1984.

ORISSA TRIANGLE, India

Orissa, a city on the shores of the Bay of Bengal, has an ancient religious history as a center of sun worship. Later it became Buddhist, but for many centuries it has been exclusively Hindu. The area is known for lavish temple architecture in a unique Orissan style; its main structural feature is a sanctuary tower rising from a square base with porches or plazas; beneath the tower is the

The Sun Temple, its relief of wheels pictured here, was erected during the reign of Narasimhadeva (1238–1265) and pays tribute to Konarak, the center of Indian sun worship. Erotic carvings, which are found throughout the temple, are clearly visible here.

room containing the image of the deity. The tower is layered and ends in a squat capstone. There are two halls: one for dancing and another for offerings. The outside is covered in carvings of animals and humans, usually in sexual poses. The sculptures on the Orissa temples, which were built between the eighth and twelfth centuries, rank among the finest artwork in India.

Orissa is intensely religious, so Westerners are often shocked by the sexual art. Hindu belief accepts sexuality and integrates sensual pleasure into religious experience, consider-

ing it quite natural to include sexual scenes in the carvings on the walls of the temples. Those at Konarak, in Orissa, are perhaps the most explicit in India. In addition, an ancient Orissan temple dance, the Odissi, which is frankly erotic, has been revived.

Bhubaneswar once had over 1,000 temples, and many are still open. The most impressive of these is the *Lingaraj Temple*. Its tower is 150 feet high, with several porches around it. Fifty smaller temples cluster around Lingaraj, all decorated with extravagant carvings of gods, spirits, and couples in passionate embrace. Though open only to Hindus, other visitors may catch glimpses of the courtyard from a viewing platform. Nearby is the *Bindu Sarovar,* or "Ocean Drop," a purification tank (actually a small lake) into which the waters of all the holy rivers of India are said to flow. Once a year, the Lingaraj image is brought to a pavilion in the lake to be ritually purified. *Vaital Temple* is dedicated to Durga (Kali), the dark manifestation of Shiva's consort. Several sculptures of various forms taken by Durga show her with eight arms, fangs, and an air of violence. In one she sits on a corpse and wears a wreath of skulls.

Konarak has always been the hub of Indian sun worship, and the immense *Sun Temple* remains its centerpiece. Its tower has collapsed, but the design is still clear: the sun god, Surya, being drawn across the sky by seven horses on a huge stone chariot that forms the temple. Even in its collapsed state, its sheer size is almost overwhelming. The entrance, a pyramid, is flanked by two colossal lions crushing elephants, a symbol of Hinduism triumphant over Buddhism. Three statues of Surya are placed to catch the rays of the sun at sunrise, midday, and sunset. There are intricate detailed carvings over every temple surface. The erotic carvings are found everywhere and range from tiny to life-size. Although most portray couples, Konarak is unusual in having some solitary figures.

Puri is the holiest place in Orissa and one of India's largest Hindu pilgrimage centers. The cult of Jagannath and its annual Rath Yatra festival dominate the town. The *Jagannath Temple* dates from 1198, and even today, over 5,000 priests and temple attendants live within its compound, grouped into 36 orders and 97 ranks. Jagannath is worshipped as Lord of the Universe, an incarnation of Vishnu, one of the high trinity of Hindu gods. The grounds are surrounded by a high wall (600 feet on each side), and non-Hindus are prohibited from entering. But, unlike many Hindu temples, Puri welcomes all Hindus, even those of low caste. Because of its sacred status, Puri permits the use of bhang, a mildly narcotic drink made from marijuana, and the government maintains five ganja shops in the town to control the trade.

The statues of the god, his brother, and his sister are ceremonially bathed in preparation for the annual festival. Every 11 to 30 years (depending on astrological signs), new statues are carved from ritually chosen perfect trees. The existing statues are then buried secretly by the priests. During the festival the statues are placed on *raths,* huge ceremonial chariots. They are pulled by 4,000 men to a temple where they spend 7 days before being returned to their own temple. The raths, 30 feet square and 42 feet high with 6-foot wheels, are then broken up and the wood set aside for use in cremation fires.

References Mano Ganguly, *Orissa and Her Remains, Ancient and Medieval.* Flushing, NY, Asia Books, 1986. David Miller and Dorothy Wertz, *Hindu Monastic Life.* Montreal, McGill-Queen's University Press, 1976. Nagendra Vasu, *Modern Buddhism and Its Followers in Orissa.* Watertown, MA, South Asia, 1987.

OUR LORD IN THE ATTIC, Netherlands

In two prosperous merchants' joined canal houses in a seedy area of Amsterdam is a clandestine chapel known as *Ons' Lieve Heer op Solder,* Our Lord in the Attic. During the Reformation period in Holland, Roman Catholics were forbidden to practice their faith openly or to have churches. But the Dutch, in a spirit of compromise, tolerated

Catholic worship so long as it was not public. In Holland, Catholicism neither disappeared, as in parts of Germany and Switzerland, nor went underground, as in England, but continued discreetly. In 1663, a clandestine chapel dedicated to St. Nicholas was built into the top two floors of a large canal house. It featured a baroque altar and a pulpit that swings out from a hiding place at the touch of a secret button. A hidden apartment for the priest includes a secret compartment in case of police raids. Peep holes permitted advance warning. The story is told that during the celebration of the Mass, each man attending would be supplied with a flagon of beer, so that in case of a raid, the group could pretend to be a social gathering! Raids were infrequent, and clearly, the police and other authorities were bribed to turn a blind eye to the chapel.

Later, the original house was joined to two smaller neighbors, and the chapel expanded across the buildings. With its balconies on either side, it can seat over 100.

The Proclamation of Freedom of Religion in 1795 allowed the construction of proper churches, but many Catholics remained loyal to the clandestine chapels of the earlier period. Our Lord in the Attic became a museum in 1888 when a large church (also dedicated to St. Nicholas) was opened in the area. Amsterdamers insisted on their right to continue the use of the chapel for special events, however. Mass is celebrated on certain feast-days, and baptisms and weddings are held regularly in the chapel. Families often bring their children to the chapel and its secret rooms and passageways, to help them understand their religious history. The house and the chapel both contain valuable and artistically important paintings, carvings, and furniture. The museum is often called the "Amstelkring," after the association of historians who led the move to preserve it in the 1880s. The only other remaining clandestine chapel of the period is in the Begijnhof.

See also Begijnhof.

came known as a great saint. His defense of the oppressed peasants took the form of political resistance, and finally he was suspended from his priesthood by Church authorities under pressure from the government. He refused to accept this suspension and continued to work in his parish until his death in 1934. His home has become both a shrine to his memory and a hostel for beggars.

Besides his reputation for holiness, Padre Cicero left a promise that someday he would return. Until then—and fully expecting his second coming from the dead—pilgrims arrive at Juazeiro seeking miracles. They recount stories of healings, and in the museum in the town they pin up *milagros*, little metal ex-votos in the shape of the favor received—an ear for a cure of deafness, a heart for a happy marriage, a leg for curing an abscess, and so on. Thousands bring photos of loved ones, seeking help or witnessing to favors. Dolls, representing children confided to the Padre's prayers, line one shelf.

The greatest pilgrimages take place on the anniversary of Padre Cicero's birth; on All Soul's Day (November 2), the feast popularly called "the day of the dead"; and on March 1, the anniversary of the first "miracle of blood." On these occasions over 100,000 people stream into Juazeiro in ancient buses and trucks, carrying posters of Padre Cicero and signs such as "Driven by God." Many have traveled for days, crossing a desert to get to the town, which turns into a raucous market for a few days. Stalls sell food, statues of Padre Cicero, religious items, "miracle waters," and the ever-popular *milagros*. The faith of the people is strong as they press into the Padre's old home, touch their medals and rosaries to his bed, and light candles.

PADRE CICERO SHRINE, Brazil

The shrine of Padre Cicero in Juazeiro, northwest Brazil, is a place of pilgrimage where the peasants' folk religion has merged with Catholicism.

In the Third World there are many religious centers where Christianity has become blended with primal religion, the ancestral faith that existed among the people before missionaries brought Western religions. They do not belong to any one religious tradition, but have developed spontaneously from some charismatic person or event. One of the largest of these centers is the shrine of Padre Cicero.

Padre Cicero Batista was sent to Juazeiro in 1872 to be its parish priest and spent the rest of his life there, admired by the people for his fervent faith. In 1889, as he was giving Communion, the sacred bread was seen to turn red, and the people immediately proclaimed it to be a miraculous vision of the Blood of Christ. This event repeated itself several times until the bishop sent an investigating team, hoping to prove it a scam. The commission shocked the Church authorities by approving the miracles, but the bishop appealed to the Vatican, which did not, declaring them "vain and superstitious." Ignoring this, the poor streamed to the town, and Padre Cicero took them in, fed them, found homes for orphans, and be-

The Catholic church takes a wary view of the pilgrimages and mixed faith of the people. Padre Cicero was forbidden to preach or function as a priest for continuing to proclaim the miracles, but the present clergy do not condemn his followers or take sides. The peasants who come to Juazeiro ignore all the arguments and believe firmly in the miracles.

References Ralph Della Cava, *Miracle at Joasiero.* New York, Columbia University, 1970. Rowan Ireland, *Kingdoms Come: Religion and Politics in Brazil.* Pittsburgh, University of Pittsburgh, 1991. José Rodrigues, *The Brazilians.* Austin, University of Texas, 1967.

PAGAN, Myanmar

The ancient ruins of Pagan lie along the Irriwady River in central Burma. Scattered across the plains, the remnants of 2,217 temples and stupas slowly molder away from centuries of disuse, the relics of a religious city that once held 13,000 sanctuaries and temples cared for by 70,000 monks. Since it also had an important university, Pagan was one of the great centers of Buddhism. The kingdom that built this enormous complex lasted from 1044 to 1278. But the vast construction project of building Pagan so exhausted the kingdom and denuded the forests that it weakened the country and made it vulnerable to invaders. In 1278, Pagan was looted and burned by Chinese raiders. Since the palaces and pavilions were made of wood, only the stone temples and stupas survived.

The remains of Pagan stretch across eight miles of the river and cover 30 square miles, at some places so clustered that one can walk among them touching shrines on either side. Though many temples and stupas are reduced to rubble, a number are in excellent condition—temples with spires thrusting to heaven, covered in white or green tile that glimmers in the sunlight. The most important of these is the Ananda Temple, built as an ascending pyramid topped by a spire. Constructed of brick covered by white stucco, it rises six terraces above its base. Pagodas and other structures are built into it, giving it mass and strength. Ananda is constructed in the form of a Greek cross, with a long corridor and two cross aisles. Small devotional chambers branch off the main corridors. In four of these are standing Buddha statues, each 31 feet tall and made of gilded teak, one for each of the four directions of the compass. They are lit by hidden skylights.

The Thatbyinnyu Temple, built in 1144, is the highest in Pagan at 201 feet. From its top terrace the visitor can see the entire plain with its complex of ruins. The effect is eerie, since Pagan draws no rush of pilgrims and few tourists. The contrast with Shwe Dagon in Yangon, a thriving and bustling Buddhist sanctuary, could not be more complete. It is not as though Pagan has no shrines that might attract the faithful, since several pagodas hold such important relics as hairs from the Buddha. But the complex is quiet, even though it remains open to visitors. It is as if the spiritual authority of the place has deserted it. The area has been developed for visitors by the present military government, resulting in the forcible removal of several thousand peasants who lived in the villages that dot the area. The final expulsion of the local population seems to have removed the last vestiges of any human dimension from Pagan.

Only one aspect of Pagan indicates a living religious tradition. Scattered among the Buddhist sites are small wooden shrines to nature spirits, often lit with simple lamps. These are spirit houses and places for the souls of the dead, all part of an indigenous nature religion that has persisted despite the dominance of Buddhism, and which many Buddhists practice alongside their more austere faith. Among the temples is an ancestor shrine in this nature tradition—the Gawdawpalin Temple, extravagantly decorated with lovely carvings. There are often pilgrims and families at Gawdawpalin to honor their ancestors. It is this last group of shrines that draws many Burmese for worship.

See also Angkor Wat; Shwe Dagon Pagoda.

References Russell Ciochon and Jamie James, "The Power of Pagan," *Archaeology* 45:5, 34–41 (September-October 1992). Wim Swaam, *Lost Cities of Asia*. London, Elek, 1966. Rudolph Wurlitzer, *Hard Travel to Sacred Places*. Boston, Shambhala, 1995.

PARAY-LE-MONIAL, France

In the east of France, not far from the ruins of the great medieval monastery of Cluny and near the modern one of Taizé, lies Paray-le-Monial, a convent and the center of Catholic devotion to the Sacred Heart of Jesus.

During the seventeenth century, a great devotion sprang up in Christian Europe around the humanity of Jesus. Traditional Christian teaching has always held that Jesus was at the same time both divine and human, a unique person, son of God and son of Mary, sent for the salvation of all people. But the various Christian faiths have experienced tension in emphasizing one or the other aspects of Christ. Because Christ had often been presented as a distant and impersonal figure, this new devotion served to balance the excess of stress placed on his divinity. One of the chief forms the new movement took was devotion to the heart of Jesus, a sign of his love. Its most prominent advocate was Margaret Mary Alacoque (1647–1690), a young French nun and mystic. Margaret Mary entered the cloistered convent after being cured of a long illness and having a vision of Christ. Her visions and ecstacies were so intense that many other sisters considered her mentally ill—a few even thought she was possessed by the devil. Only with difficulty was she allowed to stay in the community.

After taking her vows, Margaret Mary continued to have visions of Jesus, from whom she claimed to have received a mission of spreading devotion to his Sacred Heart as a sign of his love for all humanity. She was fortunate in meeting a spiritual guide who showed her that her visions were not delusions. Under his direction, she wrote an account of her mystical experiences, which he used as the basis of a book that popularized the devotion. The sisters began to support Margaret Mary and the devotion spread. After her death, Paray-le-Monial became a place of pilgrimage, and it is often included on pilgrimage tours to sites in France that include Lourdes and Nevers.

Devotion to the Sacred Heart of Jesus has been a popular Catholic form of piety, although less so since the reforms of the Vatican Council. It is usually represented in art by Jesus holding his heart on his chest. The heart itself has a crown of thorns and is surrounded by a sunburst. The devotion is directed to Christ's ardent love for his people and his willingness to suffer for them. Many Protestants and some Catholics criticize it as too sentimental and romantic.

The church of Notre Dame, in Paray-le-Monial, popularly called the Basilica of the Sacred Heart, is a large church where pilgrim services are usually held, but when the crowds are large, these are transferred to a large park behind it, which has a set of Stations of the Cross. In summer, when pilgrimages are largest, there is a diorama of the life of St. Margaret Mary. The church is a smaller copy of Cluny, the monastery that dominated religious life in the high Middle Ages. Paray-le-Monial was one of approximately 1,450 monasteries dependent on Cluny, which also controlled the major pilgrimages, especially the one to Santiago de Compostela in Spain. Cluny was destroyed during the French Revolution, but Paray-le-Monial gives an accurate model of what it was like at the height of its grandeur.

Near the basilica is the Chamber of Relics, a reconstruction of Margaret Mary's room, furnished with her bed and clothing and now kept as a shrine. In another room, a media presentation is given daily. A few steps beyond is the Chapel of the Visitation, where she received three of her visions in the 1670s. At that time it was the monastery chapel, and her body is buried there. The three chapels make up the pilgrim route.

Although people come throughout the year, the major pilgrimages are in June, near the Feast of the Sacred Heart, and on October 16, St. Margaret Mary's feast day.

References Jan Bovenmars, *A Biblical Spirituality of the Heart.* New York, Alba House, 1991. J. LaDame, *St. Margaret Mary and the Visitation in Paray.* Lyon, France, Heliogravure Lescuyer, 1977. Josef Stierli (ed.), *Heart of the Saviour.* New York, Herder & Herder, 1958.

PASHUPATINATH, Nepal

Pashupatinath is the holiest and most prominent Hindu temple in Nepal. The legendary home of Lord Shiva and Parvati, it is situated on the Bagmati River, a tributary of the sacred Ganges. There was a worship site here by 500 BCE, but the earliest traces still existing date from 477 CE.

On arriving at Pashupatinath, pilgrims immerse themselves three times in the river while reciting texts from the Hindu scriptures. The Bagmati is considered almost as sacred as the Ganges, and bathing in it assures release from a cycle of rebirth. The annual Teej Festival is limited to married women, who purify themselves by bathing, fasting, and praying to ensure the continuing love and fidelity of their husbands.

The shrine is the major one dedicated to Shiva, the god of contradictions: creation and destruction, good and evil, fertility and asceticism. He takes on 1,008 forms, but here he is shown as Pashupati, protector of Nepal and "lord of all beasts." Shiva's symbol is the phallus-shaped pillar representing fertility. Therefore, Pashupatinath's priceless treasure is its three-foot temple lingam representing Shiva's penis, a proclamation of his masculinity and fertility and a symbol of life-giving and pleasure. It rises out of a yoni, the image of the female sex organs; the union of the two shows the universe arising from pleasure. This joined image is intended to teach that love is purest enjoyment and that sexual desire is the root of enjoyment, leading to sublime transcendent joy.

On the four sides of the lingam are four faces representing differing aspects of Shiva. On top is a plain surface, actually the all-powerful fifth face that cannot be represented in art; it is said to have the magical power of the sun. Only the temple priests are allowed into the presence of the lingam. Each morning, the sacred lingam is washed with a mix of the "five nectars": ghee, yoghurt, milk, honey, and sugar. It is then bathed with waters from sacred rivers and wrapped in rich cloth. In the afternoon, food offerings are made to it. Many lesser linga are distributed about the grounds and accessible to all visitors, although none has the divine power of the one enshrined in the main temple. The lesser ones are honored by libations of milk or ghee, which drains off in the yoni from which the lingam rises.

The grounds are frequented by numerous *sadhus*, holy men who practice great austerities. They often sleep standing up or engage in strict fasts for years. One group, the "sky-clad," wanders about naked. All this is exaggerated many times over at the annual (February/March) celebration of Shivarati, the "Night of Shiva." Hundreds of thousands of pilgrims come to offer *puja* (Hindu daily prayers), and stalls and wandering vendors take over the area. Sadhus bring large amounts of *ganja*, a potent marijuana from which they make tea to share with others. Shiva approves of marijuana, although its use is not common among devotees. During Shivarati, the king presides over a review of the Royal Nepalese Army.

The temple precincts are open only to Hindus, but the surrounding area and the stairs leading up from the river, where Hindu cremations are held, are open to all. There are ramps where the dying can be laid with their feet in the water, the equivalent of bathing to cleanse the spirit of sin. Placed on biers of wood—aromatic for the wealthy, simple logs for the poor—the deceased is burnt in a fire lit by the eldest son. From these ghats the ashes are consigned to the river to flow with it to the sacred Ganges and directly to the gods. Non-Hindus may also observe the rites and see the temple from a terrace across the river. It is inhabited by tribes of monkeys, which the Hindus believe are holy. Temple monkeys are protected by law in Nepal and are allowed to steal the food offerings to the temples.

Shrines and small temples abound in the immediate area, including the Guhyeshwai Mandir, consecrated to Durga, Shiva's consort in one of her terrifying forms. Durga was said to have committed suicide after Shiva was insulted by her father. Shiva roamed the skies with her body, dropping pieces to earth, where they consecrated sacred places. Her sex organs or "secret parts" fell near Pashupatinath (*guhya* means "secret.") This is a uniquely sacred place, and also closed to non-Hindus.

References *The Hindu World*. Columbus, OH, Coronet, 1963 (video). Ormond McGill, *Religious Mysteries of the Orient*. South Brunswick, NJ, Barnes, 1976. Sacheverell Sitwell, *Great Temples of the East*. New York, Ivan Obolensky, 1963.

PATMOS, Greece

Toward the beginning of the Apocalypse or Book of Revelation in the Christian Bible, St. John the Evangelist comments on his exile to Patmos, a brief stay that has made the island a goal for pilgrims. The Greek Orthodox Monastery of St. John the Theologian is built on the supposed site of his banishment. Located a few miles off the coast of modern Turkey, the island's desolate, rocky setting made it a logical place to keep political exiles. It was one of three islands used by the Romans for deporting dissidents, and John was sent there under the Emperor Domitian around 95 CE.

In Revelation 1:9, John the Apostle says he was banished "because of the word of God and witness to Jesus." He was released after two years and returned to Ephesus, where he died. A cave on Patmos is identified as the place where John received the inspiration to write Revelation, and the monastery is built on the hilltop above. The monastery, founded in 1088 and fortified against attacks, dominates the island.

When the first hermit, St. Christodoulos, arrived to establish the monastery, the island was uninhabited, and it was granted to him by the Byzantine emperor. The emperor's edict is on display in the monastery museum amidst one of the richest collections of icons and church treasures in Greece. For centuries, the monks were the island's only inhabitants, and for 700 years they also served as its government. Because Patmos has the status of a "sacred island," the monastery, which is part of modern Greece, must be consulted on major issues. It is not a single building but a walled village with a number of chapels that feature fine frescoes. Today it is occupied by two dozen monks; at its greatest it had 150. Especially solemn celebrations are held for the feasts of Easter, the Assumption of the Virgin (August 15), and the feast of St. John.

Tradition says that John received his inspirations in terrifying dreams that came through three cracks in the ceiling of the cave, symbols of the Holy Trinity: Father, Son, and Holy Spirit. In ecstasy, John dictated the revelations to his disciple Prohoros. A chapel is built into the cave and a small monastery is built around it. Though the grotto is open to pilgrims, it is not signposted and tour buses are not encouraged to visit. The monks have successfully protected the religious atmosphere of the island and resisted the impact of tourism.

The main monastery church is shaped like a Greek cross and contains the shrine of St. Christodoulos, who is buried there. Sections of the church date from the eleventh century, and there are choice frescoes (thirteenth century) of angels with Abraham and with the Virgin Mary. The library has over 1,000 manuscripts, including a parchment of St. Mark's Gospel from the sixth century.

See also Ephesus.

References Athanasios Kominis, *Patmos: Treasures of the Monastery*. Athens, Ekdotike Athenon, 1988. Otto Meinardus, *John of Patmos and the Seven Churches of the Apocalypse*. New Rochelle, NY, Caratzas Brothers, 1979. S. A. Papadopoulos, *Monastery of St. John the The-ologian*. Patmos, Greece, Brotherhood of St. John, 1977.

PERCHERSK LAVRA, Ukraine

The first monastery founded in Russia, the Perchersk Lavra covers 75 acres of churches, monastic cells, and buildings, all set over a maze of underground caves and passages that include chapels and burial places. Founded by two monks in 1051, the Perchersk Lavra has the air of a medieval site that has weathered the ravages of Russian history. It was plundered in 1240 by the Tartars, and for two centuries it barely survived. It was then rebuilt. In the meanwhile, many Christians fled to the north, where a rival establishment, Sergiev Posad, was built in 1337. When the Russian and Ukrainian Churches separated a century later, the two monastic centers became the spiritual and cultural hearts of their respective Orthodox communities.

The Perchersk churches are magnificent examples of Byzantine architecture and contain a good collection of icons. The Assumption church, rebuilt in 1614, has the traditional golden onion domes and a fine series of frescoes along the exterior walls, protected by a walkway. The Dormition Cathedral (1089), used as a model for many other churches in the Ukraine, was destroyed in World War II, and only ruins remain. There are also several other churches, dating from the eleventh to the seventeenth centuries. Pilgrims customarily make the rounds of the monastery churches.

The caves are in two groups, Near and Far. The Near Caves are over 200 yards in length, while the Far Caves are almost 300. Along the passageways are several small chapels and a number of the cells in which hermit monks once lived. Some cells are almost walled in, leaving only a small opening for passing food and water inside. This arrangement in itself is an indication of the ancient character of the monastery, since individual hermit life was later replaced by community living in most monasteries. The complex is often referred to simply as "The Lavra," a term for this type of monasticism. The subterranean passages also contain burial places where, in monastic fashion, the bones of the monks have been separated and sorted into piles of skulls, femurs, and legs. The hermit monks were usually just left in the cells where they died, with the opening sealed up. These catacombs (the name *Perchersk* is a Slavic word for "catacomb") end in the Church of the Exaltation of the Holy Cross.

At its greatest extension, the monastery was incredibly wealthy—it owned 80,000 serfs, many villages, and a dozen other monasteries. By the nineteenth century, however, it had declined. Under Soviet Communism it was closed in 1927, although several churches were used until the 1960s. It was preserved as a museum, though some artworks were taken away, and pilgrims continued to come to the complex throughout the Communist period. Now the new Ukrainian government is returning the properties to the Orthodox Church, and plans are under way to reestablish monastic life in the Lavra.

References *Millennium of Christianity in Ukraine.* Ottawa, Canada, St. Paul's University, 1987. John Armstrong, *Ukrainian Nationalism.* Englewood, CO, Ukrainian Academic Press, 3d ed., 1990. Yaroslav Shchapov, *State and Church in Early Russia, Tenth to Thirteenth Centuries.* New Rochelle, NY, Caratzas, 1993.

PERE LACHAISE CEMETERY, France

A lovely park-like setting in northeastern Paris, Père Lachaise Cemetery contains a vast collection of mausoleums and monuments. A number of these have become objects of pilgrimage and attract a constant flow of visitors. The land formerly belonged to the Jesuits and was used as a retreat by the confessor of King Louis XIV, Père La Chaise, who donated generously to the construction of the first main buildings, now gone. The land was bought by the city of Paris and made into a cemetery in 1803. At first, no one wanted to be buried in such a distant place, so Napoleon made it fashionable by transferring the remains of prominent people, such as the medieval lovers Abélard and Heloïse. Père Lachaise now includes the graves of the composer Fréderick Chopin, the writer Honoré de Balzac, and the singer Edith Piaf, as well as public figures and French military heroes.

In 1871, after a violent uprising (the Paris Commune) had terrorized Paris, the last insurgents were cornered in the cemetery, where fierce fighting went on among the graves. The last 147 were captured and gunned down by army troops and buried where they fell along the Mur des Fédérés (Federalists' Wall). It is maintained as a memorial, and socialists and anarchists visit regularly to leave floral tributes. A political pilgrimage is held annually on the anniversary, May 28.

Nearby is an avenue of monumental sculptures, each representing a slave labor camp where deported French citizens, mostly Jews, were worked to death during World War II. The most striking represents Mauthausen in Austria, where slave labor was used to quarry large paving blocks that had to be carried up a long stairway to the mouth of the quarry. Many died of exhaustion under their burdens on the "stairway to hell," and the sculpture is modeled on a series of jagged steps.

Two of the graves constitute the leading

gay pilgrimage place in the world, the tombs of the writers Oscar Wilde (1856–1900) and Gertrude Stein (1874–1946), both of whom died in France. Wilde, exiled from England after being disgraced and imprisoned for his homosexuality, died penniless in Paris. He has become a cult figure for the gay movement, and his tomb is always marked with flowers and touching notes and ex-votos. His white sarcophagus is surmounted by a striking bas-relief sculpture by Jacob Epstein, the greatest British sculptor of the twentieth century. The tomb was erected by an anonymous woman admirer. Stein, an American writer and patroness of a generation of expatriate American writers such as Ernest Hemingway, was at the center of cultural life in Paris between the world wars. She remained in France throughout the Nazi occupation of World War II and is popular among the French as well as among gays and lesbians. Her longtime associate and companion, Alice B. Toklas (1877–1967), rests beside her.

The most recent place of pilgrimage is the grave of rock star Jim Morrison (1944–1971) of the Doors, who died in Paris while on tour. A mix of fans and rock music enthusiasts regularly visit the vault, and the surrounding tombs in all directions are marked by graffiti giving directions to the rock singer's grave. Lyrics from Morrison's songs are scrawled across neighboring vaults: "Break on through," or "This is the end." Among the ex-votos found regularly at the site are bongs and other drug paraphernalia. People pour beer or wine onto the ground around the modest grave as a kind of libation, and it is not uncommon to hear visitors humming or singing Morrison's hit, "Riders on the Storm."

References Judi Culbertson and Tom Randall, *Permanent Parisians.* White River Junction, VT, Chelsea Green,

1986. Richard Etlin, *The Architecture of Death: The Transformation of the Cemetery in Eighteenth Century Paris.* Cambridge, MA, Massachusetts Institute of Technology, 1984. Tom Weil, *The Cemetery Book.* New York, Hippocrene, 1992.

PETRA, Jordan

An ancient city in the desert wastes of Jordan, Petra was forgotten and unknown to the West from the time of the Crusades until 1812, when a young explorer followed rumors to track it down. He bribed a suspicious Bedouin tribesman to take him to the place where Abraham's brother, Aaron, was supposedly buried, saying that he wished to worship there. What he saw overwhelmed him in its beauty and untouched splendor.

Petra was settled several thousand years before Christ, but somewhere around the fifth century BCE it became a Nabatean stronghold. A complex water-supply system allowed the Nabateans to create an elaborate farming setup in the desert and a public water supply in the town. At its height, around 40 CE, Petra controlled Damascus and a large land area in what is now Syria. A shift of the Arab trade routes caused a gradual decline, and Petra later became Christian and then Muslim.

Petra is stunning. Set within a ring of mountains, its red sandstone tombs and buildings cover an area of over a square mile. Fed by a spring and easily defended, the site provided a protected trade route and a natural place for settlement. The stream, Ain Musa, is believed by local people to be the result of God's command to Moses to strike the dry rock when the Jews wandered in the desert and lacked water. It would be remarkable merely as an ancient settlement, but it was also the center of a deeply religious culture that has left some of the most striking evidence of ancient religion.

The Nabatean chief deities were the goddess Al-Uzza (Mighty One), symbolized by a lion, and Dushara, the high god. This god was represented (as was the Hebrew god, Jehovah) as a square block of rock, often referred to as "God's House," Beth-el in Hebrew. Dushara's symbolic animal was the bull. Al-Uzza was the people's deity, while Dushara was the court god of the nobility and the official cult. In the hills surrounding Petra are a number of sanctuaries known as "high places." These feature large altars of sacrifice and shaped stones representing Dushara and Al-Uzza. Around them are niches for lamps, and religious meals were held at these spots. Whether these meals were like modern picnics or sacrificed animals were eaten in some sort of ritual is not known. There are also many tombs, some massive and ornate, and these include formal eating places with benches on which diners reclined during anniversary dinners in honor of the dead. Some of these could accommodate a large group of relatives and friends.

A visitor enters Petra via the Siq, a gorge that follows the stream for slightly over a mile. Many votive niches have been carved into the canyon walls to hold offerings, some with stylized carvings of Al-Uzza. At the entry are three massive djinn (spirit) blocks, square blocks of stone sacred to the Bedouin, the nomadic people who live in the area. The visitor then comes upon the Obelisk Tomb, the first of the major burial chambers. It contains five graves set into the walls, carved into the living rock. The final entrance into Petra is very narrow and confining at first, then opens with a shock onto the brilliant, ocher-red Kasneh, a tomb with a beautifully carved classical facade. It has become the symbol of Petra. An 11-foot urn is carved above its doorway. The Kasneh was probably a temple. It has an inner chamber and sanctuary beyond its courtyard and numerous tombs, some holding as many as seventeen graves.

The center of Petra was the main public fountain, dedicated to the water spirits and surrounded by shops, which have disappeared. At the end of the street, known as the Colonnade, is the ceremonial gate leading to the sacred precincts. Within it is the Kasr el Bint, the holiest temple in Petra, built around the time of Christ. The temple is a mammoth building that honored Dushara, represented by a large god-block (no longer present). A huge hand has been excavated, indicating that the block was later replaced by a statue of the god. Some of the painted plasterwork that once covered the temple can still be seen on the walls and pillars.

A cult was once devoted to the spirit of water and was probably connected with the mountain Umm al-Biyara (Mother of Cisterns), which still has eight large water holding tanks. A short distance away is the mountain el-Barra, with a shrine on top regarded as Aaron's tomb; it is jealously guarded by the Bedouin and not open to visitors. There are over five hundred tombs in the Petra area, the most important of which is the Royal Tomb, used as a Christian church from the fifth century CE because of its vast size.

Petra also has one of the best-preserved religious sites in the ancient world, the High Place of Sacrifice. On the ceremonial path to the high plateau where it sits are two obelisks 100 feet apart and 20 feet high, carved from the same mountain top, an enormous chore that indicates the importance of honoring the deities. At 625 feet above Petra, the High Place was used for both animal and human sacrifice and was equipped with drainage to flush away the blood. A god-block, now disappeared, presided over the scene.

References Michael Berthud and Penelope Hatch, *Petra*. Turin, Italy, T.R.P., 1985. Flavio Conti, *The Closed Faith*. Boston, HBJ Press, 1979, 57–72. Avraham Negev, "Understanding the Nabateans," *Biblical Archaeology Review* 14:3, 26–45 (November–December 1988).

EL PILAR, Spain

Regarded as the site of the first apparition of Mary, Mother of Jesus, El Pilar's story begins with St. James the Apostle. Legend has it that after the death of Jesus, James went to Spain to implant the new faith—but with no success. Mary (presumably still alive in the year 40 CE) appeared to him, seated on a throne carried aloft by angels. She gave him a column of jasper and a small statue of herself with the request that a shrine be built to honor her on that spot. Folklore though the legend may be, the present Basilica of Our Lady of the Pillar in Zaragoza stands on the spot of one of the oldest shrines to Mary in Christendom.

The relation between Mary and St. James is important in Spanish tradition. James is not only the patron of Spain but also the inspiration for its liberation from Muslim occupation in a 700-year war known as the Reconquest. His shrine at Santiago de Compostela, is the other national shrine of Spain. In sharing this role, El Pilar was a nationalist rallying point in the Civil War of 1936–1939. At one point, the basilica was bombed by government forces, but when the bomb came through the roof and struck the floor, it failed to explode. The people regarded this as a miracle and kept the unexploded bomb in the church.

The present basilica was built in 1677 on the banks of the Ebro River, on the site of several previous sanctuaries. The church is decorated in baroque style, with a splendid alabaster screen behind the main altar. The statue sits in a small shrine in the center of the basilica. It is the wooden original, a mere 15 inches high and obviously of great age. Mary holds the Christ Child in her left arm, and he holds a small dove; behind them is a golden ray like a sunburst. The pillar is encased except for a small space exposing the underlying jasper so the faithful may kiss it. Newborn babies are taken to the shrine so that their first photos may be taken with the statue, in the arms of young server boys in scarlet gowns. Pilar remains a popular woman's name in Spain, and the shrine is a regular place of pilgrimage for Spaniards.

The feast day of Our Lady of the Pillar, October 12, is also the Day of the Hispanidad, commemorating Christopher Columbus' first landing in the New World. It is a national holiday and is celebrated in Zaragoza with elaborate festivities. The evening before, a solemn torch-light procession wends its way through the streets to the basilica for the singing of vespers. On the feast day, crowds pack the church, where several Masses may be offered simultaneously. Bishops come from various cities in Spain for the privilege of offering Mass in the basilica on that day. Outside, a steel framework outlines the front of the basilica. All through the day, a procession of families in traditional dress brings bouquets, which are fixed onto the frame until, by the end of the day, the church is outlined in flowers, a stunning sight. Then the festival begins, first with a dance contest with groups performing the *jota*, the traditional folk dance of Aragon. Finally, there is a bullfight for which the finest bulls have been kept. This is the official end of the bullfight season, and partying goes on through the night at sports bars near the stadium. The next evening 350 carriages with lanterns light a Rosary procession. Throughout the following week there are parades featuring giant figures up to 30 feet tall.

See also Marian Apparitions; Santiago de Compostela.

References Anselmo Gascon de Gotor, *El arte en el templo del Pilar.* Zaragoza, Molina, 1940. René Laurentin, *Pilgrimages, Sanctuaries, Icons, and Apparitions.* Milford, OH, Faith, 1994. Gerard Sherry, *The Catholic Shrines of Europe.* Huntington, IN, Our Sunday Visitor, 1986.

PILGRIMAGE

The experience of pilgrimage is common to all religions. It combines the quest for inspiration, blessing, or grace with the rigors of a demanding journey, a sacrifice made to God. A pilgrimage can be made to fulfill a promise, to plead for a cure or other favors, or simply to seek out a place imbued with the sacred.

The journey itself is as important as the goal because it is a symbol of purification. In the Celtic Christian tradition, for example, no greater sacrifice could be made than the *peregrinatio pro Dei amore,* "wandering for the love of God." Until the eleventh century, Irish Christianity was dominated by this ideal, sending monks out as missionaries and penitents into exile to atone for their sins. These pilgrims did not necessarily seek out any sacred place but journeyed for the journey's sake. This tradition still is followed by the wandering monks of Russian Orthodoxy and the holy men of Jainism and Hinduism.

Not just monks, but ordinary members of all faiths can follow in this path. Pilgrims may be seeking the place where their god's power is most concentrated or the sites of his or her life. Christians, from their earliest times, have sought out the holy places of Israel, as Jews have continued to return to the remains of the temple in Jerusalem. The crowds that throng Mecca while making the hajj, or Varanasi on the Sacred Ganges, are probably outnumbered by many other Muslims or Hindus who visit smaller and less famous shrines and holy places. Special occasions, such as the Holy Year proclaimed by Pope John Paul II for the year 2000, can bring massive numbers; 20 million are expected in Rome alone for the Holy Year. Yet, easily that many Catholics make simple pilgrimages to regional and national shrines and sanctuaries each year in Europe alone.

In the Middle Ages, pilgrimage was regarded as a suitable penance for sin, and the arduous trip to Santiago was often assigned by judges as a punishment for crime. King Edgar, around 970, decreed that such pilgrims had to go barefoot, fast, "nowhere spend a second night," and neither cut their hair nor trim their nails. Pilgrimages also led to corruption, and St. Augustine said tartly that "not by journeying but by loving we draw nigh to God." Some used the opportunity of a pilgrimage to run away from obligations, family, or debt, and criminals took the occasion to rob travelers. The Canterbury pilgrims in Chaucer's *Canterbury Tales* (c.1390 CE) traveled in a group for security.

Despite the dangers and hardships, pilgrimages flourish. Even evangelical Protestants, deeply suspicious of such spiritual works as pilgrimages, used the image of pilgrimage as a pattern of the Christian life in John Bunyan's *Pilgrim's Progress* (1684). With the reunification of Germany, the traditional Lutheran pilgrimage, the Luther Circle, has been revived.

The advent of modern means of travel, which removes the difficulties and the challenges, has transformed the pilgrimage. On one hand, it makes pilgrimages available to many who could not have made the demanding trips before. On the other hand, it reduces or eliminates the meaning of the voyage and places total focus on the sacred place at the end. Some shrines have given in to the modern approach and begun to present themselves like theme parks rather than places of mystery and encounter with the sacred.

The plastic dioramas at Kek Lok Si, the moving walkways that keep worshippers from stopping in front of the Guadalupe, and the increased use of multi-media programs show how far entertainment has wormed its way into sacred places. The development of the railroad helped create Lourdes as a major pilgrim center, and the introduction of jet aircraft and the organization of the tourism industry have made most shrines within anyone's reach. Agencies that specialize in religious tourism now dominate pilgrimages to all the most important sites in Europe and Asia, flying in large groups to visit the shrines, attend pre-arranged services, and stay in hotels booked out for them. The rise of a middle class that can afford such major trips provides a solid base for the portion of the travel industry that caters to their needs. Around such shrines as Fátima and Lourdes, as well as the holy places of Rome and Jerusalem, the religious tourist business often overwhelms the pilgrim tradition.

Those who disagree regard this argument as elitist, the argument of those who have the time and means to meander off to sacred places. They point to the new availability of the shrines to people from far corners of the world who could not otherwise undertake the journey to see their sacred places. This effect is seen in all traditions: the organized tours to the shrines of the Baha'i World Centre; the Buddhist tours of the Kumbh Mela sites from Japan, Hong Kong, and Singapore; and the massive youth gatherings every year at Taizé and various inter-national sites. But no matter how one feels about religious tourism, there is no denying that a significant shift in the concept of pilgrimage has occurred—the loss of the pilgrimage as an arduous event that tests the spirit and the advent of the new, mass-movement form of pilgrimage.

Among Catholics—and to a lesser extent, other Christians—pilgrimage programs are highly organized. Pastors or religious leaders recruit parishioners for the pilgrimage, earning a free spot on the tour for each ten persons enrolled. Tours usually include time at major holy places as well as shopping and recreational tourism, a system that leads to emphasis on those shrines with an international reputation, recognized by all and easily marketed. If that commercial element seems crass, one has only to note that such a mix of the pious and the profane has a long history. It marked many medieval pilgrimages, especially those to Mont-Saint-Michel and Santiago de Compostela. Chaucer's *Canterbury Tales* recounts the very mixed motivations of the pilgrims to that holy spot.

Traditional pilgrimages continue to thrive, however, and in recent years have undergone a revival. Some of the largest pilgrimages to Poland's Jasna Góra arrive on foot, and one youth pilgrimage to Santiago sponsored by Pope John Paul II brought several hundred thousand young people who walked, biked, and hitch-hiked from all over Europe. From Bavaria, a group of factory workers gives two weeks each year to the pilgrimage to Santiago; they gather at the last year's stopping point and continue on foot for two weeks, to reassemble again the next year until they reach their goal. To foster such groups, the Spanish government has refurbished a number of simple and crude medieval pilgrim hostels, offered free to pilgrims on the Way of St. James.

Only the hajj, the Muslim pilgrimage to the holy places of Mecca and Medina, has remained free from much influence of tourism due to strict control by the Saudi government authorities. Tourists are not allowed into Saudi Arabia, and the holy places are off limits to all non-Muslims. Mecca is a closed city at all times of the year, and as a result, the hajj has kept its purely religious character. Even here, however, the use of networks of charter flights and the availability of luxury hotels for the affluent have crept in.

See also Hajj; Varanasi.

References Ronald Finucane, *Miracles and Pilgrims*. Totowa, NJ, Rowman & Littlefield, 1977. Mary Lee and Sidney Nolan, *Christian Pilgrimage in Modern Western Europe*. Chapel Hill, University of North Carolina, 1989. Alan Morinis, *Sacred Journey*. Glenview, IL, Greenwood, 1992.

PLAINE DU NORD, Haïti

Plaine du Nord on the north coast of Haïti is a center for the cult of the Voudou *loa* (god) Ougou Feray, Yoroba god of war. In popular devotion, he has been joined to the Christian saint James the Greater, one of Jesus' apostles. James, known throughout the Spanish-speaking world as Santiago Matamoros ("James the Moor-Slayer" or "Infidel-Killer"), is honored in Spain as the divinely-sent messenger who led the Spanish to expel the Muslims in the Middle Ages. According to legend, he crossed the ocean to be seen in a vision leading the Spanish conquistadors and their Indian allies against the Aztecs in Mexico, and he is hailed as a Christian war leader. The feast in his honor is celebrated just before July 25, St. James' Day.

The shrine is Trou St. Jacques (St. James' Tub), a large mud pond created by a flood in 1909. It is considered a place of healing.

Devotees pour libations and food into the pond as offerings while others plunge themselves into the ooze, because earth and water are the elements from which life comes and which sustain it. Animals are sacrificed to the loa and the blood collected to be drunk or poured into the pond and at the four corners of the village. Chickens are held against the bodies of the sick in order to absorb their illnesses and then beheaded. Some devotees are possessed by the loa and thrown into ecstasy, and they then share their blessing with others who seek them out to have mud rubbed onto their bodies. Babies are bathed with mud to prevent illness, and the mud is also taken home after the feast and used for healing.

Women bring huge kettles of red beans and rice to distribute to the poor at the time of the feast. A little of this ends up as a food offering for the loa, along with libations of rum, wine, and red soft drinks. Red is thought a favorite color of the loas, and it is the special color of clothes that day.

See also Saut D'eau.

References Carole Devillers, "Haiti's Voodoo Pilgrimages: Of Spirits and Saints," *National Geographic* 167:3, 395–408 (March 1985). Laennec Hurbon, *Voodoo: Search for the Spirit*. New York, Abrams, 1995. *Voodoo and the Church in Haiti*. Berkeley, University of California, 1988 (video).

PLOTZENSEE MEMORIAL, Germany

During the Nazi era, the Plötzensee Prison in Berlin was the scene of over 2,500 executions, among them some of the most important Christian opponents of the regime. Although the prison compound continues in use as a juvenile detention center, the execution building and nearby areas have been set aside as a memorial to the victims of conscience, especially members of the anti-Nazi resistance movement. The movement was organized into "resistance circles," small groups who circulated pamphlets, practiced passive opposition, and fought the regime with sabotage. Among these citizens of conscience were Communists and Christians as well as a prominent group of high army officers who plotted Adolf Hitler's death in 1944 and were executed at Plötzensee when the plot failed. Among these were several strongly committed Lutherans motivated by their faith. The German government utilizes the memorial as a means of confronting German responsibility for Naziism. School groups are brought to Plötzensee in large numbers to become informed of the terrors of 1933–1945.

Those who were sentenced to death were kept in cells in the "death house" after their sentence was read out to them. From there they were led to the execution building, where they were either hanged or beheaded by guillotine. The bodies of less important people were used for the instruction of medical students, but those of prominent political and religious resisters were cremated and their ashes thrown on the fields. The meat hooks used for hangings remain in place, although the guillotine was removed after the war.

The Plötzensee Memorial attracts few visitors to honor the secular martyrs of conscience, but religious visitors come in larger numbers. In the execution building the documents of a Catholic priest are displayed, the Blessed James Gapp, an Austrian Marianist who was kidnapped while in exile in Spain and executed in 1945, with instructions from the court that his body be burned and the ashes dispersed so that no possible relics could remain. He was declared Blessed by Pope John Paul II in 1996.

Also recognized as a martyr was Blessed Alfred Delp, a Jesuit and member of the Kreisau Circle. His letters from Plötzensee are ringing affirmations of Christian opposition to the Third Reich. Among the Protestant leaders was the lawyer Helmuth Graf von Moltke, whose religious testimony at the time of his sentencing has often been reprinted. Helmuth Hübner, a devout 17-year-old Mormon youth arrested for circulating copies of British broadcasts, was the youngest to die at the prison. A remembrance day for the victims of Nazi barbarism was begun in 1996; it is observed on January 27.

A stone urn before a memorial wall contains earth taken from each of the major Nazi concentration camps. In the neighborhood, both Lutheran and Catholic shrine churches have been established as centers for prayer and education. The Confessional Church, made up of those who resisted Nazi attempts to subjugate the national Lutheran Church, became the root of the present Evangelical Lutheran Church, which has built a study center and church nearby. A Carmelite cloister, Maria Regina Martyrium, is also nearby; several tombs of the martyrs are enshrined in its crypt. It houses a bookstore about the religious resistance. As memorials to victims of Nazi barbarism, Plötzensee and the religious centers are attacked and desecrated by neo-Nazi vandals and racist skinheads. Graffiti are common, and in 1995, severed pigs' heads were left at the entrance.

References John Conway, *The Nazi Persecution of the Churches, 1933–1945*. New York, Basic Books, 1968. Alfred Delp, *The Prison Meditations of Father Delp*. New York, Macmillan, 1962. Karl Meyer, "Digging Berlin's Chamber of Horrors," *Archaeology* 45:4, 24–29 (July-August 1992).

PO LIN, Hong Kong, China

Po Lin is the site of a popular Buddhist monastery and the largest seated outdoor Buddha in the world. Founded in 1905 by three monks who fled to Hong Kong because they opposed the Manchu regime in China, Po Lin was, for many years, indistinguishable from many other monasteries. It attracted few visitors to its stunning mountaintop setting with views of the sea. But in the 1970s, after plans for the seated Buddha were announced, Po Lin began to attract larger numbers of pilgrims. Since the completion of the Buddha in 1992, Po Lin (the name means "Precious Lotus") has received several thousand pilgrims a day, rising to 15,000 on Sundays. The throngs pray and offer incense for such blessings as a needed job, success in examinations, or good health. The crowds are overwhelmingly Chinese from Hong Kong, but include every class. At Po Lin, the richly dressed mix easily with careworn workers.

The Po Lin property includes Muk Yu Hill in the highest reaches of Lantau, Hong Kong's largest outlying island, where the statue—officially the Temple of Heaven Buddha—was built. The monastery and statue are reached by an hour-long bus ride from the boat landing connecting the island to the city. The statue looks away from Hong Kong city, symbolizing the serenity and peace that come if one turns away from the hustle and commercialism of modern life. The statue was built after numerous conflicts. It was originally designed in 1974, but construction started ten years later. To maintain a structure of such stupendous size, the architect abandoned the original plan to use reinforced concrete in favor of the methods used in building the Statue of Liberty in New York harbor, a structural steel frame supporting cast bronze sheets.

There are 202 such sheets in the Temple of Heaven Buddha, each weighing over 1,700 pounds. The statue is a hundred feet high and cost some $68 million, much of it contributed by the Peoples' Republic of China. The statue sits on a three-story platform containing an ancestral hall and a memorial room where several relics of the Buddha are worshipped.

The present monastery, a collection of red-and-gold buildings spread out on the mountain, was built in 1921. It includes a collection of worship sites, temples, and prayer halls where ancestors can be honored and rituals fulfilled. Chief among these is a hall with 500 marble statues of the *lohan,* or followers of Buddha. A series of plaques depict the life of the Buddha. About a hundred monks and nuns keep up the shrines and maintain a routine of prayer while serving the needs of pilgrims.

Po Lin is Hong Kong's largest religious retreat, and many pilgrims come to spend a day or more on the grounds, worshipping, making offerings, and seeking prophecies. The monastery has a number of rooms for pilgrims and serves vegetarian meals from the common kitchen that also serves the monastery. In a sense, Po Lin is an artificial shrine, built to attract pilgrims rather than in response to a vision or historic event. In this, it mirrors Hong Kong itself, a political entity with no traditional ancestral identity.

References Heinz Bechert and Richard Gombrich (eds.), *The World of Buddhism.* London, Thames & Hudson, 1984. Ormond McGill, *Religious Mysteries of the Orient.* South Brunswick, NJ, Barnes, 1976. Robert Orr, *Religion in China.* New York, Friendship Press, 1980.

POTALA PALACE, Tibet, China

The Potala, the enormous and imposing palace of the Dalai Lama, spiritual head of

Tibetan Buddhism and exiled ruler of Tibet, towers 13 stories (330 feet) above the city of Lhasa on a tall hill. It was built in several bursts. The earliest sections can be traced to the seventh century CE, but the great building periods occurred in the late seventeenth century and the early twentieth. All of its dimensions are superlatives. With over a thousand rooms, the Potala stretches over 1,300 feet east-west and over 1,100 feet north-south. At its base, the stone walls are 16 feet thick, yet the upper stories are so finely fit together that no nails were used in the construction. As the home of the Dalai Lama and the center of his government, it was at the same time the religious and political focus of Tibet.

The Potala is divided between the White Palace and the Red Palace, which are joined by a smaller structure used to store the sacred banners hung on the face of the palace on the first and thirtieth days of the second lunar month. The White Palace contains the apartments of the Dalai Lama and other high officials, the seminary for training court and national officials, the printery for printing Buddhist scriptures, and government offices. The state treasury and the personal one of the Dalai Lama were contained in the fortified lower levels of the Potala.

The Red Palace is primarily religious and houses the lavish tombs of the Dalai Lamas. The Buddhist scriptures are preserved in special libraries; they are hand printed from carved wooden blocks and total 335 volumes. Many chapels and shrines contain the full panoply of Tibet's pantheon—Buddhas, bodhisattvas, saints, and demons. Tibetan Buddhism is a more open version than the dominant Indian form, and it has absorbed a number of deities from the ancient Bön faith, a traditional religion. Statues and shrines include a number of uniquely Tibetan figures: several

Dalai Lamas, the founders of the prominent sects of Tibetan Buddhism, and such figures as the Eight Guardians of the Faith.

In 1951, the Communist regime in China reasserted its authority by a combination of military occupation and threat. During widespread riots in 1959, the Dalai Lama fled to India with several hundred thousand followers. During the Cultural Revolution (1966–1977), thousands of monks were executed and many monasteries leveled, some used for artillery practice. The Potala was looted of many treasures and its monks expelled; its buildings also suffered some damage. A few monks have since been allowed to live at the Potala, but under strict supervision. Visitors are limited by the Chinese Communist authorities, who have recently undertaken massive reconstruction to favor tourists.

Only a few pilgrims are permitted within the Potala. By tradition, visitors may not cross a room they have entered, but must move clockwise around it. The Saint's Chapel in the White Palace, the major shrine in the Potala, contains a statue of Chenrezi, the bodhisattva of compassion and mercy. Immediately below this chapel is the room—the Dharma Cave—where King Songtsen Gampo studied the Buddhist scriptures after his conversion. The King is considered the reincarnation of Chenrezi. Both chapel and cave date from the seventh century and are the oldest part of the Potala.

The Red Palace highlights the life and works of the fifth Dalai Lama (1617–1682). It was he who unified Tibet, made the Yellow Hat sect of monasticism the state religion, and built the Potala. He is the most important figure in Tibetan history. His life is presented in murals, and in one chapel he is shown seated on a throne parallel to a seated Buddha, equal in dignity. His tomb contains his mummified body and rests in a 50-foot stupa covered with four tons of gold and studded with semi-precious stones—all this within only one of the four major chapels in the Red Palace! The tomb of the fifth Dalai Lama is rivaled only by the tomb of the last Dalai Lama, who died in 1933, after making Tibet an independent country for the first time. His stupa-tomb is a few feet shorter than the fifth Dalai Lama's, but also gold-covered and jewel-encrusted. One votive offering is a pagoda made of 200,000 pearls.

References John Avedon, *In Exile from the Land of Snows.* New York, Michael Joseph, 1984. Dalai Lama, *Freedom in Exile.* New York, HarperCollins, 1990. Thubten Jigme Norbu and Colin Turnbull, *Tibet: Its History, Religion, and People.* New York, Penguin Books, 1983.

PYRAMIDS OF GIZA, Egypt

On the edge of Cairo one of the best-known ancient sites in the world rises above the surrounding neighborhoods: the three pyramids of Giza and the Sphinx. Of the Seven Wonders of the ancient world, the pyramids are the only one still in existence. Though the purpose of this burial place is clear, the mystery attached to ancient Egyptian burial rites and beliefs and the enigma of the Sphinx make this a spiritual place today, especially for members of New Age religious groups.

Essentially, Giza is a royal necropolis made up of massive tombs that reflect the majesty and supreme power of those buried here. Architecturally, the pyramids of Giza are the high point of pyramid building, the finest examples of over 100 such tombs in Egypt and Nubia. At Giza are the tombs of the great Pharaoh Cheops, the largest pyramid at Giza, and his son and heir, Chephren, whose tomb is slightly smaller. Much smaller but still grand is the pyramid of Mycerinus, son of Chephren. Cheops was the greatest pharaoh of the Fourth Dynasty and an imperial power throughout the region. His son continued this tradition, but Mycerinus lost much royal power in squabbles with other grandsons of Cheops who claimed the right to the throne. Small pyramids were built for three of Cheops' wives, and a series of flat-topped pyramids holds the remains of his favorite children. At the end of a long causeway lined with minor tombs of court officials, a ceremonial temple was built just to mummify the pharaoh's body.

The Great Pyramid of Cheops, towering 250 feet above the plain, is built of 2.3 million stone blocks, each weighing from two to fifteen tons each. Originally, it and Chephren's pyramid were encased in polished limestone, remnants of which can still be seen. Built 4,600 years ago, the pyramids have withstood the elements but not the grave robbers, who removed their treasures in ancient times. In 1818 an Italian drove his way into the burial chamber of Chephren with a hydraulic ram, but the fabled stores of gold, jewels, and riches were long gone.

There are two kinds of pyramid myths—those of fabulous hidden treasure and those about mystical powers. Since the Great Pyramid is perfectly aligned to true north, south, east, and west, some argue that it has astrological meaning. The absence of any inscriptions has fueled speculation that there is occult or secret meaning in their dimensions, and many numerologies "prove" that the dimensions reveal secrets or can predict the future.

None of this speculation would have impressed the Egyptians. For them, the pharaoh was the living incarnation of the god Horus, son of Osiris, lord of the underworld. When the pharaoh died he joined

Of the Seven Wonders of the World, the three pyramids of Giza and the Sphinx are the only structures still in existence. Many believe that the Sphinx was designed to be a guardian of the king's tomb when it was erected 4,600 years ago.

himself to Osiris, and the tomb held all that he needed for his trip to the land of the dead: furniture, statues of servants, and boats. Five pits for funerary ships have been discovered near Cheops' pyramid. The body was mummified after the brain and internal organs were removed, so that his spirit would recognize him in the hereafter.

The Sphinx, carved from a single block of stone, is the bust of a man wearing a headdress joined to the body of a lion. It seems to be a guardian figure, protecting the tomb of the king by warding off evil spirits, although some suggest that it is a portrait of Chephren. The nineteenth-century opinion that it was an oracle has added to the Sphinx's aura of mystery. It has been weathered by the wind, and air pollution has taken its toll. During the French occupation around 1800, Mameluke troops used it for target practice for their field cannons, breaking off some of its features. Between its paws is a fifteenth-century BCE stone tablet recounting a vision given a prince who slept in the shadow of the Sphinx (and perhaps sought its divine aid) and later be-

came a pharaoh through its intercession.

No exotic spot on earth attracts New Age followers as do the pyramids. The sense of mystery that surrounds the place draws Europeans and Americans who believe in reincarnation and seek contact with divine powers and the source of their previous lives. Since 1990, private groups have been allowed into the Great Pyramid, and the majority of these have been seekers of the mystical. Taken with the harmonic mathematics involved in the pyramids' structures, which project a sense of order and evoke symmetry, peace, and human accord, many spiritual seekers at the pyramids of Giza get in touch with feelings of awe, majesty, and mystery that they fail to find in traditional religion.

See also Thebes and Luxor.

References Flavio Conti, *Breaking the Confines*. Boston, HBJ Press, 1978. I. E. S. Edwards, *The Pyramids of Egypt*. London, Penguin Books, 1991. Mark Lehner, "Computer Rebuilds the Ancient Sphinx," *National Geographic* 179:4, 32–39 (April 1991).

magnificent, the shrine itself was embellished through the centuries so that it would not be overshadowed by them. For several centuries, the shrine was a place of sanctuary where those accused of crimes could take refuge until a judgment against them was appealed. Fatimeh is held up as a role model for Shi'a women, making Qom prominent in the Islamic women's movement.

The shrine is entered through a mirrored gate, which opens onto a capacious courtyard of blue tile, surrounded by the tombs of nobles. There are actually four courtyards, and large crowds can be accommodated easily. The tomb itself has a gold dome, under which is the sepulcher, covered by a silver enclosure. Streams of the faithful reach out to touch to silver cage, then run their fingers over their faces, as if to absorb some of the holiness of Fatimeh. The shrine is made from elegant marble, with tiled passageways and alcoves covered in mirrors—an effect that is sumptuous without being gaudy.

Behind the shrine is blue-domed A'zam Mosque, used by many of the pilgrims for prayer. It is also the hub of theological teaching (up to 30,000 Islamic seminarians study in Qom), and its courtyard is the venue for important political sermons. The shrine and the mosque were hotbeds of resistance to the rule of the Shah and flashpoints in the Islamic revolution that toppled him and brought the Ayatollah Khomeini to power. When Khomeini returned from exile to lead the revolution in 1979, he first went to Qom. Since his death, the leaders of the Qom schools have set themselves up as arbiters of his legacy, quick to criticize those who, they believe, stray from the ayatollah's teachings.

Qom has supported the veiling of women, opposed the Communist party, and

QOM, Iran

Qom, a dusty town in southern Iran, is the leading center of Shi'ite Muslim theology and an important place of influence in Iranian politics. What draws multitudes of pious pilgrims there, however, is the shrine of Fatimeh, sister of the eighth imam of Shi'ite Islam.

Qom has a thousand-year tradition of politico-religious resistance, and the shrine is its spiritual embodiment. After the death of the Prophet Mohammed in 632, a crisis of leadership arose in Islam. A civil war broke out between those who believed that the community should choose its leader and those who felt that the office of imam should descend within Mohammed's family. These followed Ali, his son-in-law, and his descendants. (Though the imams are not regarded as prophets, they are believed to have divine inspiration in both spiritual and material matters.) Ali's grandson, Husayn, and his family were brutally murdered in Karbala, an act of barbarity that completed the separation of the main streams of Islam. Within this tradition, the Shi'ites have developed a cult of devotion to saints and leaders, and shrines to honor them—a tradition that most Muslims reject.

The shrine of Fatimeh dates from the Middle Ages, and important rulers considered it an honor to be buried near the holy woman. Because the royal tombs were often fought the use of alcohol and television. The religious establishment (including the shrine administration) consistently opposed the attempts of the Shah's government to modernize Iran from the 1920s to the 1970s. During this period, the government moved to take increased control of the shrine, making it a state religious center and taking over its endowments. In 1963, Khomeini was arrested, and many students were murdered by the police during the demonstrations that followed. A popular shrine devotion before the revolution was the reciting of 20,000 blessings on Khomeini and 20,000 curses on the Shah and his government, all counted on prayer beads. Since the Islamic revolution, the curses have been directed at the United States.

See also Najaf and Karbala.

References L. Bernard, *The World of Islam: Faith, People, Culture.* London, Thames & Hudson, 1976. Michael Fischer, *From Religious Dispute to Revolution.* Cambridge, MA, Harvard University, 1980. *Living Islam.* New York, BBC, 1993 (video).

The island had become overpopulated and food was scarce. Alliances were formed along clan lines until there were two rival clans, the Long Ears and the Short Ears. Prisoners were eaten, the ahu desecrated, and their statues overturned. The people believed that this robbed them of their sacred power. The final battle was within living memory of Easter Islanders when the Europeans arrived; warfare continued until 1862, when Peruvian slavers raided the island and carried off the males, reducing the population to 110. Of the traditional tales of the Easter Islanders, a third are about the clan wars and another third about cannibalism.

There are over 600 moai on Easter Island, some still on their ahu platforms, others topped and half buried. Most are about 15 feet high, but a few giants top 40 feet. They have elongated faces with jutting chins and short torsos. They were carved from soft volcanic rock, rolled somehow to the ahu, and hoisted into place. Much of what is known about them and their cult is speculative or based only on legend, and so they retain their sense of mystery.

References Paul Bahn and John Fenley, *Easter Island, Earth Island.* London, Thames and Hudson, 1992. Thor Heyerdahl, *Easter Island: The Mystery Solved.* New York, Random House, 1989. JoAnn Van Tilburg, "Moving the Moai," *Archaeology* 48:1, 34–43 (January-February 1995).

RAPA NUI, Easter Island, Chile

Only 45 square miles in size and isolated from most of the islands of the South Pacific, Easter Island boasts a mysterious cache of monumental statues. When the first white sailors contacted the few people living there in the eighteenth century, the people told a legend of having been led there 22 generations before from Polynesia—around 380 CE. The Norwegian scholar Thor Heyerdahl argued that Easter Island was settled from South America, and to prove this, he made and sailed a boat made of reeds across the Pacific. Perhaps both accounts are correct and the two peoples intermarried; certainly the recent inhabitants speak Polynesian languages and have Polynesian racial characteristics.

Along the coast, the people built stone platforms for the dead called *ahu*. There bodies were laid and left, attended by the family, until birds and weather reduced them to skeletons. Then the bones were buried in the ahu. Later, large statues (*moai*) were set up on the ahu, facing inland. These were intended as the resting places for the inner power, or *mana,* of ancestral tribal rulers. Around 1400 CE, a new cult appeared, worshipping a bird-man. Some historians believe this was a new race of people, but whether it was or not, around 1680 civil war broke out on the tiny island.

RELICS

The remembrance of the dead is a common element in most religions and takes many forms. Often people keep their ancestors present by means of some object that recalls them or where their spirit may rest. In some cases, the remains themselves are kept and revered. In the Buddhist and Christian traditions, the respect shown to the bodies of the dead evolved into a reverence for the remains of holy people or objects associated with them.

By 150 CE Christians had developed an explicit cult of the remains of the martyrs. In Rome, relics came into use as objects of reverence during the great persecutions that lasted until 313 CE. After the martyrs' execution, their bodies were taken away by the Christians to be given an honored burial in the Roman catacombs. After the barbarians sacked the catacombs several times beginning in 410, the popes began moving the relics of the martyrs to churches. The greatest relocation was the move of 28 wagonloads of Christian relics to the Pantheon, a former Roman pagan temple, in 609. In 817, Pope Paschal I had the remains of 2,300 martyrs moved to one church alone. The rising popularity of relics among Christians meant that many pilgrims to Rome began carrying them back home to be enshrined in the altars of their own churches. Churchmen began to deal in relics, and a brisk trade developed for several centuries.

During the Crusades, relics were important booty, and in 1204, Latin Christians looted the Byzantine Christian city of Constantinople of its most precious collections. This theft was followed by the sacking of the ancient Christian cities of Edessa, Antioch, and Jerusalem. In this way, powerful rulers and important pilgrimage shrines accumulated thousands of stolen items. Goldsmiths and jewelers vied with one another to produce the most beautiful reliquaries to hold the relics, and some of these are masterpieces of medieval artwork.

The custom spread of celebrating the Mass on altars into which relics of the martyrs had been sealed, in imitation of the Roman custom of holding Mass on mar-

tyrs' tombs. In the Catholic and Orthodox churches, relics are still placed into the altar stone or sewed into a cloth placed on the altar, a tradition originating from the Eastern Orthodox. The Orthodox extend this practice through the custom of having small cloths placed onto relics of the saints (*see* Rila Monastery). These "blessed" cloths are then taken home to be placed in home shrines or used in family prayer. However, Christian churches that recognize relics require them to be authenticated to avoid the excesses of the past.

Part of the Christian cult of relics stems from miracles supposedly worked by God through them. Some relics (*see* Saint Januarius) are considered sources of great power, and popular piety has always emphasized this aspect. Church theologians, on the other hand—most notably Thomas Aquinas—have taught that the relics have no sanctifying power but serve as "tangible signs" of God's love.

The continuing importance given to relics can be seen in the death sentence pronounced by the Nazi courts on James Gapp, the Austrian Marianist martyr beatified by Pope John Paul in 1996. The judge refused a request to return his body to his family for burial. Instead, he ordered that, after Gapp's execution, his body be cremated and his ashes dispersed so that the Christians would have no relics to keep and honor. Ordinarily, the bodies of anti-Nazi political prisoners were used for study in German medical schools (*see* Plötzensee).

Important artifacts can also be relics. These include tiny splinters of the Holy Cross of Christ and such supposedly genuine articles as the winding-sheet of Jesus (*see* Shroud of Turin) and the seamless robe he is described as wearing on Calvary (*see* Aachen Cathedral). Several medieval cathedrals claim to have the head of John the

Baptist. Although carbon-dating can determine the age of these items from the earliest period of Christianity, only the pieces of the Cross have any chance of being authentic. Carbon-dating gives the opportunity of exposing medieval frauds, which were numerous. Later items, such as the famous *tilma*, or woven cactus cloak, bearing the image of the Virgin of Guadalupe in Mexico, can easily be authenticated by historical and scientific methods.

Protestants in general reject the reverence given to relics as a form of superstition, and the Reformation destroyed many relics. Of the major Reformers, only Calvin tolerated their use. Despite their discomfort with relics, however, Protestants honor a few, such as the death sheet of Luther (*see* Luther Circle) and the ashes of the Ugandan Martyrs enshrined in an altar. In popular fundamentalist Protestant piety, such items as cloths, prayer shawls, and "holy oils" consecrated by the prayer and touch of prominent faith healers are a form of relic.

Islam, too, disapproves of saints and relics, since they subtract from the divine mission of the Prophet Mohammed. Relics of the Prophet are rare, although a few shrines claim to have a hair from his beard or his footprint. At Najaf and Karbala, as well as at Touba, the tombs of holy Islamic leaders are centers for pilgrimage. Throughout Turkey one finds *türbe*, the tombs of holy Dervishes, where the remains of these saints are honored.

Hinduism, with its belief in reincarnation, has no place for relics. The bodies of the dead are cremated, with any remains disposed of in sacred rivers. Despite this tradition, some of the ashes of Mahatma Gandhi, the great Indian teacher and independence leader, were kept and enshrined near Bombay until 1997.

Buddhism is the other great tradition, besides Catholic and Orthodox Christianity, that makes use of relics. After the Buddha's death there was an unseemly argument among the princes of India as to whose kingdom would be honored with the ashes and fragments of the Buddha's body. This altercation broke out as the War of the Relics, which was finally settled, according to legend, when the great King Asoka (circa 300 BCE) divided the relics into 84,000 shares and ordered the building of 84,000 stupas (shrines that contain relics). One of the most important of the relics of the Buddha is his tooth, enshrined in Sri Lanka, where a corps of priests daily conducts services in its honor, entertains it, clothes it, and offers it food and flowers. The Buddha—despite the traditional teaching that he has transcended this world—is believed to be present in his relic. Similarly, several hairs of the Buddha are enshrined at Shwe Dagon in Myanmar.

See also Holy Blood; Saint Januarius; Shroud of Turin; Tooth Temple.

References Joan Carroll Cruz, *Relics.* Huntington, IN, Our Sunday Visitor, 1983. Patrick Geary, *Furta Sacra: Thefts of Relics in the Middle Ages.* Princeton, NJ, Princeton University, 1978. David Sox, *Relics and Shrines.* London, George Allen & Unwin, 1985.

RILA MONASTERY, Bulgaria

Situated in the mountains 75 miles south of Sofia, the Rila Monastery is the center of Bulgarian Orthodoxy and the heart of Bulgaria's national spirit. It was founded in 927 CE by St. Ivan (John) of Rila as a colony of hermits, but soon became a monastic community. In 1335 a powerful local ruler built a defense tower that still dominates the courtyard, and by 1400 Rila was a feudal entity owning scores of villages and properties. It was damaged in the Turkish invasions but survived and became a symbol of the national aspirations of the Bulgarian people. The Turks regarded it warily and continued many of its medieval privileges.

In 1469, the relics of St. Ivan were returned to Rila from Târnovo, where they had been in safekeeping for several centuries. The procession became a national outpouring of faith as it moved across the country. Groups of people walked alongside the procession as it passed through their regions, and some even joined it for the entire route. This event was a turning point in the renewal of Orthodoxy during the Islamic occupation, and paintings of the cross-country trek can be found in many Bulgarian churches. At Rila, there is an important fresco showing the procession.

When the Bulgarian national and cultural revival occurred in the eighteenth and nineteenth centuries, Rila was at its center. Some of the country's most prominent writers, historians, and artists were either members of the monastery or living in its territory. In 1833 a popular campaign rebuilt the complex after a disastrous fire, with artisans settling in the region for decades to donate their skills. Bulgarian towns competed for the chance to help rebuild Rila. The Rila they restored is surrounded by multistory castle walls that face inward and form a solid defense, broken only by two gates. Along the inner courtyard are arched balconies on each level, creating a harmonious and restful atmosphere. The 200 rooms built into the walls are used by pilgrims and visitors. A few rooms originally built for local leaders from various towns are preserved. The Koprivshtitsa Room is the most elegant, the walls lined with red couches, the floors covered with hand-woven carpets below a three-dimensional carved ceiling. In the residential wings are four small chapels, also done in luxuriant style. In the nearby woods is the hermitage of St. Ivan, a cave where he lived, and several other small chapels, all richly decorated and painted.

At the center of the plaza created by the cloisters sits the Church of the Nativity of the Virgin. On three sides are galleries lavishly covered by murals whose colors are as vibrant as when they were first done. The facade takes up the theme of the Last Judgment, with drunkards, the lustful, and the fraudulent displayed in satirical scenes, while the saved bask in glory. The effect is both simple and powerful. The interior is similarly decorated with frescoes from the Bible and the history of Bulgarian Christianity, portraits of saints, and the life of St. Ivan. Hardly a square inch is left undecorated; in total there are 1,200 scenes. The iconostasis (a wall that separates the sacred interior chamber containing the altar from the people's part of the church) is richly carved and gilded. St. Ivan's relics are kept in a casket, and pilgrims bring cloths to be touched to it. An icon of the Virgin of Ossenovo is also much revered.

In 1946, the Communists took over Rila's 6,000 acres, dairy farms, and distillery, but the monastery remained open by serving tourists. An excellent museum was built containing historical documents, priceless art, and icons. Brother Raphael's cross, carved from a single piece of wood, contains 1,500 human figures, none larger than a grain of wheat. In 1991, after the fall of Communism, the government returned the monastery to the Church, and the number of monks, once down to eight, has slowly increased. In 1993, the heart of Boris III, the last king of Bulgaria, who died under suspicious circumstances in 1943, was buried in a side chapel. Most pilgrims visit and pray at his shrine, although he is not recognized as a saint.

References Flavio Conti, *The Closed Faith*. Boston, HBJ Press, 1979, 153–168. Hristo Hristov, Georgi Stojkov, and Krâstju Mijatev, *The Rila Monastery*. Sofia, Bulgarian Academy of Sciences, 1959. Margarita Koeva, *Rila Monastery*. Sofia, Borina, 1995.

ROCK OF CASHEL, Ireland

Above the town of Cashel sits a fortified hill that was a great religious center and the place from which Ireland was united in the eleventh century.

In the fifth century, Aengus, King of Munster, built a massive walled citadel here as his palace and military redoubt. It was on the Rock of Cashel in southeast Ireland that one of the great legends of Irish Christianity was acted out. When St. Patrick found the local pagans unable to grasp the truths of Christianity, he used a three-leafed clover to explain to Aengus how the Christian God was three-in-one, the doctrine of the Trinity. The young king converted in 450, and Ireland was on its way to embracing the new faith.

The Rock of Cashel—Cashel of the Kings—became central to many major events in Irish history. The first cathedral here was established by St. Declan, a disciple of Patrick's, and Cashel was a church center from the sixth century. Beginning with Aengus, many monasteries were founded from here. The great Irish hero Brian Ború was crowned at Cashel in 977. It was donated to the Church in 1101 and was the place where the English King Henry II received the homage of the Irish chieftains. During the later Middle Ages, many of the kings were bishops as well and led armies into battle.

Although there was no shrine on the Rock of Cashel, it was among the pilgrimage places to which penitential pilgrims were sent to atone for serious sins. In 1543 one Heneas MacNichaill was ordered to make a penitential pilgrimage to 16 places, including Cashel, Lough Derg, Croagh Patrick, Mount Brandon, Glendalough, and Skellig Michael, to atone for strangling his son. Cashel was a known pilgrimage center through the Middle Ages, and St. Patrick's Cross, a simple Irish high cross, was a likely station for prayer. The towers of Cormac's Chapel may have been built to protect valuable relics.

The cathedral is cross-shaped and contains what is believed to be the tomb of King-bishop Cormac (+1138), who also built the chapel that bears his name and whose remains are sheltered in its shadow. It is a remarkable example of Irish Romanesque architecture—perhaps the first Romanesque church in Ireland—with two towers and striking carvings. In 1495, the Earl of Kildare burned the cathedral, and when King Henry VII asked him why, he replied that he had done it because he thought the archbishop was inside! Enchanted by the Earl's candor, the king promptly appointed him Lord Deputy for Ireland. The cathedral contains several memorials, including the tomb of Myler McGrath (+1622), who lived to be 100 and spent 52 of those years as Anglican archbishop. He was notorious for holding title to four bishoprics and 77 other church positions, all with incomes attached.

The cathedral was pillaged by the Puritans in 1647, in a massacre where 3,000 people were killed, many of them burned alive in the cathedral. Restored yet again, it was finally abandoned in 1748. In its heyday it had a resident choir to chant the many daily cathedral services. The cathedral was originally painted in bright colors, but none of this has survived. The hilltop, which is only two acres, is covered with buildings

The Rock of Cashel, or Cashel of the Kings, is Ireland's most sacred site. The Rock was home of the kings until it was donated to the Church in 1101.

within its walls. There were two monasteries, one for Dominican preachers and another for cloistered monks, as well as a palace for the archbishop. The king's castle, three stories high, has walls thick enough to contain passages. Both Catholic and Anglican dioceses continue today, using the title of Cashel. Neither has its cathedral here, however, since the present town numbers fewer than 2,500.

References John Dunne, *Shrines of Ireland*. Dublin, Veritas, 1989. *A Guide to Celtic Monasteries*. Dublin, Irish Visions and Sounds, 1995 (video). Kenneth MacGowan, *The Rock of Cashel*. Dublin, Kamac, 1985.

ROME, Italy

The center of Catholic Christianity is the city of Rome, the residence of the pope (who is its bishop) and the repository of a rich Christian history. Its centerpiece is St. Peter's, but this grand basilica is a relative newcomer (sixteenth century) in a city is filled with hundreds of churches and sacred spots. Of the sacred places that appeal to Christians of all traditions, the most important are the catacombs and the *Coliseum*, the ancient Roman stadium where many early Christians were martyred. The Coliseum, which shows no indications of its religious connections, is maintained as a tourist spot.

Contrary to common belief, St. Peter's is not the pope's cathedral church. This honor goes to *St. John Lateran*, one of four major basilicas, the others being *St. Peter's*, *St. Mary Major*, and *St. Paul's-Outside-the-Walls*. The first St. John's was built around 313, but after several fires, earthquakes, and sackings, it is essentially a fourteenth-century church with eighteenth-century restorations. Its historical importance is not only its age; five worldwide Church councils were held here. It is considered one of the architectural treasures of Rome, and the interior features wonderful mosaics (thirteenth century), frescoes, and sculptures. The papal altar, where the pope says Mass as bishop of Rome, is sheltered by a great marble Gothic structure. Pilgrims are primarily attracted to the *Scala Santa*, a marble stairway of 28 steps. Legend says it is the stairway of Pontius Pilate, which Jesus walked on the day of his condemnation and death. It was reputedly brought to Rome in 325 by St. Helena, mother of the Emperor Constantine. Pilgrims ascend the steps on their knees as an act of devotion.

St. Mary Major was also begun in the fourth century. It is sometimes called Our Lady of Snows because of a legend that a miraculous snowfall on August fifth left an outline of the future structure. After the Council of Ephesus (431 CE) proclaimed Mary the Mother of God, the church was rededicated to her. It is known for its splendid mosaics of Christ and Mary and scenes from the Bible. These are among the oldest Christian mosaics in the city. There are also outstanding paintings, and one of these, a portrait of Mary titled *Salus Populi Romani* (Health of the Roman People), is the object of great affection and devotion on the part of the Romans.

St. Paul's-Outside-the-Walls, originally a fourth-century-building, was destroyed by fire in 1823 and reconstructed. Many of the ancient mosaics survived, as well as the bronze doors (1070) and some of the structure. The church was built over the legendary tomb of St. Paul, which lies under the high altar. Eighty granite columns frame a vast open space, ornately decorated yet simple in contrast to the baroque artistry of much of Rome. Above the columns are portraits of 265 popes.

To see an ancient Christian structure that escaped remodeling every few centuries, one visits the modest church of *Santa Costanza* (fourth century). Built as a mausoleum for one of Emperor Constantine's daughters, its original mosaics—bright and colorful—are some of the finest in the world. It was turned into a church in the thirteenth century but remained unaltered, except for the removal of Constantina's tomb.

San Clemente, near St. John Lateran, best demonstrates the historical continuity of Rome. The crypt holds the remains of a fourth-century frescoed Christian church and a small temple where Mithras, the sacred bull, was worshipped in ancient times by Roman soldiers. This was an all-male pagan cult; women were forbidden to take part. The main floor is one of the finest examples of an early Christian basilica, the original form of the first Christian churches after the Roman persecutions. San Clemente faces east toward Jerusalem.

Santa Maria della Vittoria is one of many Counter-Reformation churches. Almost excessive in its baroque decoration, it leaves no space uncarved. Overcoming this kitsch, however, is the utterly stunning Bernini sculpture of *St. Theresa in Ecstasy,* showing the Spanish mystic overwhelmed by God's love as an angel stands above her thrusting an arrow into her heart. It is both a magnificent work of art and a powerful statement of religious mystical experience.

The epitome of the baroque style, however, is the *Church of the Gesù* (1578), the mother-church of the Jesuits. Its flamboyance is breathtaking, most notably in the altar over the tomb of St. Ignatius, the Jesuit founder, which is so elaborate that it seems to move and undulate. Lapis lazuli and gold leaf abound. One fresco shows heretics, presumably Protestants, being thrown down (to hell?) when they attempt to enter heaven.

The four papal basilicas, plus *St. Lawrence, Holy Cross in Jerusalem,* and the catacomb chapel of *St. Sebastian,* make up the Seven Churches. Pilgrims make the round of them during Holy Week, saying prescribed prayers; this is a trek of 15 miles. During a Holy Year, the pilgrimage is made throughout the year and is blessed by the popes with special indulgences. During Lent, an old Roman custom, the Stations, is reenacted. It stems from the tradition of celebrating Lent as a community, with the pope gathering his people each day at a different church. It always begins with Ash Wednesday at *Santa Sabina,* and the pattern each day is invariable: Mass at dawn and a procession in the evening, with the people singing the Litany of the Saints.

See also Catacombs; St. Peter's.

References Eunice Howe and Andrea Palladio, *The Churches of Rome.* Binghamton, NY, State University of New York, 1991. Hubert Richards, *Pilgrim Rome.* Great Wakering, UK, 1994. *The Vatican and Christian Rome.* Vatican City, Vatican Polyglot Press, 1973.

SABBATHDAY LAKE, Maine

The last of what were once over twenty Shaker communities, Sabbathday Lake in Maine is a tiny but vital remnant of the major celibate religious community in the American Protestant tradition. Since the early 1990s, Sabbathday Lake has become the only living example of Shaker life.

Mother Ann Lee came to America from England in 1774, preaching a personal salvation open to all who would fashion their lives on that of Jesus Christ by the three-fold disciplines of celibacy, obedience to wise elders, and confession of sins. Mother Ann, who was illiterate, had been married but saw her four children die. Depressed and in spiritual agony, she had a vision of Adam and Eve and determined that sex was the original sin that separated humankind from God. To reclaim their spiritual birthright, Christians were to reject marriage and sexuality in order to recapture original innocence. This morally demanding regimen was to be lived in a community where all shared equally in hard work and a simple life. By the 1780s, her first farm communities had been established, and Sabbathday Lake was founded in 1792.

Men and women lived separately in the colonies, each of which was self-supporting. Some joined as adults, but many came as orphans, were raised on Shaker farms, and later

decided to enter a community. After a period of probation, each Shaker signed a covenant. Elders and eldresses led the communities, received the confessions of the members, and made major decisions. Shakers took their name from their unique form of worship. Gathered in large, austere meeting halls to await the movements of the Holy Spirit, their inspirations broke forth in ecstatic songs and a form of sacred dance in which their bodies trembled all over from the power of grace.

After 1875, Shaker communities declined, and only seven remained by 1920. Sabbathday Lake, always modest in size, had dropped to fifteen, all women, by 1950. They had made their own furniture and clothing, and after World War II there was a sudden vogue for Shaker crafts, beautifully simple chairs and cabinets, which often sold for huge sums as communities were closed and their effects auctioned off. In the face of aging and decline, the decision was made to establish a trust to support the last covenanted members in their old age. There was some fear that new members might be attracted by the large trust fund instead of by faith, and in 1965 the Canterbury, New Hampshire, community went further and decided to "close the covenant" by no longer accepting new members. Sabbathday Lake was angered by the decision and refused to accept it. Eldress Mildred Barker commented that "no one has the right to shut the door on anyone who sincerely seeks to enter it."

The division between these last two communities never healed. At one point in the 1970s, Sabbathday Lake was cut off from funds from the trust, but it persisted. Sabbathday Lake openly invited new members, and today about fifty applicants a year make serious inquiries. Few enter, however, and fewer persevere in the simple, strict

Shaker way. One who did was Theodore Johnson, a highly controversial figure who entered around 1960 and tirelessly promoted the Shaker life. Under his guidance Sabbathday Lake began a modest increase. Canterbury ordered his expulsion in 1971, recognizing that he was at the heart of Sabbathday's rejection of the closing of the covenant. Johnson died suddenly in 1986 at fifty-five, leaving the community in shock. Nevertheless, the last surviving Shaker community now has two brothers and six sisters, the youngest in her thirties. The Sabbathday Shakers believe strongly in a prophecy of Mother Ann that the sect would decline sharply, but then one day rebound in numbers and fervor.

Sabbathday Lake continues the routine of farm chores and work and attracts large numbers of visitors who come to share its spirit and to encounter the Shaker way of life. Services are conducted every Sunday and Wednesday, with men and women seated separately. It begins with hymns—Shakers have written over 10,000—and a Scripture reading. Then there is a period of silence during which anyone may speak of how the text has touched their lives. Each testimony is followed by a spontaneous hymn. Sometimes the Shakers lead a dance, not the floor-stomping, enthusiastic dances of their ancestors, but a simple rhythmic movement, palms raised to receive God's blessing, and then turned down to impart it to the earth. Shakers are pacifists and strong supporters of women's suffrage and workers' rights. They promoted progress, invented a number of labor-saving devices, and accepted electricity. Sabbathday Lake uses computers, enjoys television, and has a library of modern recordings.

Sabbathday Lake grows gourmet herbs and makes herb vinegars as well as raising sheep. The rhythm of work, prayer, and community living is unbroken. Meals are taken together, with the men and women at separate tables, and the community prays daily at 8:00 A.M. before starting work. There are 80 acres of farmland (the total land covers 1,800 acres) with 18 buildings, including barns, living quarters, and the meeting house. The community is led by one man and one woman, following Shaker tradition. As Sister Frances Carr, the female leader, comments, "There is still a group of people living in a place called Chosen Land where there have been Shakers for two hundred years, living the Shaker life."

References Cathy Newman, "The Shakers' Brief Eternity," *National Geographic* 176:3, 302–325 (September 1989). June Sprigg and David Larkin, *Shaker Life, Work, and Art.* New York, Workman, 1987. Stephen Stein, *The Shaker Experience in America.* New Haven, CT, Yale University Press, 1992.

SAINTE-ANNE DE BEAUPRE, Québec, Canada

Over a million pilgrims a year come to a tiny town on the shores of the St. Lawrence River 20 miles above Québec City, in honor of St. Ann, legendary grandmother of Jesus. The first chapel was built by early settlers in 1658, and by 1688 it was known as a place of pilgrimage for the region. By 1707, Indians (who in Canada are called the First Nations) were coming to venerate the one they called "Grandmother in the Faith." Their pilgrimage is still held each June. When the relic of St. Ann was sent to Beaupré by the pope in 1892, it stopped in New York, where an epileptic was cured on its first appearance, causing a tremendous excitement in the city. From that time, American pilgrimages to Beaupré increased tremendously. The largest pilgrimages come for the feast of St. Ann (July 26) and the

Sainte-Anne de Beaupré, named in honor of the legendary grandmother of Jesus, was built in 1658.

Sunday closest to the feast of the Nativity of Mary (September 8).

The cult of St. Ann is an ancient one, but there is no biblical authority for the grandparents of Jesus, who in tradition are named Ann and Joachim. St. Ann first appears in Christian writing around the year 150 CE, when her cult first took root in the Middle East. It developed in the West after the eighth century and was very popular in France at the time of the settlement of Québec.

The present basilica was completed in 1926, and its treasures include a number of eighteenth-century sculptures and artworks. The 240 stained-glass windows were created using a new technique that suffuses the light and brings the rest of the art into a harmonious whole. Large mosaics of the saints of Canada and 88 tableaux of the life of Jesus circle the inside of the church.

The center of devotion is the miraculous statue of St. Ann, carved from a massive single piece of oak. It is polychromed and wears a gold crown with diamonds, rubies, and pearls. She is shown carrying her child, Mary. It is not this magnificence that draws the pilgrims, however, but the miracle stories. The first was the cure of a crippled workman in 1658, and it was soon followed by the deliverance of a group of sailors from a storm. The ex-voto chapel in the basilica contains piles of crutches, canes, and folded wheelchairs, as well as paintings of instances of deliverance.

The basilica is set within a large property that includes several chapels, a sacred well, a lifesize set of the Stations of the Cross, and a replica of the *Scala Santa*, or "holy stairs," in Rome, the legendary stairs that Jesus mounted on his way to meet Pontius Pilate. There is an incessant round of prayer, with an average of eight daily Masses as well as a public Rosary, Way of the Cross, blessing of the sick with a relic of St. Ann, and a candlelight procession. Besides the places of prayer, the basilica maintains a pilgrim hostel and facilities for the sick and handicapped. The shrine policy states, "The young and the homeless must feel welcome here, for in welcoming them, we welcome Christ."

References Lucien Gagné and Jean-Pierre Asselin, *St. Anne de Beaupré*. St. Anne de Beaupré Shrine, 1984. Frances Parkinson Keyes, *St. Anne, Grandmother of Our Saviour*. New York, Julian Messner, 1955. Eugene Lefebvre, *St. Anne's Pilgrim People*. Québec, Charrier et Dugal, 1981.

SAINT ANTHONY OF PADUA, Italy

St. Anthony is one of the most popular Catholic saints, and his basilica in Padua, about 25 miles from Venice in northern Italy, attracts large numbers of pilgrims. A Byzantine-style church, it was begun shortly after his death in 1231 and was embellished by some of the finest artists of the period. Its soaring dome is covered with frescoes, and despite its size, appears light. One of its several side chapels contains the tomb of Anthony, the object of the pilgrimages. Next to it is the Lady Chapel, with a statue of a black Virgin; these medieval statues of Mary as a black woman are found frequently in Europe. The chapel is the only remaining portion of the Franciscan friary where Anthony lived. The church's main altar is adorned with a crucifix and statues by Donatello. Behind it is the Treasury, a chapel with relics of St. Anthony. In 1991, four gunmen held up the congregation and escaped with the jawbone of the saint. The raid was the work of the Mafia, who held the relic for ransom in exchange for an arrested Mafia chieftain. Within two months, a conspiracy with the Italian Secret Service had been exposed, and the relic was returned.

Anthony was born in Portugal around 1195. Shortly after he joined the Augustinian Order, he was transferred to the newly founded Franciscan Order. He was a simple but powerful preacher with the gift of touching the hearts of his listeners. Even though stories of miracles are associated with his life, it is his profoundly simple preaching that is best remembered. Sixty-eight cities and places around the world are named after him, 44 in Latin America and 15 in the United States. In popular devotion, Anthony is invoked to help find lost items. An unusual ex-voto is the custom of publishing testimonies of thanks for favors received from Anthony in newspaper classified sections. On his feast day, June 13, it is customary to bless St. Anthony Bread to be given to the poor. Today, this often takes the form of collections for food pantries.

References Lothar Hardick, *He Came to You So That You Might Come to Him: The Life and Teachings of St. Anthony of Padua.* Quincy, IL, Franciscan Press, 1989. Sarah McHam, *The Chapel of St. Anthony at the Santo and the Development of Venetian Renaissance Sculpture.* New York, Cambridge University, 1994. Charles Stoddard, *St. Anthony, the Wonder-Worker of Padua,* 2d ed. Rockford, IL, 1971.

SAINT JANUARIUS, Italy

Beneath the Cathedral of Naples, in southern Italy, lies the burial place of the patron of the city, St. Januarius, a bishop martyred under Diocletian in 305 CE. What is remarkable about Januarius is the phenomenon of his blood, which has liquified regularly since 1389. Two vials of Januarius' blood are kept in a silver reliquary, and three times a year, the larger is taken to the main altar, where it is placed near a reliquary containing the skull of the martyr. The people, led by a group of older women known as the *Zie de San Gennaro,* or "Aunts of St. Januarius," pray, often in extravagant and emotional terms, for the miracle to occur.

When the miracle takes place, the mass in the vial turns liquid and takes on a ruby-red color. It sometimes bubbles up and increases in volume, even though the vial is hermetically sealed. Scientific inquiries have failed to explain the phenomenon, though spectroscopic analysis has determined that the contents are human blood. To the people of Naples, the event is clearly a miracle. They are convinced that if the blood fails to liquify, disaster will befall Naples. To the failure of the miracle to take place they have attributed such calamities as plagues, eruptions of nearby Mt. Vesuvius, and even the election of a Communist mayor.

The story of Januarius' martyrdom is full of legends that have no basis in history but illustrate the great reverence attached to his memory. Supposedly, he was thrown into a furnace but remained untouched by the flames. After that, he and his companions were sent to the stadium, but the wild beasts there refused to attack them. The judge, who then ordered them beheaded, was struck blind, but Januarius cured him, causing the instant conversion of 5,000 people. After the beheading, the body of Januarius was taken to Naples, where it rests in a catacomb in the cathedral. This crypt chapel is decorated with frescoes and mosaics, and ornately covered with marble, gold, and bronze ornaments. The skull of Januarius and the vials of his blood are kept in a special chapel.

References Joan Cruz, *Relics.* Huntington, IN, Our Sunday Visitor, 1984. David Sox, *Relics and Shrines.* London, George Allen & Unwin, 1985. Kenneth Woodward, *Making Saints.* New York, Simon and Schuster, 1990.

SAINT JOSEPH'S ORATORY,
Québec, Canada

Originally a small, wooden chapel built by a simple brother for his healing ministry, Saint Joseph's Oratory is now a magnificent basilica on the slopes of Mont Royale in Québec. Pilgrims come from all over North America to Blessed André's shrine to pray for a cure.

Alfred Besette (1845–1937), raised in poverty and orphaned at 12, a failure at trades and then an unskilled factory worker in Connecticut in his teens, at 25 joined the Holy Cross Order, where he became Brother André. Due to poor health he could only be assigned as receptionist and doorkeeper at the Collège Notre-Dame in Montréal. But in his simple, untutored faith, he had great devotion to St. Joseph, foster-father of Jesus. Among Brother André's duties was visiting sick students, and it was noticed that those who took up his prayers to the saint were often cured instantly. As the word of his help to the sick spread, callers to the parlor became too many to accommodate, and parents grumbled that some of the sick visitors were likely to be contagious. Finally, friends arranged to purchase a vacant lot for his healing ministry, across the street from the college, on the slopes of Mont Royale. To build a chapel, Brother André raised $200 from a combination of small gifts and giving student haircuts at five cents each. From 1878, when the first cures took place, public enthusiasm was widespread.

The first wooden chapel, grandly named Saint Joseph's Oratory, measured only 15 feet by 18 feet. It was too small from the time of its opening in 1904, and almost immediately, plans for expansion were made. And the crowds came—to pray to St. Joseph, to seek cures, and to see Brother André, the miracle worker of Mont Royale.

Curiously, Brother André himself never witnessed a miracle. He counseled the sick or prayed with them, but cures took place out of his sight. He later said that this was his greatest cause of suffering. In 1916 alone, 435 cases of healing were reported. At first, Brother André was denounced as a charlatan and regarded with suspicion by both his superiors and Church authorities. A special commission to test the alleged cures and Brother André's honesty was set up in 1911. It did not comment on the faith healing, but it did recommend that the pilgrimages continue.

By 1914 a major basilica was begun, but the Great Depression halted construction after the crypt had been built. Here his body was laid when Brother André died in 1937; a million people filed past his casket despite the snow and cold of a bitter winter. In 1955 the basilica was completed, and in 1982 Pope John Paul II declared Brother André blessed, the final step before being declared a saint.

Brother André's devotion to St. Joseph was based on his own experience as a laborer and migrant worker, qualities he saw in St. Joseph. Brother André was a man of deep, constant prayer and simple faith. Though Saint Joseph's Oratory is a powerful tribute to Joseph, its devotees come as much to honor Brother André. His availability to others, often for hours on end, his unfailing good humor and sensitive kindness have left a memory that has endeared him to several generations of North Americans. The producer of the 1986 film of his life commented, "Brother André is to religion in Québec what Maurice Richard was to hockey—the *habitant* who became a superhero."

The oratory is massive, and it sits on one of the most magnificent sites in Montréal. It is the highest structure in the city, and its

Saint Joseph's Oratory, pictured here, replaced the small wooden chapel from which Brother André prayed for the sick in the early twentieth century. Although his prayers to St. Joseph were noted to have healed hundreds of people, André suffered under a great deal of suspicion from the Church.

dome is second in size only to St. Peter's in Rome. Many of the two million pilgrims who come each year climb the entrance stairs up Mont Royale on their knees. The oratory seats 4,000 with room for 10,000 more standing. Its most popular chapel contains the embalmed heart of Brother André, which was stolen in 1972 but recovered two years later. The original chapel remains, with the small apartment where Brother André lived after 1909. There are also a large outdoor Way of the Cross, a museum dedicated to Brother André, and various exhibition halls. The sculptures, stained glass (ten scenes from Canadian religious history), and artwork are outstanding. An organ with 5,811 pipes, a carillon of 56 bells in their own building, and a choir school provide concerts and liturgical music. On summer evenings, Les Jongleurs de la Montagne present a Passion play, and at Christmas a collection of 250 manger scenes, some life size, are exhibited. Brother André's tomb draws all, but many also find their way up Mont Royale to the Fountain of Redemption, where a spring of water flows from the side of a golden lamb, the biblical symbol of Christ.

References Boniface Hanley, *Brother André*. St. Joseph's Oratory, 1981. C. Bernard Ruffin, *The Life of Brother André*. Huntington, IN, OSV, 1988. Susan Stein, *The Tapestry of St. Joseph*. Philadelphia, Apostle, 1991.

SAINT PETER'S, Italy

The largest church in Christendom and a triumph of Renaissance architecture, St. Peter's is the main church of Roman Catholicism and a symbol of the papacy. It is a shrine to Catholicism itself as a community of believers, a symbolic statement in stone of what it means to be a worldwide church. Priceless art, chapels, and memorials dot the immense expanse of its interior, but the greatest shrine and the reason for the church's existence, is the tomb of Peter the Apostle, considered by Catholics to be the first pope.

St. Peter was martyred around 64 CE during the persecution of Nero, and his burial place by the Roman race track (circus) was well known. In the fourth century the Emperor Constantine built a basilica above the tomb that lasted for 1200 years. Though it was a grand church, by 1500 it was in danger of crumbling. Pope Julius II engaged the best architects to build its successor, today's St. Peter's. The first stone was laid in 1506 and the basilica was completed over a century later.

Meant to be a tribute to the unity of Christianity, it became instead the occasion of one of its greatest divisions. In order to raise the enormous sums of money needed for construction, the pope authorized a European fundraising scheme, granting indulgences to contributors. In Catholic teaching, indulgences are relief from the punishment sinners endure after death to purify them for heaven. They are normally gained by prayer or sacrifice. Many were shocked at this means of raising money and accused the pardoners, as the pope's agents were called, of selling indulgences. The scandal caused the German monk Martin Luther to challenge the authority of the Church and to denounce indulgences (*see* the entry for Luther Circle). This action was the spark that set off the Protestant Reformation.

St. Peter's was not completed until 1626. The colonnades encircling the piazza are the work of Giovanni Bernini and symbolize the open arms of Mother Church. On top are statues of saints. Beneath them are three covered walks, the middle one built wide enough for carriages. The center point is an Egyptian obelisk, now with a relic of the Holy Cross on its top, that once marked the race track where Peter was martyred. The facade, completed in 1614, projects majesty and power and adds to the sense of a triumphant Church. From a small balcony at its center the pope gives his annual blessing "To the City and the World."

Hemmed in on its sides by the offices and museums of the Vatican, St. Peter's Basilica opens its wide arms into a vast forecourt plaza. It is designed as a Latin cross with a huge nave and two side aisles with many chapels branching off them. The interior is open below a soaring dome designed by Michelangelo. There are no pews (the crowds remain standing for services); this focuses every eye upon the central shrine where pilgrims can look down on the tomb of St. Peter. At floor level is a splendid altar with a baroque wall behind it featuring a papal chair—the Throne of St. Peter—actually a reliquary for a Roman-era throne that St. Peter was alleged to have used. Nowhere else is the visitor reminded more explicitly that this basilica is a memorial of the papacy. Above the throne is an oval window representing the Holy Spirit, God hovering over and protecting the papacy. Bernini, who began his career as a stage designer, created a bronze canopy that rises 95 feet above the floor on four spiral columns; the effect is one of majesty and awe.

Besides the magnificent papal Masses, the largest of which are conducted in the

Saint Peter's, the basilica pictured here, celebrates Renaissance architecture and is the principal church of Roman Catholicism.

porch facing the plaza, Masses are celebrated in the side chapels every day by numerous pilgrim groups. Each group is provided with a song leader and assistance for holding a service that will be memorable for them.

The dome, 138 feet in diameter, above 16 windows, creates the effect of an upward movement toward the light of heaven. Around the lower rim is the Latin text of Jesus' prophecy to Peter: "You are Peter, and upon this Rock (*petros* in Greek) I will build my Church, and I will give you the keys of the Kingdom of Heaven" (Matthew 16:18–19). This text is regarded by Catholics as the biblical justification for the papacy.

Among the other memorials in the basilica is a bronze statue of a seated St. Peter as pope. It is popular with pilgrims, who have kissed its foot so often through the centuries that much of it is worn away. There are also a number of tombs of other popes, both within the church and below in a special crypt. The work of art that draws all visitors, however, is Michelangelo's *Pietà*, kept in a small side chapel and protected by bulletproof glass after an assault on it a few years ago. Sculpted from the finest marble, it shows Mary receiving the body of Jesus after he has been lowered from the Cross. The flowing lines of the Virgin's dress blend with the corpse of the dead Jesus laid upon her lap, while the detail in the marble shows the veins in Christ's arms. It is a scene of serene tenderness mixed with great sadness. Done when the artist was only 24, it is regarded as one of the world's masterpieces.

A tiny window under the main altar gives a glimpse of the grave of the Apostle, but St. Peter's tomb cannot be visited without a permit. It is constantly under study by archaeologists, and large numbers of visitors would damage the area, which is part of an ancient cemetery.

During the Holy Year of 2000, St. Peter's is expected to attract some 20 million pilgrims and visitors.

See also Catacombs; Rome.
References James Fallows, "Vatican City," *National Geographic* 168:6, 723–761 (August 1984). Michael Grant, *St. Peter, a Biography*. New York, Scribner, 1995. James Lees-Milne, *St. Peter's*. Boston, Little, Brown, 1967. Jocelyn Toynbee and John Perkins, *Shrine of St. Peter and the Vatican Excavations*. New York, Pantheon, 1957.

SAINT WILLIBRORD'S SHRINE, Luxembourg

The Basilica of St. Willibrord in Echternach honors the Christian apostle of Luxembourg and the Netherlands. Willibrord (+739), an English missionary, was archbishop of the Netherlands and responsible for the introduction of Christianity to the Lowlands. In 698, he established a monastery at Echternach with English and Irish monks. It became a center for missionary work but was also known for its illuminated manuscripts. The basilica was seriously damaged by allied bombing during the Ardennes offensive in World War II, but the crypt and tomb were unscathed, allowing complete restoration. The present monastery was built in 1949 on the pattern of the old one. During the annual feast (Tuesday after Pentecost) the people take part in the unique dancing procession that dates from the fourteenth century, though there is evidence that it goes back to Willibrord's time.

Holding scarves that link them together and accompanied by a simple polka melody, the pilgrims dance in little hopping steps, three steps forward and two back, through the town and into the plaza before the shrine church. The procession originated in prayers for protection against epilepsy, for which St. Willibrord is invoked, and it is a custom for individuals to dance on behalf of ailing relatives too sick to come to the procession themselves. Thousands of people arrive from all over the region, some coming on foot for a hundred miles or more. A reliquary containing the relics of St. Willibrord is carried in the procession as the people chant the refrains of the Litany of St. Willibrord, honoring his memory with many titles: "father of the poor . . . destroyer of idols . . . founder of churches." Willibrord's body is in a marble shrine (+739) in the crypt of the basilica near a miraculous spring, formerly used for baptisms.

References Mary Lee and Sidney Nolan, *Christian Pilgrimage in Modern Western Europe.* Chapel Hill, University of North Carolina, 1989. Dorothy Spicer, *Festivals of Western Europe.* New York, H. W. Wilson, 1958. Stephen Wilson (ed.), *Saints and Their Cults.* Cambridge, UK, Cambridge University, 1983.

SAINT WINIFRED'S WELL, Wales

A holy healing well in the town of Holywell on the northern coast of Wales, Saint Winifred's Well is one of the many memorials left by Celtic Christianity.

As Christianity expanded after the fifth century, holy men moved north in Wales to seek solitude as hermits. Most prominent among them was St. Bueno, who took up residence in the court of a Welsh king, where he began instructing the chief's daughter, Winifred, in religion. One day she was attacked by a chieftain, Prince Caradoc. She refused his advances and ran, but he overtook her and attempted to rape her. When she resisted, he was furious. He drew his sword and struck off her head. The legend of Winifred recounts that where her head fell to the ground, a well of healing waters sprang forth. The moss turned red

where the blood was spattered about and emitted a sweet odor of violets and incense. The botanist Linnaeus lists a "violet-smelling" moss that grows only in that area.

Winifred's head rolled to a small chapel, and the horrified people came out to find Caradoc standing over the murdered body. Bueno gently took up the head and reattached it to the body, praying over Winifred until she came to life again. He then placed a curse on Caradoc, who withered away to nothing in the presence of the crowd. Years later, Bueno and Winifred returned to the well and Bueno blessed it, promising that those who came to the well would receive what they prayed for, if not on their first appeal, then on the second or third. He then made her promise to weave a cloak for him each year and place it in the stream, and God would bring it to him wherever he was. Bueno then took up his staff and went forth as a wandering holy man. Every year on May Day (May 1), Winifred placed a newly woven cloak in the stream from her holy well, and it always reached him. Bueno came to be known as Bueno of the Dry Cloak from this miracle.

Winifred's Well is the only medieval sacred well that has been used by spiritual seekers uninterruptedly to the present day. The legend of Winifred dates only from the twelfth century, however, from which time her sacred well can be dated. Her relics were kept in Shrewsbury, and the monastery church there was a popular place of pilgrimage throughout the Middle Ages. The usual pilgrimage way led from Shrewsbury to Holywell. Along the way were a number of way-stations, or stops, supposedly where stones anointed with St. Winifred's blood were found. The pilgrimage was assisted by a monastery that bestowed indulgences on pilgrims whose penances were believed to free them from the purifying punishments after death that made them worthy to enter heaven. There was also a commandery of the Knights Templar, a military monastic order that provided travelers with security guards against bandits. In 1416 King Henry V went to St. Winifred's Well on foot as an act of humility and penance, but the main attraction of Holywell was its reputation as a place for miraculous cures. When King Henry VIII despoiled the shrines, the way-stations were dismantled and Winifred's relics were lost. Only one finger was rescued, kept in Rome until 1852, when it was returned and divided between Holywell and Shrewsbury.

Pilgrims continued to come to Holywell during the persecution of Catholics in the sixteenth and seventeenth centuries, despite the martyrdom of several local priests who were hanged, disemboweled, and cut into pieces. In 1629 some 1,500 came on the saint's feast day, November 3. Throughout the centuries, the sick were miraculously cured when they bathed at the well. Local priests were in residence until the Jesuits made Holywell the center of the Catholic mission to North Wales in 1670. King James II gave the shrine to his wife, the Catholic Mary of Modena, and she restored the chapel in 1683. After Catholicism was legally restored in the mid-nineteenth century, a guest house was built and the pilgrimage thrived. The popes bestowed indulgences on the pilgrims in 1851 and 1887.

The shrine is in excellent condition. It draws a steady stream of Anglican and Catholic supplicants and has several annual ecumenical pilgrimages. One of the largest of these, sponsored by Anglicans, is the annual pilgrimage for the handicapped, where hundreds volunteer to assist the frail pilgrims, most in wheelchairs, into the waters. The spring itself is inside a large structure built by the mother of King Henry VII in 1500. A chapel is on the ground level, and pilgrims descend to the sacred well, which is under a high vaulted ceiling. There is an ambulatory, or circular passage, where pilgrims circle the well before going to a large pool fed by the spring. The well itself is star-shaped. Both Catholic and Anglican parishes adjoin the well, and each day the Catholic pastor blesses visitors with the relic of St. Winifred. A Catholic pilgrim hostel is nearby, following an old tradition, since the priests during the period of persecution passed themselves off as innkeepers and maintained refuges for pilgrims.

See also Wells and Springs, Sacred.

References T. Charles-Edwards, *Saint Winefride and Her Well*. London, Catholic Truth Society, 1971. Christopher David, *Saint Winefride's Well*. Slough, UK, Kenion Press, 1969. Francis Jones, *The Holy Wells of Wales*. Cardiff, University of Wales, 1992.

SANTIAGO DE COMPOSTELA, Spain

In the far northwest corner of Spain, one of the greatest Christian shrines of the Middle Ages continues to draw several hundred thousand pilgrims each year. Santiago (St. James the Greater) is the patron saint of Spain and of all the Hispanic world, and his cult remains very popular. The shrine is the endpoint of a long and arduous pilgrimage, the *Camino,* or the Way of Santiago, that has continued for over 1,000 years. In the Middle Ages it ranked with Rome and Jerusalem as one of the three major Christian pilgrimages.

The legend of Santiago begins when James supposedly preached Christianity in Spain (*see* the entry for El Pilar) and then returned to Jerusalem, where he was martyred. His body was brought to Spain and lost after it was buried to protect it from the

Muslims. In a miraculous vision, its hiding place was revealed by a star in 844, and a chapel was built at Compostela, the "field of the star." As the Christian forces were engaged in battle at Clavijo, Santiago appeared in the sky on a white charger and led the attack against the Moors. Santiago was known thereafter as Santiago Matamoros, James the Moor-Slayer, and the reconquest of Spain had found a powerful patron saint.

Four medieval routes led to Santiago: from Vézeley, Paris, Le Puy, and Arles. Pilgrims from outside France assembled at one of these points or joined the British, who sailed to Bordeaux. Within Spain, the Way is some 600 miles long, most of it a footpath still untouched by cars, often wandering through fields. Monasteries were founded along the way to care for travelers, like Roncesvalles on the French border, where the monks washed the feet of pilgrims, fed, and housed them. The old dormitory is still there and still used. A military order of monks, the Knights of Santiago, was established to fight the Muslims. It also provided security patrols to the 500,000 to two million pilgrims who followed the Way each year during the Middle Ages.

Most people went to fulfill a vow, or out of piety, or to seek forgiveness for sins. A few went because they were forced to. Medieval courts could sentence a criminal to make the pilgrimage, requiring him to bring back evidence that he had completed it. Because a pilgrimage on foot is a test and often brings inner insight, a few criminals are still sent on it each year, usually juvenile delinquents whom the judge hopes to shock into changing their lives. To this day, a beginning pilgrim can obtain a passport that is stamped at his stopping points and finally certified at an office in the basilica.

Medieval pilgrims wore a special costume: a cloak, a broad-brimmed hat, and a walking staff with an attached water gourd. Every medieval pilgrimage had its symbol, and Santiago's was a scallop shell, worn proudly by those who made the long journey. The wealthy, of course, could ride, but most people walked, an average of three months (often more), across mountain passes and in danger from bandits and wolf packs. After the Reformation, the numbers of pilgrims dropped, and when Sir Francis Drake raided the coast in 1589, the relics were taken out of the cathedral for safekeeping. They were lost for 300 years and were authenticated and restored only in 1879.

The Way has well-marked stops, some of which have become important in their own right: the cathedral cities of Burgos and Leon, regional shrines like Conques, and villages such as Santo Domingo de la Calzada, St. Dominic of the Way. Here a local hermit built a rough hostel to shelter pilgrims (it is now a pricey government hotel). According to an old tale, a handsome youth was on the Way with his parents. When they stopped here, he was propositioned by a local bar maid. When he spurned her, she angrily planted a stolen chalice in his bags and caused him to be arrested and condemned to be hanged for thievery. His frantic parents came to the local judge's home to beg for mercy just as the judge sat down to dinner. Announcing that the boy was already executed, the judge said he could no more be brought back than the baked chickens on the table—at which, the chickens came to life and began to crow. And, of course, the virtuous youth was found alive on the gallows. From that time, the church in Santo Domingo has had a chicken coop high up near the altar, and pilgrims prize the chickens' feathers as souvenirs.

All along the route are pilgrim hostels, along with a few now expensive *paradors*, or national hotels. Some hardly changed from medieval times: simple open dormitories, sometimes serving soup and bread at the end of a long day's walk. In recent years the Spanish government has refurbished stopping places along the Way and allowed pilgrims free use of them.

Today's pilgrims are a mixed lot. About two-thirds come for religious reasons, the others for a mix of religious and cultural ones. Most come by modern transportation, but many still walk. A group of Bavarian factory workers annually spends two weeks walking; each year they take a bus to the point where they left off the year before. Two professors from the University of Rhode Island have made the pilgrimage with students five times, spending two summer months on the trek. An average of 20,000 pilgrims make the "official" walking pilgrimage each year, completing a passport of all the way-stations, but the actual numbers of pilgrims who come by plane, train, and bus are many times that. The numbers multiply further in a Holy Year, which is whenever St. James' Day (July 25) falls on a Sunday. Those who walk a minimum of 60 miles (or bike 120 miles) receive a "Compostela," the official document. In medieval times, the first to see the shrine towers cried out "Mon joie!" ("My joy!") and was named Le Roy (the king) of the group. Many a medieval pilgrim changed his name to Leroy after that experience. Today, upon entering the town, pilgrims search out a hostel, and then, after having their passports certified, they enter the great doors of the cathedral, the Port of Glory.

The cathedral is filled with spectacles and wonders. It is a riot of magnificent baroque carving, beautiful side chapels, and special places. Pilgrims stop by a pillar worn smooth by countless pilgrims before them and add their caress to the others'. At a column with a carving of the architect, they touch their heads to his with a prayer to share some of his wisdom. The next stop is the shrine of St. James above the high altar, reached by a circular staircase. Climbing up to a small room, pilgrims reach through an open space to kiss the neck of a statue of the saint above the altar. A casket with his supposed relics is in view in the crypt. The pilgrimage officially ends with the celebration of Mass in the church. At the main services, eight men lower a huge censer, the *botafumeiro,* which swings across the vast space of the cathedral a few feet above the floor. Since it is six feet high on a 100-foot rope and gives out clouds of incense, the sight is spectacular.

See also Pilgrimage.

References Georges Bernès, *The Pilgrim Route to Compostela.* London, Robertson McCarta, 2d ed., 1990. Jack Hitt, *Off the Road: A Modern-day Walk down the Pilgrim's Route into Spain.* New York, Simon & Schuster, 1995. Michael Jacobs, *The Road to Santiago de Compostela.* London, Penguin, 1992.

SAN XAVIER DEL BAC, Arizona, USA

The mission shrine of San Xavier, a few miles southwest of Tucson, was founded by Padre Eusebio Kino, the most remarkable missionary to have worked in the Spanish borderlands. San Xavier is the finest of the many beautiful churches he built between 1670 and 1710.

A member of the Jesuits rather than the dominant Franciscan friars, Kino first explored California, then came to Arizona. Unlike other missionaries, he respected the native people and refused to allow them to be taken in bondage. He taught progressive farming and spread Christianity by example and preaching but never by force or bribe.

With its large dome and two towers, the San Xavier del Bac mission is a lasting legacy to the churches Padre Eusebio Kino built between 1670 and 1710.

The churches he built are his lasting legacy. San Xavier was built in 1700 and named for the great apostle of Asia, the mission to which Kino had first asked to be sent. A century later, the present church was rebuilt completely by the Indians under the direction of the Franciscans. It remains a Tohono O'odham (Papago) mission, as it has been since its origins.

San Xavier del Bac rises from the desert like a white Moorish castle. A lovely arched gate leads to the church with its large dome and two towers, one with a cupola and the other finished. A promenade surrounds the church to provide a shaded space in the blazing sun, which is intensified as it reflects off the white walls. The fired brick is set with a mortar of sand, slaked lime, and cactus juice. The interior is a spectacular play of gold and white walls, the altar background covered with ornate baroque carving. An arched wall frames the altar space with three paintings. Recent restoration of a figure long thought to be Christ, the Good Shepherd, revealed that it was actually a portrait of the Virgin Mary.

The church attracts a steady flow of worshippers and visitors, but pilgrims come to pray at the curious shrine of St. Francis Xavier. Although it includes a 1759 statue of the saint, the focus of most pilgrims is a coffin holding a statue of the saint in death. Pilgrims come to pray for favors, leaving ex-votos as thank offerings. The most fervent walk the ten miles from Tucson.

References Alice Hall, "New Face for a Desert Mission," *National Geographic* 188:6, 53–59 (1995). Douglas Hall, *Fron-*

tier Spirit: Early Churches of the Southwest.
New York, Abbeville, 1990. Oscar Jones
and Joy Jones, *Guide to Historic Hispanic
America.* New York, Hippocrene, 1993.

SAUT D'EAU, Haïti

On the edge of Ville Bonheur ("Happiness
Town"), 60 miles from Port-au-Prince, is
Saut d'Eau, a group of waterfalls sacred to
Voudou. It has been a pilgrimage site for
over 150 years, beginning after the waterfalls were created by an earthquake in 1842.
Suppliants come to pray, beseech the spirits
for protection and success, and play in the
waters.

Followers of Voudou believe that trees
and springs are the natural temples of spirits, who must be solicited for favors and placated so that they do not harm them. During Voudou gatherings, devotees dance, play,
and sing. They hope, through these activities, to attract the *loas* (spirits) who intercede
with *Le Gran Mèt* (the Creator) to their celebration. If a loa is pleased with the disciple's service, it enters into the worshipper
and possesses him or her. The loas are identified both with ancient Yoruba (West
African) deities and with Catholic saints.
The most prominent have dual names, both
African god and Catholic saint. The Saut
d'Eau is believed to be inhabited by the
Snake God, Danbala Wedo.

During the feast of Vyèj Mirak, the Virgin of Miracles, pilgrims are anointed with
water and grain for good health by Voudou
houngon, or priests. According to tradition,
the Virgin Mary (in the dress of Our Lady
of Mount Carmel) first appeared in the top
branches of a palm tree in 1848, then annually at the time of the feast (July 16); she is
identified with the loa of love, Ezili Freda,
who also resides in the waterfall. The
Catholic church has resisted the superstitions at the site and attempted to suppress

them. The shrine also received the atten-
tions of U.S. occupation forces, who
wanted to stamp out Voudou. During the
U.S. occupation of Haiti in the 1920s,
marines were ordered to fire on the palm
tree, but the vision merely moved, until all
the palms in the area were cut down. Mary
then turned into a dove and fell into the
waterfall, consecrating it. Christians join the
pilgrimage on the feast day, but the Voudou
celebration takes place during the days preceding. Many walk the entire distance to
work off a vow or a penance they have
chosen because they have offended a loa.
Penitents refuse rides, even up the last steep
hill, and they make the pilgrimage with
only patched clothes and no money, living
from the pitifully few alms they receive on
their journey. There are various stations
along the way, including a major place of
offering to Legba, the loa of thoroughfares,
identified with St. Peter. The sacred water
from the falls is taken home for blessings
during the year.

At the site are three waterfalls, tumbling
over a hundred feet. People stand under
them to receive strength from the pounding
waters. Some bathe in the waters, shampoo-
ing themselves to wash away sin, and then
bathe their babies. The clothing they wore
into the waters is cast off, and new, blessed
clothes are donned after the ritual cleansing.
Little groups gather around candles and implore the loas for a good harvest, a successful pregnancy, or true love. A pregnant
woman will have a houngon tie a cord
around her belly, then later remove it and tie
it around a tree sacred to her favorite loa.
The more recent apparitions of the Virgin
Mary are said to take place at a sacred grove
there, St. John's Wood. It is named for St.
John the Baptist, who is also said to have appeared here. Miracles are associated with all
the sites.

Although people visit at any time, the three major pilgrimages occur on September 24, during Holy Week, and on July 16, the anniversary of the apparition. About 20,000 people visit the sacred places each year. Although anyone may come to Saut d'Eau, one must become Catholic before being initiated into Voudou rites. A pilgrimage to Saut d'Eau is a usual prerequisite to being admitted into the Voudou priesthood.

See also Plaine du Nord.

References Carole Devillers, "Haiti's Voodoo Pilgrimages: Of Spirits and Saints," *National Geographic* 167:3, 395–408 (March 1985). Melville Herskovits, *Life in a Haitian Valley*. New York, Octagon, 1964. *Voodoo and the Church in Haiti*. Berkeley, University of California, 1988 (video).

SCETE, Egypt

The monasteries of Wâdî el Natrûn in the Scete Desert, 100 miles west of Cairo, are both the heart and the backbone of Coptic Christianity, outposts of orthodoxy in a hostile Islamic atmosphere. The *wadi* is a dry river bed, centuries ago a branch of the Nile, which is now 40 miles away. Except for the irrigated farms of the monks, the place is arid, harsh, and uninviting. St. Jerome visited in 385 CE and said that "such a terrible place can be endured by none except those of total resolve and supreme constancy." Even now, access is difficult, but this remoteness has provided—and continues to provide—both solitude for monastic life and security from persecution. Today, despite their austerity and remoteness, these monasteries, among the most ancient Christian monasteries in the world, are experiencing rebirth. Many educated and talented young professionals are embracing monastic life, in the face of official oppression and Islamic fundamentalism.

The monasteries are havens of solitude, and the daily round of chanted prayer, work, fasting, and meditation goes on as it has for over 1,650 years. Monasticism originated in Egypt with St. Anthony the Great around the year 300 CE, and by 330 some of his disciples had come to the Scete Desert. At its height, the Scete had over 50 monasteries, only four of which survive. A few other monastic houses still exist elsewhere in Egypt, each with only a few monks, but the Scete is vibrant and expanding.

Each of the four monasteries follows the same rules. The day begins at 3:00 A.M. with the solemn chanting of psalms and prayers for several hours, ending at dawn with the Eucharist. Every monk also spends a period of solitary meditation each day. The monasteries, though austere, support themselves, primarily by farming. Each is surrounded by walls 40 feet high and a yard thick, a legacy of the days of frequent raids by desert nomads. As pacifists, the monks refused to defend themselves and relied on a keep—a large tower that could be entered and sealed off while the desert Bedouins looted the place.

Monastic churches always face Jerusalem, and seating is by a rigid hierarchy: the priest in the sanctuary, hidden from all by a wood screen with inlaid ivory and icons; a section for the monks and Christians; and a nave with those preparing for baptism at the front, non-Christians behind them, and the "weepers," public sinners, banished to the very back. Each of the four monasteries—the Syrian Monastery, St. Bishoi, St. Macarius, and the Virgin Mary (Baramus)—has precious artwork that has survived the many sackings. Icons from as early as the fifth century, magnificent inlaid work, and valuable libraries of ancient manuscripts can be found in all of them. In the Syrian monastery is the Door of the Virgin, made of eight ebony panels, each with eight panels of ivory, all showing Christian themes and legends. In each monastery is a cave or cell originally home to a founding saint and extensive collections of relics. Twelve of the popes who head the Coptic Church have been elected from St. Macarius.

The monks eat frugally, generally a vegetarian diet, with many long periods of fasting: the 43 days before Coptic Christmas, 3 days in remembrance of Jonah in the belly of the whale, 56 days of Lent, from Pentecost until July 12 in remembrance of the Apostles, and two weeks in mid-August in honor of the Assumption of the Virgin Mary. On fasting days there is one meal of bread and soup, with a vegetable dish added for important feast days. After at least five years in a monastery, a monk can become a hermit, living in total solitude in a cave in the nearby cliffs. Several recent Coptic popes have spent periods of years as solitaries.

In some cases, male visitors may stay at Baramus Monastery, but only with a pass from the office of the patriarch, pope of the Coptic Church. During times of fasting, all visitors are forbidden, even by day. Pilgrims, including the rich and famous, have been coming to the Scete since the earliest days.

See also Mount Sinai.

References David Knowles, *Christian Monasticism.* New York, McGraw-Hill, 1977. Otto Meinardus, *Monks and Monasteries of the Egyptian Desert.* Cairo, American University, rev. ed., 1989. James Wellard, *Desert Pilgrimage.* London, Hutchinson, 1970.

SERGIEV POSAD, Russia

Sergiev Posad, located about 45 miles outside Moscow, is the center of Russian Orthodoxy, just as the Vatican is the center for Catholicism. The Church's administrative headquarters is here as well as some of its principal places of pilgrimage. It is also one of the most beautiful religious complexes in the country—a feast of Byzantine architecture. Though its history of pilgrimages is long, Sergiev Posad only became a recognized town after the Soviet Revolution, when it was incorporated and named Zagorsk after a prominent Communist. The ancient name was restored in 1991, and today the city has about 150,000 inhabitants.

The center of Orthodoxy in Russia was originally in Kiev, but the thirteenth-century Mongol invasion left the Ukraine devastated, and by 1308, the patriarch had set up residence in Moscow, then a minor provincial town. Shortly after the fall of Constantinople (1453) reduced the influence of the Greek patriarch, Moscow and Kiev became rivals for Orthodox supremacy in Russia. Therefore, when the monk Sergius of Radonezh built the first Trinity Monastery in 1337, he provided the newer Moscow faction with a monastic heart rivaling Perchersk, the monastic focal point for Kievan Christianity. It was rebuilt in 1422, after a Tartar raid destroyed the original wooden monastery outside Moscow, and St. Sergius' relics were interred in a silver reliquary in Trinity Cathedral, which was built at the same time. St. Sergius became a national symbol of Russian and Orthodox unity, inspiring the resistance to the Tartars. In 1552, to celebrate the Tartars' defeat and the capture of Kazan, Czar Ivan Grozny (known in the West as Ivan the Terrible) ordered the construction of the Uspensky (Assumption) Cathedral. Sergius' tomb became a place of national pilgrimage, at the same time that the monastery of Trinity-St. Sergius grew into a position of political and economic power in Muscovy. Consequently, Sergiev Posad became a focus for Russia's enemies. In 1608–1609 the monastery successfully resisted a 16-month siege by the Poles, and by 1764 it had become extremely wealthy. It controlled 106,000 male serfs and their families, who tilled its fields, managed its herds, and ran its shops.

The Russian Church is headed by a patriarch, elected by bishops, who, with a council, governs for life. Sergiev Posad is his residence and the Church's central office. The patriarchate was suspended from 1721 to 1917, during which time the Church was governed by the Holy Synod, a council submissive to the Czar. The Communist period brought a brief restoration of the patriarch's office along with ruthless seizure of the Church's properties and the destruction of many churches and most monasteries. Thousands of clergy died in prison or in Siberian work camps. Since he needed the support of the Church during World War II, Stalin made important concessions, including the restoration of the patriarchate and the reopening of seminaries. After 1958, there was little persecution, even though the Church's relations to the state were tense. The ranks of the clergy and bishops were infiltrated by Communist loyalists, however, a development that generated popular suspicion.

The city's Assumption Cathedral has five blue domes with gold stars and crosses. Czar Boris Gudonov is buried there. The goal of the pilgrims to Sergiev Posad, however, is the monastery of Trinity-St. Sergius. The monastery complex has over 25 acres within its walls. Throughout the medieval period, it was a center of Byzantine art, and the Russian style of icon painting developed here, especially under the influence of Andrei Rublyov (1360s–1430), a monk of St. Sergius considered the greatest master of the form. His best work was removed to the Tretyakov Museum in Moscow by the Communists, but a great deal can still be seen in the monastery. Besides the superb icon collection, the monastery has outstanding mosaics and frescoes on its walls. It also has a rich collection of church robes, jewelry, and precious metalwork.

As part of its collaboration with the Soviets, the monastery was a secret storage depot for hundreds of art treasures looted from Germany during World War II. At no point during the Soviet era was the Zagorsk complex abandoned; it continued to draw pilgrims. In fact, from 1938 to 1950, the government embarked on extensive restoration of the monastery. In the late 1980s, it counted a hundred monks in residence, although many were elderly. With the fall of communism, younger men are entering the community.

The monastery is also the location of the Moscow Theological Academy, the main seminary and school of theology in Russia. Because it has graduate programs, it educates the professors for most of the new Orthodox seminaries springing up throughout the former Soviet Union in the wake of the fall of Communism.

There are several churches within the monastery complex, including the Smolensky, known for its icon of Our Lady of Smolensk. It, along with several other churches, the tomb of St. Sergius, and St. Sergius' Well, are a part of the pilgrimage route for visitors. Votive offerings of flowers and candles are usually placed before the icons of Christ, the Virgin Mary, or favorite saints. Icons within the churches and chapels are considered living presences of the saints they depict. They are thought to have accumulated graces from the years of prayers of earlier pilgrims down through the ages.

References Truskova Fedorovna, *The Zagorsk State Historical and Art Museum.*

Moscow, Sovetskaia Rossiia, 1971. *The Temple.* Oakland, CA, Video Project, 1987.

SHINTO SHRINES, Japan

Shinto, literally "the way of the gods," is the world's most important nature religion and the faith of nationalist Japan. Thousands of Shinto shrines dot the Japanese landscape.

Since 660 BCE, when Emperor Jimmu Tenno established his rule, the Japanese royal family has ruled in an unbroken line. Jimmu Tenno was considered a descendant of the sun-goddess Amaterasu, who presented the nation with the three symbols of its imperial line—the sacred mirror, sword, and jewels. Amaterasu created the rice fields and the water to supply them and consecrated the sacred rites that are followed to this day. Thus the emperor, as a descendant of the goddess, is believed by some to be divine and is the ultimate religious symbol in his country.

Amaterasu is the greatest of many deities who inhabit all the forms of nature—rivers, mountains, fields, and rocks, as well as storms, food and rice, and all the parts of homes. These are the *kami*, spirits who abound in everyday life, especially in unique natural formations. Specially shaped stones and trees are prized for placement in the formal gardens that are a part of every Shinto shrine, in the hope that they will attract the kami to take up their dwelling there.

Shinto shrines offer many opportunities to worship and invoke the kami, especially with offerings of rice or rice wine. A month after birth, Japanese babies are brought to major shrines or neighborhood prayer halls to be presented to the deities, and the baby will remain attached throughout his or her life to the kami of that district. The child (even as an adult, he or she will be a child to the kami) returns to this shrine to pray for success in examinations and to inform the kami of a new job, marriage, or a child in the family.

In the sixth century CE, Buddhism began to rival Shinto and eventually became predominant until the restoration of the emperor to full power in 1868, after a long period as a figurehead ruler. Shinto then enjoyed a great revival and became the state religion, tied to the fortunes of a rising Japan. Its cult became obligatory during the militaristic period ending in World War II. In 1945, the victorious Allies demanded that the emperor renounce his claims to divinity, and Shinto became one of several competing religions. Many practice its rituals alongside Buddhism, with Shinto representing reverence for ancestors and the powers of nature. However, it also has a cult following of ultranationalists who use it as an expression of imperialist politics, and its shrines are popular with war veterans. Some shrines are for the worship of the kami of a particular emperor or the souls of the war dead and feature museums glorifying military sacrifices, such as the cult of the 6,000 kamikaze (military suicides) who died for the emperor in World War II.

Approaching a shrine, a visitor passes through the *torii*, a distinctive gateway that marks the transition from secular to sacred space. The main path, always clean and beautifully landscaped, is usually flanked by two protecting stone lions. A small trough or basin flows with water for the purification rite; using a ladle, the visitor washes each hand before pouring water into a cupped hand to rinse one's mouth. Then worshippers approach the *haiden,* a raised and roofed platform where offerings and prayers to the kami are made. An offering is tossed into a box; ¥5 and ¥50 coins are considered auspicious because they have a hole

Shinto shrines, such as the Tosho-gu Shrine in Nikko, Japan, pictured here, have drawn worshippers since 660 BCE.

in them. The pilgrims twice strike a gong, bow, and clap their hands to announce their presence to the spirit god. The main shrine building is the *honden* or inner shrine, which houses the sacred object in which the spirit resides.

Japanese visit shrines on many occasions: with a newborn; for blessings of children at ages 3, 5, and 7; and on January 15 in the year one turns 20, the "day of adulthood." Marriages, even of Buddhists, are performed at shrines in the presence of a shrine priest. Priests also conduct blessings of buildings and new cars.

Shinto makes extensive use of ex-votos, and trees, braided ropes, and special boards are covered with plaques with petitions, white slips of cloth or printed papers. Small charms, sold in shrine shops, protect drivers from accidents, help in romance, or serve a variety of other personal needs. In front of the shrine hall are boxes of long, inscribed sticks, which the devotee shakes until a stick falls out. The number on the stick corresponds with slips of paper that tell fortunes. If the fortune is good, the visitor keeps it; if not, it is hung on a tree so that the wind may blow away the bad luck.

To the outsider, Shinto can be a bewildering mix of the sacred and the profane.

On the sacred path leading to the shrine at Izumo, for example, one finds a large steam locomotive that serves as a playground for both children and adults. Some shrine observances involve sumo wrestling, ritual dances, races, and tug-of-war contests.

See also Ise; Izumo Taisha Shrine; Kyoto; Nikko; Tokyo.

References Charles McCarry, "The Japan Alps," *National Geographic* 166:2, 238–259 (August 1984). Stuart Picken, *Essentials of Shinto.* Glenview, IL, Greenwood, 1994. *Shinto: Nature, Gods and Man in Japan.* New York, Japan Society, 1977 (video).

SHROUD OF TURIN, Italy

Perhaps the world's most famous relic, the Shroud of Turin is a long burial shroud— 13.5 by 4.25 feet—bearing the imprint of a man crucified and crowned by thorns. The body was placed on one half of the cloth, with the other folded over his head to cover the corpse from head to feet. Marks of nails in the crucified man's wrists are clear. The shroud has been called the burial shroud of Jesus and therefore evidence of the truth of the Gospels; it has also been called the greatest fraud ever created.

The shroud first appeared around 1380 in France, but in 1578, after being rescued from a fire, it was placed in the cathedral of Turin, where it is exposed for veneration on rare occasions. During the late Middle Ages, the shroud was assumed to be the burial shroud of Jesus mentioned in the Gospel of Matthew, and Pope Sixtus IV (1471–1484) called it "the portrait of Jesus Christ Himself." Challenges to the authenticity of the shroud arose alongside the popular approval. Already in 1389 the bishop of Troyes, in whose diocese the shroud was, denounced it as an artist's creation and forbade priests from claiming it was Jesus' bur-

ial cloth. When this dictum was appealed to the pope, he permitted display of the shroud but required that people be told that it was only a picture and not the true shroud of Jesus.

It is probable that the shroud was created, not as a fraudulent relic, but as an icon (sacred image of Jesus) for use during Holy Week ceremonies. Mystery plays were often woven into the ceremonies in the Middle Ages, and the shroud would have provided a dramatic element.

When permission was granted to photograph the shroud in 1898, a sensation followed when it was discovered that the portrait on the shroud was in fact a negative image, and the photographic negative offered a clear likeness, especially of the face. By 1903, more than 3,500 articles had been written on the shroud, the majority questioning its authenticity. The influential *Catholic Encyclopedia* (1902–1912) considered it a fabrication, but not a fraud. Many scientific theories about the shroud have been proposed, and several analyses were undertaken by laboratories. The first speculation—for many years the accepted view—was that ammonia vapors from Jesus' body after his violent death caused the negative effect. It was argued that these vapors developed the deep red-brown stains by interacting with the cloth, which was impregnated with the aloes and oil traditionally used in Jewish burials.

After World War II, interest in the shroud increased, influenced by a meticulous medical analysis of the death of Jesus undertaken by a French physician, Pierre Barbet, who based his work on the evidence of the shroud. Barbet's book became a bestseller and created a new audience for the shroud.

A series of investigations was undertaken until Church authorities agreed to carbon dating using tiny samples of several cloths.

The samples were tested by university laboratories at Oxford, the University of Arizona, and the Zurich Institute of Technology. They agreed, in independent tests, that the sample taken from the shroud was from cloth made between 1260 and 1390. Opinion on the shroud promptly divided between those who denounced it as a fraud and those who stubbornly rejected the scientific analysis and insisted it was Jesus' true burial cloth. In the media-driven controversy, the traditional argument, that it was a second image but not Jesus' shroud—still the most rational—got little hearing. Church authorities accepted the test results, saying that the shroud, as a representation of the Passion of Jesus, was a true icon but not the burial shroud of Jesus.

Questions remain unanswered, however. How does one explain that the shroud anticipates photographic technique by 500 years? It is not a painting; there are no pigments. The shroud involves gravity effects on blood stains that were only discovered in modern times by forensic medicine. How does one explain the presence in the cloth of plant pollen from first-century Palestine? Or the image of coins, one the "widow's mite" minted under Pontius Pilate, covering the eyes of the body? These could not be faked, because they were only revealed by a twentieth-century image analyzer developed by the U.S. National Air and Space Administration. The shroud raises as many questions as science has been able to lay to rest, and it is this mystery about its origins and purpose that continues to feed popular devotion. In 1996, Pope John Paul II indicated that he would allow another carbon dating test.

See also Holy Blood; Relics.

References Pierre Barbet, *A Doctor at Calvary*. Garden City, NY, Doubleday, 1953. Daniel Scavone, *The Shroud of Turin: Opposing Viewpoints*. San Diego, Greenhaven, 1989. *The Shroud of Turin*. New York, BBC, 1995 (video).

SHWE DAGON PAGODA,
Myanmar/Burma

The heart of the ancient Burmese city of Yangon (formerly Rangoon) is the elaborate Shwe Dagon Pagoda, which houses some of the most important relics of Buddha. According to legend, it was built at the time of the Buddha himself, some 500 years BCE. The Buddha supposedly gave eight hairs from his beard as a gift to two traders who carried them from India to be enshrined in Yangon. Later, a tooth of the Buddha was added to the collection. Through the years, the stupas that held the sacred relics were destroyed by fire or earthquake, but the relics always survived. The present pagoda was built in 1769.

The shrine is a forest of spires, all lovingly covered with gold leaf each year after the monsoon rains. The reliquary stupa, at 326 feet, is the highest point. It is adorned with 5,452 diamonds and 1,500 sapphires, rubies, and semiprecious stones. On its tip is a 78-carat emerald placed to reflect the last rays of the setting sun. This central stupa, containing the vault with the sacred objects, dwarfs the other spires around it. The pagoda is laid out like a compass, with eight spires surrounding the central reliquary spire. Each has a temple marked with various astrological signs.

The pagoda is a major pilgrimage site. Barefoot pilgrims in a constant stream walk clockwise around its base, then ascend by a long stairway to the terrace to leave ex-votos—paper umbrellas, incense sticks, and flowers—in honor of the Buddha. Pilgrims may bathe the Buddha statues in the pagoda before leaving offerings. Each person then seeks out the temple that is marked with his or her astrological sign, since worshipping at the temple that corresponds to one's birthday brings good fortune and strengthens character.

Shwe Dagon is a favorite place for boys' coming-of-age ceremonies. The youngster, robed in silk and with a golden crown symbolizing all his worldly potential, is carried around the pagoda. Then his head is shaved and he dons monk's garb and enters the monastery, at least for a few days.

References Richard Gombrich, *Theravada Buddhism.* New York, Routledge, 1988. Ormond McGill, *Religious Mysteries of the Orient.* South Brunswick, NJ, Barnes, 1976. E. Michael Mendelson, *Sangha and State in Burma.* Ithaca, NY, Cornell University, 1975.

SKELLIG MICHAEL, Ireland

The Skelligs ("stone splinters") are three rocky islets seven miles off Ireland's southwest coast; the largest, Skellig Michael, its two peaks thrusting up 714 feet from the sea, was the site of a Celtic monastic settlement from the seventh to the thirteenth centuries. In imitation of Christ and his Apostles it had 12 monks plus an abbot. It took its name in the tenth century, when the patronage of St. Michael the Archangel became popular among monks living on mountains (*see* the entry for Mont-Saint-Michel). According to medieval legend, a hollow stone outside St. Michael's Church was miraculously filled each day with enough wine for the celebration of Mass, a gift of the archangel.

The monastery is on North Peak, the gentler, more rounded of the two crags. Its terrain permitted a few small terraces for growing vegetables to supplement the monks' diet of birds' eggs, seaweed, and fish. Today, its remains include an ancient chapel, St. Michael's Church, two tiny prayer chapels, and six beehive-shaped huts. These were all made of dry rubble and surrounded by an unmortared wall that protected them from falling over the cliffside. The Vikings raided the settlement in 823 but evidently found little worth taking except a captive, the Abbot Eitgall. Since the poor monks had no ransom to pay for him, he was allowed to starve to death. The monastery was finally abandoned due to a shift in the climate, which brought severe storms and made growing food almost impossible. After the monks resettled on the mainland, Skellig Michael was used as a summer retreat, and pilgrimages began.

Until the late eighteenth century, Great Skellig was a place of pilgrimage for those doing penance for particularly serious sins. And penance it was, for the settlement lies at the top of 544 stairs cut into the rock. After praying by the monastic ruins, the penitent ascended the peaks, which required careful negotiation along a dangerous route. In the middle of the island the two peaks are separated by "Christ's Saddle," a U-shaped depression marked with a rock inscribed with a cross. Various reliquaries and stone crosses made up the way-stations, or places of prayer, along the pilgrim path.

A hermitage perches high up on South Peak. It is almost completely inaccessible, yet there is evidence that pilgrims went there—which required crawling through a rock chimney (The Eye of the Needle) to reach the pinnacle where a narrow rock spit projects out over the sea hundreds of feet below. The pilgrim straddled this and inched along to a cross-shaped stone, which he kissed—the last station. The hermitage itself consisted of three tiny, walled terraces and a beehive hut. The terraces were created on the cliff by building retaining walls—again without mortar—until a speck of land could be supported. The task could only have been completed by a fanatic firmly convinced that each stone brought him a step closer to God. The hermit was probably a Culdee, a prophetic guide who was installed in the hermitage as a source of spiritual power for the monastery.

In recent centuries, engaged couples went to Skellig Michael for a brief retreat before marriage and also because it was the only place where marriage was permitted during Lent. The "retreats" soon turned into frolics and an excuse for escaping Ireland's strict sexual taboos, and the Church finally suppressed the pilgrimages altogether.

References Peter Harbison, *Pilgrimage in Ireland.* Syracuse, NY, Syracuse University, 1992. Walter Horn et al., *The Forgotten Hermitage of Skellig Michael.* Berkeley, University of California Press, 1990. Des Lavelle, *Skellig: Island Outpost of Europe.* Dublin, O'Brien, 1977.

SLAVE DEPOTS

When slaves were captured in West Africa, either after battle or in raids by local chiefs, they were brought to the coast in caravans and exchanged for firearms, ironware, cloth, and alcohol. In some cases, if there was no slave ship waiting and thus no ready sale, the coastal chiefs distributed the captives to local farmers, where they worked in chains until a slave ship arrived. In other cases, the captives were sent to slave depots to await the arrival of a slave ship.

The use of slave depots—holding pens in forts and trading posts built by Western or Muslim slave traders—made the slave trade more efficient by allowing the caravans of captives to be sold immediately. It was also unspeakably cruel. The slaves were stripped, branded with red-hot irons, segregated by sex, and then crammed into small cells with their untreated running wounds.

Many slave depots had interior stairways that led from the young women's pen to the military barracks, and most of the women were raped regularly. Many captives went insane, and the death rate was high. Survival estimates vary from one-in-ten to one-in-three. Whatever the figure, the vast majority of captives perished either in the caravans, the depots, or on the voyage. Those who survived were shipped to the slave markets of the Caribbean, Brazil, America, or the Ottoman Turkish Empire.

These slave depots have become places of pilgrimage for diaspora blacks, the descendants of the survivors of this evil trade, especially for African Americans. But local Africans, too, have begun to gather at the sites, leaving offerings and occasionally holding observances in honor of the ancestors.

Bagamoyo, Tanzania, was the site of a notorious slave depot and, after abolition of the slave trade, of a village for freed slaves. Bagamoyo is a corruption of a Swahili word meaning "lay down your heart." It was at the end of the slave trade routes that brought 50,000 victims a year in chain gangs from the interior—about one-fourth of those who began the tragic forced marches. From here they were taken by *dhow* (fishing boats) to Zanzibar to be sold. Boys between eight and ten were especially prized. They were castrated to provide eunuchs for the imperial harems; perhaps one in ten survived the brutal surgery. All that remains of the slave depot at Bagamoyo is the Caravanserai, a stone slave-holding pen modeled on Arab desert camps for caravans.

Bunce Island, Sierra Leone, lies at the mouth of the Sierra Leone River, inland from the capital, Freetown. Between 1750 and 1800, Bunce (pronounced BUN-see) Island was a major slave depot. Captives were gathered from a number of inland points until there were enough slaves to fill one or more ships. The island was fought over, and the British, French, Dutch, and Portuguese held it at various times, with the British emerging as the final owners. The Gullah of South Carolina, the only slave group in the United States to retain much of their African culture, were probably shipped from Bunce, which supplied many slaves for the Carolina and Georgia rice fields. The manor house and other buildings on Bunce Island were constructed in 1795 by blacks who had fought for the British in the American Revolutionary War and were granted their freedom in exchange. But the slaves kept here were treated no better than the freedmen's ancestors had been; hobbled in chained circles in the open air, they ate from troughs and slept on the ground as they awaited their fate. After the slave trade was declared illegal in 1807, Sierra Leone became a center for recaptives—Africans kidnapped by slavers and then freed by the British when the slave ships were captured at sea by the antislavery naval squadron. They were released on the Sierra Leone coast.

Cape Coast Castle, Ghana, was built with slave labor in 1653 by Sweden and rebuilt a century later. It changed hands five times, ending up under British control. The British used it as a slave pen from 1664 to 1833. The town (now over 100,000) was built around the castle, which faces the sea and held 1,500 slaves at a time. They were shipped to Liverpool, England, to be sold. Conditions were appalling; the prisoners were stuffed into small underground dungeons, fetid and without light, where they could neither sit nor lie down. Over time, the human waste raised the level of the floor by two feet. Scratches made by the despairing captives can be seen on the walls. The church in the castle was built over a shrine to one of the coast's tutelary gods, Nana Taabiri; a stone shrine has been reestablished here. The Ghanaian government has set up a museum on the grounds and enacts a drama of the slave experience.

Christianborg, Accra, Ghana, also known as Osu Castle, is now the seat of the Ghanaian presidency and off-limits to visitors. It was built in 1647 by the Danes and used for the slave trade for a number of years. The castle, surrounded by high white walls, is elaborate and includes a fortress. The chapel was built over an indigenous shrine that has been restored. In December 1994, a gathering of chiefs was held outside Accra for a "cleansing of the stools," a sacred ceremony of purification. Carved stools are a symbol of authority in Ghana, like a Western throne, and are carried in processions and used on important occasions. The ceremony, conducted in red and black robes—the colors of mourning—was in atonement for the complicity of the chiefs' ancestors in the slave trade.

St. George's Castle, Elmina, Ghana, is the oldest European building in sub-Saharan Africa, built by the Portuguese in 1482. At first it was a trading post for gold, but by 1600 the demand for slaves in Brazil had turned it into a major slaving port. The fort was captured by the Dutch in 1637, and they, in turn, sold it to the British in 1872. By that time it had lost its value due to the abolition of the slave trade. The castle could hold 2,000 slaves after the Dutch expanded it, and they shipped some 65,000 slaves from Elmina. An impressive building visible from a distance, it was fronted by a double moat that is now dry. The slave quarters, auction room, dungeons, and governor's apartments are well maintained and open for visitors. In the women's quarters, there were separate cells for the attractive and the homely. The governor chose from among the former for his pleasures, and it seems that slave women who became pregnant were allowed to escape. Their descendants can be found in the area. A small shrine to the ancestors has been placed in one of the dungeons. The tunnel leading to the ships has been bricked up, but Africans regularly leave palm wine and flower offerings here.

Zanzibar Island, Tanzania, was the main terminus of the Arab slave routes from throughout eastern and central Africa. Throughout the nineteenth century, the Arab slavers brought an average of 50,000 slaves each year to Zanzibar for sale. Whole inland areas were depopulated by the trade, which supplied slaves for the Ottoman Empire and the Persian Gulf states. Most Arab slave depots were in lake towns and left no permanent buildings. In Zanzibar, where the sultan used slaves to work his clove plantations, an underground dungeon remains. After the British forced the end of the slave trade, and later occupied Zanzibar, they built the Anglican Cathedral over the slave market, with its altar directly above the old "whipping stone" where slaves were lashed. The cathedral also contains a cross made from the tree under which the explorer-missionary David Livingstone's heart was buried after he died in 1873. An anti-slavery campaigner, Livingstone is revered as a liberator and saint by the black Africans of the island. At Mangapwani, about six miles north of the city, are caves that were used to keep slaves being held for shipment elsewhere. The iron rings to which they were chained are still visible.

See also Gorée Island.

References Murray Gordon, *Slavery in the Arab World.* New York, New Amsterdam Books, 1989. Charles Johnson, *Middle Passage.* New York, Atheneum, 1990 (fiction). David Killingray, *The Slave Trade.* San Diego, Greenhaven, 1980. Colin

Palmer, "The Cruelest Commerce," *National Geographic* 182:3, 62–91 (March 1993).

STONEHENGE AND AVEBURY, England

The most famous megalithic monument in the world is the prehistoric stone circle at Stonehenge, in the valley of the Avon, north of Salisbury, England. Twenty-six miles further north is Avebury, enclosed by the world's largest henge, a massive earthwork 20 feet high and 1,400 feet across. Stonehenge and Avebury do not seem to be connected, though both are pre-Celtic, and their proximity and similarities have caused them to be linked together in popular imagination.

Almost nothing is known of the builders of Stonehenge. They left no records or oral history, only their awesome and enigmatic stone monuments. Stonehenge was built in three stages. The first, around 1850 BCE, was the work of a neolithic people who dug 56 holes inside a ditch and earth embankment. They raised only one stone, the Heel Stone, so named because of a unique mark on one side. A century later another group raised two concentric circles of five-ton bluestones quarried from mountains in Wales. They were brought 240 miles by raft and sledge. (To prove that the feat was possible, it was reenacted for BBC television in 1954.) The bluestones were later taken down by the Wessex people around 1650 BCE, and those that presently mark Stonehenge were quarried nearby. Thus the building stages took place about a century apart. A horseshoe of five sets of two massive pillars was raised, each set topped by a lintel. Around this was built a 94-foot circle of posts and lintels known as the Sarsen Circle. Sixteen of the uprights and five lintels remain. Hundreds of burial mounds (barrows) are scattered throughout the area, stripped of vegetation to expose the chalk undersurface. There is also a Long Barrow, which was used for ceremonial processions. No sacrifices were conducted at Stonehenge.

A computer-assisted study in the 1960s confirmed beyond a doubt that Stonehenge is an astronomical observatory of some kind. Sunrise at the solstices is easily determined, and the seasons can be defined by the settings of the stones. It is suspected that by moving posts around the holes, perhaps annually, eclipses could be predicted. Stonehenge was also used for some sort of funeral rites, and cremated remains have been discovered in the 56 holes.

For years it was believed that Stonehenge was a Druid worship center, but it has been proved that the Druids, an ancient Celtic cult, arrived many centuries after the construction of the henge. Nevertheless, contemporary New Age Druids continue the erroneous tradition and conduct services at the time of the summer solstice, the Northern Hemisphere's longest day. Tens of thousands arrive for the ceremonies, but the police have established an exclusion zone around the stones to protect them.

Stonehenge often disappoints visitors. Expecting something spectacular, they find instead a modest collection of stones with few over 20 feet high. Nevertheless, the stones weigh up to 50 tons each and their erection was an amazing feat of engineering. Though many stones have toppled through the years, some of these were raised again in 1958.

Avebury is far larger than Stonehenge, covering 28 acres bounded by a ditch 50 feet deep, and 27 of the original 100 stones still stand. The setting, however, is what sets Avebury apart. While Stonehenge is in an open plain away from habitation, Avebury has a village built in its midst. The four gateways to the henge are the entrances to the village, with their roads cutting through the surrounding earthen bank and crossing the ditch; the crossroads is the center of the town. This later development has not been kind. Early Christians knocked down the stones because they considered them part of a pagan temple, and seventeenth century Puritans broke them up for building materials. Despite this, Avebury still contains a number of stones, Europe's highest manmade hill (130 feet high, covering 5 acres), and its largest prehistoric tomb, a cigar-shaped long barrow (340 feet). Although some ritual use is certain, Avebury's exact purpose is unknown. Present-day devotees believe that standing stones can gather the earth's forces and transmit them, and so they regard Avebury as another source of earth energy, a place where that power can be encountered in a concentrated way and directed. Avebury attracts New Age worshippers for the solstices and at midsummer night.

References Richard Atkinson, *Stonehenge and Avebury and Neighboring Monuments.* London, Her Majesty's Stationery Office, 1971. Michael Balfour, *Stonehenge and Its Mysteries.* New York, Scribner, 1981. M. Scott Peck, *In Search of Stones: A Pilgrimage of Faith, Reason, and Discovery.* New York, Hyperion, 1995. *Stonehenge.* Princeton, NJ, Films for the Humanities, 1988 (video).

SWAYAMBHUNATH STUPA, Nepal

Swayambhunath Stupa is the chief Buddhist shrine of Nepal, the equivalent of the Hindu Pashupatinath Temple. Pilgrims traditionally walk from Kathmandu, the capital, a little more than a mile, along a well-marked pilgrimage path. In the summer, groups of hundreds will make the short trek from the city together, entering the temple

The eyes of the Swayambhunath Stupa are noted to keep watch over the compound and can be reached by climbing 365 stairs.

by a steep stairway. The pilgrimage is a source of merit.

Swayambhunath can be traced to the fifth century, but it is probably even older. An ancient legend says that the present-day city of Kathmandu was once a large lake, from which sprang a beautiful lotus that gave off a miraculous light, *swayambu*. When the people came to wonder, they found the gods in worship, and a wise monk covered the light with a stone and built the stupa above it. Since Buddhist custom dictates that every stupa should have a holy relic within it—a hair or tooth of the Buddha, or relics of a holy man—the confined light is regarded as the relic within Swayambhunath.

The pilgrim way leads up 365 stairs to the top of the compound, where a square structure with ever-watching eyes on all sides surveys the surrounding area. The shrine is popularly known as the "Monkey Temple" from the bands of monkeys who inhabit the grounds and scamper everywhere. Following tradition, pilgrims walk clockwise around the stupa, offering prayers. Around the base of the stupa are five shrines to the Buddha, each honoring different directions of the compass. Five other shrines are dedicated to the five elements: earth, air, water, fire, and ether. These go back further than Buddhism itself, stemming from ancient folk religions.

Besides the stupa, there are several *gompas*, Tibetan monastery-shrines, and it is here that *puja* (prayer offerings) is usually made. Announcement boards publish the day's services, and in the busy season families must schedule their puja. The most popular spot for this is the Harati Temple, dedicated to the goddess of smallpox, whom Buddha persuaded not to destroy children by giving her the best of the offerings given him. She is given the choicest food gifts. The original statue was smashed in the eighteenth century by a king whose wife died of smallpox; the present statue is a black stone representation.

References Ormond McGill, *Religious Mysteries of the Orient.* South Brunswick, NJ, Barnes, 1976. Trilok Majupuria and Indra Majupuria, *Holy Places of Buddhism in Nepal and India.* Bangkok, Tecpress, 2d ed., 1993. *Nepal: Land of the Gods.* New York, Mystic Fire, 1976 (video).

SWEAT LODGE, USA

In Native American spirituality, permanent, constructed shrines are rare. However, temporary holy places are built for special purposes and then allowed to return to the earth. Notable among these are sweat lodges, which are still built and used in the American Southwest, but have been found among most Amerindian traditions.

The lodge itself is a dome built of canvas or robes over willow saplings that holds about six people. (It is a taboo for men and women to take part together.) Prescribed rituals and prayers accompany each step in the building of the sweat lodge and in the ceremonies themselves. A fire is built in the center to heat rocks red-hot, and sometimes sweetgrass or sage is thrown on the coals to sweeten the air of the lodge and purify it. The heat is intense, and water is cast on the rocks to make a suffocating steam. Depending on the purpose of the sweat lodge, the leader may instruct young people in tribal customs and lore, or participants may pray or share their life stories. The sacred pipe is passed toward the end of the ceremony.

Among the Lakota Sioux there are seven sacred rites, including the *Inipi*, the sweat lodge ceremony, and its accompanying vision quest, *Hanbleceyapi*. An ancestral figure known as Woope (the Law), or White Buffalo Woman, gave the rites to the people over 3,000 years ago. The sweat lodge is a symbol of regeneration, renewal, and rebirth. It attempts to re-create a time before time, when there was unity in all creation, and not the fragmentation caused by selfishness, violence, and lack of reverence. It is a cleansing ceremony in which the sweat pouring from the body not only removes any physical poisons but purifies the emotions, mind, and spirit as well. Instead of leaving the participant weak, it strengthens him. The sweat lodge ceremony is also used for healing and is widely employed in Native American alcohol and drug dependency programs.

Although the sweat lodge may be used by anyone for purification or seeking wisdom, it has a special role in the Hanbleceyapi of the young warrior entering upon manhood. The sweat lodge is a purification ritual, removing the poisons from the warrior's body and freeing his mind from distraction. When a Native American youth leaves the sweat lodge to seek a vision, he wears only a breechcloth and leaves his hair unbraided as a sign of humility before the earth powers who will reveal wisdom to him. He may carry only a buffalo robe or a blanket to ward off the cold air in the high places where he will go. The purification that takes place in the sweat lodge is an important stage in the vision quest; without it, the young warrior may not perceive the vision, or the dream he is vouchsafed may be the result of some weakness in his body that has not been expelled. He spends two to four days in a high place in fasting and prayer, seeking a vision. Each summer many Native Americans from Plains tribes assemble at Bear Butte in the Black Hills, a favored spot for the vision quest.

In addition to its use as a preparation for a vision quest, a sweat lodge is conducted before a Sun Dance and other ceremonies. Amerindian Christians (the majority in modern times) incorporate it by using sweat lodge ceremonies before events such as Confirmation or marriage. The Native American Church holds sweat lodges before the use of sacramental peyote, which prevents the peyote from being taken merely as a recreational drug.

With some adaptation—often deeply resented by Native American practitioners of traditional religions—the sweat lodge is also a feature of New Age spirituality. Some of this reflects a certain "Indian chic" that appropriates rituals, often without a sense of their context. Practitioners point out, however, the universality of saunas and other uses of steam therapy for ritual and physical purification and to produce spiritual insight. Among New Age groups, the sweat lodge is also used as an adjunct to holistic healing.

References Joseph Bruchac, *The Native American Sweat Lodge.* Freedom, CA, Crossing Press, 1993. Don Doll, SJ, *Vision Quest.* New York, Crown, 1994. *Native American Sweat Lodge Ceremony.* Silver Lake, WI, Wishing Well, 1990 (video).

T'AI SHAN, China

Chinese religion identifies four imperial sacred mountains that marked off the corners of China. T'ai Shan, located halfway between Shanghai and Beijing, is easternmost and most important. For 4,000 years it has been a pilgrimage center for a mix of traditionalist, Buddhist, and Confucian believers, making it the oldest continuing pilgrimage site in the world.

Originally, the peaks were devoted to the ritual cult of the emperor, and T'ai Shan (Exalted Mountain) has always had the place of honor because it is the first to greet the sun, the source of life and symbol of the rebirth of spring. For an emperor, the ascent of T'ai Shan was the symbol that he had attained full power in China and that he could proclaim the triumph of his reign. Before he started the climb, the emperor would perform the Feng ritual, a sacrifice in honor of the heavens, at the base of the mountain. When he arrived at the summit, he would repeat the ritual. A second offering was made in honor of the earth. Along the paths leading up T'ai Shan are several remembrances of visits by emperors, including memorial groves of trees and markers attesting to the glories of their donors. The deity of T'ai Shan was the son of the Lord of Heaven, who gave the emperor his mandate to rule, and the mountain assumed the role of protector of the nation. The last emperor to proclaim his exploits through these ceremonies did so in 1008, although later rulers came on pilgrimage or to build temples. The last emperor to visit the mountain came in 1771, but by that time T'ai Shan no longer involved an imperial cult.

Because of its location between two large cities, T'ai Shan is accessible to a large population. Although its sides are rugged, it is so popular with pilgrims that it is like a vast temple yard, peopled by visitors who climb its paths, worship at its temples, and camp along its flanks. The centerpiece of devotion is a great staircase of 7,000 steps that climbs from T'ai Shan Temple, a cultural complex at the foot of the mountain, to the Emperor of Heaven Temple on the summit. This staircase is surrounded by an enormous number of temples, shrines, monuments, food stands, inns, and souvenir stalls. Every physical feature of the mountain has been named, dedicated, and associated with some aspect of religion or devotion. The total effect is less confusing than it sounds, since the focus of the pilgrim is always upward toward the summit, which is believed to be the dome of heaven. Each stage of the approach is marked by large gates. The second passage is steepest and most challenging, but the last stage is gentle. Its entrance is the impressive red brick South Gate of Heaven, and nearby is a temple marking the spot where Confucius rested on the climb, surveying the view below. Another popular shrine along the way is that of the Azure Dawn Princess, daughter of the god of the mountain and goddess of dawn. She is implored for grandchildren, and older women pray and burn paper offerings symbolizing money, so that their daughters might conceive.

Because T'ai Shan was the protector of the emperors and the common people, the god-mountain was also the supreme power over life and death. It determined success or failure in life and, in death, honor or condemnation. To the foot of the mountain came all the souls of the dead, according to folk tradition, and the mountain has always been a primary place for honoring and worshipping the ancestors.

Until the Communist period started in 1949, T'ai Shan had a vast bureaucracy at its service and temples for its worship in every town. Ten thousand people would climb the mountain each day during the spring season. The pilgrimages never stopped, even under Communist disapproval and harassment. When restrictions on pilgrimages were removed a few years ago, local officials were shocked to find that devotion to the ascent had not eroded, and thousands again flocked to T'ai Shan. The government has bowed to the inevitable and presently exploits T'ai Shan for tourism. In 1982 they built a road and cable car to the top.

T'ai Shan is often confused with Wu T'ai Shan, a Buddhist place of pilgrimage in northern China. Part of a complex of nine sacred mountains, it is dedicated to a bodhisattva, a Buddhist saint who has turned away from final bliss in order to serve the needs of struggling humans. The bodhisattva is said to appear as a series of orange globes of light in the night sky.

See also Emei Shan; Mountains, Sacred.
References Dwight Baker, *T'ai Shan: An Account of the Sacred Eastern Peak of China.* Shanghai, Commercial Press, 1925. Mary Mullikan and Anna Hotchkis, *The Nine Sacred Mountains of China.* Hong Kong, Vetch & Lee, 1973. Robert Orr, *Religion in China.* New York, Friendship Press, 1980.

TAIZE, France

Taizé is remarkable as the site of a monastic order that includes both Catholics and Protestants and has become known worldwide, particularly to young people looking for a deeper spirituality unaffected by modern materialism. The Taizé spirit incorporates meditation and faith-sharing with a respectful acceptance of a wide variety of religious traditions.

In 1940, at the onset of the Nazi occupation of France, a young Calvinist, Roger Schutz, embarked on an unusual enterprise. He founded a small religious order with monastic vows but made up of both Protestant and Catholic brothers. Brother Roger chose a tiny hamlet of Taizé, a few miles from the ruins of the great monastery of Cluny, to establish this ecumenical community. The area is poor and out of the way. During the world war the community sheltered Jews and was raided by the Gestapo.

Taizé includes no great art or architecture. Only the atmosphere is impressive. The main worship center is made of poured concrete, without adornment. The places of prayer are plain—one is an open-sided chapel in a wooded area—but they are also intense. At any hour of day or night the former village church and the large underground Church of Reconciliation are occupied by silent praying figures deep in meditation, the only light coming from small candles placed throughout the room. There are no chairs or pews. The atmosphere of contemplation is powerful yet peaceful. Each evening, vespers is celebrated in the church by candlelight, a moving event where all join in the chants as the white-robed monks enter in procession. Taizé's chants and songs have spread all over the Christian world. The style of shared prayer popularized here has spawned numerous "Taizé prayer" groups across Europe and in America.

Taizé is one of the religious phenomena of recent years. During the summer, the hill on which it sits is taken over by numbers of young people, upwards of 5,000 at once. The sight can be daunting—big tented areas with fields tramped into oozing mud. But somehow a semblance of order and cleanliness is maintained, and the spirit of harmony and joy is infectious. The visitors are by no means all Christians or even believers of any kind. Taizé brings together people of every faith and none, in its gentle way sharing what it has to offer—simple food, shared chores, prayer, and community. Realizing some years ago that the Taizé property was inadequate, Brother Roger began holding youth gatherings around Europe, often drawing over 100,000. The first of a series of smaller, regional gatherings was held in the United States at the University of Dayton in 1992.

Small communities of Taizé monks have settled in other places—in the slums of an American inner city or among Muslims in North Africa—but Taizé remains the center. The monastery sits amidst the tents and cinderblock housing, maintaining the rhythm of daily prayer. The community of about 90 is ecumenical, including Protestants of several denominations and Roman Catholics, living and sharing together without a loss of identity. Brother Roger himself and several other monks are considered leading ecumenical scholars. Catholic Mass is celebrated daily, although the vespers is the main communal prayer. The community accepts no donations or gifts but lives from its own work and the sale of publications and pottery.

References François Biot, OP, *The Rise of Protestant Monasticism*. Baltimore, Helicon, 1963. José Gonzalo-Balado, *The Story of Taizé*. New York, Seabury, 3d ed., 1988. John Heijke, CSSp, *An Ecumenical Light on the Renewal of Religious Community Life: Taizé*. Pittsburgh, Duquesne University, 1967. Roger Schutz, *The Rule of Taizé*. Taizé, France, Taizé Press, 1968.

TAJ MAHAL, India

The Taj Mahal is the mausoleum of Mumtaz Mahal, first wife of Shah Jehan, the emperor of India. Its story is a great love story. She bore him 14 children and died in childbirth with the last. Shah Jehan loved Mumtaz Mahal deeply in an age when arranged marriages meant that love was uncommon between husband and wife, and he built her mausoleum as a shrine. Not surprisingly, the Taj Mahal is a favorite with lovers and young couples.

Muslims first settled in northern India in the twelfth century, and from 1527 to 1707 the Moghuls ruled an Indian empire of splendid monuments and high culture. The fifth emperor, Shah Jehan (1627–1658) was a Muslim fundamentalist, rejecting his predecessors' policies of tolerance. He tore down Hindu temples to erect mosques, which caused resentment from his Hindu subjects. But he did follow a policy of architectural creativity. The Taj Mahal is the finest of the monuments he built.

The Taj Mahal is not only a jewel of architecture, but its placement within gardens with pools, canals and fountains at the end of a long approach sets it off. The harmonious structure of white marble is decorated outside and in with elaborate floral patterns and verses from the Qur'an, and the massive size of the building is made delicate and light as a result. Four minarets (prayer towers) anchor the corners of the compound. It took 18 years to build and involved 20,000 workers, including the best artisans in the subcontinent and from Europe. This extravagance led to Shah Jehan's being deposed by his son, and he spent his last years under house arrest, gazing from his window at his beloved wife's shrine. He is buried alongside

Surrounded by gardens, pools, and fountains, the Taj Mahal was erected as a shrine to Emperor Shah Jehan's late wife in the seventeenth century.

her in the crypt of the mausoleum. Today the Taj Mahal is threatened by air pollution and the theft of its precious inlays, and preventive maintenance has been poor.

To Westerners, the Taj Mahal seems primarily a tourist spot, and the hordes of casual visitors seem to reinforce that. However, it is also a pilgrim site, and every morning at dawn a stream of Indians come to the Taj. These are not Muslims, but Hindus from the villages, come to honor the great persons enshrined in the Taj Mahal. They leave flowers and petitions for health, success in exams, and other needs. There is also a mosque on the grounds used by Islamic pilgrims, and Fridays are active with worshippers.

References Amina Okada, *Taj Mahal.* New York, Abbeville, 1993. Raghu Rai, *Taj Mahal.* London, Times Books, 1986. *Taj Mahal: The Story of Muslim India.* Huntsville, TX, Educational Video Network, n.d. (video).

TEOTIHUACAN, Mexico

Just outside Mexico City lies the ancient city of Teotihuacán, a pre-Aztec center of culture and worship. Between 200 BCE and 650 CE it was the largest city in the Americas with a population of at least 150,000. In 650 it was sacked and burned by the nomadic Chichimecs and went into decline. The Teotihuacán language is unknown and the monuments are the only records of the people who worshipped there. But their gods were recognized and worshipped throughout Central America and are still revered among indigenous peoples. The Aztecs, who controlled the area until 1521, regarded Teotihuacán as the home of the gods but did not use it for worship. They treated Teotihuacán as a place of pilgrimage where the souls of kings were transformed into deities.

Teotihuacán is centered around a processional mall two miles long and 60 feet wide. It links two pyramids—the Temple of the Sun and the smaller Temple of the Moon—with the Temple of Quetzalcóatl, the Feathered Serpent, whose great plumed stone head juts out from the base. Each temple is approached by long, wide staircases to the top. The temple walls and stairs are decorated with stone carvings of the Feathered Serpent and Tlaloc, the rain and fertility god. The Temple of the Sun measures 720 by 760 feet at the base, approximately the size of the Great Pyramid of Giza. Built over a clover-shaped cavern believed to be the birthplace of Tlaloc, it was the site of a shrine for centuries before the Teotihuacán people arrived. Tlaloc was the chief god, though in time Quetzalcóatl rose to first place. Quetzalcóatl's temple is small but surrounded by 36 acres of ceremonial courtyards used for celebrating holy days set by the astrologer-priests. At such times the population of the city would double as pilgrims poured into Teotihuacán. Led by priests wearing feathered headdresses and bearing pots of burning incense, the people joined in begging the gods for rain and bountiful harvests.

People's social rank was indicated by how close they lived to the temples, and the city was ruled by a priest whose palace was near the Temple of the Sun. Teotihuacán was a trading empire whose influence extended well into Central America. It had over 350 workshops for obsidian, a glass-like stone that was its main export. Its trade routes served to spread the worship of its gods, and its agents built small temples modeled on its own as far away as Guatemala.

Because of later Aztec customs, many have assumed that the temples were used for human sacrifice, but Quetzalcóatl was a god of peace and gentleness who did not demand sacrifice. The legend of Quetzal-cóatl, who was a celibate god, recounts how he became drunk at a banquet and was seduced by the goddess of the magic mushroom. In despair at having given up his virginity, his claim to godliness, he marched into the sea and disappeared. The Aztecs, who worshipped a bloodthirsty warrior god who was appeased only by cutting the hearts from living human sacrifices, believed that Quetzalcóatl would someday return to usher in a new age of peace. The legend said that Quetzalcóatl would reappear in a white ship, and when the Spaniards arrived in ships with white sails, the Emperor Montezuma believed them messengers of the god. They cleverly exploited this belief to give divine approval to their assault on the Aztec empire.

Today Teotihuacán is listed on the UNESCO List of World Heritage Cultural Sites and is a major tourist destination. Its sacred tradition continues with New Age devotees, who regard it as an energy center. Teotihuacán's temples are built in mathematical relationship with one another, and the cave beneath the Pyramid of the Sun is aligned with the constellation Pleiades. An Aztec legend has it that as the sun was dying, the four creator gods refused to throw themselves into a consuming ceremonial fire that would bring forth a new sun. When a minor deity offered himself up, he became the Fifth Sun who ushered in a new age, giving order to the world. In this, New Age interpreters discover evidence of geomancy, the orientation of buildings and landscape to maximize the powers of nature. These alignments, called ley lines, point observers to further sacred power sites.

References Flavio Conti, *Centers of Belief.* Boston, HBJ Press, 1978, 105–120. George Stuart, "The Timeless Vision of Teotihuacan," *National Geographic* 188:6, 2–35 (December 1995). Peter Tompkins,

Mysteries of the Mexican Pyramids. New York, Harper & Row, 1976.

THEBES AND LUXOR, Egypt

Far down the Nile River from Cairo is the ancient Egyptian temple city of Thebes and Luxor. Modern visitors will find three ancient temple areas in the modern city of Luxor: Luxor Temple, the temples of Karnak, and the complex of Thebes across the Nile River. The site is so ancient (2000 BCE) that even Romans and Greeks visited here as tourists, amazed at the monuments and temples they found in the desert.

Thebes was a small state until one of its princes united the two kingdoms of Upper and Lower Egypt into one, ushering in a period of 250 years of prosperity. After a century of foreign occupation, the New Kingdom (1550–1150 BCE) emerged, with its capital at Thebes, as one of the great powers of the age. The capital city was embellished with grandiose temples worthy of the majesty of the pharaohs, the greatest being Karnak. The temple complex of Karnak, dedicated to Amun, was the center of his worship, and that of his wife Mut and their son Khons. Each of them had a precinct, or area, in the temple complex, although the greatest and largest belonged to Amun. There was also a precinct for Montu, the falcon-headed local god. The temple complex is huge, covering a site almost a mile by two miles. Massive size is a characteristic of ancient Egyptian monuments, and active construction went on over a period of 900 years, with each pharaoh leaving a new temple, shrine, or pylon (monumental gateway). Through several dynasties, each pharaoh added to the complex, leaving detailed hieroglyphic inscriptions across every surface of its buildings. There are over 25 temples and chapels in the complex, including separate shrines for the three boats that took

A statue of Rameses II at Luxor Temple.

the statues of the gods on their annual trip on the flooding Nile. Sanctuaries, obelisks, and groups of columns all feature accounts of the heroic deeds of the sponsoring pharaoh. Pharaoh Tuthmose III built a Wall of Records celebrating his achievements and conquests, all in the name and for the glory of Amun.

Early in this period, Tuthmose I built himself a tomb in what was to become the Valley of the Kings on the west bank of the Nile. His daughter, Hatshepsut, a rare female pharaoh, built a grand funeral temple for herself. The royal tombs were among the most important religious monuments in the kingdom, where dead pharaohs were often revered as gods. One pharaoh, Akhenaton (with his beautiful wife Nefertari), abandoned the traditional worship of Amun, the god of Thebes, and took up the worship of Aten, the Sun God. He built a temple to Aten at Karnak and moved to a new capital. After his death, the Theban priests destroyed all signs of sun worship, including the temple that defiled Karnak, and the religious center returned to Thebes.

Perhaps the most awe-inspiring sight at Karnak is the Great Hypostyle, a hall filled with 134 enormous pillars, the highest 70 feet, and each about 45 feet around. One is overwhelmed by the sheer magnitude of the entire complex. It must have impressed every visitor, Egyptian and foreign alike, with the majesty of the god who inspired it and was the state deity. In the complex was also a Sacred Lake, over 100 yards long, used by the priests for purification rites before conducting ceremonies in the temples. At one time there was also a processional Sacred Way, flanked by rows of sphinxes, that stretched the two miles from Karnak to Luxor Temple.

Luxor Temple was also dedicated to Amun, a creator god often fused with the sun-god Ra into one, Amun-Ra. Each year, to ensure the flooding of the Nile that was necessary to national prosperity, the statues of Amun, Mut (goddess of war), and Khons (the moon god) were sailed down the river to Karnak for a great festival. Luxor Temple is quite large and once housed a village within its walls. It has several pylons that are themselves some 70 yards long. The first pylon is over 70 feet high, fronted by massive statues and several obelisks. There are several open areas, once used for various forms of worship but now empty. Later inclusions are a shrine to Alexander the Great, a Roman sanctuary, and an Islamic shrine to a thirteenth-century holy man. One shrine is the Birth Room, with wall paintings showing one pharaoh's claim to have been fathered by Amun, and therefore of divine descent.

The West Bank was a vast City of the Dead, a necropolis where funeral cults were practiced and the great (and not-so-great) were buried in majestic monuments, cliff tombs, or ordinary mausoleums. Many funeral temples of the pharaohs were simply places for this cult, while the body was placed in a secret (and usually sumptuous) tomb in the Valley of the Kings. The queens were buried in the Valley of the Queens. Each tomb has a long shaft, some over 100 yards long, symbolic of entering the underworld and leading to a burial chamber. The walls were painted with themes from various books of the dead. The sun-god Ra was believed to cross the valley each night, where the dead could enter his ship if they knew the right magic texts, which were part of the wall decorations. After judgment and victory over the powers of death, the pharaoh could enter into eternal life with Amun-Ra.

Most impressive is the tomb of Hatshepsut, set into the cliffs of the mountains. This queen proclaimed herself a divine king and wore a false beard as a pharaonic sign. A 100-foot wide causeway leads to the temple, with three terraced courtyards, all covered with sculptured reliefs. Most of the carvings of the queen herself were obliterated by her stepson and successor, who hated her for the way she treated him while he was heir. There are 100 tombs in the Valley of the Nobles and 75 in the Valley of the Queens, not to mention several temple complexes, individual shrines, and many chapels. The cult of death and the lifelong preparation for the afterlife were the focus of Egyptian religion, and the West Bank tombs and sanctuaries are mute testimony to this obsession. Unfortunately, despite the best security of the age, few burial sites escaped the grave robbers.

References Lisa Maniche, *City of the Dead: Thebes in Egypt.* Chicago, University of Chicago, 1987. Bertha Porter, *Theban Temples.* Bloomington, IN, David Brown, 1972. Donald Redford, "The Monotheism of the Heretic Pharaoh," *Biblical Archaeology Review* 13:3, 16–32 (May-June 1987).

TINOS, Greece

Tinos, a small Greek island, is dominated by the national shrine of Panagía Evangelístria, whose treasure is a healing icon of the Virgin Mary. In 1823, in the midst of the Greek Revolution against Turkey, a Tiniote nun, Agia Pelagia, received two visions in dreams that revealed the hiding place of a miraculous icon. The bishop dismissed her reports until a plague devastated the island. When a third vision promised relief, he agreed to a search, and the plague ended when the icon was uncovered within the ruins of an ancient chapel. Agia Pelagia has been recognized as a saint by the Greek Orthodox Church.

Shortly after the icon was found, the imposing neoclassical shrine church was built of white marble. The icon is kept directly over the spot where it was found, a cave with a sacred spring. It shows Mary seated, with the Archangel Gabriel announcing to her that she had been chosen to be the mother of Jesus. However, it is normally covered completely by scores of gold and silver votive offerings, shielding it from view.

On March 25 (which is both Independence Day and the Feast of the Annunciation) and on August 15 (Assumption Day) major pilgrimages fill the town with worshippers, and on Assumption Day each year, several thousand worshippers are baptized. Because of the large number of visitors who come on pilgrimage year round, Tinos is sometimes referred to as the "Lourdes of Greece." Covered arcades are set up alongside the church to shield the sick from the sun as they await the daily blessing with the icon. Numerous ex-votos line the walls to testify to cures: tiny silver pieces in the forms of legs, ears, or hands that have been healed. One striking ex-voto is a silver and gold orange tree, given by a blind man who promised the Virgin an ex-voto of the first thing he saw, if his sight would be restored. The Greek government's Ministry of Religious Affairs reports two to four cures in each pilgrimage period. From the offerings of pilgrims, the shrine supports an orphanage, a home for the elderly, and a technical school for artists.

Tinos was the last bastion of Venetian power in the Cyclades, remaining under their control from 1453 to 1718, despite numerous Turkish assaults. The revelation of the Virgin at Tinos, therefore, is tied to both the Orthodox faith and Greek national aspirations. Though Tinos is operated as a religious shrine, it is supervised by an official of the Religious Affairs Ministry of the Greek government. The island population is half Latin Catholic, however, a legacy of the Venetian occupation, and the shrine is revered by both Catholics and Orthodox.

References Demetrius Constantelos, *Understanding the Greek Orthodox Church*. New York, Seabury, 1982. Jill Dubisch, *In a Different Place*. Princeton, NJ, Princeton University, 1995.

TOKYO, Japan

As the capital of imperial Japan, Tokyo became a major trade and industrial crossroads as well as the center of Japanese culture. Both Buddhist temples and Shinto shrines are prominent in the city, and often the two traditions are intertwined in a unique Japanese style. Modern Tokyo often presses around these religious centers, but they retain their vitality and popularity.

Hie Jinja Shrine honors Sanno Gongen (+1333), a legendary warrior who was declared a god at his death. Sanno became the guardian god of the Tokugawa imperial dynasty (1603–1867), and in 1882 Hie Jinja was named a government shrine. Traditionally, Sanno is offered swords and sabers as tribute, and the 31 finest of these are to be seen in the treasury. Women also come here for protection against miscarriages, and a courtyard statue of a female monkey holding her offspring is usually decorated with red scarves as thank offerings.

Kanda Myojin Shrine is small, with a number of buildings compressed into a city block and thrust up against a parking garage. The shrine honors Jizo, patron of children—a joyous and smiling god holding a sack of grain as a symbol of plenty. There is a picnic atmosphere to the place, and Kanda Myojin has always been associated with popular entertainment. Until 1945 it was in a geisha district, and later a wildly

popular detective series set in the neighborhood ran for 18 years on television. Concession stands surround the main plaza, where visitors can have their photo taken as a samurai warrior. The annual festival draws 108 neighborhood portable shrines and floats from every source—the horse-drawn Budweiser beer wagon is always featured. The temple's four-ton portable shrine is carried in rotation by 1,600 cheering men in *happi* jackets, led by geishas. The shrine has a golden cockerel on top and a little chicken coop inside.

Meiji Jingu Shrine has no roots in the nature-worshipping Shinto tradition. It enshrines the spirits of the Emperor Meiji (1867–1912) and his consort Empress Shôken, under whose reign Shinto became the state religion and the rock base of Japanese nationalism. The shrine is set in 175 acres of parkland, with 100,000 plants and trees representing every species found in Japan. The main path is flanked by ginko trees, and the shrine hall is built of finest Japanese cypress wood. A treasure house displays items from the lives of the emperor and empress, and an art gallery features scenes from their lives. Both of these are intended to evoke the virtues of the imperial couple, now revered as gods. The present structures are 1958 reconstructions.

The *Senkgakuji Temple,* founded in 1612, is the burial site of 47 samurai (warrior knights) who committed ritual suicide in 1702 to protest the unjust treatment of their leader by a feudal lord. This account of personal loyalty—a preeminent Japanese virtue—is taught to every schoolchild, and ceremonies are still held in honor of the 47 samurai.

Senso-ji Temple is in Asakusa, a neighborhood that began as a temple town centuries ago. The area has also long been the location of much of Tokyo's cheap and seedy entertainment, so the entry to the temple is abrupt and without surrounding gardens or greenery. A massive gate marks the entrance to the sacred precincts, but instead of the usual pathway, the visitor negotiates a corridor of theatrical cosmetics shops and souvenir sellers. There is a five-story pagoda and a large bronze incense burner where pilgrims purify themselves by bathing their hands and feet in the incense.

The focus of Senso-ji is the statue of Kannon, Goddess of Mercy, supposedly found in the Sumida River by the Hinokuma brothers, to whom the temple is actually dedicated. The temple was built to house the statue in 1649, but it is buried beneath the main hall and has never been seen. Since Asakusa is an entertainment district, the temple is especially beloved of kabuki actors, sumo wrestlers, and geishas. The annual Sanja Festival brings huge crowds to Senso-ji, when over 100 large shrines are carried by groups of men in a grand procession. Many men strip their tunics to the waist to expose tattooed bodies, often in the symbols of the Japanese criminal underworld.

Yasukuni Jinja Shrine, built to enshrine the spirits of Japan's military war dead, is ironically named "Peaceful Land." All priests up to 1945 were appointed by the Ministry of War and held the rank of colonel. After the war, the shrine was closed briefly and its war memorials removed. In 1957, they were restored, and as a further statement, in 1979 the spirits of Japan's executed war criminals were enshrined. In 1985, a memorial to the *kamikaze* (suicide) war cult was erected. Much of this is contained in the military museum, which features a locomotive from the Burma railway, a Zero fighter, and human torpedoes, alongside regimental flags and items from past wars.

The site itself could not be lovelier. The huge *torii* entrance arch is 80 feet high, leading to a footpath through a magnificent grove of flowering cherry trees. In Shinto shrines, the torii are wood, but at Yasukuni they are steel and bronze. The main altar is a large platform roofed and gabled in tile and decorated by imperial chrysanthemums. The inner shrine is simple by contrast, built in the style of Ise; it contains the names of 2.5 million dead, 2.3 million of whom are from World War II. Of the deified spirits, 56,000 are women, since nurses, army prostitutes, and other employees are considered war dead, though the civilians who died when the atomic bomb was dropped on Hiroshima are not eligible. Near the main shrine is the *Chinreisha,* a shrine for the military war dead of other nations; presumably the Chinese who died in Nanking or the Americans at Pearl Harbor are revered here as deities. Yasukuni's two main festivals in April and October feature sumo wrestling and Noh theater, both of which had their origins in religious rituals.

See also Shinto Shrines.

References Joseph Kitagawa, *Religion in Japanese History.* New York, Columbia University, 1966. ———, *On Understanding Japanese Religion.* Princeton, NJ, Princeton University, 1987. *Shinto: Nature, Gods and Man in Japan.* New York, Japan Society, 1977 (video).

TOOTH TEMPLE, Sri Lanka

The Temple of the Tooth at Kandy enshrines one of the most sacred relics of the Buddha. Begun in the seventeenth century to house a tooth of the Buddha, it was built up over the next 200 years. Because the temple was severely damaged by the eighteenth-century colonial wars against the Portuguese and the Dutch, the original wooden structures have been restored in stone.

From the outside, the buildings are a low-lying collection, neither magnificent nor elaborately decorated. White with red roofs, they cluster around a lake with a rectangular island that housed the king's harem in precolonial times. The inside of the shrine buildings provides a striking contrast to the plain exteriors, richly carved and decorated with inlaid woods, ivory, and lacquer. Around the entire complex is a low stone wall, delicately and simply carved with openings that give a filigree effect. During celebrations, candles are placed in the holes, lighting up the entire front. The king's palace is also in the temple compound. Nearby is the two-story inner shrine where the relic is kept, fronted by two large ivory elephant tusks. The relic rests on a solid gold lotus flower, encased in jeweled caskets that sit on a throne.

According to tradition, the tooth was smuggled into Ceylon in 313 CE, hidden in the hair of a princess fleeing the Hindu armies besieging her father's kingdom in India. Her unique gift immediately became an object of great reverence in Buddhist Ceylon and was encased in a series of nested jeweled reliquaries, each one more elaborate than the next. It was brought out for special occasions and paraded among the people on the backs of elephants, which are sacred to the Buddha. When the capital of Ceylon was moved, the tooth was taken to the new city and placed in temples built to honor it. The present temple in Kandy, in the interior of the country (named Sri Lanka since independence in 1972), is a national center symbolizing not only the Buddhist faith of the majority of the people, but also Ceylonese national identity and pride.

The tooth is only removed from its votive chapel for the annual 10-day feast of Esala Perahera, which takes place during the full moon in late July or early August. The festival brings together all ranks of Sri Lankan society in a vast throng of devotees who gather to honor the Buddha. Because of the national character of the shrine, many Tamil Hindus and mixed-blood Christians take part as an expression of their common cultural heritage. Each evening, the casket bearing the tooth is taken from the temple in a fantastic procession. Whip-cracking porters clear the way through the throngs of pilgrims, followed by musicians, jugglers, torch bearers, boy dancers and acrobats, and members of noble families in traditional Ceylonese garb. Over a hundred elephants, decked out in elaborate finery, march before the relic, which is carried on the back of a splendidly adorned elephant flanked by two perfectly matched, smaller elephants. The throng presses on every side, mixed with pilgrims burning incense and Hindu fakirs performing feats of penance, piercing themselves with skewers or walking on red-hot coals. On the last night, the procession goes from the city to the temple, led by elders in the costumes of the ancient kings of Kandy. The procession is lit by candles held by the marchers, who flow into the temple compound to encircle the shrine, following the route of the sun in its course across the skies. Attendance at the Esala Perahera is about a million, with lines of over a mile where people wait patiently for a chance to see the relic in a glass casket.

The Ceylonese Buddhists and the Tamil Hindus, who arrived in the third century, have always had a strong and sometimes bitter rivalry. Buddhist stories abound of times when the Tamils were defeated by a Ceylonese king carrying a relic of the Buddha. The kings came to be regarded as *bodhisattvas*, Buddhist saints who forgo Buddhahood in order to help their people. Armed conflict between the central government, representing the Buddhist majority, and an insurgent group called the Tamil Tigers continues and renders much of northern Sri Lanka unsafe for visitors. Twice in recent years, guerilla groups have attacked the shrine, but it has not been harmed. As a consequence, though the casket is paraded, the relic itself is rarely displayed during the feast. The last time was in 1990. The president and leaders of Sri Lanka, however, still continue the nationalist Buddhist tradition in a ceremony in which they dedicate their service to the people in the presence of the sacred relic.

References Flavio Conti, *Centers of Belief.* Boston, HBJ Press, 1978. *Man on Cloud Mountain.* Cos Cob, CT, Hartley Film Foundation, 1992 (video). Walpola Rahula, *The Heritage of the Bikkhu.* New York, Grove Press, 1974.

TOUBA, Senegal

Touba is a holy city to an important Islamic Sufi order, the Mouride Brotherhood, and is governed completely by them. The city (population about 300,000) is exempt from most Senegalese government authority and does not even appear on official maps. This status reflects its religious meaning: *Tûbâ* is the Tree of Paradise in the Holy Qur'an. It grows at the edge of the heavens that humans inhabit in the next life and the place where Allah dwells. It is the closest that a Muslim can come to Allah, and the city of Touba, therefore, is considered the abode of the most righteous, the "gate of eternity" for the faithful.

Cheik Amadou Bamba (1850?–1927) founded the Mouride Brotherhood, which now counts several million members in Senegal, West Africa. In 1886 he had several visions that made him the focus of an Islamic prophetic movement as well as a symbol of resistance to French colonial power.

He was exiled in 1895. When he was allowed to return home in 1902, his followers declared this a miracle, so the French sent him away again. During this exile he founded his brotherhood, and finally he returned to Senegal for good in 1907. Bamba taught that salvation came through hard work and total submission to the *marabouts,* or religious leaders. He commanded his followers to cultivate peanuts, which soon became the leading export crop of the country and made the brotherhood wealthy. Four of Bamba's sons have succeeded him in order, and the city is governed by their male descendants today.

The holiness of the city was supposedly revealed to Amadou Bamba in a vision, and it was here that he attained nearness to Allah. His tomb is in the Great Mosque with its towering (260-foot) central minaret, the focal point of the city and a symbolic representation of the Tree of Paradise. The entire urban plan of Touba is oriented toward Mecca, as determined by the alignment of the mosque. The mausoleum is the object of the pilgrims' veneration, because the Archangel Gabriel is believed to have been sent by Allah to reveal to Bamba that the people of the entire world would one day come to his sanctuary to be freed from their sins. Each year, Amadou Bamba's 1907 return from exile is commemorated in a pilgrimage called the *Megal.* Around 500,000 people come for it, about half the annual number of pilgrims to Amadou Bamba's mausoleum. The Megal takes place 48 days after the start of the Islamic new year (late June in 1997) and lasts three days.

Near the mosque, directly on a line toward Mecca, lies the cemetery, where the pious believe that burial assures entry into Paradise. At its center is a massive baobab tree, chosen by Bamba as the place for the burial of his first wife, whose death shortly after the foundation of Touba is regarded as the sacrifice that consecrated the city. Pilgrims carve their names on the trunk of the baobab to insure that they will be counted among the saved whom Amadou Bamba will lead into Paradise on the Last Day.

The residential areas are organized around the center and usually feature some place associated with Amadou Bamba, such as a spot where he received a vision. Several have sacred trees that are held in veneration. On the outskirts of Touba is a demonstration farm to teach modern agriculture and reinforce Amadou Bamba's teachings about self-reliance.

See also Kairouan; Nafar and Karbala.

References Ali Mazrui, *The Africans—A Triple Heritage.* Boston, Little, Brown, 1986. Donal Cruise O'Brien, *The Mourides of Senegal.* Oxford, Clarendon Press, 1971. Lamin Sanneh, *The Jakhanke Muslim Clerics.* New York, University Press of America, 1989.

UGANDAN MARTYRS' SHRINES, Uganda

One of the first modern missionary expansions of Christianity came in the late nineteenth century in what is now Uganda. It was baptized in the blood of Africa's first martyrs, and the places of their deaths have become important shrines for both Protestant and Catholic Africans.

In the 1870s, the Kingdom of Buganda had its first contact with Christianity when the American journalist and explorer Henry Morton Stanley arrived at the court. By 1880 Anglican and Catholic missions were already at the court, both gathering converts, sometimes in competition with one another or with the expanding numbers of Muslims. Until 1884 the competition was kept in balance, but that year a new ruler, Mwanga, an indecisive and impetuous youth of about 18, became kabaka or king.

Unstable yet used to absolute authority, Mwanga was infuriated and shamed when several pages of the court refused his sexual advances because they were Christian. Paranoid and fearful of Europeans, Mwanga struck back by ordering the murder of Bishop James Hannington as he was traveling to the capital to be the first Anglican prelate in East Africa. Then, in fits of irrational fury, Mwanga had several court attendants killed and began a general persecution of Christians.

For a time, the head page, Charles Lwanga, protected many of the younger boys from the kabaka's wrath, but finally Mwanga broke. He raged through the palace one day, ordering several attendants executed and others castrated. He then summoned the court attendants and commanded the Christians to step to one side. Led by Lwanga, who took the youngest boy, Kizito, by the hand, they lined up. They were taken on a forced march to Namugongo, a traditional execution spot, where they were wrapped in reed mats and burned alive with others who were arrested during the march. Thirteen Anglicans and 13 Catholics died together on June 3, 1886.

The Anglicans maintain the site at Namugongo, on the grounds of their national seminary. A group of life-sized figures representing the martyrs is arrayed on a wood pyre, each wrapped in reed mats to show the death scene. A small chapel contains the relics. Since only ashes remained, these were mixed into concrete to form an altar; the relics of the young men of both faiths are thus united in death as they were in life. In late June, there is a national pilgrimage for both Catholics and Anglicans. During it, the scene is reenacted when the soldiers arrived for Robert Munyagabyanjo, a member of the Anglican church council, who went out to greet his executioners wearing his white baptismal robe.

Matthias Kalemba of the Cane Rat Clan was overseer, or *mulumba,* of the county chief of Ssingo, a position of some importance. He was baptized at age 50 after two years of preparation. On becoming Catholic, he stayed with his first wife and sent the others away after providing for their care, and he also freed his slaves. Because of his stature in the community, his martyrdom was especially cruel. The soldiers were ordered to kill him slowly. The executioners cut off his arms at the elbows and his legs at the knees, tying off the arteries so he would not bleed to death. They abandoned him to thirst and attacks from swarms of insects. Deserted by all, Kalemba died after two days of excruciating agony. He is especially revered throughout black Africa.

A Catholic shrine is situated on a tiny island in a pond. It is located on the spot where the Kabaka Mwanga ordered the martyrdom of the pages. Another Catholic shrine has been erected in the town of Mityana, west of the capital city. It honors Kalemba and Noe Mawaggali, 35, a potter of the Bushbuck Clan who was speared and then lashed to a tree, where for hours he was attacked by dogs who ripped off chunks of his flesh until he died. Pilgrims scoop up the soil in the church from the spot where he died to keep as a souvenir.

References J. F. Faupel, *African Holocaust.* London, Geoffrey Chapman, 2d ed., 1965. Elaine Stone, *Kizito, Boy Saint of Uganda.* Nashville, TN, Winston-Derek, 1989. J. P. Thoonen, *Black Martyrs.* London, Sheed & Ward, 1941.

ULURU AND KATA TJUTA, Australia

These two Aboriginal holy places in the Australian desert are known to white Australians as Ayers Rock and the Olgas. While they remain sacred sites for the Aboriginal people of Australia, in recent years they have also taken on importance for New Age practitioners.

Uluru is a sandstone dome that rises out of the flat plains as a giant rounded outcrop. At sunrise and sunset it glows with a bright red reflection that gives it a supernatural aspect. A thousand feet high, it stretches for $2^{1}/_{3}$ miles with a width of $1^{2}/_{3}$ miles. Uluru is the largest isolated rock in the world. It is

bare without the least hint of vegetation, and this starkness adds to its arresting beauty and mysterious bearing. The base of Uluru is a contrast; runoff from the rains leaves pools around the base, nourishing a fertile circle of rich greenery and supporting a variety of wildlife. The oasis conditions have made Uluru a ceremonial place for the Aborigines, who camp in its caves and around the Rock, sustained by the waters and available food.

Aboriginal myth begins with a period called Dreamtime, in which ancestral beings roamed the earth, creating the traditional ways the Aborigines followed and the shapes of the earth itself. The physical marks that the ancestral beings left on the earth hardened into rock, and the features of the land are believed to be their dead bodies. Thus, outcrops like Uluru are considered forces that can still give life. The record of Dreamtime is found in the rock, its fissures, cliffs, and caves. These meanings are expressed in chants passed on to the youth in songs at initiation ceremonies conducted in the caves along the base of Uluru. Various outcrops represent different spirits, and by touching the rock, an Aborigine can invoke the ancestral spirits for support and blessing and put himself in communication with Dreamtime.

There are many legendary tales to account for the physical features of Uluru. Some provide mythical explanations for things that are considered gifts of the ancestral spirits, such as the boomerang. Others recount fierce battles between groups of ancestral heroes, resulting in curses such as the creation of the dingo, a wild dog that has been known to kill or carry off babies. In Dreamtime, two tribes were invited to a feast but became distracted by a group of beautiful Sleepy Lizard Women and dallied at a waterhole where Uluru now stands.

Angry at having their hospitality rejected, the waiting hosts sang evil into a mud and wattle shape until it came to life as the dingo. A hideous slaughter followed, and then a great battle, ending with the deaths of the leaders on both sides. Then the earth itself rose up to mourn the bloodshed—this rising up in grief is Uluru.

In the initiation cave are ancient wall paintings recounting this lore for the teenage initiates. Each clan has a protective animal, its totem, whose spirit oversees its affairs. The cave of those with the hare wallaby totem (*mala*), for example, is marked with dark stains, the blood of their hero ancestors who died in the great battle before time. Mala men cut themselves during cave ceremonies in unity with their ancestors.

Uluru was under government administration until 1985, when it was returned to the Aborigines. The government manages it under an Aborigine board. But the increasing pressure of 300,000 tourists annually has presented a serious problem, since Aborigines consider it sacrilegious to climb the rock. By tradition, only Mala males may climb the rock face. Despite this tradition, the government has established a regular route to the top as a hiking path for tourists. New Age practitioners often use it, since some of them have appropriated Dreamtime into their religious theory.

Kata Tjuta is nearby within the same national park but not physically related to Uluru. The name means "many heads." It consists of 36 rounded knobs of conglomerate scattered over an area of almost ten square miles. Kata Tjuta forms a kind of Dreamtime map, with many of the domes associated with events from that time of Aboriginal spiritual origins. The Aborigines follow the paths through the domes, singing traditional songs and telling stories. As they follow these tracks, or "songlines," they believe that they enter into Dreaming and unite themselves with the ancestors. Thus, the past and present become one and history is erased. The spirits present include both noble ones and evil; one cluster of stones represents the last cannibals, killed in Dreamtime by the kangaroo men.

Kata Tjuta has far more passages and entrances through the rocks than Uluru. It is also far less frequented by tourists and provides a more serene place of meditation and ritual for the Aborigines.

See also Mountains, Sacred.

References James Cowan, *The Aborigine Tradition*. Shaftesbury, UK, Element Books, 1992. Robert Layton, *Uluru: An Aboriginal History of Ayers Rock*. Canberra, Australian Institute of Aboriginal Studies, 1986. Charles Mountford, *Ayers Rock: Its People, Their Belief, and Their Art*. Honolulu, East-West Center, 1965.

VARANASI, India

According to Hindu belief, those who die in this "eternal city" on the banks of the sacred Ganges River in northern India will receive eternal life in the next world, so many devout Hindus come to Varanasi for their last days. Varanasi is preeminently the city of Shiva, the High God who is destroyer and reproducer and was born here, according to Hindu legend. In recent years, it has also become a center of the Hindu revival and increasingly politicized as a symbol of Indian nationalism.

Most pilgrims come to Varanasi to visit the long string of bathing *ghats*, platform stairways into the sacred Ganges. For three miles, more than 100 ghats stretch down the river, with shrines, pavilions, or small temples at their entrances. Each has a *lingam*, a pillar representing the sex organ of Shiva, the traditional object of worship of the god of reproduction. Several ghats are reserved for the cremation of bodies, a duty binding on every observant Hindu. The most important of these is Manikarnika, where Shiva is believed present to liberate souls from the cycle of reincarnation. The cremation pyres, lit always by the closest relative of the dead, burn constantly.

At dawn especially, pilgrims come to the river to bathe from the ghats and even to drink the polluted water, to be freed from sin by the blessing of the sacred waters. Hindu tradition says that the waters of the Ganges, even when dirty, never cause illness to a faithful person who bathes in them or drinks them. Though any and all ghats may be used, there are five which form a pilgrimage route; pilgrims bathe from them in the prescribed order and on the same day. All the ghats have unique characteristics that make them favorites of different people: one has a footprint of its god; another is dedicated to the popular monkey-god, Hanuman; a third has a well dug by Lord Shiva when his consort, the goddess Parvati, dropped an earring into it. Besides the five ghats, another pilgrimage route goes around the city in a 50-mile path, where stops for worship are taken at 108 shrines.

Varanasi has a number of other religious institutions—such as Benares Hindu University, a center of yoga, Hindu philosophy, and Sanskrit learning—and several important temples. In 1669 the Muslims destroyed the Shiva Temple with the loss of thousands of lives, but its emerald lingam was carried off and dropped into a well, around which the Golden Temple was later built. Besides the emerald lingam in the well, the Golden Temple (covered with 1,500 pounds of gold) contains a black marble lingam set into a solid silver altar. The Durga Temple honors Parvati in her dark and terrible manifestation as goddess of death and destruction. She is offered animal sacrifices. The Bharat Mata Temple honors Mother India as a goddess (it was opened by Mahatma Gandhi).

Besides the Hindu ghats on the sacred Ganges, there are several riverside Jain temples and ghats. The Jains, who share similar beliefs about reincarnation of the immortal soul but are rigorously ascetic, also practice ritual cleansing.

295

More than 100 ghats, platform stairways, line the banks of the sacred Ganges River.

See also Dilwara.

References *Benares: Steps to Heaven.* Evanston, IL, Wombat, 1987 (video). Steven Darian, *The Ganges in Myth and History.* Honolulu, University of Hawai'i, 1978. Diana Eck, *Benares: City of Light.* Princeton, NJ, Princeton University, 1982.

VERDEN, Germany

The shrine in the small town of Verden, unmentioned in any guidebook, is the worship center created by Heinrich Himmler in the suburb of Sachsenhain as part of the Nazi attempt to revive paganism. It is an antishrine, intended less to worship the ancient gods than to provide a substitute religious experience to replace Christianity.

Using slave labor, Sachsenhain was constructed in 1935, year three of the Nazi era.

Himmler, who came from a solidly middle-class Catholic family, not only turned from his faith in his youth to join the Nazi Party, but he also became a vicious anti-Catholic. He designed a complete system of religious worship, including a naming ritual to replace baptism, a Nazi wedding ceremony, and a burial service. Every effort was made to restore ancient German paganism and make it part of the doctrine undergirding Nazism. To enforce Hitler's "master race" theory, Himmler then became the author of the Holocaust, the genocidal attempt to exterminate the Jews.

The Saxon Memorial, as it is sometimes called, is made up of 4,500 standing stones that somewhat resemble Carnac. Set near a spot where the Weser and Aller Rivers come together, the stones are lined up in avenues that from time to time open out into circles. The site is the spot where Emperor Charlemagne executed 4,500 Saxons in his campaign to eradicate paganism in 782. Sachsenhain was intended as a sign of the victory of Nazi paganism over Christianity.

Shortly before the Verden massacre, Charlemagne had promulgated a harsh criminal law for the Saxons. It was antipagan and made such acts as eating meat during Lent, cremation, or performing human sacrifice all punishable by death. A Saxon revolt against Charlemagne followed, and he personally led the troops against the Saxon leader Widukind, who escaped near Verden. When news of the loss of a military column with some of his finest nobles reached Charlemagne, he was enraged. In retaliation, he ordered the execution of 4,500 Saxon prisoners. Himmler seized upon this historical atrocity against ancient Saxons to make Verden the site of his reborn pagan religion.

The solstice ceremonies held here (and at Externsteine) for up to 10,000 Hitler Youth and other disciples celebrated the birth of the sun on the ashes of the defeated Christ. Pagan hymns were composed for these ceremonies, which began with an oath of allegiance to Hitler to initiate the youth into "the religion of the Blood . . . the only racial religion of the German people." This was followed by a sermon "in poetical language," A Confession of Faith and the Hymn of Duty. The service ended with a salute to Hitler and nationalist hymns. The Winter Solstice was a reversion to the pagan Yule Feast and was intended to replace Christmas. Himmler designed a full year of such feasts, including Hitler's Birthday (April 20), the solstices, Labor Day, Harvest Thanksgiving (October), the great public ceremonies of the Nuremberg Rallies (September), and the

anniversary of the 1923 Nazi Putsch, Hitler's first attempt to overthrow Germany's democratic government (November 9). This last was the holiest day of the Nazi calendar.

A Nazi altar was erected for these services, featuring a large swastika flag, a flower arrangement symbolizing the sun, and a photo of Hitler. Neo-Nazis continue to gather at Sachsenhain each year in observance of Hitler's birthday, and in recent years have clashed with police.

See also Externsteine; Holocaust Sites.
References John Conway, *The Nazi Persecution of the Churches, 1933–1945*. New York, Basic Books, 1968. P. D. King, *Charlemagne*. London, Methuen, 1986. Peter Padfield, *Himmler*. New York, Henry Holt, 1990.

VEZELEY, France

Vézeley was one of medieval Europe's great high holy places, rising up sharply from the surrounding valley, topped by a fortified abbey built in 864 CE. During its heyday in the thirteenth century, it was the site of significant events. Bernard of Clairvaux announced the Second Crusade there with the king and queen of France in attendance, and it was the first town in France to which St. Francis of Assisi sent his friars. After the decline of the great pilgrimage to Santiago de Compostela in Spain, however, Vézeley became a backwater until the restoration of the Basilica of St. Mary Magdalene in the 1850s.

During the Middle Ages, the Santiago pilgrimage involved hundreds of thousands of people each year. Four streams of pilgrims came from starting points in Paris, Le Puy, Arles, and Vézeley. The Vézeley route crossed the River Loire and passed through Limoges and Périgueux before converging on the others near the Spanish border.

Vézeley was chosen as a gathering point because it was itself a place of pilgrimage.

It was said to have relics of St. Mary Magdalene, the disciple of Jesus who first discovered his resurrection. Popular piety has always considered her to be the penitent woman in the Bible who dramatically anointed Jesus' feet and was forgiven her sins. Folk tradition considered her great sin to have been prostitution. There is no hint of any of this in the Bible, but it made the Magdalene a powerful attraction for devout sinners, who flocked to the shrines (there were 21 in Europe) of the penitent "fallen woman."

The basilica is an outstanding example of Romanesque architecture, but there are no relics of the Magdalene there any longer. After a rival shrine claimed to have the "true" Magdalene's body, the relics were hidden (perhaps buried in the south transept) so thoroughly that they have never been recovered. The numbers of pilgrims have revived during the last 25 years along with devotion to the saint, and there is an annual pilgrimage for her feast day, July 22. The basilica is rich in sculpture, although most of it was defaced during the Huguenot Wars of Religion in the seventeenth century, when many of the statues were beheaded. The abbey had a stormy history despite the popularity of the shrine. It was burned in a peasant revolt in 1105, and the abbots ruled so oppressively that the populace did nothing to defend them when they were wiped out during the French Revolution.

See also Conques; Santiago de Compostela.

References Susan Haskins, *Mary Magdalen*. New York, Riverhead, 1993. Melanie MacMitchell, *Sacred Footsteps*. Palo Alto, CA, Opal Star Press, 1991. Marina Warner, *Alone of All Her Sex*. New York, Wallaby, 1976.

THE VRINDAVAN KRISHNA SHRINES, India

The legendary childhood home of the Hindu god Lord Krishna, Vrindavan lies near Delhi in northern India. Nearby Mathura is regarded as the place where Krishna first appeared as a manifestation of the god Vishnu, come to earth to relieve its miseries. He was born in a jail cell, but through miraculous powers he opened the gates and freed himself. His father then carried him to Vrindavan. Nearby are fields where he supposedly grazed flocks as a cowherd. Vrindavan and Mathura became important as a pilgrimage center in the fifteenth century, when devotion to Krishna was revived.

Vrindavan and Mathura have over 4,000 shrines and temples from all periods. The most recent is the temple of the International Society for Krishna Consciousness (ISKCON), known popularly in the West as the Hare Krishnas from their constant chant of that divine name. Their center is in the field where Krishna served as a cowherd during his youth, and where he flirted with the *gopis* (milkmaids), who according to tradition, were all infatuated with him. Locally, it is known as the "American temple." In addition, almost every Hindu sect has a monastery in Vrindavan, offering free meals to pilgrims.

The city lies on the Yamuna River, which has a number of bathing places (ghats) at which pilgrims purify themselves. Besides the rites of purification, pilgrims walk around the shrines, clashing cymbals and chanting. In many of the temples, devotees do an ecstatic dance in honor of Lord Krishna, with both men or women taking the part of his lover, Radha.

The most prominent of the many sanctuaries is the Bihariji Shrine, where Krishna is enshrined as the divine seducer. In his most recognized pose in Hindu art, playing his flute and leaning toward the observer, he takes the form that appeals to whatever any of his lovers seeks. The main statue, of miraculous origin, is of Krishna and his consort, Radha, in ecstatic embrace. It is believed that the statue will follow anyone of passionate devotion, so it is exposed from behind a curtain for only a few minutes at a time, lest it leave the temple in the wake of a particularly intense devotee!

The shrines offer a variety of displays. In the Kasava Deo Temple, for example, is a jail cell reproduced to show where Krishna was born 3,500 years ago. It claims to have the original stone upon which the sacred birth took place. Every conceivable event in Krishna's life has been associated with a place, including the spot where Krishna's diapers were washed, the place where he rested after killing the wicked king who had imprisoned his parents, and above all, the riverside spot where he stole the gopis'

clothes as they bathed, teasing them to come out uncovered. One temple, forbidden to visitors after dusk, is where Krishna and Radha return each night to make love. Visiting these sites is a common pilgrim activity, but there is a set pilgrimage route, the *Parikrama,* a five-mile circle that passes the main temples. Evidence of religious tourism is found side-by-side with the temples, such as mechanical puppet shows of the Bhagavad Gita, the Hindu scriptural epic that recounts the legend of Krishna, and endless stalls selling religious trinkets. As in all Hindu holy places, any clothing of leather—shoes, belts, and so on—is strictly prohibited.

References Enrico Isacco (ed.), *Krishna, the Divine Lover.* Boston, David R. Godine, 1982. Ormond McGill, *Religious Mysteries of the Orient*. South Brunswick, NJ, Barnes, 1976. *Understanding Hindu Traditions.* Huntsville, TX, Educational Video Network, n.d. (video).

By 1538, however, Henry VIII was suppressing religious houses and appropriating their wealth. Walsingham Priory surrendered its property to the crown, the Holy House was destroyed, and the statue of Our Lady of Walsingham was burnt in the presence of Thomas Cromwell, the king's chief agent. Pilgrimages were prohibited, and Philip, Earl of Arundel, who died for the old faith in 1595, left this requiem among his papers: "Weep, weep O Walsingham, whose days are nights / Blessing turned to blasphemies, holy deeds to despites." Only a few ruins remained when John Wesley, the founder of Methodism, preached there in 1781, lamenting: "Had there been a grain of virtue or public spirit in Henry VIII, these noble buildings need not have run to ruin."

WALSINGHAM, England

Nestled in East Anglia north of London lies the small village of Walsingham, the site of a Marian shrine since 1061. Its uniqueness arises because, after a long period of suppression, it has enjoyed a modern revival that has taken an ecumenical form. It draws over a quarter-million people a year.

The original legend is told in a fifteenth-century manuscript, *The Ballad of Walsingham*. Mary appeared to the lady of the manor, Richeldis, showing her a replica of the home of the Holy Family in Nazareth, where the angel announced the coming of Jesus. Richeldis built a simple wooden copy of the building she saw in the vision, and around 1153 her descendants brought in Austin Canons to care for the Holy House. By the fifteenth century a stone building had been built over it to protect it, and pilgrimages had begun. The pilgrimage route included stations, or small chapels for rest and worship. Of the two that remain, one is the Slipper Chapel, now the Roman Catholic shrine. Here the pilgrims took off their shoes and walked barefoot the final mile to the Holy House.

Royal pilgrimages began in 1226; Edward I came 11 times. Henry VIII came on pilgrimage in 1511, walking the "holy mile" barefoot and leaving a necklace for the statue. Among other famous pilgrims was Erasmus of Rotterdam, who left a poem in praise of the Virgin.

Restoration began in the late nineteenth century. The Slipper Chapel was reclaimed by Catholics from use as a barn, and in 1897 a new statue of Our Lady of Walsingham was erected. Pilgrimages were slow to start up until 1931, when a remarkable man, the Anglican vicar, Fr. Hope Patten, built another shrine in the village near the original site. A replica of the Holy House, including its protective outer building, was constructed, and a sacred well opened. The church, modeled on that of the original priory, has 15 altars, one each for the mysteries from the life of Jesus and Mary associated with the Rosary. Anglican nuns care for the shrine, which also has a pilgrim hostel and a hospice for the sick. Father Patten had to overcome opposition from his bishop and many evangelical Protestants, who opposed the idea of a Marian shrine under Church of England sponsorship. Even today, evangelicals harass and disrupt the national Anglican pilgrimage. Ironically, the opposition has spurred Anglican-Roman ecumenism; leaders of both Churches insist that there is only one shrine, Walsingham itself, with several centers of devotion. People of all faiths join together, and there has been an Orthodox chapel at the shrine since 1931.

In 1934, the Slipper Chapel was declared the national Catholic shrine, and 10,000 came to dedicate it. The custom of making the "holy mile" between the chapel and the shrine was resumed, and the walking pilgrimage from London, following the medieval route, was revived. In 1947, participants in a Pilgrimage of Peace carried 14 large crosses from all over England to be erected on the grounds. A pilgrim center and the Chapel of Reconciliation accommodate the crowds.

The original site with its ruins is privately owned but open to the public. One of the arches of the chapel remains, and the spot where the Holy House stood is marked. The wells also remain, although they are now dry. One was used as a sacred well, the other as a wishing well where pilgrims cast in a coin when praying for a favor, an ancient, pre-Christian custom.

The feasts of the Annunciation (March 25) and the Assumption (August 15) are major pilgrimage days, beginning with a torchlight procession around the churches of the village—Anglican, Catholic, Methodist, and Orthodox—the night before. Other important pilgrimages are the national Anglican pilgrimage (May) and the Catholic one (September), one for Christian members of Parliament (May), and the Pilgrimage for the Sick (July). At Easter there is the "Student Cross," a pilgrimage for university students. Besides these large events, groups of pilgrims come on most weekends. Although they avoid receiving sacraments outside their own faiths, people freely share activities across denominational lines. A typical Anglican pilgrimage involves a sung Mass, candlelight procession, and sprinkling at the well, in addition to prayer services and a visit to the Holy House. Catholics begin in the village and go in procession to the Slipper Chapel for a reconciliation service, Mass, adoration, and litanies and prayers. Both programs last through the weekend.

See also Marian Apparitions.

References Henry Gillett, *Walsingham.* London, Burns, Oates, & Washbourne, 1950. Elizabeth Ruth Obbard, *The History and Spirituality of Walsingham.* Norwich, Canterbury, UK, 1995. Colin Stephensen, *Walsingham Way.* London, Longman & Todd, 1970.

WAT PO, Thailand

Close by the Temple of the Emerald Buddha is Bangkok's second major temple, that of the Reclining Buddha. It was built in 1860, although the first buildings on the site date from the sixteenth century. The largest temple compound in Bangkok (20 acres), Wat Po is the residence of a large group of monks who maintain an active schedule. Despite the bustle, there is an atmosphere of serenity and gentleness here that the crowded and more popular Emerald Buddha Temple cannot match.

The walls have 16 gates, two open to the public. There is a long arcade of golden Buddha statues, all identical, massed in serried rows of devotion. Around the grounds are numbers of stone statues of sages carved in Chinese style, originally imported as ballast on ships trading with China. The *chedis*, pagoda-like spires that contain royal relics, are of varying sizes and stand in rows, covered by reflecting colored mirrors and bright tiles. Seventy-one small chedis contain the ashes of members of the royal

Chedis, pagoda-like spires that contain royal relics, vary in size and are covered with reflecting colored mirrors and bright tiles.

family, and 20 large ones contain relics of the Buddha. No attempt has been made at architectural uniformity, and what is harmonious at the Emerald Buddha is here mixed and unmatched. To the Thai, however, these artistic and aesthetic issues are beside the point. Wat Po's seeming jumble of buildings mirrors its variety of activities.

One of Wat Po's early purposes was general education for the people, and as a consequence, it includes a series of 20 knolls that illustrate rock formations from around the kingdom. Plaques provide instruction in astrology, literature, and Thai traditions. The most prominent part of this cultural aspect of Wat Po is its program of instruction in folk medicine. Not only are there plaques with information about home remedies for simple ailments, but one small hill has a series of 80 statues showing methods of massage as practiced in ancient Thailand. Wat Po remains the nationally recognized center for traditional medicine, and every afternoon, traditional healers are available at its monastery for consultations and treatment. During the mid-nineteenth century, the compound was the medical teaching center of the country, but it lost that function as modern medicine was introduced. Traditional medicine is closely interwoven with religious belief in Thai society, however, and Wat Po continues that heritage. The government today recognizes Wat Po in this role as its official teaching center. In particular, the monks are adept at the techniques of ancient Thai massage, and it is offered for a modest fee. Thai massage is based on principles of energy flow, similar to Chinese acupuncture, and is intended to remove negative forces from the body by opening blocked circulation. It includes sharp, chiropractic-type moves.

Though Wat Po is not the pilgrimage center that the Emerald Buddha is, the Re-clining Buddha remains a major object of popular piety. It is imposing—145 feet long and 45 feet high, covered with gold leaf. The soles of its feet—in Thai culture the least-valued part of the body—are inlaid with mother-of-pearl emblems of the Buddha.

References Gerald Roscoe, *The Monastic Life: Pathway of the Buddhist Monk.* Bangkok, Asia Books, 1992. Alistair Shearer, *Thailand: The Lotus Kingdom.* London, John Murray, 1989. Steve Van-Beek and Luca Tettoni, *The Arts of Thailand.* London, Thames & Hudson, 1991.

WELLS AND SPRINGS, SACRED

Springs and wells have been objects of reverence from earliest times, as sources of healing and the abodes of spirits and gods. In ancient Greece, when questioners approached the oracle at Delphi for advice, they first had to wash in the sacred waters of the Castalian Spring before presenting offerings to the priestess. Wells were especially revered in Roman Britain. The Romans encouraged them and built a major shrine dedicated to the goddess Coventina alongside a fort in Hadrian's Wall. When Coventina's Well was excavated in 1876, a hoard of Roman coins was found, along with a number of bronze heads and a human skull. The last two items indicate that the well was probably old enough to have been part of ancient Celtic cults that worshipped the human head and often offered the severed heads of the dead to win the goddess's favor. The coins indicate that the spring was used as a wishing well, one where the divine power could be implored through an offering.

Although Christianity rejected the power of the goddesses, sacred wells continued in use, often connected with a local saint. In Ireland alone, it is estimated that there were once 3,000 of these. People would approach the well after saying five decades of the Rosary, going around it on their knees, offering prayers. Finally, a small container of the holy water was drunk and refilled to be taken home. Small chapels or stone-piles were built near some of these wells, or sacred trees planted. A pilgrim would visit it, leave a small offering at the tree (a rosary, symbolic cloth, or a coin hammered into the tree), or add a stone to the pile. Between 1750 and 1850, the Catholic clergy attempted to restrain pilgrimages to holy wells, because many had become occasions for partying and drunkenness. Priests continued to encourage prayers and vigils.

The waters of many saints' wells (or springs) were considered to have healing properties, often helpful for rashes and skin diseases. St. Bueno's in Wales has such a well, with steps leading down into it; it is reputed to have the power to cure children's diseases. Bueno ("The Good") was the uncle of St. Winifred, whose well is perhaps the best known in the United Kingdom.

The Reformation generally attacked sacred wells and springs as superstitious and pagan, and they were closed in Britain and Ireland. Nevertheless, many continued to be used by Catholics in secret, and some Anglicans also frequented them.

Though denying any spiritual importance to the spring itself, some Protestant groups require that the central rite of baptism be done by immersion in living water, a spring or river. The Catholic church, which rarely uses immersion, does provide for baptism in "the area where the baptismal font flows," which implies that many churches were built over springs in early times.

Healing springs or wells have appeared at the places of a number of Marian apparitions. There were two springs at Walsing-ham, and a generous flow of water at Lourdes still supplies visitors with Lourdes Water, much prized as a blessed souvenir of pilgrimage. In the garden of the simple cottage of Sister Lucia, the last remaining seer of the visionaries of Fátima, there remains a blessed well over which Lucia received an apparition of an angel. Water from the well is today eagerly sought.

The most common means of honoring sacred wells is by gift-offering. Among the Mayans (300–900 CE) and other peoples of Central America, this included the offering of human sacrifices. A modern version of the custom of placating wells is the popular notion of the "wishing well," where a small offering accompanied by a wish is supposed to make the wish come true. It is such a universal custom in modern society that even decorative fountains in shopping centers are scattered with coins. Often, a local charity will be named to receive the gifts, to avoid the embarrassment of what is seen as superstitious practice.

In Derbyshire, England, the custom persists of "dressing" wells. Elaborate panels are decorated for a feast day or some other traditional date—always in the summer—and erected over the holy well, usually with a floral garland. These panels often depict biblical scenes, using flower petals, seeds, bark, and other natural elements. The "dressing days," of which there are about twenty each summer, are accompanied by Anglican religious services.

See also St. Winifred's Well.

References Janet Bord and Colin Bord, *Sacred Waters: Holy Wells and Water Lore in Britain and Ireland.* London, Paladin/ Collins, 1986. Francis Jones, *The Holy Wells of Wales.* Cardiff, University of Wales, 1992. *Sacrifice and Bliss.* New York, Mystic Fire Videos, 1988.

WESTMINSTER ABBEY, England

One of the most visited sites in England, often mistakenly considered the Anglican cathedral of London, Westminster Abbey is the chapel of parliament and the Chapel Royal. Until the suppression of the monasteries under Henry VIII, it was also an important abbey, and parliament met in its monastic meeting hall. The buildings, close by today's Parliament, are crowded into one of the busiest commercial districts in London, and almost none of the original sense of peace and contemplation can be retained. Nonetheless, along with Canterbury and York Minster, it is one of the great symbols of worldwide Anglicanism and its "middle way" between Protestantism and Catholicism. It is also a national shrine, housing tombs of the famous and the infamous, and 400 memorials to English heroes.

There has been a monastic church on this site since about 750. St. Edward the Confessor, the second-last Saxon king, completed the abbey a few weeks before his death. Within a year, England was occupied by the Norman William the Conqueror, who was the first to be crowned in Edward's abbey church. Edward was canonized in 1163 as St. Edward the Confessor, and it was decided to build a shrine worthy of the sainted king. The present church, 530 by 200 feet and 95 feet high, was built between 1243 and 1375 in French Gothic style. The twin towers were added in 1722. Because it has the title of "Royal Peculiar," meaning that it is directly under the authority of the sovereign, Westminster Abbey escaped the vandalism and destruction of the Reformation.

The shrine of Edward the Confessor was consecrated in 1269. It remains substantially in its original form behind the high altar, though its gold and mosaic coverings were lost during the Reformation. Throughout the Middle Ages and well beyond, the shrine was considered a place of healing. Pilgrims came to touch the tomb, and the sick were left there overnight in hopes of a cure. Around the shrine are the tombs of the medieval Plantagenet kings, and across from it is the coronation throne, used in every coronation since 1296. Inside the throne is the Stone of Scone, the sacred coronation stone of Scotland, brought to the Abbey after Scotland was conquered by England and incorporated into the United Kingdom.

Westminster Abbey is a national resting-place for the greatest people of British history. Almost all are laid under the paving stones, trod by every visitor. The tomb of the Unknown Soldier is marked off by a frame of poppies and may not be walked on; the Unknown is buried in earth brought from the battlefields of France. The aisles hold monuments to generals, prime ministers, and politicians, although the Methodist founder, John Wesley, lies among them. Memorials and monuments crowd the walls, including one to a painter who refused burial at Westminster because "they bury fools there." For many visitors, the highlight of the abbey is the Poet's Corner, where sculpted monuments to Shakespeare and Handel contrast with simple floor plaques marking the graves of Tennyson, Robert Browning, and T. S. Eliot. Chaucer (+1400) has the earliest tomb.

The Chapel of Henry VII was added in the early 1500s. It contains the tombs of the Tudor and Stuart sovereigns. High windows make it light, rising to a carved stone ceiling so intricate that it seems like lace. It has been called "the loveliest jewel of Christendom." It is decorated with banners of the knights of the Order of the Bath and also holds a memorial to the heroes of the Battle of Britain in World War II. The statuary

The Poet's Corner, part of Westminster Abbey, pictured here, marks the graves of Chaucer, T. S. Eliot, Robert Browning, and Tennyson.

was not defaced during the Puritan period and includes fine medieval sculpture. Elizabeth I and her half-sister and bitter rival, Mary, lie in a joint marble tomb.

References Flavio Conti, *Splendor of the Gods.* Boston, HBJ Press, 1978. Keith Spence, *Cathedrals and Abbeys of England and Wales.* New York, Norton, 1984. Christopher Wilson et al., *Westminster Abbey.* London, Bell & Hyman, 1986.

Church, York Minster also features many tombs, monuments, and war memorials to British heros.

Although the St. William window is one of the finest, the largest (and the largest stained-glass window on earth) is the Great East Window. It covers an area the size of a tennis court, presenting the beginning and end of the world in over 100 scenes. York Minster gives perhaps the best opportunity for a visitor to experience the meaning of medieval stained glass as a means of learning faith while being inspired by it. The stained glass, Britain's largest and best collection, survived a terrible fire that destroyed part of the Minster in 1984. Because the cathedral's soaring nave is one of the widest in Europe, its ceiling had to be made of wood to reduce weight, making it vulnerable to fire. The restoration has erased the damage of the fire, but a memorial cross of fire-scarred timbers is kept on display as a reminder.

Every four years, the Minster presents the York Cycle of Mystery Plays, using 100 members of the local community to perform biblical tales. The next performance will be in 2000, for about two weeks after Corpus Christi Day. Mystery plays originated at York in the Middle Ages.

See also Canterbury Cathedral.

References G. E. Aylmer, *A History of York Minster*. Oxford, UK, Clarendon, 1977. Charles Kightly and Michael Cyprien, *A Traveller's Guide to Places of Worship*. London, Routledge & Kegan Paul, 1986. Gilbert Thurlow, *Cathedrals and Abbeys of England*. Norwich, UK, Jerrold, 1990.

YORK MINSTER, England

The cathedral church of the Anglican Communion's second archdiocese, York Minster is a magnificent structure with a rich history, and the goal of many pilgrims. It is built over a small holy spring (*see* Wells and Springs, Sacred) used for baptisms in early times (bishops were recorded there by the third century). Throughout the Middle Ages, Canterbuy and York contended for supremacy in the English Church, a matter that was settled in the fourteenth century by accepting the primacy of Canterbury but permitting equal standing for the two prelates. Archbishop William FitzHerbert was canonized in 1226, giving York a saint whose relics would attract pilgrims, just as Canterbury's shrine of St. Thomas à Becket did. The chief relic, the head of the saint in a silver reliquary, disappeared at the time of the Reformation, when the shrine was broken up. It was replaced in the last century with a simple tomb where both Anglican and Catholic services are held. The major remaining memorial to St. William is a large stained-glass window recounting his miracles. Because of its role in the Anglican

Z

ZAGORSK

See Sergiev Posad.

ZEBRZYDOWSKA CHAPEL, Poland

A small monastery chapel near Kraków is home to a sacred icon that attracts hundreds of pilgrimages annually and up to 40,000 for its intense Holy Week ceremonies.

According to legend, in the seventeenth century a local provincial chief near Kraków had a vision of three fiery crosses on a hill in the foothills of the Carpathian Mountains. The area reminded the nobleman of the hills of Jerusalem, and in 1600 he began to build an elaborate "holy city" on that model, after sending agents to Jerusalem to measure the path of Jesus' last journey. The heart of the complex is the Bernardine monastery and church (1603), which are the focus of pilgrimages so extensive that Kalwaria Zebrzydowska has become the second Polish religious center after Czestochowa. A series of chapels was built atop the surrounding hills; 42 survive.

The monastery church is baroque, its every surface covered by carving, imagery, and design. The object of pilgrimage during much of the year is the miraculous painting of the Virgin Mary in the Zebrzydowska

Chapel. It has a reputation as a "weeping icon," one that sheds tears that have the effect of bringing observers to penance and conversion. All the major feasts of Mary are occasions for large pilgrimages, especially September 8 (Nativity of Mary) and August 13–15, which closes with the Solemnity of the Assumption. August 15 is a national holiday, and the custom is to make the round of many of the chapels before coming to greet the miraculous painting. The monastery is near Kraków, and Pope John Paul II often visited the shrine as a young man and later as its archbishop.

Kalwaria is famous also for its Passion play during Holy Week, which has been an annual event since the seventeenth century. Events begin on the Sunday before Easter (Palm Sunday) and reach a climax during the last days of the week. Between 30,000 and 40,000 people take part. The great procession in Kalwaria begins on Holy Thursday, moving along to half of the chapels, with a scene from the Passion of Jesus acted out at each by the monks and local residents. Again on Good Friday, beginning at dawn, the procession makes the stations, calling at another 20 or more chapels. The Passion play is in the tradition of the medieval mystery plays, a mixture of theater and deep religious piety. The crowd becomes animated and involved, and it is not unusual for pilgrims to be carried away and attempt to protect Jesus from the Roman soldiers who have come to arrest him on the Mount of Olives.

References Mary Craig, *Lech Walesa and His Poland*. New York, Continuum, 1987. Tad Szulc, *Pope John Paul II: The Biography*. New York, Scribner, 1995.

Sacred Sites Listed by Religious Tradition

Note: Sites set in capital letters are entries in the text.

SACRED SITES OF PRIMAL AND NATURE RELIGIONS

Bear Butte, South Dakota, USA
BIGHORN MEDICINE WHEEL, Wyoming, USA
BLACK HILLS, South Dakota, USA
CAHOKIA MOUNDS, Illinois, USA
Canyon de Chelly, Arizona, USA
CARNAC, France
Casa Riconada, New Mexico, USA
CHACO, New Mexico, USA
CHIMAYO, New Mexico, USA
DOGON CLIFFS, Mali
Effigy Mounds, Iowa, USA
EXTERNSTEINE, Germany
Fajada Butte, New Mexico, USA
Futaarasan Shrine, Japan
GGANTIJA, Malta
Hie Jinja Shrine, Japan
ISE, Japan
IZUMO TAISHA SHRINE, Japan
Kanda Myojin Shrine, Japan
Kasuga Taisha Shrine, Japan
KILAUEA, Hawaii, USA
Lizard Mound, Wisconsin, USA
Majorville Medicine Wheel, Alberta, Canada
Meiji Jingu Shrine, Japan
Moose Mountain Medicine Wheel, Saskatchewan, Canada
Mound City, Ohio, USA
MOUNT FUJI, Japan
MOUNT KAILAS, Tibet, China
Mount Kilimanjaro, Tanzania
MOUNT SHASTA, California, USA
NAN MADOL, Pohnpei
NAZCA LINES, Peru
NEWGRANGE, Ireland
Newark Earthworks, Ohio, USA
PAGAN, Myanmar/Burma
PLAINE DU NORD, Haïti

Pueblo Bonito, New Mexico, USA
RAPA NUI, Easter Island, Chile
El Rincon, Cuba
ROCK OF CASHEL, Ireland
SAUT D'EAU, Haïti
Serpent Mound, Ohio, USA
SHINTO SHRINES, Japan
STONEHENGE AND AVEBURY, England
T'AI SHAN, China
Toshogu Shrine, Japan
ULURU AND KATA TJUTA, Australia
Wanuskewin, Saskatchewan, Canada
Yasakuni Jinja Shrine, Japan

SACRED SITES OF ANCIENT RELIGIONS

ACROPOLIS, Greece
CHICHEN ITZA, Mexico
CUZCO, Peru
DELOS, Greece
DELPHI, Greece
MACHU PICCHU, Peru
Mount Olympus, Greece
OLYMPIA, Greece
Pantheon, Italy
PETRA, Jordan
PYRAMIDS OF GIZA, Egypt
TEOTIHUACAN, Mexico
THEBES AND LUXOR, Egypt

HINDU SITES

Allahabad (Prayag), India
ANGKOR WAT, Cambodia
Bhubaneswar, India
CHANGU NARAYAN TEMPLE, Nepal
ELLORA CAVES, India
EMEI SHAN, China
ERAWAN SHRINE, Thailand
GUNUNG AGUNG, Indonesia
Hardwar, India
JANAKPUR, Nepal

Konarak, India
MEENAKSHI TEMPLE, India
MOUNT KAILAS, Tibet, China
Nasik, India
PASHUPATINATH, Nepal
Puri, India
Ujjain, India
VARANASI, India
VRINDAVAN KRISHNA SHRINES, India

BUDDHIST SITES

AJANTA, India
Bodh Gaya, India
BODHNATH STUPA, Nepal
BOROBUDUR, Indonesia
CAVES OF THE THOUSAND BUDDHAS, Dunhuang,
    China
CHOGYESA TEMPLE, Korea
EIGHTY-EIGHT TEMPLES PILGRIMAGE, Japan
ELLORA CAVES, India
EMEI SHAN, China
EMERALD BUDDHA, Thailand
HASEDERA TEMPLE, Japan
Horyu-ji Temple, Japan
JOKHANG TEMPLE, Tibet, China
KEK LOK SI, Malaysia
Kushinagar, India
LAKMUANG SHRINE, Thailand
Lumbini Park, Nepal
MOUNT FUJI, Japan
MOUNT KAILAS, Tibet, China
PAGAN, Myanmar/Burma
PO LIN, Hong Kong, China
POTALA PALACE, Tibet, China
Rinno-ji Temple, Japan
Sarnath, India
Senkgakuji Temple, Japan
Senso-ji Temple, Japan
SHWE DAGON PAGODA, Myanmar
SWAYAMBHUNATH STUPA, Nepal
T'AI SHAN, China
Todai-ji Shrine, Japan
TOOTH TEMPLE, Sri Lanka
WAT PO, Thailand

JEWISH SITES

ANNE FRANK HOUSE, Netherlands
AUSCHWITZ-BIRKENAU, Poland
BABI YAR, Ukraine
Belzec, Poland

Bergen-Belsen, Germany
BUCHENWALD, Germany
Chelmno, Poland
DACHAU, Germany
HEBRON, Palestinian Authority, Tomb
    of the Patriarchs
Jasenovac, Croatia
Kraków, Poland
Majdenek, Poland
MASADA, Israel
Mauthausen, Austria
MOUNT SINAI, Egypt
Mount Zion, Israel
Paneriai, Lithuania
Plaszow, Poland
Sachsenhausen, Germany
Salaspils, Latvia
Sobibór, Poland
Tomb of Rachel, Palestinian Authority
Treblinka, Poland
Warsaw Ghetto, Poland
Western (Wailing) Wall, Israel
Yad Vashem, Israel

ISLAMIC SITES

Blue Mosque, Turkey
DJENNE, Mali
Dome of the Rock, Israel
HEBRON, Palestinian Authority, Ibrahim Mosque
KAIROUAN, Tunisia
KONYA, Turkey
MASJID AL-BADAWI, Egypt
Mecca, Saudi Arabia
Medina, Saudi Arabia
THE MEZQUITA, Spain
Mount Arafat, Saudi Arabia
MOUNT SINAI, Egypt
NAJAF AND KARBALA, Iraq
QOM, Iran
Süleymaniye, Turkey
TAJ MAHAL, India
Timbuktu, Mali
TOUBA, Senegal
Yeni Camii, Turkey

ROMAN CATHOLIC SITES

AACHEN CATHEDRAL, Germany
Akita, Japan
ASSISI, Italy
AVILA, Spain

APPENDIX A

Banneux, Belgium
BEGIJNHOF, Netherlands
BETHLEHEM, Palestinian Authority
BOM JESUS, Portugal
CATACOMBS, Italy
CHIMAYO, New Mexico, USA
EL COBRE, Cuba
CONQUES, France
CONSOLATRICE, Luxembourg
CROAGH PATRICK, Ireland
Dominus Flevit, Italy
EINSIEDELN, Switzerland
EPHESUS, Turkey
FATIMA, Portugal
Garabandal, Spain
THE GARGANO MASSIF, Italy
GLENDALOUGH, Ireland
Grotto of the Nativity, Palestinian Authority
GUADALUPE, Mexico
GUADALUPE, Spain
HILL OF CROSSES, Lithuania
HOLY BLOOD, Belgium
Holy Sepulchre, Israel
INFANT JESUS OF PRAGUE, Czech Republic
IONA, Scotland
JASNA GORA, Poland
KIBEHO, Rwanda
Knock, Ireland
KOREAN MARTYRS' SHRINES, South Korea
La Salette, France
LINDISFARNE, England
LISIEUX, France
LOPPIANO, Italy
LORETO, Italy
LOUGH DERG, Ireland
LOURDES, France
MARTYRS' HILL, Japan
MEDJUGORJE, Bosnia & Herzegovina
Miraculous Medal Shrine, France
MONTE CASSINO, Italy
Monte Sant'Angelo, Italy
MONT-SAINT-MICHEL, France
MONTSERRAT, Spain
MOUNT BRANDON, Ireland
Mount of Olives, Jerusalem
MOUNT SINAI, Egypt
Mount Zion, Israel
NAZARETH, Israel
OBERAMMERGAU, Germany
OUR LORD IN THE ATTIC, Netherlands
PADRE CICERO SHRINE, Brazil
PARAY-LE-MONIAL, France

PATMOS, Greece
EL PILAR, Spain
PLOTZENSEE MEMORIAL, Germany
Pontmain, France
Portiuncula, Italy
ROCK OF CASHEL, Ireland
SAINT ANTHONY OF PADUA, Italy
Saint Bernadette, France
SAINT JANUARIUS, Italy
Saint John Lateran, Italy
SAINT JOSEPH'S ORATORY, Québec, Canada
Saint Mary Major, Italy
Saint Paul's-Outside-the-Walls, Italy
SAINT PETER'S, Vatican City
SAINT WILLIBRORD'S, Luxembourg
SAINT WINIFRED'S WELL, Wales
SAINTE-ANNE DE BEAUPRE, Québec, Canada
San Clemente, Italy
San Giovanni Rotondo, Italy
SAN XAVIER DEL BAC, Arizona, USA
Santa Costanza, Italy
SANTIAGO DE COMPOSTELA, Spain
Scala Santa, Italy
SHROUD OF TURIN, Italy
SKELLIG MICHAEL, Ireland
UGANDAN MARTYRS' SHRINES, Uganda
Via Dolorosa, Israel
VEZELEY, France
WALSINGHAM, England
ZEBRZYDOWSKA CHAPEL, Poland

EASTERN ORTHODOX SITES

AXUM, Ethiopia
BETHLEHEM, Palestinian Authority
CATACOMBS, Italy
COPTIC CAIRO, Egypt
DEBRA LIBANOS, Ethiopia
EPHESUS, Turkey
Grotto of the Nativity, Palestinian Authority
HAGIA SOPHIA, Turkey
Holy Sepulchre, Israel
METEORA MONASTERIES, Greece
MOUNT ATHOS, Greece
Mount of Olives, Israel
MOUNT SINAI, Egypt
NAZARETH, Israel
PATMOS, Greece
PERCHERSK LAVRA, Ukraine
RILA MONASTERY, Bulgaria
Saint Catherine's Monastery, Egypt
SCETE, Egypt

SERGIEV POSAD, Russia
TINOS, Greece
Zeitoun, Egypt

PROTESTANT SITES

BEGIJNHOF, Netherlands
BETHLEHEM, Palestinian Authority
CANTERBURY CATHEDRAL, England
CATACOMBS, Italy
CORRIE TEN BOOM HOUSE, Netherlands
EPHESUS, Turkey
Eisenach, Germany
Eisleben, Germany
Erfurt, Germany
GENEVA, Switzerland
Grotto of the Nativity, Palestinian Authority
Holy Sepulchre, Israel
IONA, Scotland
LINDISFARNE, England
LUTHER CIRCLE, Germany
MORIJA, South Africa
Mount of Olives, Israel
MOUNT SINAI, Egypt
NAZARETH, Israel
NIDAROS, Norway
OBERAMMERGAU, Germany
PATMOS, Greece
PLOTZENSEE MEMORIAL, Germany
SABBATHDAY LAKE, Maine, USA
ST. WINIFRED'S WELL, Wales
TAIZE, France
UGANDAN MARTYRS' SHRINES, Uganda
WALSINGHAM, England
WESTMINSTER ABBEY, England

Wittenburg, Germany
YORK MINSTER, England

NEW AGE SITES

AACHEN CATHEDRAL, Germany
ANGKOR WAT, Cambodia
BIGHORN MEDICINE WHEEL, Wyoming, USA
BLACK HILLS, South Dakota/Wyoming, USA
CAHOKIA MOUNDS, Illinois, USA
CARNAC, France
CATHAR SITES, France
CHACO, New Mexico, USA
CHICHEN ITZA, Mexico
CUZCO, Peru
DOGON CLIFFS, Mali
EASTER ISLAND, Chile
EXTERNSTEINE, Germany
IONA, Scotland
KILAUEA, Hawaii, USA
MONT-SAINT-MICHEL, France
Montségur, France
MOUNT FUJI, Japan
MOUNT KAILAS, Tibet, China
MOUNT OLYMPUS, Greece
MOUNT SHASTA, California, USA
MOUNT SINAI, Egypt
NAN MADOL, Pohnpei
NAZCA LINES, Peru
NEWGRANGE, Ireland
PYRAMIDS OF GIZA, Egypt
Serpent Mound, Ohio, USA
STONEHENGE AND AVEBURY, England
Timbuktu, Mali
ULURU AND KATA TJUTA, Australia

APPENDIX B
Entries Listed by Country

Note: Small caps signify that the site is included as an entry in the text.

Australia
    ULURU AND KATA TJUTA
Austria
    HOLOCAUST SITES
    Malthausen
Belgium
    Banneux
    HOLY BLOOD, Brugge
    MARIAN APPARITIONS
Bosnia and Herzegovina
    MEDJUGORJE
Brazil
    PADRE CICERO SHRINE, Juazeiro
Bulgaria
    RILA MONASTERY
Cambodia
    ANGKOR WAT
Canada
    Majorville Medicine Wheel, Alberta
    Moose Mountain Medicine Wheel
        Saskatchewan
    SAINT JOSEPH'S ORATORY, Montréal, Québec
    SAINTE-ANNE DE BEAUPRE, Québec
    Wanuskewin, Saskatoon, Saskatchewan
Chile
    RAPA NUI, Easter Island
China
    CAVES OF THE THOUSAND BUDDHAS, Dunhuang
    EMEI SHAN
    JOKHANG TEMPLE, Lhasa, Tibet
    MOUNT KAILAS, Tibet
    PO LIN, Hong Kong
    POTALA PALACE, Lhasa, Tibet
    T'AI SHAN
Croatia
    HOLOCAUST SITES
    Jasenovac
Cuba
    EL COBRE
Czech Republic

    INFANT JESUS OF PRAGUE
    Theresienstadt
Egypt
    COPTIC CAIRO
    MARIAN APPARITIONS
    MASJID AL-BADAWI, Tanta
    MOUNT SINAI
    PYRAMIDS OF GIZA, Cairo
    St. Catherine's Monastery, Sinai
    SCETE, Wâdî el Natrûn
    THEBES AND LUXOR, Luxor
    Zeitoun, Cairo
Ethiopia
    AXUM
    DEBRA LIBANOS
    LALIBELA
France
    CARNAC, Ménec
    CATHAR SITES
    CONQUES
    La Salette
    LISIEUX
    LOURDES
    MARIAN APPARITIONS
    Miraculous Medal Shrine, Paris
    MONT-SAINT-MICHEL
    Montségur
    PARAY-LE-MONIAL
    PERE LACHAISE CEMETERY, Paris
    Pontmain
    St. Bernadette Shrine, Nevers
    TAIZE
    VEZELEY
Germany
    AACHEN CATHEDRAL
    Bergen-Belsen
    BUCHENWALD, Weimar
    DACHAU, Munich
    Eisenach
    Eisleben
    Erfurt
    EXTERNSTEINE
    HOLOCAUST SITES

LUTHER CIRCLE
OBERAMMERGAU
PLOTZENSEE MEMORIAL, Berlin
Ravensbrück
Sachsenhausen, Oranienenberg
VERDEN
Wittenburg
Ghana
    Cape Coast Castle, SLAVE DEPOTS
    Christianborg, SLAVE DEPOTS
    St. George's Castle, SLAVE DEPOTS
Great Britain
    CANTERBURY CATHEDRAL, England
    IONA, Scotland
    LINDISFARNE, England
    SANIT WINIFRED'S WELL, Holywell, Wales
    STONEHENGE AND AVEBURY, England
    WALSINGHAM, England
    WESTMINSTER ABBEY, London, England
    YORK MINSTER, England
Greece
    ACROPOLIS, Athens
    DELOS
    DELPHI
    METEORA MONASTERIES
    MOUNT ATHOS
    Mount Olympus
    OLYMPIA
    PATMOS
    TINOS
Haïti
    PLAINE DU NORD
    SAUT D'EAU, Ville Bonheur
India
    AJANTA
    Allahabad
    Bodh Gaya
    ELLORA CAVES
    DILWARA
    GOLDEN TEMPLE, Amritsar
    Hardwar
    HEARTH OF BUDDHISM
    Kushinagar
    KUMBH MELA SITES
    MEENAKSHI TEMPLE, Madurai
    Nasik
    ORISSA TRIANGLE
    Sarnath
    TAJ MAHAL, Agra
    Ujjain
    VARANASI
    VRINDAVAN KRISHNA SHRINES

Indonesia
    BOROBUDUR, Java
    GUNUNG AGUNG, Bali
Iran
    QOM
Iraq
    NAJAF AND KARBALA
Ireland
    CROAGH PATRICK, County Mayo
    GLENDALOUGH, County Wicklow
    LOUGH DERG, County Donegal
    Knock, County Mayo
    MOUNT BRANDON, County Kerry
    NEWGRANGE, County Meath
    ROCK OF CASHEL, County Tipperary
    SKELLIG MICHAEL, County Kerry
Israel
    BAHA'I WORLD CENTRE, Haifa
    JERUSALEM
    MASADA
    Mount Zion, Jerusalem
    NAZARETH
    Yad Vashem, Jerusalem
Italy
    ASSISI
    CATACOMBS, Rome
    THE GARGANO MASSIF
    LOPPIANO
    LORETO
    MONTE CASSINO
    Monte Sant'Angelo
    ROME
    SAINT ANTHONY OF PADUA
    SAINT JANUARIUS, Naples
    Saint John Lateran, Rome
    Saint Mary Major, Rome
    Saint Paul's-Outside-the-Walls, Rome
    SAINT PETER'S, Rome
    San Clemente, Rome
    San Giovanni Rotondo
    Santa Costanza, Rome
    Scala Santa, Rome
    SHROUD OF TURIN
Japan
    Akita
    EIGHTY-EIGHT TEMPLES PILGRIMAGE
    Ginkakuji, Kyoto
    HASADERA TEMPLE
    HIROSHIMA PEACE MEMORIAL
    Kinkakuji, Kyoto
    KYOTO
    ISE

APPENDIX B

IZUMO TAISHA SHRINE
MARTYRS' HILL, Nagasaki
MOUNT FUJI
NARA
NIKKO
Ryoanji Temple, Kyoto
SHINTO SHRINES
TOKYO
Jordan
  PETRA
Kenya
  MOUNT KENYA
Korea
  CHOGYESA TEMPLE, Seoul
  KOREAN MARTYRS' SHRINES
Lithuania
  HILL OF CROSSES
  Paneriai, Vilnius
Luxembourg
  CONSOLATRICE, Luxembourg City
  SAINT WILLIBRORD'S, Echternach
Mali
  DJENNE
  DOGON CLIFFS
Malaysia
  KEK LOK SI, Air Itam
Malta
  GGANTIJA, Xaghra, Gozo
Mexico
  CHICHEN ITZA
  GUADALUPE, Mexico City
  TEOTIHUACAN, Mexico City
Myanmar/Burma
  PAGAN
  SHWE DAGON PAGODA, Yangon
Nepal
  BODHNATH STUPA, Kathmandu
  CHANGU NARAYAN TEMPLE, Kathmandu
  HEARTH OF BUDDHISM
  JANAKPUR
  PASHUPATINATH, Kathmandu
  SWAYAMBHUNATH STUPA, Kathmandu
Netherlands
  ANNE FRANK HOUSE, Amsterdam
  BEGIJNHOF, Amsterdam
  CORRIE TEN BOOM HOUSE, Haarlem
  OUR LORD IN THE ATTIC, Amsterdam
Norway
  NIDAROS, Trondheim
Palestinian Authority
  BETHLEHEM
  Grotto of the Nativity, Bethlehem

HEBRON
  Tomb of Rachel, Bethlehem
Pohnpei
  NAN MADOL
Poland
  AUSCHWITZ-BIRKENAU, Kraków
  Belzek
  Chelmno
  HOLOCAUST SITES
  JASNA GORA, Czestochowa
  Kraków
  Majdenek
  Sobibór
  Treblinka
  Warsaw Ghetto
  ZEBRZYDOWSKA CHAPEL, Kalwaria
Portugal
  BOM JESUS, Braga
  FATIMA
Peru
  CUZCO
  MACHU PICCHU
  NAZCA LINES
Russia
  SERGIEV POSAD
Rwanda
  KIBEHO
Saudi Arabia
  THE HAJJ, Mecca and Medina
Senegal
  GOREE ISLAND, Dakar
  TOUBA
Sierra Leone
  Bunce Island, SLAVE DEPOTS
South Africa
  MORIJA, Transvaal
Spain
  AVILA
  Garabandal
  GUADALUPE
  THE MEZQUITA, Córdoba
  MONTSERRAT
  EL PILAR, Zaragoza
  SANTIAGO DE COMPOSTELA
Sri Lanka
  TOOTH TEMPLE, Kandy
Switzerland
  EINSIEDELN
  GENEVA
Tanzania
  Bagamoyo
  Mount Kilimanjaro

APPENDIX B

Zanzibar
Thailand
    EMERALD BUDDHA, Bangkok
    ERAWAN SHRINE, Bangkok
    LAKMUANG SHRINE, Bangkok
    WAT PO, Bangkok
Tunisia
    KAIROUAN
Turkey
    EPHESUS
    HAGIA SOPHIA, Istanbul
    ISTANBUL MOSQUES
    KONYA
Uganda
    UGANDAN MARTYRS' SHRINES
Ukraine
    BABI YAR, Kiev
    PERCHERSK LAVRA, Kiev
United States
    Bear Butte, South Dakota
    BIGHORN MEDICINE WHEEL, Wyoming

BLACK HILLS, South Dakota / Wyoming
CAHOKIA MOUNDS, Illinois
CHACO, New Mexico
CHIMAYO, New Mexico
Effigy Mounds, Iowa
KILAUEA, Hawaii
Lizard Mound, Ohio
MEDICINE WHEELS
MORADA
MORMON TEMPLE, Salt Lake City, Utah
MOUND-BUILDERS
Mound City, Ohio
MOUNT SHASTA, California
NATIVE AMERICAN SACRED PLACES
Newark Earthworks, Ohio
SABBATHDAY LAKE, Maine
SAN XAVIER DEL BAC, Arizona
Serpent Mound, Ohio
SWEAT LODGE
Vietnam
    CAO DAI TEMPLE, Tay Ninh

APPENDIX C
Entries on the UNESCO World Heritage List of Cultural Sites (1997)

The United Nations Educational, Scientific and Cultural Organization (UNESCO) maintains a list of the most important sites for world culture, and helps to raise funds for their preservation and protection.

Aachen Cathedral, Germany
Acropolis, Greece
Ajanta Caves, India
Angkor Wat, Cambodia
Atomic Bomb Dome, Hiroshima
Auschwitz, Poland
Ávila, Spain
Axum, Ethiopia
Bodhnath Stupa, Nepal: Kathmandu Valley
Borobudur, Indonesia
Cahokia Mounds, Illinois, USA
Canterbury Cathedral, England
Chaco, Peru
Changu Narayan: Kathmandu Valley
Chichén-Itzá, Mexico
Cuzco, Peru
Delos, Greece
Delphi, Greece
Djenné, Mali
Dogon Cliffs, Mali
Ellora Caves, India
Emei Shan, China
Ggantija Temples, Malta
Gondar, Ethiopia
Gorée Island, Senegal
Guadalupe, Spain
Horyu-ji Temple, Japan
Istanbul: Islamic Sites and Hagia Sophia, Turkey
Jerusalem: Old City, Israel
Kairouan, Tunisia
Kandy, Sri Lanka
Kathmandu Valley, Nepal

Konorak Sun Temple, India
Kyoto, Japan
Lalibela, Ethiopia
Luther Memorial Towns, Germany
Machu Picchu, Peru
Native American Sacred Places: Mesa Verde, Colorado, USA
Meteora Monasteries, Greece
Mezquita, Spain
Mont-Saint-Michel, France
Mount Athos, Greece
Nazca Lines, Peru
Newgrange, Ireland: Bend of the Boyne
Olympia, Greece
Orissa Triangle, India: Sun Temple, Konorak
Pashupatinath, Nepal: Kathmandu Valley
Perchersk Lavra, Ukraine
Petra, Jordan
Potala Palace, Tibet, China
Pyramids of Giza, Egypt
Rapa Nui, Easter Island, Chile
Rila Monastery, Bulgaria
Rome Historic Center, Italy
Santiago de Compostela, Spain, and the Way of Santiago
Sergiev Posad, Russia
Skellig Michael, Ireland
Stonehenge and Avebury, England
Swayambhunath, Nepal: Kathmandu Valley
T'ai Shan, China
Taj Mahal, India
Teotihuacán, Mexico
Thebes, Egypt
Tooth Temple: Sacred City of Kandy, Sri Lanka
Uluru and Kata Tjuta, Australia
Vatican City: St. Peter's
Vézeley, France
Westminster Abbey, England

GLOSSARY

Allah The One God proclaimed by Mohammed, the Prophet who first preached Islam. Allah, the creator and sustainer of all, is pure spirit and may not be represented in art.

Ambulatory A walkway around the shrine in medieval shrine churches. It symbolizes the final steps of the pilgrim's journey and final purification. Pilgrims circle the shrine several times (often a sacred number, such as three or seven) before approaching the shrine itself.

Ancestralist A follower of a primal religion that either worships or honors ancestor spirits and believes that they affect those who are still alive.

Angel A created, bodiless spirit that serves as a messenger of God. The existence of angels is revealed in the sacred scriptures of Christianity, Judaism, and Islam.

Apparition A vision in which one sees a person or object that is ordinarily invisible. Though the vision may be a natural phenomenon (optical illusion), most religions recognize the possibility of supernatural apparitions.

Ascension Day A Catholic feast celebrating Jesus' rising into heaven 40 days after his Resurrection. It is often observed with processions and is a legal holiday in many European countries.

Aura An atmosphere, sensed but not usually seen, surrounding a person or any center of power or energy. Sometimes it is manifested as an electro-magnetic field.

Baptismal font A mounted basin of water used for baptism in Christian churches. Elaborate ones may have flowing waters.

Bible The sacred scriptures of Christianity. The Hebrew scriptures (called the Old Testament by Christians) and the New Testament together form a collection believed by Christians to be the revealed word of God, inspired by the Holy Spirit.

Bodhisattva A Buddhist saint who has freely renounced nirvana in order to help others toward salvation.

Buddha Siddhartha Gautama, who received enlightenment and became the founder of Buddhism.

Byzantine Churches The leading form of Eastern Orthodox liturgy and theology, arising from the Byzantine Empire, which flourished from the sixth to fifteenth centuries with its capital in Constantinople.

Celibacy A religious commitment to abstain from sex and especially to forgo marriage. Required of monks and nuns (and sometimes priests) in Catholic, Orthodox, Buddhist, and other religions.

Corpus Christi The Catholic observance of the Body and Blood of Jesus, which are believed to be literally present in the Eucharistic bread and wine. In many Catholic countries, large public processions are held on the feast (second Thursday after Pentecost), in which the consecrated bread is carried in an elaborate golden monstrance, or portable shrine.

Cross A simple crossbar that represents redemption or salvation to Christians, since it was the instrument of Jesus' death. Crosses are often worn as jewelry or used decoratively to demonstrate faith.

Crucifix A representation of the body of Jesus nailed to the cross, the manner in which he was martyred. It symbolizes for Christians Jesus' supreme sacrifice, which brought redemption and is a common theme in Christian art. Some evangelical Protestants reject it, believing that since the Resurrection of Jesus, only the cross remains a valid symbol.

Dalai Lama   In Tibetan Buddhism, the spiritual leader believed to be the reincarnation of the Celestial Buddha. Though he does not manage or direct his followers, the Dalai Lama is regarded as the master spiritual guide. Until 1949, he was also the ruler of Tibet.

Dervish   A member of a Muslim Sufi order who enters into contact with Allah through ecstasy brought on by a whirling dance and the recitation of the Ninety-nine Names of Allah.

Devil   An angel who followed Satan in rejecting the authority of God and who tempts the faithful and tests their fidelity.

Equinox   The dates (March 21 and September 22) when the sun crosses the equator, making day and night everywhere on Earth of equal length.

Eucharist   The central act of Christian worship, in which bread and wine are shared in remembrance of Jesus' Last Supper (also called Communion in some Protestant denominations). Liturgical religions believe that Jesus is somehow present in the bread and wine, and Catholics and Eastern Orthodox Christians worship him in these elements. The celebration of the Eucharist, called the Mass by Catholics, is the major ceremony at Catholic and Orthodox shrines.

Ex-Voto   An offering at a shrine, especially at a tomb. It may be a bouquet of flowers, a prayer candle, a letter appealing for aid, or a badge symbolizing a favor granted by the saint.

Feast day   The annual observance of a saint's day or some religious event, such as Christmas (the birth of Christ) among Christians; the solstices among New Age followers; Yom Kippur (the Day of Atonement) among Jews; Diwali (the Feast of Lights) among Hindus. *Also see* Mawlid.

Fetish   In many primal religions, especially in Africa, a bundle of items such as bones, feathers, and stones believed to have magic powers.

Gaia theory   A New Age concept, named for the Greek goddess of earth, that proposes that all matter, either animate or not, composes a single living being. Within this living earth, sacred sites are energy centers where power is concentrated and made available to those who use them.

Ganesh   Elephant-headed god of prosperity in the Hindu pantheon, the son of Shiva and Parvati. A very popular god.

Ghat   A Hindu bathing place for purification rites, either a pond or steps leading down to a sacred river.

Hajj   The pilgrimage to Mecca required once during the life of every able-bodied Muslim.

Harmonic Convergence   A New Age event in 1987, in which thousands of people converged on a number of "power points" around the world to draw together cosmic energies and focus them on initiating a new age of peace and harmony.

Hebrew scriptures   The inspired books of the Jewish Bible, made up of the Torah (first five books or Books of Moses), the prophets, the Psalms, and various historical books. They represent the revelation of God to the Jewish people and are also accepted as revealed by Christians, who refer to them as the Old Testament.

Holocaust   The Nazi campaign to eradicate the Jewish people during World War II by systematic genocide and wholesale slaughter; over six million died.

Holy water   Water that has been blessed for use in prayer and ritual as a sign of purification. Christians also consider it a sign of baptism.

Holy Week   The final days of Christian Lent leading up to Easter, during which the Last Supper, death, and Resurrection of Jesus are celebrated. In many countries, the liturgical ceremonies are accompanied by Passion plays, pageants, and processions.

Holy Year   In Jewish tradition, a year of jubilee was proclaimed every fifty years (Leviticus 25:8–24), when "each of you shall return to his family." In Catholicism, this is a year of pilgrimage to the holy places of Rome. The Holy Year of 2000 is expected to draw about 20 million to Rome from around the world.

Icon   A representation of Christ or the saints that has the power to take on the presence of the one shown, creating an aura of grace around it. Icons are honored in Orthodox shrines and churches as the presence of holiness.

Idol A representation of a god or goddess, usually a statue, which is the object of worship because the god resides within it or the god's power rests on it.

Intercession Prayer offered for the good of others by a believer or by a saint in heaven. Christians believe that Christ above all intercedes before God for the human race.

Jesus The prophetic teacher who began Christianity, preaching a doctrine of salvation through faith and forgiveness of sins. He claimed to be the Messiah and was executed by the Romans by being crucified. Three days later he was raised from the dead. Christians believe Jesus to be the Christ, the son of God, and one of the members of the Trinity.

Ka'bah The most sacred sanctuary of Islam. It contains the black rock that tradition teaches was given to Ishmael by the Archangel Gabriel.

Kali The consort of the god Shiva in Hinduism, she is both the goddess of destruction and the Great Mother, giver of life. She is represented as a black goddess wearing a necklace of skulls and with fangs dripping blood. Because of widespread wars and the threat of nuclear destruction, many New Age adherents refer to the present time as the Age of Kali.

Kiva Sacred ceremonial rooms of Pueblo Amerindians symbolizing the womb of Mother Earth. A small hole in the floor represents the umbilical cord and the underworld from which humankind emerged. The kivas are used for discussions and prayer and can be either communal or limited to a certain clan.

Koran *See* Qur'an.

Lama The monks who guide Tibetan Lamaism, a blending of Buddhism and ancient animist beliefs. The lamas also traditionally governed Tibet.

Lent The Christian period of forty days of prayer and penance leading up to Holy Week and Easter.

Ley lines In New Age religions, geological lines of spiritual force that are associated with sacred places, such as megaliths, sacred mountains, and springs.

Libation A drink, usually wine or beer, poured out as an offering to a god or to ancestor spirits. It can be either a sign of respect or a means of appeasing the power of the spirits.

Lingam A pillar representing the sex organ of Shiva, one of the Hindu trinity. It is regarded as the source of fertility and pleasure and is shown erect, rising out of the yoni.

Liturgy The ritual celebration of religious observances, usually following a cycle of seasons, such as the cycle of Advent, Christmas, Lent, Easter, and Pentecost, which commemorates the life cycle of Jesus in Christian faiths.

Loa A voodoo god or goddess that can manifest itself by possessing a devotee.

Magic The use of supernatural powers, through spells and rituals, to achieve some goal or to harm someone.

Martyr A believer who sacrifices his or her life rather than abandon his faith. The word means "witness."

Mary, Mother of Jesus Honored by Christians and Muslims, Mary is especially revered by Catholics and Orthodox Christians, who have built many shrines and churches in her name. She, as well as her son, is considered a powerful intercessor in Catholic and Orthodox traditions, and she has a special role of bringing Jesus' call to conversion to people through apparitions, visions, and miraculous manifestations.

Mass Popular word for the Eucharist, the Christian ritual celebration of the body and blood of Jesus. Catholics, Orthodox, and some Anglicans regard it as the reliving of the sacrifice of Jesus; most Protestants regard it as a memorial of that event. *See also* Eucharist.

Mawlid The annual celebration or feast day of an Islamic saint or prophet. Except for the mawlid for Mohammed, which is observed internationally, most are kept at the shrines of the saint. The mawlid is usually on or around the saint's birthday, although some Muslim cultures observe the anniversary of the saint's death instead.

Medicine man or **woman** In most primal religions, a practitioner of herbalism who is in contact with the spirits of plants, so that through incantations, their healing properties are invoked.

Messiah In Jewish and Christian teaching, the holy one sent from God to deliver his people. *See also* Jesus.

Midsummer Night In northern Europe, the longest day of the year, when there is often no more than an hour of darkness, is a time for all-night festivities going back to pagan customs. It was believed that if someone slept that night, evil spirits could cast a curse on them. Usually observed June 23–24, the night before the feast of St. John. In Spain, England, and elsewhere, St. John's Day is a festival time, traditionally observed with bonfires.

Miracle An event with spiritual meaning that defies natural explanation, an intervention in the events of the world by a divine power. At shrines, miracles often take the form of cures without medical explanation, but they can also be suspensions of the laws of nature such as the spinning of the sun or a snowfall in summer.

Mohammad The prophet and apostle of Islam, who received the Qur'an, the inspired word of Allah, in the seventh century and formed and inspired the Muslim community.

Monastery The residence of a community of monks or nuns, vowed to celibacy and living with common sharing of goods, and engaged in prayer and worship as their primary daily activities.

Moroni An angel sent to the founder of Mormonism, Joseph Smith (1805–1844), to help him translate the golden plates on which the Book of Mormon was inscribed. Moroni ordained Smith the first Mormon priest.

Mosaic A picture made with closely fitted colored stones or pieces of tile.

Mystic A believer who seeks direct, personal experience of God through prayer, meditation, or spiritual discipline.

Nirvana A state of fulfillment in Buddhism in which the restlessness of existence ceases, and the soul becomes enlightened and moves beyond any form of human experience.

Occult The teachings and practices of cults that stress the mysterious. These practices can be known only by an elite of enlightened persons.

Oracle A prophetic voice that speaks through a medium, usually a special person who is in a trance.

Orthodox Literally, one who holds to true faith, but generally used to refer to Christians of various Eastern churches, especially the Byzantine churches that accept the leadership of the patriarch of Constantinople while remaining autonomous. The most observant branch of Judaism is also called Orthodox.

Pagan One who follows an ancient religion with multiple gods and goddesses who are ordinarily represented as idols endowed with divine power.

Pagoda A Buddhist shrine built over a sacred relic.

Passion play A religious pageant of the last days of Jesus, reenacting his Trial, Passion, Crucifixion, and Resurrection.

Pentecost The Christian feast celebrating the descent of the Holy Spirit upon the Apostles of Jesus, as recounted in the Bible in Acts 2.

Pillars of Islam The five duties required of every observing Muslim: professing the creed that Allah is the only God and Mohammed is his prophet; ritual prayer; almsgiving; fasting for the month of Ramadan; and making the hajj, or pilgrimage to Mecca, at least once in life.

Prayer Communication with God or saints, either verbally or though interior silence. It may be expressed through formulas (such as the Lord's Prayer), worship, meditation, or mystical experience.

Prayer wheel In Buddhist ritual, a cylinder bearing the inscription, "Om mani padme hum" (Hail to the jewel in the lotus). The devotee spins the wheel, setting the prayer into eternal repetition.

Primal religion The religious faith of traditional, preliterate peoples who have no sacred writings. They are tribal, revering spirits and natural powers as well as ancestors.

Prophet One who announces a message or warning from God. In Jewish tradition, the ancient prophets called the people back from heresy and proclaimed justice. The Prophet is also the title of Mohammed, who was the vehicle for Allah's revelation to the world.

Qur'an The holy book of Islam, regarded as the literal word of Allah revealed to Mohammed.

Ramadan The month in the Islamic calendar during which Muslims fast from sunup to sundown, abstaining from all food, liquids, tobacco, or sexual pleasure, as a period of purification.

Ramayana A great epic in Hindu sacred writings that tells the life story of Rama.

Reincarnation The doctrine that souls are reborn at death and pass through a number of lives before achieving a final state of perfection. Taught by Hindus, Jains, and many New Age religions.

Rosary A string of beads for repeating prayers. Catholic rosaries have five "decades," or sets of ten beads, on each of which the Ave Maria is recited. Each decade is separated from the others by the Lord's Prayer. There are three groups of five mysteries, traditional scenes from the life of Christ or Mary, to be used for meditation while reciting the prayers. A Muslim rosary has thirty-three beads for reciting the Ninety-Nine Names of Allah, a litany of praise.

Sacrament The external, ritual sign of an inward, spiritual grace, believed to have been established by Christ. All Christians accept baptism and the Eucharist (the Lord's Supper) as sacraments; Catholics and Orthodox Christians also accept confirmation, marriage, priestly ordination, confession of sins, and the anointing of the sick. Among some Anabaptists, foot-washing is considered a sacrament.

Sacred A sense of awe, holiness, and dependence upon a supernatural being—God—that is the most basic characteristic of religion. The experience of the sacred calls forth a response: worship, moral living, and membership in a religious community.

Sacrifice A ritual offering, either real or symbolic, that allows the faithful to enter into communion with the divine.

Sadhu A Hindu holy man, a wandering ascetic who lives a life of austerity.

Saint A holy person who is revered by believers and considered a channel of contact with divine grace or blessing. In Christian tradition, there are recognized saints who have died as heroes of faith and are considered to be in the presence of God. Liturgical religions usually celebrate saints' feast days.

Sanctuary A consecrated place dedicated to a god or saint.

Santería A Caribbean religion blending ancient West African worship of Yoruba gods with Christianity. Similar to Voudou, it uses animal sacrifice and an elaborate system of rituals to engage the powers of natural forces on behalf of the worshippers.

Satan The personification of all evil; an angel who rejected God in Christian, Jewish, and Muslim belief and became a force for sin.

Scriptures The sacred writings of a religion, usually believed to have been directly inspired by God and to contain the wisdom and teachings of the faith. The Jewish Torah, the Christian Gospels, and the Muslim Qur'an are all examples.

Shaman A practitioner of sacred magic, able to invoke the powers of nature because of an inborn ability to move between the world of the living and that of the dead. Through magical powers a shaman diagnoses illness, lifts curses, and finds lost persons and objects. Shamans are found among Amerindians and the Inuit (Eskimos) and the traditional peoples of Siberia and Japan.

Sikhism An Indian religion, founded by Guru Nanak in the 1500s and found primarily in India. The men do not cut their beards or hair, which they wear in a turban. The religion has many Hindu aspects, but it is monotheistic and rejects caste distinctions.

Solstice The longest or shortest days of the year, in which the sun expands or declines in its power. In the Northern Hemisphere the summer solstice is June 21 and the winter solstice is December 22; the dates are reversed in the Southern Hemisphere.

Spell A magic charm or incantation believed to have power over natural forces, usually invoked through a secret formula of words or syllables.

GLOSSARY

Spirit   A living soul without a body, either that of the dead, such as an ancestor spirit, or an angel or devil. In primal religions, every living thing is believed to have a spirit.

Station   A stop along a pilgrimage way, used for prayer and various spiritual activities. It might be a chapel, a small shrine or memorial, or a special site, such as the Mount of Olives outside Jerusalem. The popular devotion of the Way of the Cross has 14 stations of the Passion and death of Jesus.

Stupa   A Buddhist religious structure that is a solid white mound with a spire on top, usually marking a holy place or a relic. It has 13 conical rings for the 13 degrees of wisdom necessary to attain nirvana.

Sufi   A member of an Islamic brotherhood that follows a common mystical practice by which members attain direct experience of Allah. The practice, or *tariq,* might be chanting verses from the Qur'an, ecstatic dancing, the recitation of the Ninety-nine Names of God, or similar acts.

Syncretism   The growing together of two religious traditions that produces a mixture of both. Voudou, for example, consists of elements of African primal religions and Roman Catholicism.

Tabernacle   A small chest, usually decorated, that contains sacred objects. In Catholic churches, it is used to hold the Communion host, believed to be the body of Christ.

Totem   In primal religions, a guardian spirit that inhabits certain animals and protects the tribe or clan. In some African cultures, it is forbidden to eat the meat from the clan's totem. Amerindians of the Pacific Northwest erected tall totem poles on which ancestors and totem animals are carved. These are sometimes used in graveyards to honor the ancestors, or as protectors.

Türbe   The tomb of a Muslim holy man, especially a dervish master.

Virgin Mary   *See* Mary, Mother of Jesus.

Vision quest   In some Amerindian religions, a solitary spiritual search that ends when a vision of a sacred totem is received or appears in a dream. Sometimes the vision gives the seeker his or her permanent name, and in a few traditions, it is a part of initiation rites.

Voodoo   A religious system brought from Africa to the Caribbean by slaves. It worships and seeks help from divine power through *loas,* deities who manifest themselves by possessing worshippers. Animal sacrifices are made to the loas.

Way of the Cross   A popular Catholic devotion involving prayer and meditation on 14 scenes from the Passion and death of Jesus, from his arrest to his Crucifixion and removal from the cross. The way is marked by pictures or statues, called stations, and individuals or groups walk from scene to scene.

Wicca   The religion of modern witchcraft. It has many connections with contemporary New Age religions.

Witchcraft   The religion, with ancient pagan roots, that worships the powers of nature and has rituals to use these powers for the benefit of the human race, although curses and black magic are also possible.

Worship   Prayer directed at honor and praise of God or a sacred object rather than petitioning for the needs of the faithful.

Yoni   A representation of the sex organs of the Hindu goddess Parvati, Shiva's consort. It symbolizes the power of nature. *See* Lingam.

FURTHER READING

Adair, John. *The Pilgrims' Way: Shrines and Saints in Britain and Ireland*. New York: Thames and Hudson, 1978.

Altschuler, David, ed. *The Precious Legacy*. New York: Summit, 1983.

Amin, Mohamed, Duncan Willetts, and Brian Tetley. *Journey through Nepal*. London: Bodley Head, 1987.

Bernbaum, Edwin. *Sacred Mountains of the World*. San Francisco: Sierra Club, 1990.

Bonnefoy, Ives. *Mythologies*. 2 vols. Chicago: University of Chicago Press, 1991.

Booz, Elizabeth. *Tibet: Roof of the World*. Lincolnwood, IL: Passport Books, 1994.

Bottomley, Frank. *Explorer's Guide to the Abbeys, Monasteries and Churches of Great Britain*. New York: Avenel Books, 1981.

Braunfels, Wolfgang. *Monasteries of Western Europe*. London, Thames & Hudson, 1972.

The Catholic Encyclopedia. 16 vols. New York: Appleton, 1907–1912.

Cavendish, Richard, ed. *Men, Myth and Magic*. 11 vols. New York: Marshall Cavendish, 1983.

Coleman, Simon, and John Elsner. *Pilgrimage Past and Present in the World's Religions.* Cambridge, MA: Harvard University Press, 1995.

Cruz, Joan Carroll. *Miraculous Images of Our Lady*. Rockford, IL: Tan Books, 1993.

Davies, J. G. *Temples, Churches and Mosques*. Oxford, England: Basil Blackwell, 1982.

De Rivieres, F. Philipin. *Holy Places: Their Sanctity and Authenticity*. London: n.p., 1874.

Devereux, Paul. *Secrets of Sacred and Ancient Places*. London: Blandford, 1992.

Durham, Michael. *Miracles of Mary*. San Francisco: Harper San Francisco, 1995.

Eliade, Mircea, ed. *The Encyclopedia of Religion*. 16 vols. New York: Macmillan, 1986.

Freedman, David Noel. *The Anchor Bible Dictionary*. 6 vols. New York: Doubleday, 1992.

Gilbert, Martin. *Atlas of the Holocaust*. Rev. ed. New York: William Morrow, 1993.

Gillett, H.M. *Famous Shrines of Our Lady*. 2 vols. Westminster, England: Newman, 1952.

Graber, Linda. *Wilderness and Sacred Space*. Washington, DC: Association of American Geographers, 1976.

Gutman, Israel, ed. *Encyclopedia of the Holocaust*. 4 vols. New York: Macmillan, 1990.

Harbison, Peter. *Pilgrimage in Ireland*. Syracuse, NY: Syracuse University Press, 1991.

Harpur, James. *Atlas of Sacred Places*. New York: Henry Holt, 1994.

Hastings, James, ed. *Encyclopaedia of Religion and Ethics*. 13 vols. New York: Scribner's, n.d.

Higgins, Paul. *Pilgrimages to Rome and Beyond*. Englewood Cliffs, NJ: Prentice-Hall, 1986.

Hirschfelder, Arlene, and Paulette Molin. *The Encyclopedia of Native American Religions*. New York: Facts on File, 1992.

Hollis, Christopher, and Ronald Brownrigg. *Holy Places*. New York: Praeger, 1969.

Jarrow, Rick. *In Search of the Sacred*. Wheaton, IL: Theosophical Publishing, 1986.

Joseph, Frank, ed. *Sacred Sites*. St. Paul, MN: Llewellyn, 1992.

Kightly, Charles. *Traveller's Guide to Places of Worship*. London: Routledge & Kegan Paul, 1986.

Klieckhofer, Richard, and George Bond, eds. *Sainthood: Its Manifestation in World Religions*. Berkeley: University of California Press, 1988.

Kubler, George. *The Religious Architecture of New Mexico*. Albuquerque: University of New Mexico Press, 1940.

Laurentin, René. *Pilgrimages, Sanctuaries, Icons, and Apparitions.* Milford, OH: Faith, 1994.

Leeming, David, and Margaret Leeming. *Encyclopedia of Creation Myths*. Santa Barbara, CA: ABC-CLIO, 1994.

Lehrman, Frederic. *The Sacred Landscape*. Berkeley, CA: Celestial Arts, 1988.

Li, Hans. *The Ancient Ones.* New York: City of Light, 1994.

FURTHER READING

MacMitchell, Melanie. *Sacred Footsteps*. Palo Alto, CA: Opal Star Press, 1991.

McNaspy, C. J. *A Guide to Christian Europe*. 2d ed. Chicago: Loyola University Press, 1984.

Majupuria, Trilok, and Indra Majupuria. *Holy Places of Buddhism in Nepal and India*. 2d ed. Bangkok: Tecpress, 1993.

Marshall, Richard. *Strange, Amazing and Mysterious Places*. San Francisco: Collins, 1993.

Miller, Sherrill. *The Sacred Earth*. Stillwater, MN: Voyageur Press, 1991.

Mirsky, Jeannette. *Houses of God*. New York: Viking, 1965.

New Catholic Encyclopedia. 19 vols. New York: Mc-Graw-Hill, 1967–1979.

Nolan, Mary Lee, and Sidney Nolan. *Christian Pilgrimage in Modern Western Europe*. Chapel Hill: University of North Carolina Press, 1989.

O'Carroll, Michael. *Theotokos*. Wilmington, DE: Michael Glazier, 1982.

Peck, M. Scott. *In Search of Stones: A Pilgrimage of Faith, Reason, and Discovery*. New York: Hyperion, 1995.

Pepin, David. *Discovering Shrines and Holy Places*. Aylesbury, UK: Shire, 1980.

Peterson, Natasha. *Sacred Sites*. Chicago: Contemporary Books, 1988.

Quilici, Folco. *Children of Allah*. Secaucus, NJ: Chartwell, 1979.

Rice, Edward. *Ten Religions of the East*. New York: Four Winds, 1978.

Scanlon, Christopher, ed. *Video Source Book*. 2 vols. 18th ed. Detroit: Gale, 1997.

Schele, Linda, and Mary Ellen Miller. *The Blood of Kings*. London: Thames & Hudson, 1992.

Sherry, Gerald. *The Catholic Shrines of Europe*. Huntington, IN: Our Sunday Visitor, 1986.

Sitwell, Satcheverell. *Great Temples of the East*. New York: Ivan Obolensky, 1963.

———. *Monks, Nuns and Monasteries*. New York: Holt, Rinehart & Winston, 1965.

Sox, David. *Relics and Shrines*. London: George Allen & Unwin, 1985.

Spence, Keith. *Cathedrals and Abbeys of England and Wales*. New York: Norton, 1984.

Spicer, Dorothy. *Festivals of Western Europe*. New York: H. W. Wilson, 1958.

Streep, Peg. *Sanctuaries of the Goddess*. Boston: Little, Brown, 1994.

Swadling, Mark, ed. *Masterworks of Man & Nature*. New York: Facts on File, 1994.

Tóibín, Colm. *The Sign of the Cross: Travels through Catholic Europe*. New York: Pantheon, 1995.

Walker, Benjamin. *The Hindu World*. New York: Praeger, 1968.

Walker, Charles. *Atlas of Secret Europe*. New York: Dorset Press, 1990.

Westwood, Jennifer, ed. *The Atlas of Mysterious Places*. New York: Weidenfeld & Nicolson, 1987.

Woodward, Kenneth. *Making Saints*. New York: Simon & Schuster, 1990.

Wurlizter, Rudolph. *Hard Travel to Sacred Places*. Boston: Shambhala, 1995.

ILLUSTRATION CREDITS

INDEX

INDEX

INDEX

INDEX

springs, sacred, 61, 101, 156–158, 163, 164, **304–305**, 309
Station Island (Ireland), 57, 155–156
Stations of the Cross, 27, 85, 127–128, 178, 217, 248, 328
Stein, Gertrude, 222
Stonehenge (England), 204, **271–272**
Story of a Soul (book), 153
Subiaco (Italy), 175
Sufi mystics, 142–143, 167–169, 198, 239, 289–290, 328
Süleyman the Magnificent, 121–122
Süleymaniye Mosque (Istanbul), 121
Sultan Ahmet Mosque, 121
Sun Dance, 200, 275
Sun Temple (India), 212–213
Sunni Islam, 197
Suryavarman, King, 8, 9
Swayambunath Stupa (Nepal), **272–274**
sweat lodge, 25–26, 170, 195, 274–275

T'ai Shan (China), 185–186, **277–278**
Taizé (France), 217, **278–279**
Taj Mahal (India), **279–281**
Tay Ninh (Vietnam), 37
Tekla Haymanot, Saint, 60
Temple Mount (Jerusalem), 129–131, 195
Ten Boom, Corrie, 55–56
Teotihuacán (Mexico), **281–282**
Teresa of Avila, Saint, 15–16
Thatbyinnyu Temple, 216
Thebes (Egypt), **282–285**
Thérèse (Martin), Saint, 152–153
Theresienstadt concentration camp (Czech Republic), 114
Thousand Buddhas, Caves of the, **43–44**
Three Gates Mosque (Kairouan), 137
Thugs, 71, 145
Timbuktu (Mali), 67
Tinos (Greece), **285–286**
Todai-ji Shrine (Japan), 200
Toklas, Alice B., 222
Tokyo (Japan), **286–287**
Toltecs, 47–48
Tombs of the Prophets (Jerusalem), 133
Tooth Temple (Sri Lanka), 239, **287–289**
Tosho-su Shrine (Japan), 207
Touba (Senegal), 239, **289–290**
Treblinka concentration camp (Poland), 114
Trondheim (Norway), 205–206
Tucson (AZ), 258–259

Ugandan Martyrs' Shrines (Uganda), **291–292**
Ujjain (India), 145
Uluru (Australia), **292–293**
UNESCO, 3, 10, 93, 321
Ustaša, 112

Vaital Temple (India), 213
Valley of the Kings (Egypt), 284
Valley of the Queens (Egypt), 284
Varanasi (India), 105, 138, **295–296**
Varlaam, 173
Verden (Germany), **296–297**
Vézeley (France), 257, **297–298**
Via Dolorosa (Jerusalem), 128
Vishnu, 46, 97, 213, 298
vision quest, 24, 25–26, 274–275, 328
votive offerings. *See* ex-votos.
Voudou, 227, 260–261, 328
Vrindavan (India), **298–299**

Wâdî el Natrûn (Egypt), **261–262**
Wailing Wall (Jerusalem), 131–133, 167
Walsingham (England), 80, **301–302**, 305
Wanuskewin (Canada), 169–170
War of the Relics, 239
Warsaw (Poland), 114
Wartburg Castle (Germany), 159
Wat Phra Keo (Thailand), 73–74
Wat Po (Thailand), **302–304**
wells, sacred, 47, 70, 129, 137, 255–256, 263, 295, 301, **304–305**
Wesley, John, 301, 306
Western Wall (Jerusalem), 131–133, 167
Westminster Abbey (England), **306–307**
Wilde, Oscar, 222
William of York, Saint, 309
Willibrord, Saint, 254–255
Winifred, Saint, 255–256, 305
Wittenberg (Germany), 158–159
Wobbelin concentration camp, 111 (photo)
World Council of Churches, 88
Wu T'ai Shan (China), 278

Yad Vashem (Jerusalem), 114, 133
Yasukuni Jinja Shrine (Tokyo), 287
Yan Chi-Chung, 144
Yeni Mosque (Istanbul), 122
Yevtushenko, Yevgeny, 19
yoni, 218–219, 328
York Minster (England), **309**
Young, Brigham, 181–182

341

INDEX